The Hungarian Agricultural Miracle?

The Harvard Cold War Studies Book Series
Series Editor: Mark Kramer, Harvard University

Recent Titles in the Series

Mao and the Sino-Soviet Partnership, 1945–1959: A New History
Zhihua Shen and Yafeng Xia

The Soviet Union and the Horn of Africa during the Cold War: Between Ideology and Pragmatism
Radoslav A. Yordanov

The Power of Dynamic Détente Policies: U.S. Diplomacy between the Military Status Quo and the Transformation of Europe, 1964–1975
Stephan Kieninger

The Tito–Stalin Split and Yugoslavia's Military Opening toward the West, 1950–1954: In NATO's Backyard
Ivan Laković and Dmitar Tasić

Bridging the Baltic Sea: Networks of Resistance and Opposition during the Cold War Era
Lars Fredrik Stöcker

US–Spanish Relations after Franco, 1975–1989: The Will of the Weak
Morten Heiberg

Stalin's Legacy in Romania: The Hungarian Autonomous Region, 1952–1960
Stefano Bottoni

Mao and the Sino-Soviet Split, 1959–1973: A New History
Danhui Li and Yafeng Xia

A Cold War over Austria: The Struggle for the State Treaty, Neutrality, and the End of East-West Occupation, 1945–1955
Gerald Stourzh and Wolfgang Mueller

The Soviet Invasion of Czechoslovakia in 1968: The Russian Perspective
Edited by Josef Pazderka

Stalin's Double-Edged Game: Soviet Bureaucracy and the Raoul Wallenberg Case, 1945–1952
Johan Matz

The Red Army in Austria: The Soviet Occupation, 1945–1955
Edited by Stefan Karner and Barbara Stelzl-Marx

The Hungarian Agricultural Miracle? Sovietization and Americanization in a Communist Country
Zsuzsanna Varga

The Hungarian Agricultural Miracle?

Sovietization and Americanization in a Communist Country

Zsuzsanna Varga
Translated by Frank T. Zsigó

LEXINGTON BOOKS
Lanham • Boulder • New York • London

Published by Lexington Books
An imprint of The Rowman & Littlefield Publishing Group, Inc.
4501 Forbes Boulevard, Suite 200, Lanham, Maryland 20706
www.rowman.com

6 Tinworth Street, London SE11 5AL, United Kingdom

British Library Cataloguing in Publication Information Available

Library of Congress Cataloging-in-Publication Data

Names: Varga, Zsuzsanna, 1970–, author. | Zsigo, Frank T., translator.
Title: The Hungarian agricultural miracle? : Sovietization and Americanization in a communist country / Zsuzsanna Varga ; translated by Frank T. Zsigó.
Description: Lanham : Lexington Books, [2020] | Series: The Harvard Cold War studies book series | Includes bibliographical references and index. | Summary: "This book examines the success of the Hungarian agricultural miracle, a hybrid agricultural system created by transfer processes of Sovietization and Americanization"—Provided by publisher.
Identifiers: LCCN 2020036308 (print) | LCCN 2020036309 (ebook) | ISBN 9781793634351 (cloth) | ISBN 9781793634375 (paperback) | ISBN 9781793634368 (ebook)
Subjects: LCSH: Agriculture and state—Hungary—History—20th century. | Agriculture—Economic aspects—Hungary. | Agricultural systems—Hungary.
Classification: LCC HD1940.5 .V37 2020 (print) | LCC HD1940.5 (ebook) | DDC 338.109439—dc23
LC record available at https://lccn.loc.gov/2020036308
LC ebook record available at https://lccn.loc.gov/2020036309

Translation funded by the László Tetmájer Fund of the Hungarian Studies Program, Department of Central Eurasian Studies, Indiana University–Bloomington.

Contents

Preface

I began my research into agrarian history[1] at a special moment in history. As a consequence of the fall of socialism and "system-change," both central and local archives of the party-state had been opened, hence, when writing my doctoral dissertation, I had access to documents that had previously been classified as secret and had been inaccessible to researchers. The 1990s also opened up fantastic opportunities for conducting interviews, as the majority of the most important figures in agrarian policy were still alive. As well as interviewing national leaders, my local researches also gave me the opportunity to interview collective farm presidents and members.

This was a time when interest in the West in respect of Central and Eastern Europe grew and, thanks to scholarships and invitations to conferences, my generation was quick to establish relations with the international circuits of scientific life. I greatly valued the experience of meeting in person researchers such as Martha Lampland, Nigel Swain, and Chris Hann whom I had previously only known from their publications. Cooperation with them, that is still ongoing, strengthened in me the conviction that historians who address the transformation of agriculture and rural society have a great deal to learn from professional interaction with sociologists and anthropologists.

In writing this monograph my intention was to prepare a synthesis which extended across the whole socialist period of Hungarian agriculture, from 1949 to 1989. The majority of publications on this theme focus only on one or another of the subperiods within these four decades, and then extend the conclusions that they have drawn to the whole era. The debates which emerged from this sort of approach were greatly instrumental in stimulating me to write a monograph that covered the whole period.

László Borhi and Nigel Swain were particularly helpful in turning my manuscript into a book that is accessible to an Anglo-Saxon audience. Over the course of writing the manuscript I received valuable advice and suggestions from individuals too numerous to list, but special thanks go to: György Földes, János Honvári, Lajos Izsák, Pál Juhász, György Kerekes, Edit Nagy, György Péteri, Attila Pók, István Simon, and Gyula Varga. Finally I would like to thank Mark Kramer for including my book in the Cold War Studies Series published at Harvard University.

Introduction

In December 1955, amid the first East–West détente of the Cold War after the death of Joseph Stalin in March 1953, unusual guests arrived at an American farm: a three-person delegation from Communist Hungary on a fact-finding visit. The farm's owner, Roswell Garst, who was widely recognized as an innovative farmer specializing in hybrid-corn production, had already received a Soviet delegation the same year; and he took seriously their invitation to him so that, later in 1955, he did in fact visit the Soviet Union, stopping off in Hungary en route.[1] This could be the beginning of a gripping spy novel, but it is a story of a something different. After a full decade had passed, a new Hungarian delegation made up of high-level ministerial and economic leaders visited Garst's farm, as part of a monthlong study visit. This time it had an additional goal: with the permission of the Hungarian Socialist Workers' Party (the ruling Communist Party), it purchased the most modern corn-production technology of the era.[2] This equipment, which had been developed in capitalist agriculture, was then transplanted into a Soviet-bloc agricultural system that was performing very poorly as a consequence of forced collectivization. Yet it was adapted so successfully that in the mid-1970s U.S. Secretary of Agriculture Earl E. Butz became interested in it and paid a visit to Hungary.

The research on which this book is based calls attention not only to a unique case of how to pull success out of failure within the Soviet bloc. Analysis of the origins of the "Hungarian agricultural miracle" has wider implications. This book as a work of transnational history examines not just high politics and trade deals, but exchanges, research visits, enterprise managers, and academic links. It draws attention to the fact that ordinary people and interest groups had agency even in a totalitarian regime. As a consequence of their actions the Iron Curtain was considerably more permeable than is commonly thought. To different extents, at different periods, the possibility to cross the divide existed for individuals and specialist groups, and mutually advantageous exchanges of knowledge and experience began.

It was not just ideologies and weapons that played important roles in the competition between the two global systems of socialism and capitalism, so too did consumer goods; and in this domain, the countries of the Soviet bloc struggled with serious deficiencies throughout. The economics of shortage (János Kornai's term) revealed itself most dramatically in the supply of basic foodstuffs, as was evident when the Soviet Union was forced in the 1970s to use some of its gold reserves to finance food imports. For example, food shortages were a near permanent problem in Romania during the Nicolae Ceauşescu era, and in Poland sugar and many other basic food products were still being rationed as late as the beginning of the 1980s.

Food shortages, rationing, and queuing were also commonplace in Hungary, which was compelled to import bread grains and meat until the middle of the 1960s. However, by the 1970s a fundamental change had taken place as a result of technology and know-how transfer from the West: domestic food supplies became stable and Hungarian agricultural exports began to grow, both to Eastern and Western markets. According to statistics from the United Nations Food and Agricultural Organization (FAO), Hungary's agricultural output was unrivaled within the Soviet bloc. The Western press even began to refer to the "Hungarian agricultural miracle." Yet, during this period, Hungary's government always denied the existence of a unique Hungarian model because it did not want to get into an ideological conflict with the principle of Soviet agricultural superiority. Works on agricultural history written during the Communist era could therefore engage in only tangential discussion of this phenomenon. Following the collapse of communism, researchers dealing with the contemporary era focused primarily on political history. Until recently, the investigation of more specialized topics receded into the background.

The opening of archives in Hungary after 1989 makes it possible to address this formerly taboo subject. Yet the Hungarian literature on collectivization has been dominated by two mutually exclusive positions: "success story" and "dead end." The followers of the "success-story" approach acknowledge that collectivization was accompanied by economic, administrative, and physical force (coercion), but nevertheless emphasize the production results from the late 1960s, claiming collective farms had achieved modernization. Given that no other agricultural sector in the Soviet bloc had been able to demonstrate a similar production success, the concept of the "Hungarian model" began to spread. However, it was never precisely clarified how this model differed from the kolkhoz exemplar, nor when divergence began. The other position focuses on the genesis story of the establishment of collectivized agriculture during three campaigns (1949–53, 1955–56, 1959–61), laying out in detail the tools, spread, and consequences of state violence. Works that take this position also agree that through reoccurring campaigns of violence the Stalinist kolkhoz system was transplanted into Hungary, and it remained in place in an unchanged form until regime change. The (even by international standards) outstanding production results of the 1970s and 1980s cannot be explained in this interpretive framework, and for this reason these analyses for the most part skip this period in their analyses.

It is clear that both explanations emphasize different periods in the four-decade history of Hungarian agricultural producer cooperatives, yet try to apply the conclusions drawn from these periods to the entire history of socialist agriculture. A different approach is required which moves beyond the two diametrically opposed positions found in the literature.

The methodological novelty of this book resides in its use of the concept of transfer and multidimensional historical comparison. In the title of this monograph there are two terms highlighted, Sovietization and Americanization, however the concept of transfer became the main analytical category of this research project, as it can be used to present both Soviet determinants and Western influences. Although there was a brief period when Hungary, along with the other socialist countries, was so to speak hermetically sealed off from the Western half of Europe, this situation gradually changed after Stalin's death. No examination of the period between 1949 and 1989 can be undertaken without taking into consideration relations between the socialist East and the capitalist West. And indeed a growing number of researchers have sought to uncover economic, technical, and cultural, etc., transfers, even between divergent political systems. Thus, for example, the number of works examining transfers across the Iron Curtain increased significantly.[3]

Historical research into transfers represents a kind of response to comparative history, making the point that comparisons are too static, whereas historical reality is much more pliant and constantly in motion. The reason such researchers prefer an approach, which places transfers at the forefront, is that it is capable of pointing to processes and mutual effects. The response of the followers of the comparative orientation to this is that so-called entangled or transnational approaches dealing with transfers do not separate out adequate units for this sort of analysis, given that they claim that processes between countries are inseparably and mutually interconnected. Their conclusion is the following: without explicit comparison, historical studies of transfers and of entanglements are in danger of becoming airy and thin. Over the last decade a lively debate has unfolded between the two positions, particularly in Germany, which has resulted not in a reinforcement of opposing stances but in an emphasis on the connections between the two methods and their integrated utilization. This is reflected in the appearance of the expression "transnational comparison" which is gaining currency.[4]

Despite agreement on the importance of this approach, it has inspired few empirical studies. This monograph represents an attempt to produce transnational comparison in history on a solid empirical basis. The same procedure is adopted for both Eastern and Western transfers. First, the object under investigation in its old context is elucidated in considerable detail. Then the causes, channels, and actors involved in transfers are analyzed together with the methods applied. Transfers are a continuous feature of societies, yet each transfer has its particular actors, who have specific motivations. Driving forces may come from the society of origin (push factors) as well as from the recipient society (pull factors). Great emphasis is then placed on adaptation processes and the interactions between the intermediaries and recipients. Finally, economic and social consequences, just like results of transfers are examined. Transfers might be unsuccessful and may yield only partial results.

A macro-level approach is required for the exploration of the party-state decision-making processes, but meso- and micro-historical level research has been included in order to investigate the perspectives of those affected by, and participating in, the transfers: the networks of intermediaries (for example what became known as the agrarian lobby) involved in the causes, fields, and selection of transfers.

The analysis of Eastern and Western model transfers in this book has made use of the official documents of both former party and state organizations as well as the press and oral sources. The first group of official written sources used was the minutes of the supreme decision-making bodies in Hungary. Documents from more specialized organizations and institutions, such as the Agricultural Department of the party headquarters and the agricultural ministry, were examined in order to introduce the intermediaries of these transfers. Research for this monograph was also conducted in the archival fonds relating to the Foreign Department of the party headquarters and the Foreign Ministry. These are all located in the Hungarian National Archives. The second group of official written sources was the records of the authorities that directed and supervised the secret police and other organizations enforcing state power (e.g., the Ministry of the Interior and the Administrative Department of the party headquarters) as well as those of the state-security organizations engaged in the "prevention of agricultural sabotage" located at the Historical Archives of the Hungarian State Security. In addition to the study of national-level documents, meso- and micro-level research was conducted in the county archives of three different regions in Hungary, in Nógrád, Hajdú-Bihar, and Zala counties.

In addition to archival research, the contemporary Hungarian press was also examined, including the official party daily and the specialist agricultural press. Articles relating to Hungary and Eastern Europe in the Soviet Party daily *Pravda* and American newspapers (the *New York Times*, the *Los Angeles Times*, and the *Christian Science Monitor*) were also studied. Research was conducted at the Hungarian Radio Archives, the Archives of the Hungarian Academy of Sciences and the specialist archive located at the largest agricultural university in Hungary, Szent István University in Gödöllő. Surveys "for internal use" and studies prepared at the former institutes of agricultural economics and sociology also proved to be significant sources of valuable information.

Research for this monograph relied to a considerable degree on oral sources. Interviewing first began as long ago as the 1990s. Those interviewed included officials from the socialist-era agricultural ministry, agricultural researchers and practical specialists, the former leaders of state farms and agricultural cooperatives as well as people who had worked in these enterprises.[5] Notes, documents, photos, etc., received from the interviewees provided a considerable amount of nonofficial written and visual sources. The recordings of interviews regarding agriculture kept at the Oral History Archives of the 1956 Institute in Budapest were also used in this monograph.

HISTORIOGRAPHY

There is an extensive literature available in Hungarian on the history of agricultural producer cooperatives between 1949 and 1989, in which can be found a wide range of not only historical, but also sociological, ethnographic, and sociographic analyses. A historiographical overview is impossible without resort to the specialist terminology associated with collectivization. The following paragraphs will therefore clarify a number of key terms that are used here and throughout this monograph.

Western academic literature on the collectivization of agriculture tends to adopt Soviet terminology, such as *kolkhoz* (the abbreviation for *kollektivnoie khoziaistvo*) meaning collective farming. But the kolkhoz operated as a form of producer (rather than consumer) cooperative, and politicians in East Central Europe in the 1940s were keen to stress the cooperative origins of the new method of farming, partly because most countries had a strong cooperative tradition (although not of producer cooperatives) and partly to distance themselves from the negative connotations already associated with the kolkhoz. Hungary, like other countries in the region, therefore adopted cooperative terminology. Its full name for the equivalent of the kolkhoz (although this monograph later devotes a lot of space to interrogating equivalence) was "mezőgazdasági termelőszövetkezet" which translates as "agricultural producer cooperative."

In this monograph cooperative terminology is used, not just because this is what is used by the Hungarians (and Germans, and Czechs and Poles, etc), but because it also draws attention, as Nigel Swain has argued, to two fundamentally important ways in which agricultural producer cooperatives in the region differed from the Soviet kolkhoz.[6] First, they did not operate on nationalized land, but rather on land that remained, if only formally, in the private ownership of peasants. Second, for a long time many types of cooperative form were allowed to remain in existence, while in the Soviet Union, at the end of the period of collectivization, only one version of the umbrella term *kolkhoz* had become general, and that was the *artel'*. This difference is also reflected in the existence of a law obliging the kolkhoz to operate in a prescribed manner.

It is also important to note that the transformation of Eastern European agriculture (termed at the time the socialist transformation of agriculture) did not simply mean taking over the kolkhoz model. Works on collectivization pay little attention to elaborating the fact that from the end of the 1940s it was a question of taking over the Stalinist system of socialist agriculture in its entirety. One element of this was the creation of a specific economic and political environment (by price, tax and investment policy, etc.) in which agriculture was subordinated to the interests of industrial development and the agricultural population counted as second-class citizens compared to the industrial working class. Within the peasantry, *kulaks* were separated out: because of their wealth they counted as "exploiters."

The Stalinist system of agriculture brought into being three entities to replace individual peasant farms. Two of these embodied the highest form of state property: the state farms and the machine and tractor stations (MTS), which enjoyed a monopoly on machinery ownership and also fulfilled an important role of political control in the countryside. The third entity was the cooperative or communal farm, which was made up of two parts. The first was the farming that took place on the lands that had been put into common indivisible ownership, and this took place on the basis of communal work organization (in brigades and work groups), for which the members received remuneration. In addition to this, members were allowed to keep for their own use a certain limited area of land and restricted number of animals. This was called the household plot, and there the members decided themselves what to produce and what to do with it (consume it themselves or sell it). Originally the communal farm engaged primarily in crop production and animal husbandry, but later their sphere of activities expanded significantly to units engaged in processing, trade, and other services. These were termed ancillary enterprises.

Returning to the literature on the Hungarian collectivization, it is appropriate for an assessment of this literature to begin in the 1970s, because it was at this time that publications on the socialist transformation of Hungarian agriculture based on the analysis of primary sources began to appear. The first of these was Sándor Orbán's *Két agrárforradalom Magyarországon: Demokratikus és szocialista agrárátalakulás 1945–1961* [Two agrarian revolutions in Hungary: Democratic and socialist agrarian transformation 1945–1961], published in 1972, which was based on extensive archival research.[7] In the introduction the author made clear his initial historical judgment and analytical premise. "Who can deny that the democratic agricultural conditions that replaced the feudal latifundia, and then the creation of socialist large-scale forms to replace and surpass village-level small-scale production, signified two separate agrarian revolutions?"[8] A quarter of Sándor Orbán's book is dedicated to land reform of 1945, while the other three-quarters cover collectivization campaigns. The first two collectivization campaigns are covered in a single chapter, with another dedicated to the third. Regarding the Soviet model, he satisfied himself with the observation that from 1948 the Hungarian Workers' Party (HWP) had utilized the model that had been established in the Soviet Union in the course of a collectivization drive which had taken place under very different conditions.[9] His interest in social history and his earlier research on the peasantry permitted him occasionally to compare the central resolutions and measures of those in power with their expected and unexpected economic and social consequences.

Another highlight of the 1970s literature was the research conducted by Ferenc Donáth. Donáth was well known as one of the Communist Party's leading agriculture policy experts until his arrest in 1951. After his release in 1954 he became the deputy director of the Institute of Economics of the Hungarian Academy of Sciences, which was being established at the time. In 1956, after the revolution, he was jailed again for being a member of the Imre Nagy group. After his subsequent release he engaged with issues of agricultural history and agricultural economics.[10] The first result of this work was his 1969 book on land reform, which he actually completed in 1965.[11] In it he merged macro- and micro-level approaches by collecting materials on every county and amalgamating them with analysis of national decision-making organizations. In the latter half of the 1960s he worked increasingly intensely on the history of collective farms. Donáth felt the time had come to write a comprehensive history of Hungarian producer cooperative movement as it was termed at the time. He felt that an appropriate foundation for this large-scale undertaking would be the histories of collective farms that were being prepared throughout the country at the time.[12]

Donáth's own synthetic work was published in 1977.[13] In this review of agricultural history, he began, like others, with the land reform of 1945. But he did not close the study in 1962, as Sándor Orbán had done, choosing rather to take it up to 1974.[14] The essentially chronologically structured volume also contained thematic chapters. This approach paid off, in that it allowed him to truly examine the key processes and problems of the structural transformation of Hungarian agriculture after 1945. His source base was primarily the publications of the Central Statistical Office. A novelty of Donáth's book was that he examined agricultural cooperative workplaces not only in terms of production and management but also as a field of interest-group politics.

Donáth's book had a significant effect on Western sociologists and anthropologists who, beginning in the mid-1970s, started to visit Hungary to research socialist agriculture. In their subsequent publications, Donáth's *Reform and Revolution* is often mentioned as indispensable to fieldwork. One of these scholars, Chris Hann, studied a *szakszövetkezet* (specialist cooperative) specializing in vineyards and orchards. Since 1976 he has regularly visited Tázlár in Bács-Kiskun County, primarily to analyze local events as a participant observer.[15] Nigel Swain also arrived in Hungary in 1976 with the goal of analyzing agricultural producer cooperatives from the point of view of labor organization. He was interested in issues like the system of relations between collectives and households, or the appearance of a new type of technocratic leadership stratum in producer cooperatives.[16] He later directed and researched for an international research project investigating post-socialist rural transformation in 54 villages in East Central Europe[17] and wrote with his brother a multiply republished general history of Eastern Europe since 1945.[18] Martha Lampland came to Hungary in the 1980s and studied Sárosd in Fejér County, focusing on the effect that the collectivization of agriculture had on the work culture of various groups in village society.[19] These foreign researchers, who at the time were quite young, established professional relations with Hungarian ethnographers and sociologists.[20] The reason why these research results are worthy of attention from the perspective of model transfer issues is that they record effects on the communities receiving the transfers, so facilitating the analysis of geographical difference, particularly differences between settlements.[21]

As the 1970s turned into the 1980s, an increasing number of books were produced by Hungarian researchers which reflected a changing interpretive framework. Péter Simon's short monograph based on primary sources analyzed the prehistory of collectivization, i.e., the agricultural policy of the 1946–1949 period,[22] but it is still worth noting, because he used the term *kolkhozization* to describe the organization of agricultural producer cooperatives beginning in 1949. This was a breach of the norm, in that the dominant terms in use to that point were *socialist reorganization* and *transformation of agriculture*. A gradual distancing from ideological expectations could also be felt in agricultural economics and agricultural sociology research on household plots.[23]

The most outstanding and in many ways still relevant summary of the history of the transformation of Hungarian agriculture since 1945 was written in the mid-1980s.[24] Sándor Szakács had been researching issues of post-1945 agricultural history since the 1960s. He authored a book on the land reform, and then worked on the history of state farms.[25] In the 1970s his attention increasingly turned to collective farms. This shift is apparent in his study published in 1975 in *Agrártörténeti Szemle* [Agricultural History Review], in which he endeavored to write the micro-history of the Jókai Agricultural Producer Cooperative.[26] The synthesis of Sándor Szakács's agricultural history work took shape in the general economic history of Hungary since 1945—planned as two-volumes—that he coauthored with Iván Pető.[27] The most obvious novelty of this work lay in its consistent avoidance of an ideological interpretive framework. For the most part they adopted the conceptual apparatus of descriptive economics. The majority of their sources were the materials of economic administrators and statistical data. When examining post-1945 agricultural history Sándor Szakács consistently sought to separate the history of agricultural policy from the history of agricultural production. In this way he was able to indicate at several points the economic and social "costs" of agricultural restructuring and the radical changes taking place in the spheres of ownership and production.

Writing more critical than this could only be published in institutional publications intended for internal use, or as samizdat. A good example of the former is Ferenc Donáth's 1979 working paper published in the series of the Cooperative Research Institute titled "The relationship between work and property in industrializing agriculture."[28] At the end of *Reform and Revolution* Donáth had already touched on the issue of efficiency in industrialized agriculture, but he did no more than pose the question. In this working paper intended for internal use, however, he could express himself more openly. Even his approach was provocative, in that he was comparing the Hungarian agricultural sector to Western agricultural development. While on Hungarian state farms and cooperatives, increasing expenditure on materials and equipment was associated with decreasing efficiency, Western trends pointed to the opposite. In capitalist production, modernization and profitability could not be separated long-term. From this he drew the conclusion that, to the extent that a decrease in efficiency could only be observed in Eastern European agricultural sectors, the phenomenon must be related to collectivization in some way. From here it was only a short step to the question of property relations.

He referred to a data series that showed that the decrease in efficiency was consistently more severe on state farms than on agricultural producer cooperatives; in consequence, economic practice did not support the ideological axiom of the superiority of state ownership. Donáth's criticism of existing ownership structures went further in that he also claimed that increased use of material and equipment of industrial origin meant the agricultural sector was increasingly dependent on the industry, but that this dependence was completely different in the West, where real competition existed, unlike socialist economies, where the collective farms worked with enterprises that enjoyed monopoly positions.

The Cooperative Research Institute, headed by Antal Gyenes gave space to several research projects that questioned official positions.[29] Tibor Simó, for example, studied social processes and interest patterns on collective farms from the unique standpoint of formal and informal interest politics.[30] Research by Pál Juhász and Bálint Magyar provoked a response from a wider audience. They also published together, for example on the situation of small producers in Poland and Hungary.[31] In the second half of the 1980s they both started participating in the increasing amount of fieldwork that was taking place at the time, conducting research jointly in Dunapataj, while Pál Juhász was a regular participant in the village research camp in Homokmégy.[32] The results of the latter research project were made available mainly as workshop studies, but Tibor Valuch prepared an independent monograph with the title *Rekviem a parasztságért* [Requiem for the peasantry].[33] In these publications the huge scale of peasant opposition to collectivization was unambiguously revealed, as was the widespread and multilayered state violence that accompanied it.

This discussion of the literature so far supports, that agricultural history reached regime change with fewer "blemishes" than contemporary history generally. This explains why 1989–90 does not represent a sharp dividing line in the agricultural history literature. Thanks to the effects of research projects employing new approaches launched in the 1980s, agricultural history saw some outstanding monographs published on the changes that had taken place, unlike political history of the post-1945 period where access to sources dramatically increased only in the 1990s. In 1992 Gyula Erdmann, the director of the Békés County Archives, published his well-documented monograph on the history of compulsory deliveries.[34] Although the title indicates that his analysis starts in 1945, the author also emphasizes continuity with the compulsory delivery system that developed at the time of the Second World War. This is followed by an extraordinarily detailed explanation of how the Communist Party utilized this tool of the wartime economy in the interest of introducing the Stalinist system of socialist agriculture.

Another important element of the Stalinist system of socialist agriculture, namely the machine and tractor station, was covered in an outstanding monograph by János Honvári.[35] The virtues of his work include not only his extensive use of sources, but, after clarifying the criteria of the Soviet model, the consistent attention he pays to similarities and differences between it and the Hungarian system.

László Urbán similarly pulled together earlier research when he wrote about the establishment of the first collective farm towns.[36] He successfully forged together macro- and micro-level sources and paid a great deal of attention to the long-term environmental effects of socialist large-scale farming.

Meanwhile, in the context of restitution and privatization, the 1990s saw collective farms catapulted into the crossfire of intense political and public debate. They were increasingly labeled "Stalinist kolkhozes," or were characterized as having been support pillars for a dictatorial regime. However, few such one-sided approaches entered the historical literature. This is underscored by the three large-scale agricultural historical summaries that were published after regime change. In 1996, an extensive volume, edited by István Orosz, Lajos Für, and Pál Romány,[37] covered the entire period from the Conquest (circa the 9th century) to regime change. Within this large time interval, the reader encounters the socialist period and the years of the regime change the most.

The second of the three was edited by Péter Gunst and originally prepared in English for the American book market, but then subsequently published in Hungarian.[38] The third also starts with the emancipation of serfs and moves up to the EU-accession in its coverage of agricultural history.[39]

Research projects after regime change, however, were influenced by the felt need in society for greater knowledge on the suffering and tragedy of peasant society about which there had previously been silence. This was reflected in the István Hajnal Circle's 1991 conference in Gyula, which was dedicated to the topics of peasant opposition and self-organization.[40] The presenters and commenters in the section which dealt with the post-1945 period continued their research programs for a number of years. Zsuzsa Hantó and her colleagues worked on the history of kulak families deported to labor camps in the Hortobágy region with the help of archival sources, interviews, and reminiscences.[41] Gyöngyi Farkas, studying the regional and micro-level processes of collectivization, paid particular attention to making use of the sources of state security organs.[42] Although a number of other publications on the oppression of kulaks saw the light of day in the 2000s, research interest was not restricted to this group. József Ö. Kovács undertook a systematic study of the suffering and persecution of the whole peasant society, a topic that had been taboo for decades.[43] The great strength of his research work is his use of a wide range of sources: he collected sources from every county archive and also made intensive use of oral history. Referring back to the distinction in the historiography between "success story" and "dead end," it can be stated that these are more at the "dead end" of the spectrum, while the earlier ones were more "success story," with Donáth being neither at one end nor the other. Interest in the process of collectivization in Hungary peaked on its 50th anniversary. An interdisciplinary conference was held at which historians, sociologists, and legal experts joined economists and ethnographers to report on their latest research findings.[44] The collection of studies published from the conference represents a snapshot of the key directions and methods of current research projects. The volume also contains studies examining how communities of Hungarians in neighboring countries were affected by agricultural collectivization.[45] A further conference held on December 12, 2012, in the Institute of History of the Hungarian Academy of Sciences with the title *Collectivization and state violence* resulted in the publication in 2015 of an edited collection under the title "Állami erőszak és kollektivizálás a kommunista diktatúrában" [State violence and collectivization in the communist dictatorship].[46]

These two conferences are worthy of note because they signify two new directions of research on collectivization. One of these concentrates on temporal and spatial changes in the use of state violence. A particularly significant moment in the preparation for the transfer of the Soviet model was the purge of the Ministry of Agriculture which took place in 1948. Éva Cseszka's contribution analyzed the so-called FM (Ministry of Agriculture) trial.[47] István Papp's study conducted in the Historical Archives of the Hungarian State Security is a noteworthy examination of the role of the political police. Specifically, he examined the organizational history of the Agricultural Sabotage Prevention Department following 1956.[48] In his more recent research projects he worked on the political biography of the leading figure of the agrarian lobby, Lajos Fehér.[49]

The unique aspect of the second new direction in recent research is that it prioritizes primarily meso- and micro-level steps over macro-level analysis. András Schlett wrote the company history of the Bábolna State Farm, well known as a "flagship" of Hungarian agriculture and a key player in Western transfers.[50] Two recently published volumes of a new book series Vidéktörténet [The history of the countryside] contain several case studies at county or district-level, and some of them adopt a micro-level approach.[51] Almost thirty years after the collapse of socialism, it is still the case that the dichotomy of "success story" versus "dead end" is present in the Hungarian specialist literature, yet these meso- and micro-histories demonstrate the significance of local conditions and individual villages and individual personalities in adapting to Eastern and Western transfers.

Two conference volumes should also be mentioned, which aim to integrate the latest research from the region on collectivization into the English-speaking scholarly world.[52] These two books are important too because, although in different measure, they demonstrate the need for systematic comparison. Nigel Swain's study represents a useful starting point in such a process.[53]

Finally this author's own contribution to the Hungarian language historiography might be mentioned. Her research began with a study of interest relations in agriculture.[54] By combining oral history with an analysis of archival documents that became accessible at the beginning of the 1990s, she uncovered dimensions of conflicting interests being resolved between central power and the peasantry, which not only went beyond the totalitarianism approach but formed the basis of her later investigations into how various groups pursued and achieved their interests under state socialism. This resulted in her monograph *Az agrárlobbi tündöklése és bukása* [The Rise and Fall of the Agrarian Lobby under State Socialism] published in 2013.[55] Locating her Hungarian expertise in a comparative perspective, she jointly edited with Anssi Halmesvirta a Finnish-Hungarian volume.[56]

STRUCTURE OF THE BOOK

Generally, when studying economic and social processes, it is difficult to establish periods bracketed off by specific years. However, what follows is an examination of a political system in which all large-scale economic and social transformation processes were launched through specific party decrees, which makes it easier to mark out such years. The starting point of the monograph is 1949. The leadership of the HWP had been working on accelerating the Sovietization of agriculture in the second half of 1948. In the spring of 1949 a final political decision was reached on the pace and methods of collectivization. The closing year is 1989 because that was the year in which the socialist elite, still in power, broke with a number of ideological axioms regarding collective farms, landownership and land use that had stretched back to the Stalinist period.[57]

The book is constructed chronologically, and so sequential order is an important organizing principle; but it is important to emphasize that Eastern and Western model transfers cannot be strictly separated in time. For this reason, appreciation of simultaneity plays an important role in the analysis.

The monograph begins with a historiographical and methodological introduction and contains seven substantive chapters. Chapter 1 outlines the broader context in which the Hungarian case can be embedded: examining, on the one hand, the main features of the kolkhoz system, and on the other, placing the Hungarian case into an Eastern European comparative framework. Both contexts are vital to study the fundamental question: was it really a kolkhoz (system) that was created in Hungary? Although they disagree about whether later a convergent or divergent development took place, both the success-story and dead-end narratives in the scholarship mentioned above consider it self-evident to give a positive answer to this question. So the starting point is the same in both cases: they accept without clarification the relation between the Stalinist-type kolkhoz and the collective farm created in Hungary.

By clarifying the original content of the Soviet model, chapter 1 offers a new insight into the whole transfer process. As Nigel Swain pointed out: "In the case of collectivization, however, we are saved the methodological chore of constructing for ourselves an 'ideal type' collective farm because Stalin provided a concrete and prescriptive model in the form of the Model Charter for collective farms of 1935."[58] The Soviet Union exported the other elements of the Stalinist system of socialist agriculture too, along with the kolkhozes. Thus the transfer of the kolkhoz model can only be interpreted as a part of the whole, i.e., socialist agriculture. Familiarity with the whole also requires consideration of the subordinated (inner colony) role of agriculture within the socialist economy and the hierarchical order of the new operational units (state farms, machine and tractor stations, kolkhozes).

The causes of collectivization in East Central Europe have been well-known in the literature for a long time. On the one hand, the existence and persistence of smallholders was in sharp contradiction with the ideology of the communist party. On the other, transforming private farms into socialist large-scale state or collective farms in late 1940s served mainly the purposes of preparing for the next world war. Our knowledge of the actors involved in transferring the Stalinist agricultural system is very limited. So far, research has emphasized rather the role of the recipient peasant society in the process. Chapters 2, 3, and 4 cover all three phases of the prolonged and violent process of introducing socialist agriculture in Hungary between 1949 and 1961, special attention is paid both to the intermediaries and the social groups affected.

Chapter 5 analyzes the initial phases in the transfer of Western knowledge and technology following the conclusion of collectivization. Chapter 6 introduces the preparations made for the transfer of "closed production systems" from the United States as well as the implementation of this model and its consequences. Chapter 7 contextualizes the "Hungarian Agricultural Miracle"—both its successes and limitations.

Its combination of historical comparison with transfer studies permits this volume to analyze how Hungarian cooperatives, which had been created through forced collectivization, managed to integrate highly developed industrial-style production models of capitalist agriculture in the 1970s. The closed production system represented the practical synthesis of biological and technical science. It aimed at the rapid, significant, and economical increase in a specific output of arable and/or livestock farming. This required a close coordination and continuous updating of all factors of production. The closed production system is interpreted in this book as a model, because when it was imported, it was compulsory to implement every element of it in a precisely prescribed order. The monograph follows the dissemination of these new production systems. Special attention is paid in these chapters to the differences and similarities between the Hungarian agricultural producer cooperatives and the kolkhozes. The chosen temporal reference points allow for systematic comparison. The concluding part of the monograph aims to collect experiences and reflections on how comparative and transfer studies can be combined in the field of the transnational history.

NOTES

1. Richard Lowitt and Harold Lee, eds., *Letters from an American Farmer: The Eastern European and Russian Correspondence of Roswell Garst* (DeKalb, IL: Northern Illinois University Press, 1987).
2. The name of the Communist Party in Hungary change as follows: 1945–1948, Hungarian Communist Party (HCP); 1948–1956, Hungarian Workers' Party (HWP); and 1956–1989, Hungarian Socialist Workers' Party (HSWP).
3. Sari Autio-Sarasmo–Katalin Miklossy, eds., *Reassessing Cold War* (London–New York: Routledge, 2011); Patryk Babiracki and Kenyon Zimmer, eds., *Cold War crossings: international travel and exchange across the Soviet bloc, 1940s–1960s*, Introduction by Vladislav Zubok (College Station: Texas A&M University Press, 2014); Michael David-Fox, *Crossing borders: modernity, ideology, and culture in Russia and the Soviet Union* (Pittsburgh: University of Pittsburgh Press, 2015); Theodora Dragostinova and Malgorzata Fidelis, "Beyond the Iron Curtain: Eastern Europe and the global Cold War," *Slavic Review* 77, no. 3 (2018): 577–87; Gertrude Enderle-Burcel, Piotr Franaszek, Dieter Stiefel, and Alice Teichová, eds., *Gaps in the Iron Curtain: Economic relations between neutral and socialist countries in Cold War Europe* (Kraków: Jagiellonian University Press, 2009); Maximilian Graf, *Österreich und die DDR 1949–1990: Politik und Wirtschaft im Schatten der deutschen Teilung* (Vienna: ÖAW, 2016); Bernd Greiner, Christian Th. Müller, and Claudia Weber, eds., *Ökonomie im Kalten Krieg*, Studien zum Kalten Krieg 4 (Hamburg: Hamburger Edition, 2010); Aaron Hale-Dorell, *Corn crusade: Khrushchev's farming revolution in the post-Stalin Soviet Union* (New York: Oxford University Press, 2018), 167–96; Anssi Halmesvirta, *Co-operation across the Iron Curtain: Hungarian-Finnish Scientific Relations of the Academies from the 1960s to the 1990s* (Jyväskylä: University of Jyväskylä, 2005); Walter Hixson, *Parting the curtain: propaganda, culture, and*

the Cold War, 1945–1961 (Basingstoke: Macmillan, 1998); Suvi Kansikas, *Socialist countries face the European community: Soviet-bloc controversies over East-West trade* (Frankfurt am Main: Peter Lang Edition, 2014); Fruzsina Müller, *Jeanssozialismus: Konsum und Mode im staatssozialistischen Ungern* (Göttingen: Wallstein Verlag, 2017); Ludlow N. Piers, ed., *Ostpolitik/Westpolitik: European integration and the Cold War, 1965–1973* (Abingdon: Routledge, 2007); György Péteri, "Nylon Curtain: Transnational and Trans-Systemic Tendencies in the Cultural Life of State-Socialist Russia and East-Central Europe," *Slavonica* 10, no. 2 (2004): 112–23; György Péteri, ed., *Imagining the West in Eastern Europe and the Soviet Union* (Pittsburgh: University of Pittsburgh Press, 2010); Villaume Poul and Westad Odd Arne, eds., *Perforating the Iron Curtain: European Détente, Transatlantic Relations and the Cold War, 1965–1985* (Copenhagen: Museum Tusculanum Press, 2010); Karsten Rudolph, *Wirtschaftsdiplomatie im Kalten Krieg: Die Ostpolitik der Westdeutsche, Großindustrie 1945–1991* (Frankfurt: Campus, 2004).

4. This is underscored by the English-language volume edited by Heinz-Gerhard Haupt and Jürgen Kocka that presented the innovative cooperation that developed between the new approaches and comparative historical research. The volume contains not only theoretical-methodological pieces but also six 20th-century analyses to consider the opportunities inherent in renewing comparative historical writing. Heinz-Gerhard Haupt and Jürgen Kocka, eds., *Comparative and Transnational History: Central European Approaches and New Perspectives* (New York–Oxford: Berghahn Books, 2009).

5. Interviewees have been anonymized where no explicit permission was given to publish their comments.

6. Nigel Swain, "Eastern European Collectivization Campaigns Compared, 1945–1962," in *The Collectivization of Agriculture in Communist Eastern Europe: Comparison and Entanglements*, eds. Constantin Iordachi and Arnd Bauerkämper (Budapest and New York: CEU Press, 2014), 497–534.

7. Sándor Orbán, *Két agrárforradalom Magyarországon: Demokratikus és szocialista agrárátalakulás 1945–1961* [Two agrarian revolutions in Hungary: Democratic and socialist agrarian transformation 1945–1961] (Budapest: Akadémiai, 1972).

8. Ibid., 8.

9. Ibid., 71.

10. Tibor Valuch, ed., *Ferenc Donáth: A Márciusi Fronttól Monorig: Tanulmányok, vázlatok, emlékezések* [Ferenc Donáth: From the March Front to the so-called Monor meeting: Studies, sketches, memoirs] (Budapest: MTA Közgazdaságtudományi Intézet–Századvég, 1992), 13–18.

11. Ferenc Donáth, *Demokratikus földreform Magyarországon 1945–47* [Democratic land reform in Hungary, 1945–47] (Budapest: Akadémiai, 1969).

12. The initiative was launched in the Hungarian Academy of Sciences' Agricultural History Committee. In 1969 it passed a decision calling for the preparation and writing of the socialist transformation of agriculture based on case studies. Donáth's commitment to the project is reflected by the fact that not only did he take on editorial responsibilities when the Museum of Hungarian Agriculture launched its series

Termelőszövetkezeti tanulmányok [Producer Cooperative Studies], he also authored a lengthy methodological study in which he both laid out the history of the development of Hungarian socialist agriculture and attempted to clarify methodological issues for further research. See: Ferenc Donáth, "A magyar szövetkezeti nagyüzemi mezőgazdaság kialakulásának vázlatos története (1949–1970)" [A brief account on the history of socialist large-scale agriculture in Hungary, 1949–1970], *Agrártörténeti Szemle* 14, no. 3–4 (1972): 292–330.

13. He originally wrote it, as he later claimed, to inform "the intelligentsia of developed capitalist and developing countries." In truth, the Hungarian-language edition was published first, with the English version published three years later. Ferenc Donáth, *Reform és forradalom: A magyar mezőgazdaság strukturális átalakulása, 1945–1975* (Budapest: Akadémiai, 1977). In English: Ferenc Donáth, *Reform and revolution: transformation of Hungary's agriculture 1945–1970* (Budapest: Corvina, 1980).

14. Within the more than 10 years between 1962 and 1974 he viewed the 1968 New Economic Mechanism as a divider between eras.

15. Chris Hann, *Tázlár: a village in Hungary* (Cambridge: Cambridge University Press, 1980). He continued his fieldwork research in rural Hungary after the regime change and has published numerous papers on the post-socialist period. One of his latest publications also deals with this topic: Chris Hann, "Morality and economy: work, workfare, and fairness in provincial Hungary," *Archives Européennes de Sociologie* 59, no. 2 (2018): 225–54.

16. Nigel Swain, *Collective Farms Which Work?* (Cambridge: Cambridge University Press, 1985).

17. Nigel Swain, *Green Barons, Force-of-Circumstances Entrepreneurs, Impotent Mayors: Rural Change in the Early Years of Post-Capitalist Democracy* (Budapest–New York: CEU Press, 2013).

18. Geoffrey Swain and Nigel Swain, *Eastern Europe since 1945*, 5th ed. (London: Palgrave, 2018).

19. Martha Lampland, *The object of labor: Commodification in Socialist Hungary* (Chicago and London: The University of Chicago Press, 1995). She continued to work on Hungary-related topics, which resulted in 2016 in a new monograph: Martha Lampland, *The value of labor: The science of commodification in Hungary, 1920–1956* (Chicago: The University of Chicago Press, 2016).

20. Mihály Sárkány, "A társadalomnéprajzi kutatás hazai története" [The history of social anthropology in Hungary], in *Magyar néprajz* [Hungarian Anthropology], ed. Attila Paládi-Kovács, vol. 8, *Társadalom* [Society] (Budapest: Akadémiai, 2000), 29–66.

21. A review of later works published abroad—mostly based on fieldwork conducted in the 1980s—is appropriate: Peter D. Bell, *Peasants in Socialist Transition: Life in a collectivized Hungarian Village* (Berkeley, Los Angeles, and London: University of California Press, 1984); Marida Hollos and Bela C. Maday, eds., *New Hungarian Peasants? An East Central European Experience with Collectivization* (New York: Columbia University Press, 1983); Ildikó Asztalos Morell, *Emancipation's Dead-End Roads? Studies in the Formation and Development of the Hungar-*

ian Model for Agriculture and Gender (1956–1989). Acta Universitatis Upsaliensis 46 (Uppsala: Uppsala Univ. Library, 1999); Ildiko Vasary, *Beyond the Plan: Social Change in a Hungarian Village* (Boulder, CO: Westview Press, 1987).

22. Péter Simon, *A magyar parasztság sorsfordulója, 1946–1949* [The Hungarian peasantry's change of fortune] (Budapest: Kossuth, 1984).

23. János Juhász, *A háztáji gazdálkodás mezőgazdaságunkban* [The household farming in our agriculture] (Budapest: Akadémiai, 1980); Imre Kovách, *Termelők és vállalkozók: Mezőgazdasági kistermelők a magyar társadalomban* [Producers and entrepreneurs: Agricultural small producers in the Hungarian society] (Budapest: Társadalomtudományi Intézet, 1988); Gyula Varga, ed., *A mezőgazdasági kistermelés helyzete és jövője* [The present and the future of the small-scale farming] (Budapest: Mezőgazdasági, 1979).

24. Iván Pető and Sándor Szakács, *A hazai gazdaság négy évtizedének története 1945–1985* [The History of Four Decades of Domestic Economy, 1945–1985], vol. 1, *Az újjáépítés és a tervutasításos irányítás időszaka 1945–1968* [The Period of Rebuilding and Command Economic Planning, 1945–1968] (Budapest: Közgazdasági és Jogi Könyvkiadó, 1985).

25. Sándor Szakács, *Földosztás és agrárfejlődés a magyar népi demokráciában 1945–1948* [Land distribution and agrarian development in the Hungarian people's democracy], Marx Károly Közgazdaságtudományi Egyetem közleményei 5 (Budapest: KJK, 1964); Sándor Szakács, *Állami gazdaságaink helyzetének alakulása 1945–1948* [Development of our state farms, 1945–1948] (Budapest: Akadémiai, 1969); Sándor Szakács, *A népi demokratikus agrárfejlődés kezdetei Magyarországon 1945–1948* [The beginnings of the democratic agrarian development in Hungary] (Budapest: Akadémiai, 1971); Sándor Szakács, *A földművesszövetkezeti mozgalom története 1945–1949* [The history of land recipient cooperatives, 1945–1949] (Budapest: Szövetkezeti Kutató Intézet, 1976).

26. Sándor Szakács, "A nagyigmándi Jókai termelőszövetkezet története" [The history of the Agricultural Producer Cooperative in Nagyigmánd], *Agrártörténeti Szemle* 17, no. 1–2 (1975): 54–128.

27. Unfortunately the second volume of this monumental economic historical summary was never written. A few years later Sándor Szakács published a study of wide scope, which was in all likelihood the foundation for the agriculture-related chapters of the planned second volume, given that he summarized processes that had taken place in the agricultural economy from 1968 to the mid-1980s. Sándor Szakács, "A reform kérdése és a termelés: Meghatározottságok és adottságok a magyar mezőgazdaságban 1968–1985" [The question of the reform and the production. Determining factors and facilities of the Hungarian agriculture 1968–1985], *Agrártörténeti Szemle* 31, no. 1–4 (1989): 56–117.

28. Ferenc Donáth, *A munka és tulajdon kapcsolata az iparosodó mezőgazdaságban: Tulajdon és hatékonyság* [Connections between the labor and the property in the industrialized agriculture] (Budapest: Szövetkezeti Kutató Intézet, 1979).

29. Gyenes himself participated in such research programs. See: Antal Gyenes, *A B.-i Mezőgazdasági Termelőszövetkezet: Monográfia* [The Agricultural Producer Cooperative in B.: Monograph] (Budapest: Szövetkezeti Kutató Intézet, 1977).

30. Tibor Simó, *Érdekérvényesítés a termelőszövetkezetek formális és informális szervezetében* [Assertion of interests in formal and informal organization of producer cooperatives] (Budapest: Szövetkezeti Kutató Intézet, 1981).

31. Pál Juhász and Bálint Magyar, "Néhány megjegyzés a lengyel és a magyar mezőgazdasági kistermelők helyzetéről a hetvenes években" [Some remarks on the situation of Polish and Hungarian small producers in the 1970s], *Medvetánc* 4, no. 2–3 (1984): 181–208.

32. As reflected in the titles listed below, the authors substituted the real names of the fieldwork settlements with fictive names (Dunaapáti) as placed in the titles. Pál Juhász, "Dunaapáti—egy elsüllyedt mezőváros" [Dunaapáti—a sunk agrarian town], in *Emberek és intézmények: Két zsákutca az agráriumban.* [People and institutions: Two dead ends in the agriculture] (Budapest: Új Mandátum, 2006), 300–10; Bálint Magyar, *Dunaapáti 1944–1958: Dokumentumszociográfia* [Dunaapáti 1944–1958: Document-sociography], 3 vols. (Budapest: Művelődéskutató Intézet–Szövetkezeti Kutató Intézet, 1988).

33. Tibor Valuch, *Rekviem a parasztságért* [Requiem for the peasantry], Határ Füzetek 3 (Debrecen: Kossuth Lajos Tudományegyetem, Debrecen, 1988).

34. Gyula Erdmann, *Begyűjtés, beszolgáltatás Magyarországon, 1945–1956* [Compulsory deliveries in Hungary, 1945–1956] (Békéscsaba: Tevan, 1993).

35. János Honvári, *A gépállomások története, 1947–1964: A gépállomások és a magyar mezőgazdaság gépesítésének története 1947–1964* [The history of the machine and tractor stations: The machine and tractor stations and the mechanization of the Hungarian agriculture] (Győr: Távtan, 2003).

36. László Urbán, *Az első termelőszövetkezeti városok agrárpolitikai szerepének kialakulása, változásai, gazdasági és környezeti hatásai* [The agrarian policy role of the first socialist agricultural towns, and their economic and ecological impacts] (Szolnok: MTA Jász-Nagykun-Szolnok Megyei TudományosTestülete, 2002).

37. István Orosz, Lajos Für, and Pál Romány, eds., *Magyarország agrártörténete: Agrártörténeti tanulmányok.* [The agricultural history of Hungary: Studies on agricultural history] (Budapest: Mezőgazda, 1996).

38. Péter Gunst, ed., *Hungarian Agrarian Society from the Emancipation of Serfs (1848) to the Re-privatization of Land (1998)* (New York: Columbia University Press, 1998). The Hungarian version was published in the same year under the same title.

39. János Estók, György Fehér, Péter Gunst, and Zsuzsanna Varga, *History of Hungarian Agriculture and Rural Life, 1848–2004* (Budapest: Argumentum Publishing House–Museum of Hungarian Agriculture, 2004).

40. Gyula Erdmann, ed., *Paraszti kiszolgáltatottság—Paraszti érdekvédelem, önigazgatás* [Peasants' defenselessness—Safeguarding of peasants' interests, self-governing] (Gyula: Békés Megyei Levéltár, 1994).

41. Zsuzsa Hantó et al., ed., *Kitaszítottak* [Outcasts of the socialist society], vol. 1, "Magukkal fogjuk megzsírozni a földet" (Budapest: Alterra, 2001). In this series there were another four volumes published, which contained mostly document and interview collections.

42. Gyöngyi Farkas, *Lázadó falvak: Kollektivizálás elleni tüntetések a vidéki Magyarországon, 1951–1961* [Rebellious villages: Demonstrations against collectivization in rural Hungary, 1951–1961] (Budapest: Korall, 2016).

43. József Ö. Kovács, *A paraszti társadalom felszámolása a kommunista diktatúrában: A vidéki Magyarország politikai társadalomtörténete, 1945–1965* [The elimination of the peasant society in the communist dictatorship: The political-socio history of the rural Hungary, 1945–1965] (Budapest: Korall, 2012).

44. András Schlett, ed., *Földindulások—Sorsfordulók: Kollektivizálás, agrárvilág és vidéki változások a XX. század második felében* [Earthquaking—transformations: Collectivization and rural changes in the second half of the 20th century] (Budapest: Szent István Társulat, 2012).

45. See chapters by Teréz Kovács, István Gaucik, and Márton László in the volume.

46. Sándor Horváth and József Ö. Kovács, eds., *Állami erőszak és kollektivizálás a kommunista diktatúrában* [State violence and collectivization in the communist dictatorship] (Budapest: MTA Bölcsészettudományi Központ, 2015).

47. Éva Cseszka, *Gazdasági típusú perek, különös tekintettel az FM-perre (1945–1953)* [Economic show trials, with special regard to the trial against the leaders of the Ministry of Agriculture] (Budapest: Gondolat, 2012).

48. István Papp, "A BM II/7 (Mezőgazdasági Elhárító) Osztály" [The Agricultural Anti-Sabotage Department (II/7) of the Ministry of Interior], in *A megtorlás szervezete: A politikai rendőrség újjászervezése és működése, 1956–1962* [The organization of reprisal: Reconstruction of the political police and its actions, 1956–1962], ed. Imre Okváth (Budapest: L'Harmattan–Állambiztonsági Szolgálatok Történelmi Levéltára, 2013), 181–209.

49. István Papp, *Fehér Lajos: Egy népi kommunista politikus pályaképe* [Lajos Fehér: A political biography of Lajos Fehér] (Budapest: Kronosz–ÁBTL, 2017).

50. András Schlett, *Sziget a szárazföldön: A Bábolnai Állami Gazdaság története 1960 és 1990 között* [An island on the continent: The history of the Bábolna State Farm between 1960 and 1990] (Budapest: Szent István Társulat, 2007).

51. Gergely Krisztián Horváth, ed., *Életvilágok és társadalmi gyakorlatok a 18–20. században* [Everyday life and social practices in the 18th–20th centuries], Vidéktörténet 1 [The History of the Countryside 1] (Budapest: MTA Bölcsészettudományi Központ, 2017); Gergely Krisztián Horváth, ed., *Vakvágányon: A "szocializmus alapjainak" lerakása vidéken a hosszú ötvenes években* [Laying the foundations of the socialism in the countryside], Vidéktörténet 2 [The History of the Countryside 2] (Budapest: MTA Bölcsészettudományi Központ, 2018).

52. Constantin Iordachi and Arnd Bauerkämper, eds., *The Collectivization of Agriculture in Communist Eastern Europe: Comparison and Entanglements* (Budapest and New York: CEU Press, 2014); Sorin Radu and Cosmin Bundeanca, eds., *Countryside and Communism in Eastern Europe: Perceptions, Attitudes, Propaganda* (Berlin: LIT Verlag, 2016).

53. Swain, "Eastern European."

54. Zsuzsanna Varga, *Politika, paraszti érdekérvényesítés és szövetkezetek Magyarországon 1956–1967* [Politics, the Assertion of Interests in the Peasantry and Agricultural Cooperatives in Hungary between 1956 and 1967] (Budapest: Napvilág, 2001).

55. Zsuzsanna Varga, *Az agrárlobbi tündöklése és bukása az államszocializmus időszakában* [The Rise and Fall of the Agrarian Lobby under State Socialism] (Budapest: Gondolat, 2013).

56. Zsuzsanna Varga and Anssi Halmesvirta, eds., *Agriculture and Rural Life in Finland and Hungary* (Loimaa: Sarka, 2018), 97–112.

57. Between May 30 and June 2, 1989, Parliament modified Act II of 1971 on producer cooperatives (1989: XV tc), Act I of 1987 on land (1989: XIX tc), and Act III of 1967 on agricultural producer cooperatives (1989: XX tc).

58. Swain, "Eastern European," 502.

Chapter One

The Stalinist System of Socialist Agriculture and Its Export to East Central Europe

THE WHOLE AND ITS PARTS

Economic and Social Inheritance

Any presentation of the birth of the kolkhoz model necessarily requires an overview of the economic and social relations that characterized rural areas of the Tsarist empire at the beginning of the 20th century.[1] On the eve of the October Revolution, Russia's peasant society of nearly 120 million encompassed a wide range of farming methods and cultures across a vast empire, covering rural areas with differing historical pasts and natural endowments. Alongside this heterogeneity, there was a general problem: at the beginning of the 20th century only a small fraction of the peasantry had been able to become true landowners, a consequence partly of the terms and provisions that governed the emancipation of the serfs in 1861, and partly of the persistence of the village community (*obshchina* or *mir*), which dated back to feudal times. The *obshchina* was on one hand an agricultural community based on ancient joint property and individual usage of land, and on the other an organization of self-government (*mir*). That is to say it was at once a property rights and administrative community.

The Missing Actor—The Landowning Peasant

The settlement of 1861 had divided the land between landlords and serfs, but the latter were obliged to redeem their share in installments. Liberated serfs could only take full ownership of the land they had been allocated after paying the redemption fee; and even then they were not fully independent but remained within the obshchina, where the heads of families supervised land use. Furthermore, there was a prohibition on selling or mortgaging allotted land until the redemption fee had been paid. Nor was personal freedom complete in that peasants could only leave their villages with council authorization, which was given only restrictively because the village community was jointly liable for taxes and for redemption fees.[2]

The response of various groups within the peasantry to the new situation depended on the size of their allotted land, the scale of payment commitments, the conditions of redemption, and the nature of land use.[3] Peasants who could find an additional occupation were able to rent land from those who had moved to cities and over time purchase land from nobles; in this way they rose materially above the others. Poor peasants (*bednota*) termed them *kulaks* or *miroed*s.[4] Poor peasants constituted almost two-thirds of the total; for them the redemption price and tax payments represented such a heavy burden that their outstanding redemption payments increased year on year. At the same time, they could not renounce their expectation of land from the emancipation, because they could not leave the obshchina without paying the majority of the balance of the redemption fees.[5] Because the tradition of periodically redistributing land within the obshchina persisted,[6] it was not in the peasants' interest to make investments of any kind, and in consequence agriculture remained at its previous low level, even though village populations were dynamically growing. Meanwhile, in the interest of financing industrialization, Russia undertook massive grain exports, which, given the poor production results of the time, could only be realized at the cost of low domestic consumption.[7]

These gathering tensions took visible form in the peasant riots and land seizures of 1905–1906. Stolypin, who from 1906 was both prime minister and minister of the interior, implemented reform measures designed to resolve the peasantry's problems. He decreased and then finally abolished redemption fees, so creating the opportunity for peasants to be owners of their holdings, to migrate freely and to freely exit the village community.[8] By 1916, however, in the 40 European provinces of Russia, only a quarter (24%) of families had left their obshchina. The majority of those who did leave were commodity-producing peasants, to a considerable extent from Ukraine and the North Caucasus. By the middle of the 1910s—largely in these two areas—a significant stratum of better-off, commodity-producing peasant proprietors had come into existence.[9]

The Socialization of Land and the New Economic Policy

Tensions grew in the villages throughout the First World War. Peasants opposed having to supply the government with produce for which they were paid in depreciating rubles. But, as illegal peasant land-seizures demonstrated, there was also a deep-seated demand for the distribution of the landlords' land. It is no wonder that one of the first acts of the October Revolution of 1917 concerned that most important factor of agrarian production: the land. A decree passed on November 8 of 1917 by the Second All-Russia Congress of Soviets of Workers' and Soldiers' Deputies confiscated without compensation the land of the landed nobility and transferred it to those who worked it, on the basis of equality; no family could have more than it could cultivate since the hiring of labor was forbidden.[10] The land became the "property of the whole people."[11] Bolshevik leaders did not agree with giving the land to individual use on ideological grounds, but they would not win peasant support unless they did. In doing so, they took over the agrarian policy of the SRs.

The next step in legal regulations concerning land was the "Declaration of the Rights of the Working and Exploited People" passed at the Third Congress of Soviets.[12] The first point of its second article, which was later included in the Constitution, reinforced the abolition of the private ownership of land, and further announced that model farms and agricultural companies had become national property. On February 9, 1918, the same Third Congress passed a fundamental law on the social ownership of land.

In the span of about half a year, therefore, enormous changes took place in respect of landownership and ownership rights. All ownership rights rooted in feudalism, together with all bourgeois ownership rights, ceased. Land could no longer be bought or sold, and neither could it be rented. Of necessity, it could not be mortgaged either. All land—including that held by peasants—was expropriated without compensation; it became the property of the whole people, and was transferred to the use of those who worked it. It was divided up on the basis of labor and consumption norms appropriate to local conditions; and it was redistributed from time to time in accordance with population growth. Land use rights were granted to all citizens (regardless of sex) who desired to cultivate it, with their own labor, with the help of their families, or by pooling it into a cooperative. The hiring of labor was prohibited. In theory choice of land use forms—individual or communal—was free. It is important, however, to point to Article 11 of the act on the "socialization" of land, which made it clear that, in the interests of transforming to a socialist economy, collective production would be developed at the expense of individual production, collective production being advantageous from the perspective of the economic use of labor and products. This preference was further confirmed by Article 20, which stated that when land needs were being addressed, collective users, communes, and cooperatives would have priority.

The redistribution of 150 million hectares of noble, tsarist, and church estate land began in 1918. The land of the industrial and commercial bourgeoisie (approximately 19 million hectares) was confiscated in addition to that of large estate owners. During the civil war a further almost 50 million hectares were confiscated from kulaks. The division of land was carried out largely by the peasants themselves, in local land committees, soviets, and the obshchina. Implementation did not take place at the same time across the country but rather extended over time, partly as a consequence of the Civil War and foreign intervention.[13]

Allied intervention and the Civil War also resulted in a collapse of production and transportation and the destruction of market relations, leading to severe shortages and inflation. The ensuing system of War Communism was accompanied by the introduction of rationing and the banning of private trade in certain foodstuffs. In order to procure food and especially grain at a time of very low nominal prices, the Bolsheviks introduced a system of compulsory deliveries (*prodrazvërstka*) under which each peasant household was obliged to deliver its surplus to the state. Peasants naturally resisted and numerous riots broke out. Despite all the efforts to requisition bread grain, a severe famine broke out in 1920–21, compounded by unfavorable weather.[14]

When the Civil War ended, the Bolsheviks became masters of an exhausted country full of severe tensions. Peasant revolts exploded across the country in early 1921; the peasant masses opposed compulsory deliveries with increasing force. The New Economic Policy (*novaia ekonomicheskaia politika, NEP*) was introduced to address this problematic situation, offering temporary exemptions for market mechanisms and the private sector. From March of 1921, *prodrazvërstka* was replaced by a tax in kind (*prodnalog*), which represented a considerably smaller burden than the delivery quota. (In 1924, the tax in kind was replaced by a monetary tax.[15]) Once the tax had been paid, peasants were free to sell their produce. Given Russia's great distances and poor transportation links, only a few producers were able to sell directly on urban markets, and thus it was also necessary to legalize private trade. The rebuilding of agriculture progressed quickly, helped too by the authorization of land rental and the hiring of labor. But there was a major shift in industrial and agricultural prices in 1923. In the first two years of NEP the peasantry had enjoyed an advantage in the trade between villages and cities, but after 1923 a gap between agricultural and industrial prices grew quickly, to the detriment of villages: the agricultural price scissors had opened.[16]

By this point those in the party leadership who opposed the NEP were increasingly making themselves heard. In these circles, Preobrazhensky's notion of "primitive socialist accumulation" emphasized the significance of imbalanced trade between industry and agriculture. Bukharin vehemently criticized this concept, which would have subordinated agriculture to colonial status in the interests of accelerating economic growth.

Collectivization and "Primitive Socialist Accumulation"

The Preobrazhensky-Bukharin debate gained particular significance in the political situation of the time. By the mid-1920s it was becoming ever clearer that, as the European revolutionary wave waned, the Soviet Union would be forced to build the socialist system alone. In light of the antagonistic international environment, strengthening the country's defense capacity became its primary goal, together with the accelerated development of industry necessary to achieve it. A decree on the development of national defense was passed at the Third All-Russian Congress of Soviets in 1925, and this priority was confirmed at the 13th Party Congress in 1924. In accordance with this, at the 14th Party Congress in December 1925, the development of the metal and engineering industries was made the basic principle of economic policy.[17] In his closing remarks to the Congress Stalin stated: "The essence of our guiding principle is to transform our country from an agrarian country to an industrial one capable of producing the equipment it needs using its own resources. We must strive . . . to change our country from one that imports equipment into one that manufactures it."[18]

The Agriculture as an "Inner Colony"

The real question was: how could the resources necessary for rapid industrialization be procured? Could Soviet Russia's attempt to close the gap be accelerated using the slow, balanced, decentralized, peasant micro-accumulation recommended by Bukharin, or by state macro-cumulation implemented to the cost of these same small producers?

The grain crisis that peaked in 1927–28 confirmed that the market logic unfolding under NEP was at odds with the interests of the Soviet state. In 1926–27 purchase prices in the agricultural sector continued to fall. The state, as the largest purchaser, radically reduced the price of wheat and cereals, by 20–26%.[19] Peasant producers responded by withholding their stocks. By January 1928 the Soviet state had purchased more than one million (metric) tons less grain than the year before, even though the 1927 crop had been outstanding. Not simply was supply for urban workers and the army at risk, but so too were grain exports, and these were considered a necessary condition for Soviet industrialization.[20]

This situation clearly illustrated the legal relationship of peasants to the land: peasants had not enjoyed private ownership of the land since 1917, yet they remained owners by dint of the fact that they produced food surpluses on their individual farms.[21] As the Soviet state started moving toward extractive price and tax policies, it became apparent that over 20 million small and midsized peasant farms could not be forced to sell more grain to the state at reduced prices, nor to consume less.[22] During the debate on the grain crisis Stalin gave a number of speeches in which he spoke bluntly about the true stakes in the emerging conflict with the peasantry.[23] One of the most important such speeches was given at the Soviet Communist Party Central Committee plenum on July 9, 1928.

> In capitalist countries industrialization was usually achieved, in the main, by robbing other countries, by robbing colonies or defeated countries, or with the help of substantial loans from abroad circumscribed by more or less usurious conditions. You know that for hundreds of years Britain amassed capital from all of her colonies and from all parts of the world, which permitted her to make extra investments into her industry. . . . One respect in which our country differs from the capitalist countries is that it cannot and must not engage in colonial robbery, or the plundering of other countries in general. That way, therefore, is closed to us.
>
> Neither, however, does our country have or want to be fettered by foreign loans. So, that path, too, is closed to us.
>
> What path remains? Only one: to develop industry, to industrialise the country from *internal* accumulation. . . . But where are the chief sources of this accumulation? As I have said, there are two such sources: firstly, the working class, which creates value and takes industry forward; and secondly, the peasantry.
>
> As far as the peasantry is concerned, our current situation is as follows: first, the peasantry not only pays the state the usual direct and indirect taxes, it also *overpays* in the relatively high prices of manufactured goods, and, second, it is more or less *underpaid* in the prices for agricultural produce.
>
> This is an additional tax levied on the peasantry for the sake of promoting industry, which serves the whole country, the peasantry included. It is something in the nature of a "tribute," of a supertax, which we are compelled to levy for the time being in order to preserve and accelerate our present rate of industrial development. . . .
>
> It is an unpalatable business, there is no denying. But we should not be Bolsheviks if we glossed over it and closed our eyes to the fact that our industry and our country cannot at present dispense with this additional tax on the peasantry.[24] [Emphasis in the original]

Peasants, Kulaks, and Class War

In addition to the planned "inner colony" role of agriculture, Stalin touched, in the second half of his speech, on several other questions through which he essentially laid out the ideology of collectivization. It is important to note these because later a number of them became unquestionable dogma.

One such tenet concerned the unviability of small-scale production. Stalin unambiguously connected the agricultural crisis threatening Soviet economic growth with the dispersed nature of productive forces in agriculture.

> *The basis of our grain famine lies in the increasingly scattered and divided character of agriculture.* It is a fact that agriculture, especially grain farming, is growing ever smaller in scale, becoming increasingly less profitable and less commodity producing. Before the revolution we had approximately 15–16 million peasant farms, now we have some 24–25 million, and the trend towards subdivision is becoming more marked.[25] [Emphasis in the original.]

After supporting this point with further data, he turned to the issue of the scale of farming:

> Small-scale farming is less profitable, less commodity producing, and less stable than large-scale farming. It is a well known tenet of Marxism that small-scale production is less profitable than large-scale production, and this is wholly true of agriculture too. That is why, from the same area of land, a small-scale peasant farm yields much less marketable grain than a large-scale farm.[26]

Stalin did not restrict the issue of farm size simply to economic issues, rather he connected it to social consequences that would define the very nature of socialism.

> Today the Soviet system rests upon two heterogeneous foundations: united socialized industry and *individual* small-peasant farming based on the *private* ownership of the means of production. . . . Lenin states that so long as individual peasant farms, which give birth to capitalists and capitalism, predominate in the country, the danger of a capitalist restoration will persist.[27] [Emphasis in the original.]

Stalin used the Leninist thesis of the peasantry as the "last capitalist class" to derive the immediate tasks for the worker-peasant alliance.

> The alliance of the proletariat with the peasantry under the conditions of the dictatorship of the proletariat is not an alliance with the whole of the peasantry . . . Such an alliance cannot be effected without a struggle against the capitalist elements of the peasantry, against the kulaks. . . . That is why the alliance between the workers and the peasants under the present conditions of the dictatorship of the proletariat can be effected only in accordance with Lenin's well-known slogan: rely on the poor peasantry for support, establish a firm alliance with the middle peasant, do not for a moment relax the fight against the *kulak*.[28]

The logical consequence of this interpretation was the thesis of intensifying class struggle, which in itself encapsulated the necessary role of state violence. Stalin often stressed that the grain crisis was proof that Soviet power still had enemies, and what is more, that these enemies were increasing in number and becoming more aggressive. What could the Bolshevik Party do?—he asked.

> Naturally, our policy must by no means be regarded as a policy of inflaming class struggle. Why? Because inflaming class struggle would lead to civil war. . . . But this in no way implies that class struggle has been abolished, nor that it will not grow sharper. Still less does it imply that the class struggle is not the decisive factor in our advancement . . . the more we advance, the greater will be the resistance of the capitalist elements and the sharper the class struggle . . . the advance of the working class towards socialism cannot but cause the exploiting elements to resist it, and the resistance of the exploiters necessarily and unavoidably leads to the sharpening of the class struggle.[29]

Stalin also linked the long-term goal of the worker-peasant alliance to collectivization:

> The purpose of the bond is to bring the peasantry closer to the working class, the leader of our entire development, to strengthen the alliance of the peasantry with the working class, the leading force in the alliance, gradually to remold the peasantry, its mentality and its production, *in the spirit of collectivism,* and thus to bring about the conditions for the abolition of classes.[30] [Emphasis in original.]

Two State-Owned Pillars of Socialist Agriculture

Stalin accorded the socialist units of large-scale agriculture a significant role in reeducating the peasantry in the spirit of collectivism, and further hoped to use them to replace the grain production of the kulak farms that were being eliminated, often terming them grain factories for this reason. According to official ideology state (all people's) ownership was of a higher order than cooperative ownership, and thus the *sovkhoz* was the organization within Soviet agriculture with the most socialist content. The name itself reflected this, sovkhoz being a contraction of *sovetskoe khoziaĭstvo*, or soviet farm. It counted as the highest form of property in agriculture.

The prioritized development of the sovkhoz can be illustrated by the fact that in spring of 1928 there were 3,124 sovkhoz in the country, while by the spring of 1931 their number had increased to 5,383. Their operations were financed out of the state budget, meaning that sovkhoz workers received regular monthly salaries irrespective of whether the farm made a profit or a loss.[31] Their privileged status is reflected in the fact that they received a significantly higher proportion of agricultural investment than their share in production. Sovkhozes were established for grain or industrial crop farming, mostly in steppe areas where they operated on a largely mechanized, extensive basis. There were also specialized animal husbandry sovkhozes. However, in the first half of the 1930s their actual results in both crop farming and animal husbandry fell far below what the party leadership expected of them.

The second pillar in the socialist structure of agriculture was the system of state-owned machine and tractor stations (MTS), and it was equally significant in terms of accumulating state resources. In March 1929, on the eve of collectivization, a decree was passed on the establishment of MTS. In 1930 there was a total of 158 MTS in the Soviet Union. By 1931 this number had risen to 1,228 and three years later in 1934 it had reached 3,326. By this point these stations were providing machine services to nearly two-thirds of kolkhoz. [32] Because kolkhozes could not own large-scale machinery, they became dependent on these stations for machinery work, the services of which had to be paid for in kind, usually in the form of a percentage of the harvest. In this way, by the second half of the 1930s, the state acquired over half of the grain produced in kolkhozes via MTS payments.[33] This all contributed to the elimination of the role played by money in the economy.

The party also accorded an important political role to MTS, treating them as advanced fortresses of the working class in the countryside. The background to this was that the small number of party members in kolkhozes could not guarantee party influence. Political control was therefore ensured through the political deputy director of the MTS, and in 1933 political departments (*politotdel*) were established in MTS. These only functioned until 1934, although in the years of the Second World War (November 1941–May 1943) the system was reintroduced.[34]

Creating Collectivized Agriculture

In light of the hierarchy of property forms in the official ideology, it is legitimate to ask why sovkhozes were not created immediately out of peasant farms. The specialist literature emphasizes that this solution would have entailed too high a burden on the state budget in terms of both investment and salaries.[35] Collectivization nevertheless created a production basis for large-scale farming by gathering together the equipment and animal stock of small peasant farms.

In the mid-1920s approximately 90% of peasants still lived in essentially unchanged conditions in about 350,000 obshchina. The technical level of agriculture remained at its prewar level, the traditional three-field system was general, and crop rotation was only used sparsely.[36]

In the mid-1920s, the three most widespread forms of communal farm (*kollektivnoe khoziaĭstvo*, or kolkhoz for short) organized from peasant farms had been the *kommuna*, the *artel*, and the TOZ. The *kommunas* were not only joint farming units, but also consumer communities; in fact, members often lived together and raised children communally. Farming in the *artel* took place jointly, but members also held small individual plots that they cutivated themselves. They could also raise a few animals and keep the equipment necessary for this. The TOZ (*Tovarishchestvo po sovmestnoĭ obrabotke zemli* literally Association for Joint Cultivation of Land) was a looser form of agricultural association, where only certain procedures were carried out jointly.[37] Barely 1% of the peasantry was amassed in communal farms, most in TOZes. Data from 1926 indicate a lot about the preparedness of the different peasant strata for joint farming. Close to three-quarters of the members of kommuna were landless persons who owned neither a horse nor a cow; in the case of artels, approximately a third of members were landless, a third were poor peasants (1–3 ha), and the final third were middle peasants (3–15 ha). Here too the proportion of peasants with neither horse nor cow approached 50%.[38]

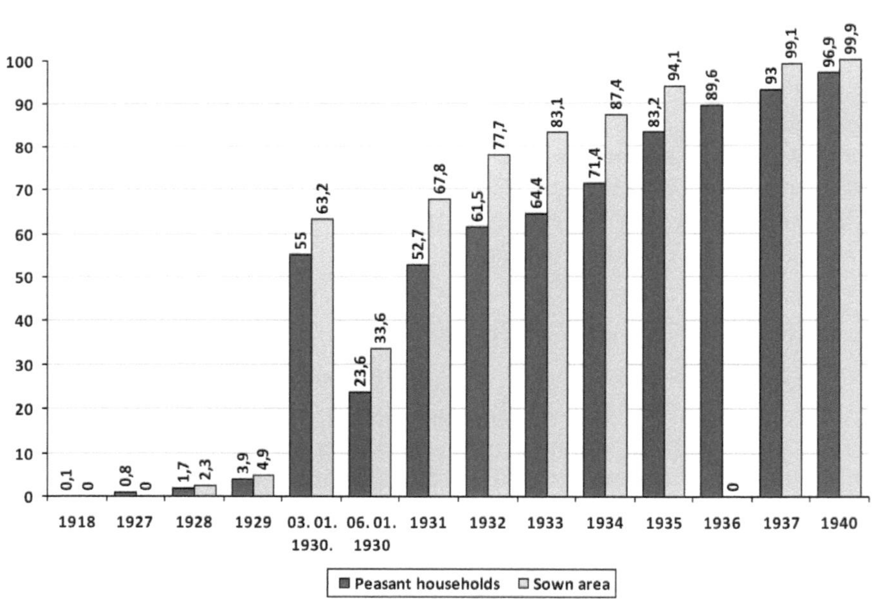

Figure 1.1. Degree of Agricultural Collectivization in the Soviet Union (1918–1940). Source: Nove, *An Economic History*, 172, 174.

By the end of the first five-year plan (1932) the proportion of collectivized peasant farms had risen to 61.5%, which in terms of area sown represented a jump from 2.3% to 77.7%. Some 95.9% of the new collective farms were of the artel type, 2.1% were the simplest association, and only 2% were kommuna—compared to the 25% initially planned.[39] By the end of the second five-year plan in 1937, almost 93% of former peasant farms operated on a collective basis, utilizing 99% of the country's sown area.[40] As already mentioned in the introduction, by the end of collectivization the artel had become the most widespread form of collective farming. Thus, when references were made to kolkhozes they usually meant artel. Kolkhoz became the synonym for artel, and in time it was the former term that spread.

Nevertheless, behind the columns of statistics, extends one of the greatest dramas in Russian history, one which imposed enormous suffering and privation not only on kulaks who were stripped of their property and deported to areas distant from their homes, but also on peasant society as a whole. Ever more new monographs and collections of source documents are being published on Soviet collectivization to this day.[41] The focus of this monograph is on an analysis of the transfer of the kolkhoz model however, so it touches on the historical events of collectivization only to the extent that they were significant for the formation of the kolkhoz model.

Refining the Kolkhoz Model

At the beginning of collectivization, the party leadership worked out a concrete program for the elimination of the kulaks as a class, but it did not clarify sufficiently what types of communal farm should be organized by local organizations. In early October 1929, 62% of communal farms in operation were of the TOZ type, but the Stalinist leadership did not view this loose type as "collective" enough, and thus encouraged the creation of kommunas and artels. Several variations of artel existed in practice, however. Although initially there were wide variations in the proportion of livestock and equipment that was collectivized in individual artels, by December of 1930 central directives required 100% collectivization of draft animals and cows.[42] Collectivization was already at its height when the first model charter (*primerniĭ ustav*) was made public,[43] on March 2, 1930, the very day that Stalin signaled retreat in his Pravda article, "Dizzy with Success."[44] During the first big campaign, at the turn of 1929–30, more than half of all individual farms had been collectivized in just a few weeks. This meant that by late February and early March, 1930, the original five-year plan for collectivization had already been overfulfilled two to three times. The degree of associated violence can be approximated from the fact that following the party decree criticizing collectivization, members left the kolkhozes en masse.[45]

Prompted by the experiences of the first drive, an important measure took place over the summer. On June 30, 1930, a decree was passed to stop the old village community organizations (obshchina, mir) from operating within the framework of collectivization. According to the land act of 1922, the decision to move to large-scale farming on consolidated land (that is to establish a kolkhoz) belonged to the competences of the obshchina. It soon became clear that even the obshchina council members with voting rights—that is the land community already "cleansed" of kulaks—did not support the establishment of kolkhozes. In consequence "Stalinist agricultural policy opted for the 'violent death' of the obshchina."[46]

In August 1932 the scope of the law on the defense of socialist property was extended to the kolkhoz. An amendment to Article 58 stated that the maximum punishment for pilfering kolkhoz property (including the harvest in the fields, stocks, animals, etc.) was loss of freedom (prison or camp) for not less than ten years, together with confiscation of all property. Such draconian sanctions were related to the fact that in several places the response of peasants to renewed violent collectivization had been to slaughter their animals before joining. The introduction of the internal passport in December 1932 sought to place a barrier in front of a second form of peasant opposition, namely escaping from the village.[47] These measures were closely related to preparations for a new comprehensive collectivization campaign. As noted above, in January 1933, political departments had been established in the MTS to facilitate control over kolkhozes. The political deputy directors of these newly established departments were agents of the political police (OGPU), whose responsibilities included, in addition to supervising and checking compulsory deliveries, uncovering those who damaged socialist property and sabotaged state planning tasks. Less food and fodder than ever before remained with rural population, while the Soviet Union continued to export grain in large quantities to pay for the imports of essential capital goods. This sweating of the peasantry caused a famine in Ukraine and Kazakhstan in 1933–34.[48]

Toward the end of 1934 the Central Committee decided that the hastily issued model charter of March 1930 had become obsolete. They planned to draft new rules which would include the experience gained over the previous four and a half years. With this goal in mind the Second All-Russian Congress of Outstanding Kolkhozniks was called in February of 1935.[49] Although kolkhoz members themselves chose delegates, it was local party organs that decided which kolkhozes could actually send them.[50] Even so, the congress was less formal than the first one had been in 1933. It proved to be not only a forum where middle level and local leaders could meet, but also negotiate to an extent; and this despite the fact that, as is emphasized in the specialist literature, the Central Committee's Agricultural Department had not included peasant representatives when elaborating the plans for the new model charter. The delegates were presented with the document on the first day of the congress. The final text was drafted over the course of the congress by a 170-member body, chaired by People's Commissar for Agriculture Mikhail

Chernov, but effective coordination was carried out by I. A. Iakovlev, who at that time was made head of the Party Center's Agricultural Department. Stalin was present throughout the committee's deliberations and took an active role in writing the final text. It is no misnomer to refer to it as the Stalinist kolkhoz model charter.

There were three areas of lively debate: household plots (*lichnoe podsobnoe khoziaĭstvo*), maternity benefits, and accepting kulaks into membership. A common feature is apparent from all three, namely that party leaders were open to concessions to peasant needs, while the kolkhoz activists took a more dogmatic position. This is well illustrated by the debate on the scale of household plot farming. In the discussions of the 170-member drafting body, it was Stalin himself who strove to convince the delegates to allow household plots of larger dimensions. He argued that the majority of peasants lacked the progressive thinking of their delegates. For this reason, attention still had to be paid to their desires, and 0.1 hectares was not enough for them to have a little household fruit or vegetables. Stalin recommended that the size of the household plot should be set at between 0.2 and 0.5 hectares. Indeed, in certain areas he thought that one hectare might even be permissible.[51]

One result of the debate was that it concretized the extent of maternity benefit, which the plan had only approached in a general fashion. Expectant mothers were granted a month's leave before birth, and a further month after, during which time they would receive half of their average income.[52] The draft model charter also contained provisions for the acceptance of kulaks who had been stripped of their property into the kolkhoz. It was unclear, however, which of the three categories of kulak this applied to: those banished to the gulag, those deported from their villages to other regions, or those simply stripped of their property but who had remained in their homes. In the end a flexible wording was adopted into the model charter. It was possible to take into membership kulaks together with their family members who had previously been deported if they demonstrated their support for the policies of the Soviet government through three years of conscientious work.[53]

It should be noted that the model charter as accepted, stressing compromises reached with the peasantry, never became obligatory for kolkhozes. Nor did it ever appear as an official law, for example in the form of a government decree. The party leadership was able to make this gesture, since by this time the vast majority of the peasantry had already been forced into kolkhozes.

The 1935 Kolkhoz Model Charter

The kolkhoz model charter statute made public on February 17, 1935, was broken into eight sections that regulated the life of the kolkhoz in detail.[54] It became the "basic law" that influenced several generations of kolkhoz peasants, in that the next model charter was passed over three decades later, in 1969.[55] Its short definition of kolkhoz was as follows: the kolkhoz, that is to say artel type of communal farm, is a community of persons who are the joint users of a given municipality's nationalized land, who have placed their farming equipment and animals (in large part) into communal use, and receive payment from the kolkhoz for the work they carry out together—in the framework of brigades and work teams. The unit of measure for work completed was the *trudoden'*, which literally meant labor day. This labor day unit expressed both time expended and the nature and quantity of the given piece of work, while simultaneously bearing no relationship at all to the quality of the work performed. Neglect of work could be punished by the leadership in accordance with kolkhoz internal rules, while damage to state or kolkhoz property fell under the jurisdiction of Soviet criminal law.[56]

The members received an ownership share in the kolkhoz because of the goods that they contributed, the value of which, in theory, had to be paid in money should they leave the kolkhoz.[57] The reason why the artel type communal farm was deemed to be a lower order and not consistently socialist form of ownership compared to the sovkhoz was that it represented the property of a small community or group, not of society as a whole. For this reason, official ideology considered the artel to be a temporary solution, which, with time, would develop further to become a sovkhoz.

In theory the general assembly of the kolkhoz members was its highest forum, which elected its president and leadership in open ballots. However, practice revealed that the choice of leaders took place centrally. Control of the kolkhozes was ensured on the basis of political reliability by the party leadership through party members sent from towns to the villages or poor peasants elevated to the status of party cadres.[58]

In order to realize the will of the state, two areas of kolkhoz life had increasingly to be controlled: production on the one hand and the distribution of goods once produced on the other. From the spring of 1930 kolkhozes were given mandatory seeding plans, which permitted the internal structure of plans to be prescribed with the force of law. This law and the regulations supplementing it integrated agricultural production into the planned economy.[59] The state, therefore, wanted to dispose over the crop and animal products produced by the kolkhoz as if it were the owner of the farm, despite it being the group property of its members. This was made possible by the specific system of income distribution prescribed in the model charter. In a system that became known as the residue principle, kolkhoz incomes had first to be used to make compulsory deliveries to the state, then to pay—mostly in kind—the work fees of the MTS; and then, to the prescribed extent (10–15%), seed and fodder funds had to be created for the next year of farming. Distribution to the membership could only be made out of the residue that remained.[60] A similar order of payments was implemented for the monetary income of the kolkhoz: state taxes, insurance premiums, interest on loans and so on had to be settled first. The residue principle thus ensured that state interests would supersede all others. Further, any production losses would also, in the end, burden the membership.

The subordinate position of kolkhoz membership found expression in several points of the model charter. For one thing, the kolkhoz membership was not guaranteed fixed salaries, unlike workers and employees, including sovkhoz workers. They were guaranteed a tax-free minimum wage by the state, above which there was progressive taxation to an upper limit.[61] Furthermore, while the workers were paid monthly, the kolkhoz membership received an income only once a year after harvest, and its level could not be planned in advance because of the prior claim of contributions to the state at unknown levels. This explains why the value of labor day units on collective farms was always determined retrospectively, and was very often lower than had been planned.[62] As a consequence, the household plot had a huge significance in terms of members' livelihoods. A certain portion of the nationalized land under kolkhoz use (a quarter to a half a hectare per family) was handed over for personal use. On these household plots families could keep a cow and a calf, a pig and a piglet, four sheep, and unlimited numbers of rabbits and poultry. The equipment, stables, and sties needed for such household plot farming were exempt from collectivization. Members received the fodder necessary for keeping animals as an in-kind share.[63]

The disadvantageous treatment of the kolkhoz peasantry was not limited to income relations. Members were obliged to work, but the kolkhoz was not required to provide work.[64] Should a peasant wish to seek work elsewhere, that is to say to leave the kolkhoz, this could not be done freely. The local Soviets only issued internal passports in exceptional cases.[65] A further problem was that a workbook was required for taking on industrial labor but kolkhoz members did not have them. They were only permitted to leave if there was a state labor-recruitment campaign in the region.[66]

Soviet labor rights applied only to workers and employees, not to kolkhoz members. This not only meant that labor rights problems had to be resolved within the kolkhoz, but also that members could not rely on state-financed social security and pension provision.[67] The model charter required the formation of a social and cultural fund from kolkhoz income. Adherence to this regulation was not strictly controlled, and as a result this fund was quite minimal in poor kolkhozes. It was only in 1964 that the state began to supplement them.

Kolkhoz membership therefore was not simply an employment category, but a special legal status within Soviet society, which, in several respects, reflected a continuation of the situation of serfdom.[68] The most obvious aspect of this was that kolkhoz members—like serfs—had to seek permission to leave the village.[69] Kolkhoz membership, however, also enjoyed advantages over other social groups. Although at the end of the 1930s urban workers too were granted access to small parcels of land, the household plots of kolkhoz members were bigger.[70] Further, kolkhoz members had the right to sell their produce.[71]

A further aspect that can be regarded as an extension of old Russian and Tsarist peasant rights is the fact that, according to the 1935 model charter, the right to a household plot was enjoyed not by the member, but by the household. Yet, in the 1930s it appeared that the peasant household (*dvor*) would lose its earlier significance, reflected in the fact that kolkhoz membership, unlike that of the mir, was based on individuals.[72] At the same time, from the point of view of the peasant, the basic unit of village society remained the household.[73] Every peasant household which included a kolkhoz member was considered a kolkhoz household, which meant both that its tax burdens were lower than those of the individual peasant, and that it had the right to a household plot that was bigger than those of any other social stratum. Village families with mixed sources of income became quite common.[74]

The kolkhoz system struggled to consolidate, suffering from both a weak work morale and an absence of expertise. Traditional expertise disappeared as kulaks were deported, and the trustworthy cadres brought in from the towns to head the new large-scale farms often lacked the necessary agricultural knowledge. This situation was made even worse during the purges of 1934–38. On the one hand, the mass arrests resulted in constant flux within the state and party apparatus, on the other local leaders were burdened by intense psychological pressures.[75]

It is clear from the above that from the beginning the kolkhoz system suffered from serious structural problems.[76] These had their origins, on the one hand, in the subordinate status of the kolkhoz when compared to the sovkhoz or the MTS. On the other, they were the consequence of the conception which subordinated agriculture as a whole when compared with industry. Ever focused on the interests of industry, Stalin treated agriculture as an inner colony, from which he extracted both material and human resources. This all intensified with the outbreak of the Second World War. A serious labor shortage emerged in agriculture during the war. In order for the women and elderly who remained on the kolkhoz to work harder to supply the army and the urban population, concessions were introduced to Stalin's model charter in respect of both household plots and labor remuneration. These modifications were not retained after the war, however, and kolkhozes were obliged to return to the original model charter.[77] The model charter of 1935 remained untouched until 1969. This explains why, at the end of the 1940s, it was Stalin's original kolkhoz model charter that was exported to East Central European countries together with the other elements of the Stalinist agricultural system.

TRANSFERRING SOCIALIST AGRICULTURE TO THE EASTERN BLOC

Land Reforms after the Second World War

When the Soviet Union appeared as the victorious power in East Central Europe at the end of 1944 and beginning of 1945, it faced a situation in which communist parties enjoyed weak support even among urban workers, and considerably less among the village population. It was precisely in the interest of winning over peasant support that the Soviet leadership was interested in quickly implementing land reforms. Land distribution was in fact contrary to communist ideology which called for the abolition of private property. This is why the literature occasionally contains the claim that the Soviet Union deliberately influenced the post-1945 land reforms to increase the number of economically unviable properties so as to facilitate future collectivization. The fact of Soviet intervention is undeniable, however it has not yet proved possible to confirm that a preconceived, general plan of this kind existed.

Land reform was radical in countries where extensive large estates had remained in place after the post-WWI land reform.[78] This group included Hungary, the eastern half of Germany, and Poland. Proportionately, the largest-scale land reform took place in Hungary, for there, in the interwar period, close to half of cultivated land was concentrated in the hands of large and middle estate owners.[79]

Interwar Agriculture and Land Reform in Hungary

Following the First World War, land reforms had been introduced in East Central European countries to remedy the unequal distribution of land. The motivation was primarily political: to avoid possible revolution by ending rural destitution.[80] In Hungary the bourgeois revolution of 1918 included land reform in its program, but the law—declaring the expropriation of estates over 500 *kataszträlis hold* (kh) (285 ha)—was never enacted.[81] Instead of land reform, the Hungarian Bolshevik Government in 1919 issued a decree nationalizing all large and medium-sized estates and creating cooperatives on them. The conservative regime which came to power after the Hungarian Soviet Republic, also implemented a land reform in 1920. But it affected a mere 8.5% of the country's arable land, so barely changing the unequal structure of landholding.[82] This proportion was much smaller than those in neighboring countries; 27% of arable land in Romania, and 16% in Czechoslovakia had been redistributed after the First World War.[83]

The Hungarian land reform had left the bulk of large estates untouched, and the new Hungary became Europe's large-estate country in the most extreme sense of the word. Nearly half of the country's arable land was owned by a few dozen aristocratic families, yet the proportion of nonaristocratic large estates was also high.[84] By contrast, only about 20% of total arable land belonged to the small estates, under 10 kh (5.7 ha), that made up some four-fifths of all agricultural holdings. This highly skewed distribution of landed property explains why only about 30% of the agrarian population was able to maintain a family from the crops produced on its own land.[85] In mid-1930s, about 70% of agrarian society consisted of people with very little or no land who, as a consequence, were compelled to work as wage labor for others.[86]

It is, thus, very important to stress that at the time of the land reform at the end of the Second World War, two-thirds of the Hungarian agrarian population had not been peasants in the western European sense. Nevertheless, they considered themselves to be peasants and held on to their tiny strips of land (1–2 hectares in size) even if farming them had not paid off. This was because, in agrarian society landownership was paramount, and smallholders whose holdings were so small that they were termed "dwarf-holders" were nevertheless held in higher esteem than agricultural laborers, even if the latter had a higher annual income.

The modernization of agricultural production between the wars progressed at a very slow pace because of the combination of the enormous surplus of (consequently) cheap agricultural labor and unfavorable market conditions which resulted in a large gap between agricultural and industrial prices, and such progress as occurred was devastated by the Great Depression. In the interwar period, nonmechanized capstan threshers were replaced gradually by steam and internal combustion engine threshers. Between 1925 and 1929 the number of tractors increased from 1,189 to 6,800, however in the first half of the 1930s barely more than 100 vehicles were added to the tractor fleet. The spread of harvesting machines was similarly hindered by the availability of very cheap labor. As a consequence of the Great Depression the consumption of artificial fertilizers dropped from 26 kg to 3.5 kg/hectare. The persistence of prewar cultivation methods and a neglect of soil melioration measures explain the stagnation in crop production in the interwar period.[87]

The land reform decree, passed on March 17, 1945, affected close to 35% of the country's agricultural land. Estates bigger than 575.5 hectares (1,000 kataszträlis hold) were expropriated without compensation, as were estates owned or rented by large companies, and the landholdings of war criminals, Arrow Cross members, and far-right political leaders. Gentry estates in excess of 57.55 ha (100 kataszträlis hold) and peasant holdings in excess of 115 ha (200 kataszträlis hold) were expropriated in return for nominal compensation. The difference between them depended on the social origins of the owner. Participants in the anti-fascist resistance were treated as an exception and were allowed to keep 172.65 ha (300 cadastre acres).[88] Almost 60% of the 5.6 million kh (3,222,800 ha) of land seized was distributed among 642,342 claimants—largely agricultural laborers, servants on the large estates and dwarf-holders—while the other 40% (mostly forest and grazing land) became state or cooperative property. Equipment, tools, buildings, seed, and feed originally belonging to the expropriated estates were also taken over in addition to land, as were large machinery stocks and supplementary operations (e.g., mills, grinders, distilleries, etc.): these too became the property of land recipients' cooperatives (in Hungarian: *földművesszövetkezet*). [89]

The land reform resulted in the birth of a new agrarian society: the proportion of landless groups within the peasantry fell from the 1941 level of 46% to 17%, while those in the category of smallholders rose from 47% to 80%, but the new landowners received on average 5 kh less than 3 ha.[90]

Postwar Land Reforms Elsewhere in the Region

The land reform carried out in the Soviet occupation zone in Germany (the future GDR) was similarly radical and affected 30% of total land. The distribution of Junker large estates began on September 3, 1945. The limit on land that could be retained was set at 100 ha, although estates of war criminals were confiscated in their entirety. A total of 2.2 million ha was distributed among 560,000 claimants. In 1939 small and middle peasant farms made up 37.5% of agricultural area; by 1946 this proportion had increased to 66.5%.[91]

While, in Hungary, the new proprietors received land that was registered as private property in the land register, in east Germany a state land fund was created out of the requisitioned large estates, from which land was distributed to land claimants for individual use. Even though this was recorded in land registers, it did not equate to a full property right. Land that had been distributed under the land reform (*vererbbares Eigentum*) could not be sold, rented, or mortgaged. It could be passed on to descendants, but only if they committed to farming, and land could only be given up if the owner found a new farmer to take over the farm.[92]

In Poland, the key feature of the land reform was the breakup of German estates.[93] Three-quarters of distributed land had formerly been German-owned, so it is not surprising that, of the 5.6 million hectares that was divided up, 4.5 million hectares was in the western "Regained Territories." The bulk (483,000) of the 788,000 new peasant farms were established in former German territories. In total, the land distribution affected 20% of national territory.[94]

The Czechoslovak land reform was smaller in scale than in the previous two, but nevertheless resulted in significant structural transformation as a result of the confiscation of lands in German and Hungarian ownership. A third of Bohemian-Moravian territory was divided up, as was a tenth of Slovak territory. Furthermore, land distribution did not end in 1945. In July 1947 and March 1948, the time came for further land seizures as the upper limit on landownership was reduced, eventually, to 50 hectares.[95]

The countries of the Balkans were less affected by the wave of post-1945 land reforms. There the vast majority of land was in peasant hands, either because peasant farms already dominated at the end of the 19th century, as in Yugoslavia and Bulgaria, or because radical land distribution had been carried out after the First World War, as in Romania. In Romania the Law on Agricultural Reform and Colonization of March 22, 1945, redistributed 8% of cultivated land. The act ordered the confiscation of the lands of German war criminals and those landowners who had left Romania after August 23, 1944; and maximum property size was set at 50 hectares.[96] In accordance with the Yugoslav land reform decree of August 23, 1945, close to 400,000 ha of German-owned land was redistributed, and at the same time the upper limit of properties was set at 25–35 ha, depending on the quality of the soil.[97] The most modest land reform took place in Bulgaria, the home the dwarf-holder. As a consequence of the decree of March 12, 1946, which reduced the upper limit to 20 hectares (30 ha in Southern Dobruja), 200,000 ha of land was distributed to 127,000 families.[98]

In total, on the territory of Central and Eastern Europe, 20 million hectares of land was expropriated, of which 12 million hectares were redistributed among three million peasant families.[99] Although the majority of newly established farms were too small to be viable, the land reform had tremendous significance because of its sociopsychological effect. The groups that gained landownership viewed the land reform as a form of historical justice that gave them the chance to become property-owners and independent farmers.[100] Consciousness of private ownership liberated tremendous forces within them. As a result, postwar governments were able to pass the burdens of agricultural reconstruction over to the peasantry. Between 1945 and 1948, years of capital and equipment shortage, peasant farms, old and new alike, ensured the necessary conditions for relaunching production by restricting family consumption

Table 1.1. Land Reforms in East Central Europe after the Second World War

Country	*Time*	*Upper limit for individual use (hectare)*	*Unique characteristics*
Bulgaria	March 12, 1946	20	30 ha in Southern Dobruja. Decree of April 15, 1945, on lower type collective farms.
Czechoslovakia	June 21, 1945	50	Mainly German and Hungarian estates were taken.
Hungary	March 17, 1945	115	For gentry-owners: 58 ha
Poland	September 6, 1944	100	Three-quarters of territory taken was German owned.
Romania	March 22, 1945	50	A quarter of territory taken was German owned.
Yugoslavia	August 23, 1945	45	41% of territory taken was German owned.
Soviet Occupation Zone of Germany	September 3, 1945	100	Landowners stripped of their property were also expelled from their homes.

Source: Nigel Swain and Zsuzsanna Varga, "Postwar Land Reforms in Comparative Perspective," *Öt kontinens: az Új- és Jelenkori Egyetemes Történeti Tanszék Tudományos Közleményei* 11, no. 1 (2013): 141–58.

needs. The results of this could be seen in the rapid regeneration of agricultural production.[101]

The Specificities of Model Transfer in East Central Europe

The small peasant farm thus became the dominant player in the postwar agricultural production structure, but at the same time, cooperative forms were not alien to individual farmers. There were a wide variety of cooperatives in the region, the majority of them consumer, sales, and credit cooperatives, which had already been formed in the first half of the century. Following the land reforms these were supplemented by new ones, but production cooperatives remained uncommon. Examples of the latter were to be found only in Bulgaria and Yugoslavia. As early as the fall of 1944, 579 agricultural producer cooperative farms operated in Bulgaria, the only country in the region with any tradition of this form.[102] In Yugoslavia cooperatives of war veterans were established on expropriated estates. By the end of 1946 there were close to 500 cooperatives of various types. The Yugoslav government then decided that in the future it would only support the establishment of cooperatives similar to the Soviet kolkhoz form, and by the end of the first five-year plan (launched in 1947) half of productive land was collectivized.[103] Albania, which was under powerful Yugoslav influence in this period, also began organizing collective farms in 1946.[104]

Imposing Soviet Control

This all indicates clearly that when the Soviet-Yugoslav conflict erupted, the Soviet charge, that the Tito leadership did not want to collectivize agriculture, was unfounded. In public the Soviet side criticized the Yugoslav Communist party's agrarian policy, whereas very much less was said about the real background to the conflict, Tito's independent foreign policy ambitions. As Soviet–American tension intensified, the Soviet leadership regarded national independence in its sphere of influence as a risk factor.[105]

It was important, therefore, to demonstrate what would be faced by any country that did not fully submit to Soviet desires. It is well known that Yugoslavia was sharply criticized earlier, on June 18, 1948, and then, under Soviet pressure, was expelled from Cominform in 1949.[106] In addition, following this, Moscow launched a series of show trials in the countries of the region to get rid of communist leaders who wanted to adopt the Soviet model but mould it to national interests and characteristics.[107]

As was noted in the introduction, the processes that were carried out in the political, economic, and social lives of the countries that had come into the Soviet sphere of influence in the second half of the 1940s are termed Sovietization in the literature.[108] Sovietization in political life signified a shift from a multiparty system to a Bolshevik-type, one-party system. In the economic sphere, the goal was the abolition of private property and the market economy, and the construction of a planned economy based on state and collective ownership; because the persistence of production based on private ownership by wide social groups was incompatible with Communist Party ideology.[109]

After the Second World War, several waves of nationalization made it possible to exclude market relations and move to a system of centrally managed production and distribution, where companies, now owned by the state, would receive compulsory plan directives on what and how much to produce.[110] The official ideology held that the great advantage of socialism was that the abolition of private ownership of the means of production and the market would make possible an ordered national economy and in doing so insulate them from problems such as overproduction, unemployment and so on.[111] The promise held that, by adopting the Soviet model, the underdeveloped agrarian and agro-industrial countries of the region would quickly become industrial ones. In reality pursuing its military-security and great-power interests, the Soviet Union strove to create an easily controllable bloc which on one hand would become independent of the capitalist West, that is self-sufficient, and on the other dispose of a significant heavy industry and military industry base. Preparation for military conflict in the near future played a significant role in both endeavors.

Those who became the leaders of the Sovietization process were the communists who had spent long periods as émigrés in the Soviet Union between the two world wars, those who had not only embraced the ideology, but also had had the occasion to get to know Soviet-type political, social, and economic structures. Following the Second World War they moved into the leading positions of the local Communist parties. The Soviet Union sent numerous advisors to various ministries, but also to the military and the political police, in order to both assist them in their work and control them.[112] The institution of Soviet advisors in Hungary, as in Romania and Bulgaria, was established within the framework of the Allied Control Commission's Soviet section.[113] A turning point was reached in 1949, when the construction of a long-term system of advisors was accelerated and expanded, first in the military and state security, but eventually also in economic fields. They were tasked with managing and supervising the Stalinist-style transformation of economy and society.[114]

Russian archival sources reveal that, after 1949, not a single significant socioeconomic decision was made in the East-Central Europe region without the participation of Soviet advisors, whether this concerned long-term or short-term development plans, the collectivization of agriculture or the reorganization of the system of social administration. At the same time Soviet advisors fulfilled an important role as information channels for both the Moscow leadership and the Communist Party leadership of Eastern European countries.

The Stalinist Model of Socialist Agriculture Transferred, but Not Entirely

Although the Cominform decree condemning Yugoslavia had not contained any direct orders to launch collectivization, in the second half of 1948 all of the Communist parties of Central and Eastern Europe took decisive steps in this direction. In Spring 1949, collectivization was begun in Romania, Czechoslovakia, Albania, and then Hungary.[115] The Polish party leadership thought in terms of a gradual reorganization.[116] The only exception was the GDR, where, thanks to the uncertain future of Germany, the party leadership was advised by Stalin to delay collectivization.[117]

The restructuring of agriculture along Soviet lines represented a task for the Communist parties of the region for which even the Soviet Communist

Table 1.2. Collectivization in East Central Europe

Country	*Beginning of collectivization*	*Temporary delay of collectivization*	*Completion of collectivization*
Yugoslavia	1945–48	1953	—
Bulgaria	1945–48	1953–55	1958
Albania	1949	1953–57	1966
Poland	1949	1956	—
Czechoslovakia	1949	1953–55	1959
GDR	1952	1953	1960
Hungary	1949	1953–54, 1956–58	1961
Romania	1949	1953–55	1962

Party did not have a well-established recipe, despite the existence of a clear Soviet model.[118] In the Soviet Union, including areas incorporated into the Union after 1945 the private ownership of land had already been abolished before collectivization began. And, as already mentioned, the wording of the Model Charter presupposed nationalized land. But in Central and Eastern Europe, this was not so. Here it was a question of persuading peasants who owned land to join collective farms. What is more, the land reforms of 1945 had further strengthened the system of peasant farming. The conflict that developed as a result explains both the prolonged nature of Central and Eastern European collectivization and the fact that it was interrupted several times.[119]

What is striking when the process of transferring the Stalinist agrarian model to East Central Europe is examined is the primacy of the "inner colony status." The first step was the construction of an environment of economic extraction. This was facilitated to a large degree by the continuation into the postwar years of the wartime system of compulsory deliveries which, from 1948, was increasingly operated on a "class war basis," which is to say that the burden on peasant strata with more land was gradually increased. The system of compulsory deliveries meant that an increasing proportion of goods was acquired by the state almost free, or at a merely symbolic price. At the same time, income was channeled from agriculture to industry through the pricing and taxation systems. The principle of progressivity increased the burden on wealthier farmers and exceeded any normal understanding of progressive taxation: tax rates and delivery quotas reached penal levels, which translated into severe discrimination against kulaks. This was no accident, for the Communist parties of the region had also taken over in its entirety from Soviet collectivization practice the necessity of class war in the village, that is to say war against rich peasants who had been declared kulaks.

The verdict on this group was strongly influenced by the fact that the state above all sought to get hold of its property, for this formed the foundation for the newly established collective farms.

The construction of the elements of the Stalinist system of socialist agriculture was launched under the banner of modernization. On the one hand existing state farms were further developed. One basis for these was the fact that the land reforms after the Second World War had not distributed all of the land that they had seized. State farms were established everywhere, but not to the same extent. Their goal was to promote the improvement of production through quality seed production and plant breeding. In Poland and Czechoslovakia state farms had an 11% share of the land, while in Romania, for example, it was only 5%. On the other hand, in the name of modernization, starting in 1948, there was an upsurge in the construction of a Soviet-style system of MTS, the second pillar in the Stalinist system.

The artel had become the third and most important unit in the Stalinist system, and this undoubtedly served as a model in Central and Eastern Europe too; but there were two significant differences in the initial phase of collectivization. One of these concerned landownership. In Central and Eastern Europe private peasant landownership remained in place, although it must be noted that in the majority of countries this was merely a formality.[120] Ownership was not accompanied by true rights of disposal, that is to say land could not be sold or rented.

The second difference was the authorization of several types of collective farm, which again can be explained by the desire to forestall conflict between those in power and the peasantry.[121] With the exception of Bulgaria, where from 1950 only one form existed, which was very similar to the Soviet kolkhoz, all countries permitted at least two, but in some places three or four types of cooperative.[122] They were termed simply type I, type II, type III. and type IV cooperative. It is important to note that the four types did not exist in all countries, and that the types did not mean the same thing in every country. The essential difference lay in what portion of activity was carried out collectively, and, related to this, what proportion of income was allocated on the basis of labor executed or land contributed. In types III and IV the vast majority of income was based on labor executed, even if some symbolic sum was paid as a rental for land contributed. These higher order types (III and IV) were most similar to the kolkhoz form. Their model rules can be considered to be copies of the 1935 kolkhoz model charter statute.[123] Livestock and farming equipment had to be contributed to the communal farm, labor had to be carried out collectively in accordance with the labor organization and remuneration systems set out in the kolkhoz model charter. Types I and II referred to lower order producer cooperatives. In type I only certain operations (such as ploughing and sowing) were carried out jointly, and thus, when distributing income, the amount of land contributed played the key role. In type II farms, draft animals and farming equipment had to be contributed to the common farm, but livestock could still be held privately. Initially this was called the "Bulgarian" type, despite the fact that it quickly disappeared from Bulgaria.

These national differences aside, there is no questioning the fact that, from the end of the 1940s, the Sovietization of agriculture in East Central Europe took the form of all key elements of the Stalinist system of socialist agriculture, including the kolkhoz, as prescribed in the Soviet Union in the 1935 model charter.

NOTES

1. This section relies heavily on the following works from the international literature: Roger P. Bartlett, ed., *Land commune and peasant community in Russia: communal forms in imperial and early Soviet society* (New York: St. Martin's Press, 1990); Robert William Davies, ed., *From tsarism to the New Economic Policy: continuity and change in the economy of the USSR* (Ithaca, NY: Cornell University Press, 1991), 47–65, 79–91; Mikhail D. Dolbilov, "Zemel'naya sobstvennost' i osvobozhdeniye krest'yan," in *Sobstvennost' na zemlyu v Rossii: Istoriya i sovremennost'*, ed. Dmitriy Fedorovich Ayatskoy (Moskva: Rosspen, 2002), 45–152; Nikolai M. Dronin and Edward G. Bellinger, *Climate Dependence and Food Problems in Russia 1900–1990: The Interaction of Climate and Agricultural Policy and Their Effect on Food Problems* (Budapest and New York: Central European University Press, 2005), 1–84; Wendy Goldman and Donald Filtzer, eds., *Hunger and war: food provisioning in the Soviet Union during World War II.* (Bloomington: Indiana University Press, 2015); Boris B. Gorshkov, *Peasants in Russia from Serfdom to Stalin: Accommodation, Survival, Resistance* (London: Bloomsbury Academic, 2018); Carol Scott Leonard, *Agrarian reform in Russia: the road from serfdom* (Cambridge and New York: Cambridge University Press, 2009); David A. J. Macey, *Government and peasant in Russia, 1861–1906: the prehistory of the Stolypin reforms* (DeKalb, IL: Northern Illinois University Press, 1987); Judith Pallot, *Social change and peasant land-holding in pre-revolutionary Russia* (Oxford: University of Oxford, School of Geography, 1982); Pavel Nikolayevich Zyryanov, "Pozemel'nyye otnosheniya v russkoy krest'yanskoy obshchine vo vtoroy polivine XIX–nachale XX veka," in Ayatskoy, *Sobstvennosti*, 153–95; for Hungarian-language literature on the topic see: György Kövér, "Az orosz obshchina történetéhez: Áttekintés a hetvenes évek szovjet szakirodalmáról" [The history of the Russian obshchina: An overview on the Soviet historiography of the 1970s], *Történelmi Szemle* 21, no. 2 (1978): 338–54; György Ránki, "Oroszország gazdasági fejlődése, 1861–1917" [The economic development of Russia], *Századok* 118, no. 3 (1984): 433–85; Endre Tanka, *Az obscsinától a társasgazdálkodásig: Az orosz földviszonyok fejlődési vázlata* [From the obshchina to the collective farming] (Budapest: Szövetkezeti Kutató Intézet, 1988).

2. Macey, *Government and peasant*, 5–40.

3. The basic principle was that the peasants received their homes and house plots without the need to pay compensation. As far as arable land was concerned, the coun-

try was divided into three belts, and the belts were divided into four to nine regions each. The maximum and minimum that peasants were to be granted were defined differently for each belt. Leonard, *Agrarian reform in Russia*, 43–51.

4. For more on this concept which would become highly politicized, and later it was part of the package that was transferred to the socialist countries, see: Lynne Viola, "Collectivization in the Soviet Union: Specificities and Modalities," in Iordachi and Bauerkämper, *The Collectivization of Agriculture*, 58–60.

5. It is interesting to note that in 1905 barely one-quarter of the land theoretically marked for the peasantry in European Russia's 50 governing territories was being used on private land principles.

There was a concentration of obshchina-free lands in the western part of the empire, in a belt extending from the Baltics to the Black Sea (essentially along the banks of the Dnieper). Ibid., 48.

6. A law was passed in 1893 whereby land could only by redistributed by the obshchina every 12 years.

7. M. R. Dohan, "Foreign trade," in Davies, *From tsarism*, 212–36.

8. Abraham Ascher, *P. A. Stolypin: the search for stability in late Imperial Russia* (Stanford, CA: Stanford University Press, 2001), 208–60; David A. J. Macey, "'A wager on history': the Stolypin agrarian reforms as process," in *Transforming peasants: society, state and the peasantry, 1861–1930*, ed. Judith Pallot (Houndmills, Basingstoke: Macmillan, 1998), 149–73.

9. Dorothy Atkinson, *The end of the Russian land commune, 1905–1930* (Stanford, CA: Stanford University Press, 1983), 71–113.

10. In the Hungarian-language literature Sándor Szakács and Endre Tanka point out that the passages of the decree on land are often interpreted as nationalization, but that there was at the time no talk of national ownership or state ownership. Sándor Szakács, "A Szovjetunió mezőgazdasága (1917–1939)" [The agriculture of the Soviet Russia], *Agrártörténeti Szemle* 23, no. 1–2 (1979): 95–141; Tanka, *Az obscsinától*, 76–80.

11. Karl-Eugen Wädekin, "The Agrarian Question in Marxist and Leninist Thought," in *Agrarian Policies in Communist Europe: A Critical Introduction*, Studies in East European and Soviet Russian agrarian policy, vol. 1 (The Hague–London: Allanheld, Osmun Publishers and Martinus Nijhoff Publishers, 1982), 4–13.

12. The Congress was held in Petrograd from January 10 to 18 (23–31), 1918.

13. Moshe Lewin, *Russian Peasants and Soviet Power* (London: Allen & Unwin, 1968), 81–107.

14. Alec Nove, *An Economic History of the U.S.S.R.* (London: Penguin Books, 1975), 59–63.

15. Ibid., 105–13.

16. "The price divergence (i.e., "price scissors") reached its peak by October 1923, when industrial prices were three times higher, relative to agricultural prices, than they had been before the war." Nove, *An Economic History*, 93–96.

17. Robert William Davies, Mark Harrison, and Stephen G. Wheatcroft, eds., *The economic transformation of the Soviet Union, 1913–1945* (Cambridge: Cambridge University Press, 1994), 136–58; Andrew Sloin and Oscar Sanchez-Sibony, "Econ-

omy and Power in the Soviet Union, 1917–39," *Kritika: Explorations in Russian and Eurasian History* 15, no. 1 (2014): 7–22.

18. *J. V. Sztálin művei* [Collected works of Stalin], vol. 7 (Budapest: Szikra, 1950), 277–79.

19. Moshe Lewin, "Taking Grain: Soviet Policies of Agricultural Procurements before the War," in *The Making of the Soviet Union* (New York: Pantheon, 1985), 142–77.

20. Stephan Merl, "The role of agriculture in Soviet industrialization," in *Communist agriculture: Farming in the Soviet union and Eastern Europe,* ed. Karl-Eugen Wädekin (London and New York: Routledge, 1990), 3–22; Elena Osokina, *Our Daily Bread: Socialist Distribution and the Art of Survival in Stalin's Russia, 1927–1941* (Armonk, NY: M.E. Sharpe, 2001), 28–41.

21. Lenin addressed this problem in late 1919 at the first meeting on party work in villages: ". . . although we have abolished private land ownership, the peasant is still an owner, mainly because this group of peasants has a remaining food product surplus. The middle peasant produces more food than he needs, and as such, through having grain surpluses, becomes the exploiter of the starving worker. This is the key problem, the key contradiction." V. I. Lenin, "Beszéd a falusi pártmunka kérdésében tartott I. Összoroszországi tanácskozáson, 1919. november 18-án" [Speech at the first all-soviet meeting dedicated to the questions of the rural party work], in *V. I. Lenin művei*, vol. 30, *1919. szeptember–1920. április* (Budapest: Szikra, 1953), 133.

22. James R. Millar and Alec Nove, "A Debate on Collectivization: Was Stalin Really Necessary?," *Problems of Communism* 25, no. 4 (July–August 1976): 49–62.

23. Lewin, *Russian Peasants*, 214–50.

24. J. V. Sztálin, "Az iparosításról és a gabonaproblémáról (1928. július 9.)" [Industrialization and the Grain Problem, July 9, 1928], in *J. V. Sztálin művei* [Collected works of Stalin], vol. 11, *1928–1929. március* (Budapest: Szikra, 1950), 171–73.

25. Ibid., 195–96.

26. Ibid., 196.

27. J. V. Sztálin, "A gabonabegyűjtésről és a mezőgazdaság fejlődésének távlatairól (1928. január)," [Grain procurements and the prospects for the developments of agriculture], in *J. V. Sztálin művei*, 11: 6–7.

28. J. V. Sztálin, "A gabonafronton: A Vörös Tanárképző Intézet, a Kommunista Akadémia és a Szverdlov Egyetem hallgatóival 1928. V. 28-án folytatott beszélgetésből," in *J. V. Sztálin művei*, 11: 104.

29. J. V. Sztálin. "Az iparosításról és a gabonaproblémáról (1928. július 9.)" [Industrialization and the Grain Problem, July 9, 1928], in *J. V. Sztálin művei*, 11: 185–87.

30. Ibid., 176.

31. "Under the Soviet system . . . large grain farms, being at the same time state farms, do not at all require for their development either the maximum profit or the average profit, but can content themselves with a minimum profit (and sometimes do without any profit at all for a while), and this, coupled with the absence of absolute ground rent, creates exceptionally favorable conditions for the development of large grain farms." J. V. Sztálin, "A munkás-paraszt összefogásról és a szovhozokról: Az

SZK(b)P KB plénumán 1928. július 11-én mondott beszédből" [On the bond between the workers and peasants and on state farms: A speech delivered at the plenum of the Central Committee of the CPSU], in *J. V. Sztálin művei*, 11: 210.

32. For more, see: Robert F. Miller, *One Hundred Thousand Tractors: The MTS and the Development of Controls in Soviet Agriculture* (Cambridge, MA: Harvard University Press, 1970).

33. Nove, *An Economic History*, 180–81.

34. Ibid., 182–83.

35. Robert Conquest, *The Harvest of Sorrow: Soviet Collectivization and the Terror-Famine* (Oxford: Oxford University Press, 1986), 87–114, 144–63; Robert William Davies, *The Socialist offensive: the collectivisation of Soviet agriculture, 1929–1930* (London: Macmillan, 1989), 372–81; L.V. Izyumova, "Gosudarstvennaya politika v kontekste sotsial'noy modernizatsii kolkhoznoy derevni v 1930–1960-ye gg," in *Gosudarstvennaya agrarnaya politika v Rossii XX veka v kontekste modernizatsionnogo protsessa* (Vologda: Rus', 2006), 78–101; Karl-Eugen Wädekin, "Soviet Agriculture under Stalin: Collectivization and Its Results," in *Agrarian Policies*, 14–30.

36. 5.5 million farms still used wooden ploughs. Lewin, *Russian Peasants*, 214–50.

37. Davies, *The Socialist offensive*, 51–56.

38. Vladimir F. Stanis, *The Socialist Transformation of Agriculture* (Moscow: Progress Publishers, 1976), 85–86.

39. Nove, *An Economic History*, 172–74.

40. Ibid., 238–40.

41. Among these is most significant is a five-volume collection of documents, the volumes of which were published from 1999 to 2006. This grandiose publication of sources is attention worthy not only for having been prepared in a cooperative project between Western and Russian scholars and archivists, but also because, beyond materials from central archives, it offers a rich collection of documents from local archives. Viktor Petrovich Danilov, ed., *Tragediya sovetskoy derevni: Kollektivizatsiya i raskulachinanie: Dokumenty i matieriali v 5-kh tomakh. 1927–1939*, 5 vols. (Moskva: Rosszpen, 1999–2006). A selection of materials from the first two volumes was published in English: Lynne Viola, Victor Petrovich Danilov, Nikolai A. Ivnitskii, and Denis Kozlov, eds., *The War Against the Peasantry, 1927–1930* (New Haven: Yale University Press, 2005).

42. Nove, *An Economic History*, 161–62.

43. The first version of the Model Charter was drafted in December, 1929, based on Stalin's recommendations. They were passed on January 5, 1930. Robert William Davies, *The Soviet collective farm, 1929–1930* (London: Macmillan, 1980), 75–97.

44. Davies, *The Socialist offensive*, 269–90.

45. Ibid., 311–30. On the tools of state violence and peasant opposition see: Lynne Viola, *Peasant Rebels under Stalin: Collectivization and the Culture of Peasant Resistance* (New York and Oxford: Oxford University Press, 1996).

46. Tanka, *Az obscsinától*, 100.

47. Ibid., 195–98.

48. Robert William Davies–Stephen G. Wheatcroft, eds., *The years of hunger: Soviet agriculture, 1931–1933* (New York: Palgrave Macmillan, 2003), 358–60.

49. Sheila Fitzpatrick dedicated a separate chapter to this Congress in her 1994 book. See: Sheila Fitzpatrick, *Stalin's Peasants: Resistance and Survival in the Russian Village After Collectivization* (New York–Oxford: Oxford University Press, 1994), 117–27.

50. One-quarter of the 1,433 participants were kolkhoz presidents, and another quarter were brigade leaders. The others were from the kolkhoz membership, but primarily activists who earlier had joined and were tightly connected to the kolkhoz. With the proportion of party members dropping from 44% to 27% the party leadership tried to demonstrate that it was interested in the opinions of the peasants. Ibid., 118–19.

51. Ibid., 121–22.

52. Stalin's speech on this matter was published by Pravda on March 13. Ibid., 123.

53. Later, on several occasions, Iakovlev warned local leaders to take care "not to let wolves in sheep's clothing reenter the kolkhoz." Ibid., 123–24.

54. I. Goals and tasks; II. On the land; III. On farming tools; IV. The operation of the artel and artel management; V. On membership; VI. The artel's financial tools; VII. The organization and payment of labor, and labor discipline; VIII. Artel management. See: "Primernyĭ sovet sel'khoztekhniki," in *Sobranii zakonov i rasporyazheniy rabot-krest'yanskogo pravitel'stva SSSR* 1935. goda 11. In Hungarian: *A szovjet mezőgazdasági artelek minta-alapszabálya* [The model charter of the Soviet agricultural artel's] (Budapest: Földművelésügyi Minisztérium, 1952).

55. On the characteristics of the operations of kolkhoz see: M. A. Beznin and T. M. Dimoni, *Agrarnyy stroy Rossii 1930–1980-kh gg* (Moscow: Lenand, 2014), 12–38; Davies, *The Soviet collective farm*, 1–14, 56–67; Fitzpatrick, *Stalin's peasants*, 103–51; Stephan Merl, *Bauern unter Stalin: Die Formierung des Kolchossystems 1930–1941* (Berlin: Duncker & Humblot, 1990); Jenny Leigh Smith, *Works in Progress: Plans and Realities on Soviet Farms, 1930–1963* (New Haven: Yale University Press, 2014), 32–146; Karl-Eugen Wädekin, "The Soviet Kolkhoz: Vehicle of Cooperative Farming or of Control and Transfer of Resources," in *Cooperative and Commune,* ed. Peter Dorner (Madison: The University of Wisconsin Press, 1977), 95–116.

56. In August, 1932, the scope of the act on the defense of socialist property was extended to the kolkhoz.

57. At the abovementioned 1935 congress there was a debate over what was to be done with those late joiners who had neither equipment nor animals at the time of joining, because they had either sold them or lost them due to tax arrears. For such cases it was finally prescribed that joiners pay a monetary fee upon entry.

58. The party leadership sent 25,000 urban workers to the countryside from 1928 to 1930. For an excellent overview of this process: Lynne Viola, *Best Sons of the Fatherland: Workers in the Vanguard of Soviet Collectivization* (New York–Oxford: Oxford University Press, 1987), 121–51.

59. Wädekin, "The Soviet Kolkhoz," 109–10.

60. See Section VII and further Davies, *The Soviet collective farm*, 131–58.

61. Nove, *An Economic History*, 244–50.

62. Davies–Wheatcroft, *The years of hunger*, 375–82; O. M. Verbitskaya, *Rossiyskoye krest'yanstvo ot Stalina k Khrushchevu, seredina 40-kh–nachalo 60–kh godov* (Moscow: Nauka, 1992), 10–39.

63. See Section III. Further: Vladislav Alexandrovich Belyanov, *Lichnoye podsobnoye khozyaystvo pri sotsializme* (Moskva: Ékonomika, 1970), 3–54; Karl-Eugen Wädekin, *The Private Sector in Soviet Agriculture*, 2nd ed. (Berkeley and Los Angeles and London: University of California Press, 1973), 35–60; S. V. Yakhnovskaya, "'Ochen' mnogo razvelos' skota u rabochikh . . . Iz opyta gosudarstvennogo regulirovaniya LPKh," *Rodina* 24, no. 3 (2012): 157–160.

64. In 1939 the minimum compulsory work-unit was legally regulated. Wädekin, *The Soviet Kolkhoz*, 106–7.

65. The decree on domestic passports was passed in December, 1932. Fitzpatrick, *Stalin's peasants*, 95–102.

66. Ibid., 90–95.

67. Lewin, *Russian Peasants*, 406–521.

68. Sheila Fitzpatrick, "Ascribing Class: The Construction of Social Identity in Soviet Russia," *Journal of Modern History* 65, no. 4 (1993): 745–70.

69. At the same time, should the kolkhoz member have left the village and found an urban job, he/she did not need to keep kolkhoz membership a secret, because it improved his/her labor status, given that it proved he/she was not a kulak. Ibid.

70. During the war, thanks to a labor shortage, certain concessions were introduced. One of the effects of this was a significant expansion in individual land use. Not only could kolkhoz members use land individually, but so could workers and employees in cities and in territories near urban spaces. There was an effort to put an end to these concessions after the war, beginning in 1946. Andrei Markevich, "Finding additional income: subsidiary agriculture in Soviet urban households, 1941–1964," in *A dream deferred: new studies in Russian and Soviet labour history*, ed. Donald Filtzer et al. (Bern and New York: Peter Lang, 2008), 385–416.

71. This was made possible by the institution of the kolkhoz market, introduced in 1932. As such, once the kolkhoz fulfilled all its responsibilities to the state and had surpluses for the next year, it could sell its produce in this market. These applied to kolkhoz members and individual farmers. Nove, *An Economic History*, 184–85.

72. Fitzpatrick, *Stalin's peasants*, 130–36.

73. This was legally confirmed in Stalin's 1936 constitution by introducing the concept of the kolkhoz household (*kolhoznij dvor*). Wädekin, *The Soviet Kolkhoz*, 103–6.

74. There were cases where the head of the family became a kolkhoz member while the sons continued to farm independently, or took on work in the mines or the railroad. Fitzpatrick, *Stalin's peasants*, 164–72, 218–24.

75. Sheila Fitzpatrick, "How the Mice Buried the Cat: Scenes from the Great Purges of 1937 in the Russian Provinces," *The Russian Review* 52, no. 3 (1993): 299–332.

76. Wendy Goldman and Donald Filtzer, eds., *Hunger and war: food provisioning in the Soviet Union during World War II* (Bloomington: Indiana University Press, 2015).

77. Viola, "Collectivization in the Soviet Union," 76.

78. Paul Brassley, "Land reform and reallocation in interwar Europe," in *Contexts of Property in Europe: The Social Embeddedness of Property Rights in Land in Historical Perspective*, eds. Rosa Congost and Rui Santos (Turnhut, Belgium: Brepols, 2010), 145–64; Dietmar Müller, "Bodeneigentum und Institutionenwandel in Ostmittel- und Südosteuropa 1918–1945–1989," *Zeitschrift für Ostmitteleuropa-Forschung* 61, no. 3 (2012): 332–55.

79. Under pressure from the Soviets, this far-reaching decision was accepted not in the form of an Act, but as a government decree (decree 600/1945. M. E. sz.). On the political background of the decision see: Donáth, *Demokratikus földreform*, 57–71; Imre Kovács, *Magyarország megszállása* [Occupation of Hungary] (Budapest: Katalizátor Iroda, 1990), 234–39; Orbán, *Két agrárforradalom*, 22–45.

80. Brassley, "Land reform and reallocation," 145–64.

81. In Hungary before 1972 the official unit of land measurement was *kataszträlis hold* (abbreviated: kh) or "cadastral yoke" (1.42 English acres, or 0.57 hectare). Figures are also given in hectares (abbreviated: ha), to facilitate comparison with other countries.

82. Miklós Szuhay, "Evolution of Hungarian Agriculture during the Inter-War Years (1918–1945)," in *Hungarian Agrarian Society from the Emancipation of Serfs (1848) to the Re-privatization of Land (1998)*, ed. Péter Gunst (New York: Columbia University Press, 1998), 177–90.

83. The neighboring states could afford to be more generous, relying on the estates formerly owned by Austrian and Hungarian aristocrats. Ákos Bartha, "A két világháború közti csehszlovák, jugoszláv és roman földbirtokrendezés" [The land reallocation in the interwar Czechoslovakia, Yugoslavia and Romania], *Valóság* 55, no. 10 (2012): 96–111; Marchut, "Land reforms in the little entente;" Dietmar Müller, "Property between delimitation and nationalization: the notion, institutions and practices of land proprietorship in Romania, Yugoslavia and Poland, 1918–1948," in *Property in East Central Europe: Notions, Institutions and Practices of Landownership in the Twentieth Century*, eds. Hannes Siegrist and Dietmar Müller (New York: Berghan, 2015), 117–43.

84. Szuhay, "Evolution of Hungarian Agriculture," 178–79.

85. Gábor Gyáni, "Social History of Hungary in the Horthy Era," in *Social history of Hungary from the reform era to the end of the twentieth century*, eds. Gábor Gyáni, György Kövér, and Tibor Valuch (New York: Columbia University Press, 2004), 271–507.

86. Martha Lampland gives a deep insight to the ambitions and life strategies of these social groups: Lampland, *The object of labor*, 35–108.

87. Michael Kopsidis, "Agricultural development and impeded growth: The case of Hungary, 1870–1973," in *Agriculture and economic development in Europe since 1870*, eds. Pedro Lains and Vicente Pinilla (London and New York: Routledge, 2009), 286–94; Szuhay, "Evolution of Hungarian Agriculture," 179–80.

88. Sándor Szakács, "From Land Reform to Collectivization (1945–1956)," in Gunst, *Hungarian Agrarian Society*, 285–97.

89. Ibid., 325–29.

90. Tibor Valuch, *The Social History of Hungary in the Second Half of the 20th Century* (Budapest: Osiris, 2001), 200–207. Peter Kenez, *Hungary from the Nazis to the Soviets: the establishment of the Communist regime in Hungary, 1944–1948* (Cambridge, and New York: Cambridge University Press, 2006), 110–15.

91. For summaries of the latest research on East German land reforms see: Arnd Bauerkämper, *Ländliche Gesellschaft in der kommunistischen Diktatur: Zwangsmodernisierung und Tradition in Brandenburg 1945–1963* (Köln, Weimar, and Wien: Böhlau Verlag, 2002), 68–122; Maria Hetzer, Elisabeth Meyer-Renschhausen, Leonore Scholze-Irrlitz, Laura Stoye, and Viktoria Müller, *Transitzone Dorf: Ein Ort zwischen Bodenreform und Kollektivierung* (Leipzig: Zank, 2015) Jonathan Osmond, "From Junker estate to co-operative farm: East German agrarian society 1945–1961," in *The workers' and peasants' state: communism and society in East Germany under Ulbricht, 1945–1971*, eds. Patrick Major and Jonathan Osmond (Manchester and New York: Manchester University Press, 2002), 135–39.

92. This approach was in many ways similar to the implementation of the 1917 land decree. Jochen Laufer, "Die UdSSR und die Einleitung der Bodenreform in der Sowjetischen Besatzungszone," in *"Junkerland in Bauernhand"? Durchführung, Auswirkungen und Stellenwert der Bodenreform in der Sowjetischen Besatzungszone*, ed. Arnd Bauerkämper (Suttgart: Franz Steiner Verlag, 1996), 21–36.

93. On September 6, 1944, the Lublin Committee ordered the division of large estates. The decree differentiated the limits of personal use by region. In Poland's middle and eastern territories estates larger than 50 ha were divided, while in western areas only estates above 100 ha were affected. In the interest of repopulating one-time German-held large estates in the west, masses of Poles were transferred from western Belorussia and western Ukraine. Antony Polonsky and Bolesław Drukier, *The Beginnings of Communist Rule in Poland* (London and Boston: Routledge & Kegan Paul, 1980).

94. Andrzej Korbonski, *Politics of Socialist Agriculture in Poland: 1945–1960* (New York and London: Columbia University Press, 1965), 74–80.

95. The process of distributing land in Czechoslovakia is analyzed in detail in István Gaucik, "A csehszlovákiai magyarság gazdasági státuszvesztése (1945–1948)" [The economic status losses of the Hungarian minority in Czechoslovakia] (PhD thesis. ELTE TDI, Budapest, 2011).

96. David A. Kideckel, "The Socialist Transformation of Agriculture in a Romanian Commune, 1945–1962," *American Ethnologist* 9, no. 2 (1982): 320–40.

97. Teréz Kovács, "Az 1945 utáni jugoszláv agrárpolitika hatása a délvidéki magyarokra" [The effects of the post-1945 agrarian policy on the Hungarian minority in Yugoslavia], in Schlett, *Földindulások—sorsfordulók*, 138–40.

98. Gerald W. Creed, "The Politics of Agriculture in Bulgaria," *Slavic Review* 54, no. 4 (1995): 843–68.

99. Iván T. Berend and György Ránki, *Economic development in East-Central Europe in the 19th and 20th centuries* (New York and London: Columbia University Press, 1974), 343–46.

100. Erik Mathijs, "An historical overview of Central and Eastern European land reform," in *Political Economy of Agrarian Reform in Central and Eastern Europe*,

ed. Johan Frans Maria Swinnen (Brookfield, VT: Ashgate Publ., 1997), 33–54; Hannes Siegrist and Dietmar Müller, "Introduction: Property in East Central Europe: notions, institutions and practices of landownership in the twentieth century," in Siegrist and Müller, *Property in East Central Europe*, 1–28.

101. Włodzimierz Brus, "Postwar Reconstruction and Socio-Economic Transformation," in *The Economic History of Eastern Europe 1919–1975*, eds. Michael Charles Kaser and Edward Albert Radice, vol. 2 (Oxford: Clarendon, 1986), 564–641.

102. Karl-Eugen Wädekin, "The Early Postwar Period in Eastern Europe," in *Agrarian policies*, 31–34.

103. Melissa Bokovoy, *Peasants and Communists: Politics and Ideology in the Yugoslav Countryside, 1941–1953* (Pittsburgh: University of Pittsburgh Press, 1998), 47–54.

104. *Örjan Sjöberg, Rural Change and Development in Albania* (Boulder, CO: Westview, 1991).

105. László Borhi, *Hungary in the Cold War, 1945–1956: between the United States and the Soviet Union* (Budapest: CEU Press, 2004); Stefano Bottoni, *Long Awaited West: Eastern Europe since 1944* (Bloomington: Indiana University Press, 2017), 10–56; Mark Kramer, "Stalin, the split with Yugoslavia, and Soviet East European efforts to reassert control, 1948–1953," in *Imposing, maintaining, and tearing open the Iron Curtain: the Cold War and East-Central Europe, 1945–1989*, eds. Mark Kramer and Vít Smetana (Lanham, MD: Lexington Books, 2014), 51–102; Miklós Mitrovits, "A népi demokráciától a proletárdiktatúráig: A csehszlovák–lengyel–magyar eset összehasonlító vizsgálata" [From the people's democracy to the proletarian democracy: The comparative analysis of the Czechoslovakian, Polish and Hungarian cases], in *Sztálin árnyékában: A szovjet modell exportja Kelet-Közép-Európában (1944–1948)* [Under the shadow of Stalin: The export of the Soviet Model to the East-Central-Europe] (Budapest: Országház Könyvkiadó, 2018), 9–32.

106. Cominform is the abbreviation for the Communist and Workers' Parties Information Bureau. This Moscow-directed international body was set up in late September 1947 in a Polish town of Szklarska Poreba.

107. György Hódos, *Show trials: Stalinist purges in Eastern Europe, 1948–1954* (New York: Praeger, 1987).

108. The term *Sovietization* originally meant the takeover of power by workers' and soldiers' councils (Soviets) during and after the 1917 Revolution. It was later used to describe the spread of the Soviet practice of power, pertaining, for example, to the Baltic states. Over time the term was used in an ever-wider sense—concerning economic, social, and cultural aspects. After the Second World War Western literature used the term Sovietization to describe that process through which the Soviet Union forced its own political, economic, and social systems upon countries that had entered its sphere of influence (occupied or annexed). Émigré authors spread the term, attaching a strongly negative meaning to it. This was particularly characteristic of West German literature. After the collapse of the Soviet Union the term was once again used more intensively, but with a much more neutral character. Balázs Apor, Péter Apor, and E. A. Rees, eds., *The sovietization of Eastern Europe: new perspectives on the postwar period* (Washington, DC: New Academia Publishing,

2008); Michael Lemke, "Einleitung," in *Sowjetisierung und Eigenständigkeit in der SBZ/DDR (1945–1953)* (Cologne and Weimar and Vienna: Böhlau, 1999), 13–14; Krysztof Brzechczyn, ed., *New Perspectives in Transnational History of Communism in East Central Europe* (Berlin: Peter Lang Verlag, 2019); Norman Naimark, "The Sovietization of Eastern Europe, 1944–1953," in *The Cambridge History of the Cold War*, vol. 1, *Origins*, eds. Melvyn P. Leffler and Odd Arne Westad (Cambridge–New York: Cambridge University Press, 2010), 175–97.

109. David Mitrany, *Marx Against the Peasant: A Study in Social Dogmatism*, 2nd ed. (New York: Collier Books, 1961); Nigel Swain, "The Fate of Peasant Parties during Socialist Transformation," in *Bauerngesellschaften auf dem Weg in die Moderne: Agrarismus in Ostmitteleuropa 1880 bis 1960*, eds. Angela Harre–Helga Schultz (Wiesbaden: Harrasowitz, 2010), 163–76.

110. Berend and Ránki, *Economic development*, 347–52.

111. János Kornai, *The socialist system: the political economy of communism* (Oxford: Clarendon Press, 1992), 140–59.

112. On the construction of the advisor system see: Norman M. Naimark, *The Russians in Germany: a history of the Soviet Zone of occupation, 1945–1949* (Cambridge, MA: Belknap Press of Harvard University Press, 1995).

113. Between 1945 and 1947, the Allied Control Commission, comprising delegates from the Allied Powers, had the rights to "regulate and control" implementation of the armistice terms in the interim until a definitive peace settlement was reached. Since the Commission in Hungary was headed by a Soviet general, this amounted to legitimizing direct interference in the country's internal affairs.

114. On Hungary see: Magdolna Baráth, *A szovjet tényező: Szovjet tanácsadók Magyarországon* [The Soviet factor: Soviet advisors in Hungary] (Budapest, Gondolat, 2017); Pál Germuska, "Szovjet tanácsadók magyar hadiipari vállalatoknál az 1950-es években" [Soviet advisors in the Hungarian military industry], *Századok* 142, no. 6 (2008): 1465–81.

115. Swain, "Eastern European Collectivization," 501–39.

116. Dariusz Jarosz, "Polish Peasants versus Stalinism," in *Stalinism in Poland, 1944–1956: Selected Papers from the Fifth World Congress of Central and East European Studies*, Warszawa, 1995, ed. trans. A. Kemp-Welch (Basingstoke and London: Macmillan; New York: St. Martin's Press, 1999), 59–77.

117. Elke Scherstjanoi, *SED-Agrarpolitik unter sowjetischer Kontrolle, 1949–53* (München: Oldenbourg Verlag, 2007).

118. The Soviet leadership faced a similar challenge only in the Baltic states, but collectivization there went hand in hand with the nationalization of land. David Feest, "The Collectivization of Agriculture in the Baltic Soviet Republics, 1944–1953," in Iordachi and Bauerkämper, *The Collectivization*, 81–113.

119. Richard J. Crampton, *Eastern Europe in the Twentieth Century—and after*, 2nd ed. (London and New York: Routledge, 1997); Karl-Eugen Wädekin, "Collectivization in Eastern Europe: The Common Pattern and the Deviations," in *Agrarian Policies*, 63–81.

120. Swain, "Eastern European Collectivization."

121. At the beginning of Soviet collectivization a looser form of association, the TOZ, was still recognized, but later on the artel form was clearly preferred. In the Baltic states this was the only authorized form. Kestutis K. Girnius, "The Collectivization of Lithuanian Agriculture, 1944–1950," *Soviet Studies* 40, no. 3 (1988): 460–78; David Feest, *Zwangskollektivierung im Baltikum: Die Sowjetisierung des Estnischen Dorfes 1944–1953* (Vienna: Böhlau, 2007); Anu Mai Kõll, *The Village and the Class War: Anti-Kulak Campaign in Estonia* (Budapest: CEU Press, 2013); Geoffrey Swain, "Deciding to Collectivize Latvian Agriculture," *Europe-Asia Studies* 55, no. 1 (2003): 39–58.

122. Four types were designed in Yugoslavia in May of 1949. Type IV was based on joint ownership of the land, while the other three saw private property remain, for which various levels of lease fees were paid. Bokovoy, *Peasants and Communists*, 120–25.

123. Swain, "Eastern European Collectivization," 507–8.

Chapter Two

Transplanting the Soviet Model

The First Attempt at Collectivization (1949–1953)

DEBATES ON THE ADOPTION OF THE KOLKHOZ MODEL, 1948/49

With the intensification of the Soviet–American confrontation, the demands from Moscow were clearly articulated for the acceleration of Sovietization in the region.[1] After the founding of the Cominform in 1947, the Muscovite group within the Hungarian Communist Party[2] monitored and strove to conform with every detail of Soviet change; they increasingly sensed that the Stalinist model had to be applied not only to political structures, but also to the transformation of the economy. Companies employing more than 100 workers were nationalized without warning in March 1948. Following this, agriculture remained the only sector of the national economy where private property continued to dominate.

The bulk of peasant society, which included middle peasants with plots of 15–20 kh (8.6–11.4 ha), as well as the mass of old and new smallholders with 5–10 kh (2.9–5.7 ha), unequivocally rejected the kolkhoz. This was an enormous challenge for the Communist Party, since these 600,000 farms accounted for two-thirds of all agricultural land.[3]

The hostility of the Hungarian peasantry to collective farming was so well known to the leaders of the Communist Party that they avoided the topic from the start and strove to avoid even appearing to be preparing to introduce the Soviet kolkhoz system. Nothing was said about the matter to the public or the party membership. Furthermore, the Hungarian Communist Party's relationship with villages and peasant society had always been one of its weak points, and this tended the party toward caution. The party's Muscovite agricultural expert, Imre Nagy, counted on a long transition. Thanks in part to his family background and in part to his rural experiences in the 1920s, he had deep knowledge of Hungarian peasant society.[4] His view was that the three sectors of agriculture (private, cooperative, state) would exist alongside one another for a long time, and that people's democracy "could not, for economic or political reasons, give up on the economic development of the decisive branch of the capitalist sector represented by petty-commodity-producing small farms, nor strengthening the alliance with middle peasants on this basis."[5]

At the beginning of 1948 the Village (from May 1948 Agrarian Policy) Committee headed by Imre Nagy was commissioned to prepare the guiding principles of cooperative policy.[6] The document that it prepared argued for a gradual, slow transition. The guiding principles accepted at the April 22, 1948, meeting of the Politburo were as follows:

> In our country the conditions for generally replacing individual farms with producer cooperatives have not yet been reached. . . . The transition from individual farms to cooperative farming is a slow process that requires voluntary resolve on the part of the peasants and further patient re-education . . . the cooperative sector cannot play a decisive role in agricultural production for a good time to come.[7]

The section on cooperatives of the program of the new Workers' Party, the Hungarian Workers' Party (HWP) was similar in content.[8] (The forced merger of the Hungarian Communist Party and the Social Democratic Party formally took place on June 12, 1948.)

They did not have long to wait before the Soviet verdict arrived. According to L. Baranov, deputy head of the CPSU Foreign Affairs Department:

> With only rare exceptions, the draft program statement refers to the peasantry in a unified, undifferentiated manner. The document does not define party relations with the poor peasantry, the middle peasantry and the kulaks. There is no mention of kulaks and the struggle against them . . . we also see as improper the fact that in the establishment of plan-based agriculture . . . priority was given to technical measures (land improvement, fertilizer, and so on) instead of issues of a social nature (developing all forms of cooperatives, providing credit facilities, etc.).[9]

The Cominform decree of June 18, 1948 condemning Yugoslavia acted as a further warning, as a result of which the leadership of the HWP quickly revised its agrarian policy. At the end of June, HWP First Secretary Rákosi informed both the Politburo and the Central Committee (CC) of the Cominform meeting. A month later the public was informed of the changes brewing in agrarian policy. Timed to coincide with the celebration of new bread, Mátyás Rákosi gave a speech that cited was many times in later years. We should examine the contents of this famous speech of his given in Kecskemét on August 20, 1948.

> There are two paths open to the Hungarian peasantry. One is old, familiar, and exaggerated individual farming, where everyone only cares for themselves, where the fundamental principle is "might is right." The unavoidable, ineluctable consequence of this is that the big fish will devour the little fish, the big kulak farms will get even stronger, even richer and destroy the poorer working peasantry. . . . Democracy not only supports the cooperativization of the working peasantry, but also arranges things so that the trees of the kulak big producers do not reach the sky, so that kulak expansion is kept within limits.[10]

Behind the scenes, in the leading bodies of the HWP, the timetable for collectivization was being concretized, as a part of the debate between Imre Nagy and Ernő Gerő (the secretary responsible for the economic policy), which dated back to November 1947, reached a new stage. On September 10, 1948, the Politburo ordered Nagy to submit within four weeks a written statement of his position on the party collectivization policy, peasant property, the peasantry as a historical category, and people's democracy.[11] Although a debate on Imre Nagy's views would only take place months later, Magdolna Baráth notes, "there was a general sense that Imre Nagy was being side-lined when questions related to agriculture were being debated, and Gerő was increasingly becoming the master of this territory."[12]

At the November 27, 1948 meeting of the CC of the HWP, in the context of an analysis of the international and domestic situation, Mátyás Rákosi stated that a move toward Soviet-style collectivized agriculture was one of the most pressing tasks. In his closing comments Rákosi set out a concrete schedule: "Within three to four years we must get this question to the point where 90% of the Hungarian peasantry and 95% of Hungarian land is cultivated through proper socialist, joint, collective farming."[13]

In order to document this strategic decision for the other "fraternal parties," Ernő Gerő published an article in the Cominform journal at the end of 1948 with the title *The Policy of the Hungarian Workers' Party in the Villages*. In it, although without mentioning his name, he sharply criticized Imre Nagy's views on agrarian policy.

> Although it was fully clear to the leadership of our party that, in villages too, we are moving toward a sharpening of the class struggle . . . there was still a comrade in the Politburo who held that the path of capitalist development in the Hungarian village had already been blocked. Naturally he drew from this mistaken position the conclusion that there was no class war in villages and no need to intensify the fight struggle the kulaks. The Politburo rejected this right-wing opportunist position.[14]

By the end of 1948, therefore, the HWP leadership had freed itself of the "dissenting opinion" represented by Imre Nagy.[15]

LAYING THE FOUNDATIONS OF STALINIST AGRICULTURE: STATE FARMS AND MACHINE STATIONS

As noted in chapter 1, at the pinnacle of the Stalinist system of socialist agriculture stood the state-owned, large-scale farms, the sovkhozes. They represented the highest order of ownership, and the embodiment of state property. In interwar Hungary a number of state-owned, "treasury estates" had been in operation. Some specialized in horse breeding (Kisbér, Bábolna, Mezőhegyes), and there were others that dealt with plant breeding and the supply of seeds; and in animal husbandry their activities extended to cattle, sheep, and pigs. Their common task was to promote the development of agricultural production.[16]

After the 1945 land reform, the state agricultural estates were given tasks similar to those of the earlier treasury estates: to ensure smallholders were supplied with quality seeds and pure breeding stock, and to provide good examples of how to use modern production procedures. The Communist Party intended them to serve as model large-scale farms, and so, in 1948, the re-structuring of state estates became part of the plan of the HWP Agriculture and Cooperative Policy Department. As a first step they were reorganized into farming organizations operating with an independent corporate form, termed national companies. Development plans including land expansion plans were worked out and a new wage and accounting system was introduced. This, however, proved to be only a temporary stage on the path to conforming with system of the planned economy. Within the Ministry of Agriculture, they were first administered by the State Farming Center, and then the State Farms' Directorate. Under the provisions of Law XXV on the first five-year plan, they were to be developed as model farms. Paragraph 35 of the Law stated:

> Over the plan period, state farms must be developed into significant economic forces, which, as socialist large-scale farms, should serve as model farms and nodes for the scientific operation of agriculture, as examples of good farming; and should assist the working peasantry, and in particular the producer cooperatives, with breeding stocks and quality seeds, and at the same time contribute to ensuring provision of necessary food supplies to the non-farming population.[17]

This explains why the largest portion of agricultural investment (42.4%) went to state farms, but it was not enough to counter the exceptional growth in the acreage that they farmed.[18]

Table 2.1. The Number of State Farms and the Development of Their Territory Between 1949 and 1956

Year	*Number of farms (at the end of the year)*	*Total territory (thousands of kh)*	*Ploughing area (thousands of kh)*	*Percentage of the country's arable land*
1949	299	554	389	4.1
1950	375	827	582	6.1
1951	396	1,067	767	8
1952	501	1,600	1,164	12.1
1953	469	1,677	1,189	12.5
1954	494	1,693	1,198	12.6
1955	472	1,684	1,181	12.6
1956	466	1,682	1,166	12.4

Source: Központi Statisztikai Hivatal, *A szocialista mezőgazdasági üzemek működése, 1956, Statisztikai időszaki közlemények 7* (Budapest: KSH, 1957), 13.

At the same time the farms also began to specialize, yet they could not reach the results expected of them. Their yields, for example, did not reach those of landed estates of over 1,000 kh (570 ha) between the wars. Despite this, they played a significant role in the central procurement of food stocks. In 1951 they cultivated 8% of arable land, but provided from it 15% of all produce collected.[19] It should also be noted that where state farms were located close to large-scale industrial plants of various kinds, they played a direct role in alleviating their supply problems. A leading agrarian politician of the Kádár-era, remembered the early phase of his career on a state farm in Borsod county: "We had a very hard headed first secretary there by the name of József Prieszol. He had an industrial mentality, and always had an eye for the interests of industrial workers. When he called me on the phone I knew to ask 'Comrade Prieszol, how many wagons of porkers shall I send?'"[20]

Their production was not helped either by the fact that, under the banner of constant vigilance, experts deemed "class alien" before 1945 were sacked or pushed into the background. They were replaced by cadres who lacked the appropriate expert training but were politically trustworthy. In the mid-1950s hardly more than 10% of directors had a university education. Managers were also replaced rather frequently.[21]

There was another change in the management of the farms in early 1952: the State Agriculture and Forest Farms Ministry, which would become the State Farms and Forests Ministry half a year later, was established alongside the Ministry of Agriculture, and András Hegedüs—from the party center—was named Minister. The party leadership explained this subdivision of responsibilities by claiming that the management of individual farms and cooperatives required different methods from state farms and forests in state hands, a difference that could not be resolved with a single ministry.[22]

An even bigger role in the implementation of collectivization than that of the state farms devolved to the machine stations, the Hungarian version of the Soviet machine and tractor stations (MTS). The first machine station was opened on November 23, 1947 in Kisszállás, the hundredth on December 5, 1948, in Tard, and the three-hundredth on May 14, 1950, in Lovasberény.[23]

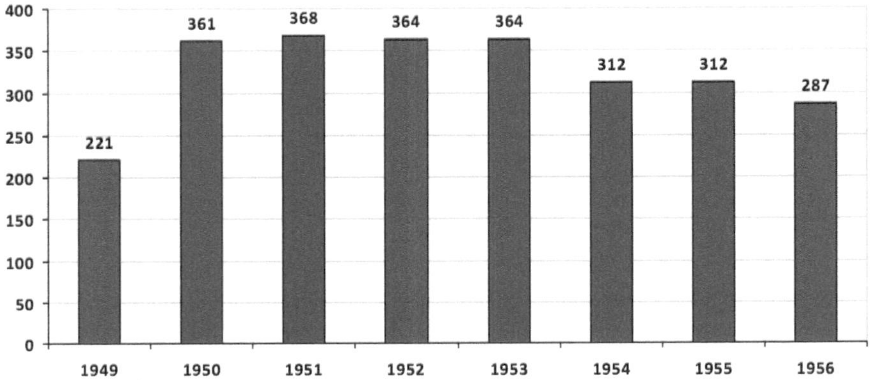

Figure 2.1. Number of Tractor Stations (1949–1956). Source: Központi Statisztikai Hivatal, *A szocialista mezőgazdasági üzemek, 1956*, 88.

Initially their role was to assist individual farmers, especially new landholders, by hiring them equipment. At the end of July 1948 the Cooperative Policy Department of the HWP prepared a submission for the Politburo's Administration Committee in which it was emphasized that: machine stations, as the advanced bastions of the working class, will be one of the most important tools in the socialist transformation of agriculture.[24] They did indeed take on significant roles in both the collectivization campaigns and the management of newly established producer cooperative groups and producer cooperatives. The work of the machine station network was assisted by two Soviet advisors, A. D. Zadvarnov and A. E. Alalikin.

The consequence of copying the Stalinist model in this case was that the mechanization of Hungarian agriculture was resolved exclusively through the use of state-owned large machines.[25] At the beginning of the process, neither individual farmers nor producer cooperatives could purchase new machines.[26] Then the land recipients' cooperatives, which in 1945 had received the expropriated machinery of large estates, responded to a central directive and "offered" their tractors, threshing machines, and all equipment with motor traction to the state sector. At the same time, privately owned engines and machinery were confiscated. The implementation of this was outlined by Ernő Gerő, the leader of the Agricultural Department, as follows:

> We have taken numerous economic measures to limit and push back the kulaks. . . . But all these orders have not fundamentally attacked the kulaks. . . . The current situation is that kulaks (and exploiting village elements similar to them) own 7,000 tractors and approximately 13,000 threshing machines at a time when the state in its machine stations has at most 1,200–1,400 tractors and about 250–300 threshing machines.

Judging inadequate the measures taken so far, he continued:

> We must go further and bring together the entire stock of large-scale agricultural machinery into the hands of the state. . . . Taking into state ownership need not take the form of confiscation, that is to say, we do not have to do what was done when nationalizing industrial plants. . . .[27]

But this was the path followed in practice. If, for example, an owner did not meet the ploughing requirement prescribed in decrees, or did not return his machines to working order by a given deadline, or failed to use his engine for "appropriate activities in the interest of agricultural production," then the machines concerned could be confiscated.[28]

By creating a state machinery monopoly, both producer cooperatives and individual farms were placed in a position of dependence. This was reflected in the fact that the very high fees for machine station work were set centrally, and usually had to be paid in kind. In this way, the machine stations also played an important role in state procurement.[29] Furthermore, they played a wide-ranging management role in the life of producer cooperatives. They had a detailed say in farming decisions and supervised how production plans were met. For this reason, the leaders of machine stations were chosen primarily on political grounds, mostly from factory workers. Initially they underwent a two-week training course, but then from 1949 they were trained at the Agricultural Academy, organized on Soviet lines.[30]

A great deal of tension was generated by the fact that, when the employees of machine stations worked on producer cooperative land, their primary concern was to fulfill as quickly as possible their own quantitative plans, so consequently they paid little attention to the impact of their work the next year's crop. This was also affected by the fact that tractor drivers were unqualified. The young drivers, from poor peasant families and with a few months' training, had minimal knowledge and were for the most part unable to maintain their machinery or carry out minor repairs.[31] The introduction on a campaign basis of female tractor drivers also only served to increase the operational problems;[32] and all this had a very negative impact on the wear and tear of the machinery stock.

Like state farms, machine stations operated at a loss. This, however, did not impact the fact that, after state farms, they received the biggest share of agricultural investments of the first five-year plan (25.8%). An indication of their exceptional status was the fact that when, in 1952, their national center was merged into the Ministry of Agriculture as a main department—with the name State Agricultural Machinery Works—it was given its own separate floor that could only be entered with a special permit.[33]

GRADUALISM AND PRODUCER COOPERATIVE TYPES

The third pillar of the Stalinist system of socialist agriculture was the producer cooperative sector. The HWP worked out its initial tactics in light of the Hungarian peasantry's fear of the kolkhoz and the strength of its ties to the land. It was well known that a half of agricultural laborers and estate servants had not received land in 1945, and an attempt had been made to push this poor peasantry toward cooperative production in order to satisfy their hunger for land. The governmental decree of August 29, 1948, on renting agricultural land had set an upper limit of 25 kh (14.25 ha). Where the total of rented and owned land exceeded 40 kh (22.8 ha), the amount above that level could similarly be confiscated. The decree gave preference in the use of this newly freed land to joint cultivators over individual small-scale renters, to land-renting cooperatives or land-renting groups within farming cooperatives.[34] Such groups cultivating collectively could share in concessions when using machine station services and signing production contracts. Of the 245,000 kh (139,650 ha) confiscated, 60% was put to indivisible common rental, while 40% went to individual use. The largest proportion of land confiscated on this basis was in Szolnok, Csongrád, Békés, and Hajdú counties. Communal land leasing and cultivation was most common in Szolnok, Hajdú, Bihar, Békés, Csongrád, and Szabolcs counties. Individual small-scale rental dominated in the counties west of the Danube.

Some months later it became apparent that owners of small and dwarf farms who had opted for the cooperative format had not put their own land into communal production. A report submitted to the Agriculture and Cooperative Policy Committee stated: "*The poor and disorganized state of the jointly farming producer groups established to date threatens to compromise and ruin the reputation of the producer cooperative movement and make future development difficult.*"[35] [Emphasis in original.] Responding to this situation the committee decided that centrally elaborated regulations must create a clean slate.[36] Initially it was intended to introduce two types of collective farming. But the Ministry of Agriculture decree released at the end of December, 1948, partly responding to experiences in Bulgaria, identified three types of producer cooperative group (*tszcs*).[37] Type I was termed the "general producer cooperative group." The name of Type II was "average distribution producer cooperative group" and Type III was termed "joint producer cooperative group." All three types functioned within the framework of land recipients' cooperatives, and therefore did not have an independent legal identity.

In Type I *producer cooperative groups*, fertilizing, ploughing, and sowing which could be done by machine (grains, small seeds, etc.) was carried out jointly, while other work and harvesting was executed individually. The goal was to produce a single crop on a consolidated parcel of land. After sowing, the parcels were divided up for individual harvesting by drawing lots. Members were individually responsible for paying the cooperative group's costs of joint work on their land, and they also contributed to the operations and investment savings fund for the following year.

In Type II *producer cooperative groups*, farming was similar to that of the Type I groups in many respects. After joint fertilization, ploughing, and sowing, the land was parcelled out for individual cultivation, but harvest was largely common, and joint threshing was mandatory. The true difference came in how the harvest was distributed. Joint farming costs and an amount earmarked for reserve were first deducted from the harvested product. The rest was split among the members in proportion to their sowed land, but on the basis that they received a share "according to the average" yield of the whole parcel.

In Type III *producer cooperative groups* joint farming was extended to all the members' land, with the exception of household plot of one and a half kh (0.3 ha). All draft animals and livestock in excess of those permitted for household plot use,[38] together with the more important items of agricultural equipment (carts, sowing machines, ploughs, harrows, etc.) had to be contributed into the common stock. Fifteen percent of the value of property items was placed in the cooperative's indivisible common fund, while 85% was paid in installments to the members, generally over four years. All work was to be carried out jointly, in cooperative work structures. A maximum of 25% of the income remaining after deducting costs and reserve fund contributions could be distributed in accordance with the amount of land contributed, the rest had to be distributed in relation to the amount of labor performed. The labor share was calculated, according to the Soviet model, on the basis of labor day units. In the spring of 1950 permission was given for Type III producer cooperative groups that had sufficient territory to be capable of large-scale and mechanized production to become independent. These independent producer cooperatives came closest to the Soviet model, the kolkhoz, as will be discussed in more detail below.

At the end of 1948 and beginning of 1949, the approximately 500 producer groups that had been created within the cultivating and land-recipients'

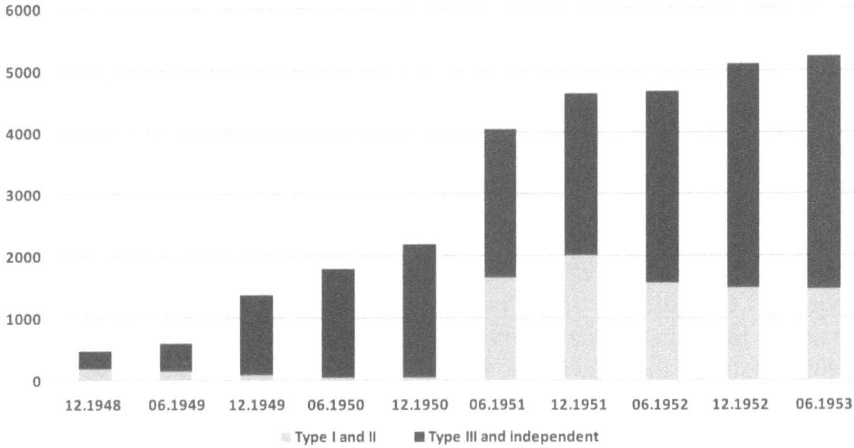

Figure 2.2. Number and Share of Producer Cooperatives December 1948–June 1953. Source: *A szocialista mezőgazdasági üzemek, 1956*, 47.

cooperatives had to choose which cooperative model to adopt for their future farming. It is striking how many areas opted for the Type III groups—93% in Transdanubia, for example.[39] The fact that these types were promised the most state support undoubtedly also contributed to this preference. A national study also revealed that a third of families that joined were landless peasants, while two-thirds owned dwarf farms of under 7 kh (4 ha). These Type III producer cooperative groups were provided with land and necessary equipment by the state and land recipients' cooperatives. At the same time, it was also discovered that where smallholders established Type III producer groups, "property-owning working peasants do not contribute their own land to joint cultivation. . . . Most often, they engage in intensive farming on the privately cultivated land kept out of the cooperative, and extensive farming on the land placed into the group."[40]

The Ministry of Agriculture's Producer Cooperative Department prepared a statistical report at this time on the extent to which members undertook private farming outside their group. It revealed that in the northern regions (Abaúj, Borsod, Heves, Nógrád, Zemplén) more than half the members held a private farm, of on average of 4.6 kh (2.6 ha). In areas east of the Tisza River this proportion was 20–25%. In the area between the Tisza and Danube (Bács-Bodrog, Pest) two-thirds of members had plots averaging 5 kh (2.85 ha), while this level was lower in areas west of the Danube, at approximately 30%.[41]

The HWP Agriculture and Cooperative Policy Committee expressed the tasks at hand as follows: "This year must be viewed as a probationary period in this respect, but in the fall external private farming in all three types must be restricted, and less liberal conditions must be placed on the state's considerable support."[42]

It was no coincidence that 1949 was seen as a probationary period. As mentioned above, the party at this point did not have a well-constructed national apparatus, but just as big a problem was the fact that a significant mass of the party membership itself had to be convinced of the necessity of collectivization. At this point the communist leaders' vehement tactical denial in the years following the war that they were planning to introduce the soviet system backfired. In this situation the only task which the party leadership could embark on with any chance of success was class war in the villages following the Stalinist model. By this it could visibly demonstrate to the Soviet leadership that it had distanced itself from the Yugoslav Communist Party's peasant policy.

With the launch of the first five-year plan on January 1, 1950, the Hungarian Party leadership adopted Stalinist economic policy, which based economic growth on internal accumulation and subordinated agriculture to the role of "inner colony."[43] In addition to restricting consumption on the part of the population, it was hoped that the necessary material base for growth could be created by draining income from agriculture. The new price system that was introduced in 1946 to stabilize the currency had already had a detrimental impact on agricultural prices. In addition, the system of compulsory deliveries, a hangover of the war economy but endowed increasingly since 1948 with a class war role, also served to divert income from agriculture. The principle of progressivity was used to place a disproportionate burden on better-off groups; and, by setting procurement prices at levels that did not even cover costs, the state did not even pay average agricultural producers for the goods they produced.[44]

The system of compulsory deliveries and the distorted price system together played a significant role siphoning off peasant incomes, but it should not be forgotten that classic income-extraction was also in operation in the form of the tax system. Between 1949 and 1953 the tax burdens on the peasantry tripled.[45]

The "inner colony" role of the agricultural sector was also reflected in the investment policy of the first five-year plan. According to the law that implemented the five-year plan, over five years, 8 billion forints or 15.7% of investment was to be directed to agriculture.[46] Individual peasant farms, which were to be terminated, received nothing for investment. State farms, the highest-order property form, received 42.4% of investments, followed by machine stations, which received a quarter of investments. It is evident therefore that disproportionately little remained for the producer cooperatives

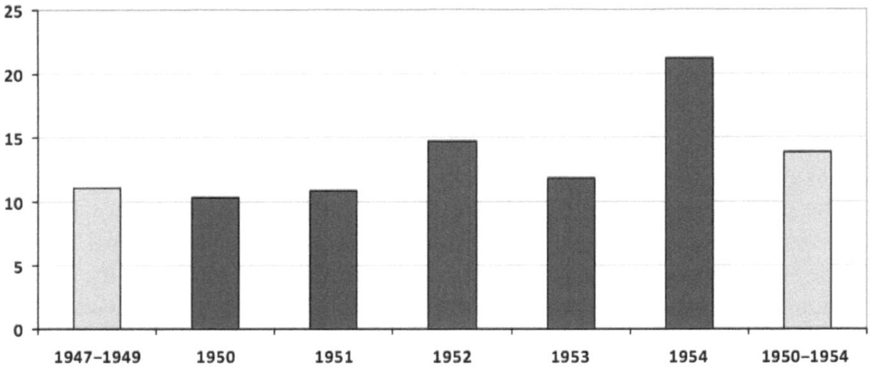

Figure 2.3. Share of Agriculture in Total Peoples' Economy Investments (%) 1947–1954. Source: Központi Statisztikai Hivatal, *Adatok és adalékok a népgazdaság fejlődésének tanulmányozásához, 1949–1955*, 40–41.

which had been created to replace private farms; yet they had been allotted a sizable task in the planned 150% growth in agricultural production.[47] According to the five-year plan, by fall of 1953, 55–60% of agricultural land was to be under producer cooperative cultivation.

THE FIRST COLLECTIVIZATION CAMPAIGN: MOVING TOWARD THE SOVIET MODEL CHARTER

Faced with rather modest results in the first year of model transfer, Rákosi decided to make a change to the collectivization methods used so far. In 1950, the party decided in advance how many producer cooperative groups to establish in each county in a given year. To prepare for this they endeavored to give the impression that there was mass demand in Hungarian peasant society to create cooperatives, and that the party leadership was merely responding to grassroots demand. To demonstrate this demand, the first national congress of producer cooperative groups and machine stations was held in Budapest on January 24–25, 1950. Mátyás Rákosi addressed the congress:

> The land recipients' producer cooperative movement in Hungary has passed the test, stood its ground and developed deep roots . . . this congress shows that the members of producer cooperative groups are convinced that the path that our Party led them on was the right one, as was that path we aimed for, that which the peasantry of our liberator the great Soviet Union had taken.[48]

The event received wide publicity. It was covered intensively in various radio programs and in the press.[49] The message directed at the peasantry was clear:

> The first national congress of the members of producer cooperative groups and machine stations has come to an end. The delegates have returned home . . . and now are, with new vigor, setting to the task of . . . the strengthening and reproduction of socialist-style agricultural large-scale production, the construction of socialist agriculture. . . . As long as agriculture is composed of petty-commodity-producing peasant farms—which daily give birth to capitalism—the state power of the working class only stands on firm socialist-economy ground on one leg. For us to firmly stand on both legs, capitalism must be eliminated in villages too, socialism must be built.[50]

Following this, it appeared entirely logical for the HWP Politburo to pass a decree on January 26, 1950, setting the pace of development in numerical terms. It was planned to increase the number of producer cooperative groups from 1,350 to 2,500–2,700, and expand their acreage from the then 400,000 kh (228,000 ha) to 7–800,000 kh (399,000–456,000 ha) with the number of families affected rising from 50,000 to 100,000.[51] In the interest of achieving the planned target, a land consolidation campaign—considerably larger in scale than in the previous year—was set out: "In order for autumn to pass smoothly, it is necessary for a land consolidation process similar to last year's to be implemented in 1,000 villages on the behalf of 1,200 producer cooperative groups, also for property restructuring in 200 villages for 200 producer cooperative groups."[52]

As is well known, the original aim of land consolidation was to unify fragmented farm plots into a single parcel in the spirit of promoting more rational farming. In contrast, the function of land consolidation when part of collectivization campaigns was to loosen peasants' ties to the land. The primary goal of land consolidation in this context was to acquire the best village lands for the producer cooperatives under formation, and create a contiguous area out of them. In order to do this, they could seize land of individual farmers who did not want to join the collective farm and offer them exchange land from another part of village land. Although the legal regulations stressed that exchange land had to be of equal quality and value, in practice it was often of poorer quality and remote. What is more, the rules for implementing land consolidation held that kulaks' affairs had to be handled last.

In light of the experiences of 1949, the government organs in charge of model transfer made every effort to get peasants to join Type III farms, which

Table 2.2. The Number of Partial and General Land Consolidations 1949–53

Type	*1949*	*1950*	*1951*	*1952*	*1953*
Partial	463	1,013	714	834	104
General	—	352	200	311	98

Source: Az FM jelentése a tagosításokról, 1953. április 25. [Report on the land consolidations given by the Ministry of Agriculture] MNL OL, M-KS 276. f., 74. cs., 10. ő. e.

resembled most the kolkhoz, rather than joining simpler cooperative farms, which were seen as hiding places for individual farmers.[53] At the same time a new need was formulated for the elaboration of a cooperative form closer to the kolkhoz than any before. The Politburo also dealt with this matter in early 1950. The relevant decree stated:

> In the spring of 1950, after necessary preparation, based on the democratically expressed resolution of the membership, 10–15 of the most economically and politically developed producer cooperative groups must be transformed into the more developed type, the Agricultural Producer Cooperative, *which will differ from the kolkhoz type of cooperative only in the fact that it will cultivate land that is not nationalized.*[54] [My emphasis]

A good month later, the Agriculture and Cooperatives Department reported to the Politburo on the state of developments. By this time, they had worked out everything about which it was expected that the Ministry of Agriculture would articulate centrally published operational regulations. The key guiding principle was as follows: "1) When preparing model rules, the starting point must be the kolkhoz model charter."[55] According to their submission, the most developed Type III producer cooperative groups would free themselves from the ties of land recipients' cooperatives, and over the course of 1950 transform into independent producer cooperatives with their own legal identity.

The regulations for independent producer cooperatives were drafted over the spring,[56] but this text contained not a single reference to the example of the soviet kolkhoz. The argumentation pointed to the economic advantages of large-scale production, the increasing income arising as a result, and the improving living conditions of the peasantry.[57] Its structure was also simpler than that of the 1935 model statute.[58] The requirement to contribute land was set out explicitly, as was payment of nominal rent for the land. The maximum for land in individual use, termed "in household cultivation" at the time, was allowed to remain at 1/2 to 3/4 kh (0.3–0.4 ha), but at the same time no limits were put on privately held livestock. This was clarified in the government decree released on August 11, which stated: "Members can, to meet their own and their family's household needs, keep: one cow, one calf, one sow and her piglets, five sheep or goats, an unlimited number of poultry, rabbits and bees, and further, in proportion to the family's needs, one or two fattening pigs."[59] From this point on the term "household plot" became general.

The spring decree already contained the regulation that communal labor had to be carried out in the frame of labor brigades and work teams, and further that members' labor should be measured and valued in labor day units. The mandatory labor minimum was only introduced by further revisions in

August.[60] It was clear from the start, however, that, at year end, the amount that could be used for distribution on the basis of accumulated labor units in cash or kind was that which remained after obligations to the state had been made and funds necessary for future farming set aside: the residue-of principle income distribution, as noted above in the Soviet case.

Adoption of the Stalinist kolkhoz model was made difficult not only by the fact that all its essential elements were foreign to Hungarian circumstances, but also because legal regulation was in a rather chaotic state in 1950. Minister Ferenc Erdei's memorandum on this topic indicates: ". . . unified model rules can be edited together from a total of eight sources, but only in a way where numerous important details cannot be taken from any laws but must be reformulated on the basis of party decrees. This makes the question so complicated that we must consider strengthening the summary unified text in a law."[61] The model rules for producer cooperatives and the operational regulations for producer cooperative groups were issued as an ordinance by the Minister of Agriculture in a single unified text at the beginning of 1951.[62] This meant that the regulations for both covered the following groups of questions: the cooperative's landholdings and level of equipment; the membership; the cooperative's organs; the organization and evaluation of labor, labor discipline and income distribution. The regulations stated explicitly that kulak and other exploiters could not be members of cooperatives farms.[63] This regulation also introduced a prohibition on leaving within three years.

INTERMEDIARIES—THE AGITATION AND PROPAGANDA APPARATUS IN ACTION

An important part of the preparations for the collectivization drive during the fall of 1950 was the theoretical and practical training of the party apparatus. At the beginning of April, the HWP village seminars had to dedicate two sessions to working through teaching material titled *The Socialist Agriculture of the Soviet Union*. A report was prepared based on experience in six counties (Fejér, Békés, Zala, Somogy, Hajdú, Szabolcs) which provides a picture of the effects of the course. In many places it was reported that the seminars were not held, and generally "the material was covered only superficially, with the repetition of key phrases, without theoretical questions being supported by practical examples and without introducing actual problems. For example, the issue of work units, which appeared rather confusing, was in essence not discussed in any of the seminars."[64]

At the same time a massive campaign was launched to provide education and training on the most foreign element of the kolkhoz form, the work unit.

Table 2.3. The Comparison of Kolkhoz Model Charter (1935) and Agricultural Producer Cooperative Model Charters (1950–51)

Kolkhoz Model Charter (1935)	*Agricultural Producer Cooperative Model Charters (1950–51)*
After three years of good behavior kulaks can be accepted into the kolkhoz, but priests and their children cannot.	Kulak and other exploiters cannot become members
The member cannot leave the kolkhoz freely (domestic passport system). Leaving is equivalent of exclusion: requiring a 2/3 majority of the membership.	Ban on leaving for three years.
Leadership elected by the general assembly for 2 years.	Leadership elected by the general assembly for 2 years.
Land in the hands of the state.	Land remains in private hands, but is used collectively, for which the collective farm pays land rent to the owner.
Duty to contribute farming equipment, draft animals and livestock.	Duty to contribute faming equipment, animals.
Area for household plot: 1/4–1/2 hectare	Area for household plot: 1/4–1/2 kh (0.14–0.28 ha)
Animals allowed: 1 cow, 1 calf, 1 pig, 1 piglet, 4 sheep, unlimited poultry and rabbits.	Animals allowed: 1 cow, 1 calf, 1 sow and her piglets, 5 sheep or goats, unlimited poultry, rabbits and bees, 1–2 fattening pigs.
Sphere of activity: crop production, livestock farming, household industry.	Sphere of activity: crop production, livestock farming, processing and selling own produce.
Compulsory sowing plans.	Compulsory sowing plans.
Duty to deliver produce to state.	Duty to deliver produce to state.
Residual remuneration.	Residual remuneration.
Remuneration based on work unit system, once a year, advances payable within certain limits.	Remuneration based on work unit system, once a year, advances payable within certain limits.
Collective labor organization (brigade, labor team).	Collective labor organization (brigade, labor team).
Disciplinary punishment (admonition, warning, reprimand, rescinding of work units, fine, exclusion).	Annual labor minimum (initially 80, then 120 work units).

The Ministry of Agriculture sent work-unit-teaching brigades to the countryside through the winter.[65] The radio program *Village Radio* also took part in the campaign.[66]

At the same time, programs singing the praises of Soviet agriculture became daily fare on the radio. A good opportunity for this was the visit of the latest 200-strong peasant delegation to the Soviet Union, which Rákosi announced at the end of January at the first congress of producer cooperative groups and machine stations. The official goal was for the participants to get to know the Soviet Union's socialist agriculture, the system of kolkhozes, sovkhozes, MTSs, and scientific institutes.[67] The delegation was split into five groups. The first traveled to Ukraine, the second to Kyrgyzstan; the third group visited large-scale farms in the vicinity of Moscow, the fourth visited the Michurinsk area, while the fifth traveled in Uzbekistan and Tajikistan.[68] The members of the delegation had to write regular reports on the kinds of direct experiences they had gained regarding "development surpassing all imagination" taking place in Soviet agriculture and in Soviet villages. Naturally, this was not all that delegation was entrusted with. It might be said that their work only began in earnest upon their return to Hungary. They had to undertake a tour of Hungary, providing reports to individually farming peasants on the results of Soviet agriculture.

Meanwhile, the question of creating the apparatus necessary to transfer the soviet model remained unresolved. In a decree of March 29, 1950, the Secretariat responded to it. "One of the most decisive tasks for specialist agricultural training is to turn adult cadres—largely from industrial worker and poor peasant backgrounds—into leaders with an understanding of specialist issues, for service in the socialist sector of agriculture and agricultural administration." The other important task marked out was to "train a large pool of middle level specialists from young people mainly of industrial worker and poor peasant origin."[69]

From 1947 onward, young Hungarians were sent to soviet higher educational institutions with the aim of training professional cadres, but because their studies were expected to last five to six years, they could only be counted on in the medium term.[70] In order to solve collectivized agriculture's mass demand for cadres as quickly as possible, a Soviet-style Agricultural Academy was established in Hungary. Three specialisms were created: machine station, state farm, and producer cooperative group (the latter also trained cadres for the agricultural administration). In 1950 the Agricultural Academy moved to Gödöllő, a small town, near Budapest.[71] The renovation and preparation of necessary buildings began in the spring, and at the same time the search for the academy's director, deputy directors, and department heads was launched and the curriculum prepared.[72]

The largest task, however, was the selection of students. This was coordinated by the Ministry of Agriculture's Professional Education Department. It was a guiding principle that 40% of the academy's students be industrial workers, 55% poor and middle peasants, and 5% other workers. It was intended that 650 students be invited to apply, of which 500 would be enrolled in the fall. A three-month preparatory course was organized between July 4 and September 23. The department wanted to use this not only to prepare students for their studies, but also to get to know them from a cadre perspective.[73]

It was hoped that an existing institution would solve the issue of training middle-level specialists. Agricultural secondary schools were to be transformed into three-year technical schools. The teaching staff was vetted in the spirit of dutiful vigilance, and in mid-June an order was issued to write the 46 textbooks, amounting to 10,400 pages(!), that were needed, with a deadline of September 20.

After 11 months' study, students received certification as "agricultural technicians." Technical schools were established specializing as follows: 24 in crop production, 16 in animal breeding, 8 in horticulture (vegetables, fruits, viticulture), and 3 in forestry. The plan was to train 2,000 students in the first academic year of 1950–51.[74] In the end, 3,000 applied, and their social composition was satisfactorily aligned with political expectations, because the desire was for this technical school education to be imparted, for the most part, to young people of industrial worker and poor peasant origin, and the schools took on children of: workers (30%), workers in the socialist sector of agriculture (20%), poor peasants (30%), middle peasants (10%), and intellectual and "other" categories (10%).[75]

In the summer of 1950 increasingly concrete plans were prepared by the party apparatus for how to implement that fall's "numerical development." At the same time, measures were taken to impose order on already functioning producer cooperative groups whose operation did not conform to expectations. The view of the party leadership was that producer cooperative groups where members refused to put their animals into collective use, or where household plots were too large, etc., set a bad example for the upcoming fall campaign, and therefore wanted to enforce their compliance with the model rules (which had been made even stricter) over the summer.

On July 10, 1950, the Agriculture and Cooperative Policy Committee recommended supplementing the model rules of producer cooperatives and producer cooperative groups in order to resolve the following operational questions: "The question of household plot farming; the question of farming and ploughing equipment and livestock no longer needed for household plot farming; the question of minimum labor day units; the question of elderly, and temporarily incapacitated members and those on study leave."[76] The Ministry of Agriculture was required to prepare a decree on the matter by July 25, and then to ensure that the changes were made known throughout the country. These amendments to the model rules were to be communicated partly through the agitation and propaganda apparatus and partly through the press before the fall collectivization campaign commenced.

The campaign to popularize the results of the kolkhoz movement was intensified in the summer of 1950. The Central Committee's Agitation Department worked out its policies and in early June these were made known to the leaders of the press, radio and film production companies. The youth and women's mass organizations were also included in organizational work.[77] At the same time, measures were also taken to prepare the workplace party organizations that were to be sent to villages for their agitation tasks. A series of presentations on the principles of party peasant policy were held for them through June and July.

The organizational situation of the institutions involved in agricultural transformation had also improved. In 1949, the establishment of agricultural departments in district-level party committees was just beginning, and so county-level organs had to deal directly when organizing collective farms. By 1950, however, district party committees and district agricultural departments could be counted on. A problem persisted in local government, however, in that its reorganization along soviet lines had only just been completed in 1950. Under the 1949 constitution, the old bodies of local government were replaced by the Russian-style soviets that had already been tried out in Hungary in 1919, with soviets or councils (*tanácsok*) being elected at county (*megye*), district (*járás*), municipal/city (*város*), and community/village (*község*) level. The HWP's own hierarchy was built from community/village, municipal/city level upward as a mirror of the state administrative structure.[78]

VIOLENCE AND RESISTANCE

Continued persecution of kulaks formed an integral part of the collectivization drive in the fall of 1950. A kulak was defined as a farmer whose land reached or exceeded 25 kh (14.25 ha), or whose net cadastral income reached or exceeded 350 gold crowns. The traditional unit of measure for land value in Hungary was the "gold crown."[79]

When it became apparent that there would be a shortfall in harvest delivery plans (which were broken down to the county level), the Minister of Domestic Trade directed audit committees primarily toward producers classified as kulaks.[80] Their task was to carry out an audit of the whole quantity produced on the land farmed by the kulaks and further to hunt out any possible hidden quantities. The Ministry of Justice soon joined the struggle to complete the compulsory deliveries plan. Ministry publications called the attention of local judges and prosecutors to the need, when considering inadequate compulsory deliveries, to distinguish clearly between kulaks and small or middle peasants. The latter were to be punished less severely.[81]

This class-based differentiation was also used in proceedings launched in so-called anticollective incitement cases, the number of which increased significantly when the fall collectivization drive was launched.[82] The Ministry of Justice issued directives on this matter on October 7, 1950.

> Incitement against a producer cooperative group is a crime which, in our current phase of political and economic development, must be met with the weapons of criminal justice principally against kulaks, who commit this crime in full consciousness, because they are aware that the establishment and strengthening of producer cooperatives will bring an end to their economic power. . . . It would be completely improper to indiscriminately employ criminal procedures and strict punishments against all those small and middle peasants who, in their ignorance, make statements that are criminal according to §1. of Government Decree 2560/1949.[83]

By 1950–51 the authorities had brought kulaks to a point of economic incapacity. This is well reflected in the fact that in 1950–51 they offered their lands to the state en masse. The amount of land in kulak hands fell by 70% compared to the figure for 1948, and by 1952 more than one-third of kulaks had become completely landless. The share of kulak land farmed decreased most in Békés and Szabolcs-Szatmár counties.[84]

These examples were supposed to act as a deterrent, but they were not followed by broad masses of the peasantry moving toward collective farming.

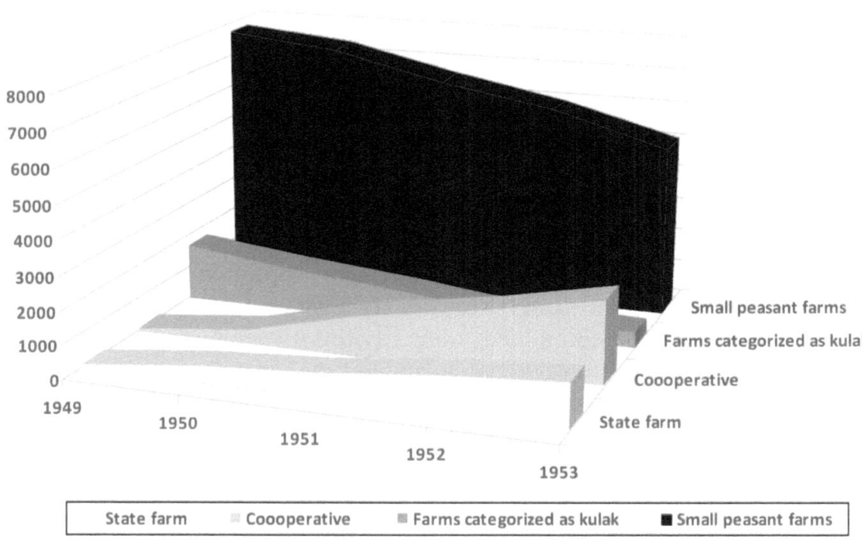

Figure 2.4. Distribution of Arable Land by Farm Type (Thousands of kh), 1949–1953. Source: *A szocialista mezőgazdasági üzemek, 1956*, 5–12.

The response of those in power to this was gradually to put middle and small peasants too under the press.[85] This intention became clear in the 1951 decree on compulsory deliveries.[86] The limit below which land was exempt from compulsory deliveries (for those paying land tax only) was reduced from five cadastral yokes to one, but for certain products (such as milk and eggs) even the smallest holdings had to make deliveries. At the same time the burden on farms of over 5 kh was tripled, with the requirements placed on farms between 5 and 15 kh (2.85–8.55 ha) increasing most.[87] This also meant that less and less produce remained for sale on free markets, where prices could be many times higher than compulsory delivery prices.

The compulsory delivery system in fact became a sort of a universal tool of state intervention that influenced significantly not only production, but also how the goods produced were used. Earlier, after harvest, it was the farmer himself who decided how much the family would consume, how much would be used for the following year's seed corn, for feed for the livestock, and how much would be taken to market. The farmer also decided what to do with the monetary income left after taxes had been paid. Should income be saved or invested: buying machinery or equipment? The constantly changing and ever-heavier compulsory delivery burdens rendered it completely uncertain how much of the year's production and monetary income would remain in the hands of the farmer.

In the light of this drastic increase in burdens, it is no surprise that ever-increasing numbers within peasant society were unable to meet the demands placed on them. Accumulating shortfalls in compulsory deliveries and tax arrears, however, had their consequences. Over the course of 1951, reprisal measures, directed at individual farmers who insisted on retaining their individual farms, increased as never before.[88] It became increasingly common for them to be called in to and threatened at the local council headquarters—on occasion accompanied by a beating—and harassment of landowning peasants became permanent. Not only were financial penalties levied and prison terms imposed for compulsory delivery and tax arrears, but they could also be occasioned on all kinds of pretexts ("suspect dog without a muzzle", public hygiene offenses, failure to exterminate autumn webworms, fire code violations, and so on).

In light of the above, it is no surprise that over 1951–1952, the reason that people joined producer cooperatives was mostly to free themselves from burdens that they could not meet. Others could only be forced in by violent pro-producer cooperative agitation. The agitators who swarmed into villages were steeled with the following ideological logic. Those who do not join a producer cooperative obstruct the construction of socialism, and those who obstruct, by that very act prove that they do not want socialism; those who do

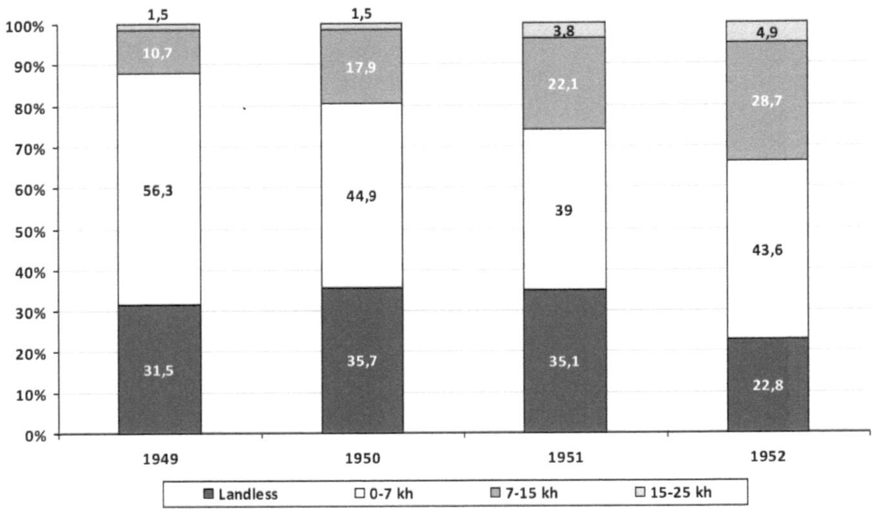

Figure 2.5. Families Joining Cooperative by Farm Size 1949–1952. Source: *A szocialista mezőgazdasági üzemek, 1956,* 49.

not want socialism are in reality enemies of socialism, and enemies should expect no mercy. The last link in the chain in effect granted free choice of which "agitation" tools to employ. Discussions, convincing and promising were soon replaced by crude threats, and then by the use of administrative and in many cases physical compulsion and violence.[89] In Hungary the prime instrument of the terror was the special force, State Security Authority (Államvédelmi *Hatóság*). As an indication of its size, the State Security Authority had its own units in every county, larger town, and even in bigger districts.[90]

A particularly intense campaign unfolded in early 1951 on the occasion of the 2nd Congress of the HWP.[91] A "great agitation" was launched on January 21 in the town of Túrkeve on the Great Plain, in which, on this day, 100, on January 23, 150, and on January 24, close to 300 "popular educators" took part.[92] On February 19, Túrkeve became a "socialist town," a fact that a town delegation personally reported to Rákosi himself. A third of the members who had been violently forced to join either never worked for the producer cooperative, or left it after a few months to work in industry. Cegléd too became a "socialist town" using similar methods: there a number of the Great Stalin Producer Cooperative members were put on the membership list "by copying names from the cemetery headstones, while others never showed up in the cooperative again after signing the membership form."[93] The producer cooperatives of these two municipalities were among the ten producer cooperatives which were identified by the Politburo at the end of the year

Table 2.4. The Regional Dynamics of the First Collectivization Drive

1951		*1952*		*1953*	
Annual arable land growth compared to previous year					
Szolnok	363.9	Szabolcs	290.6	Békés	133.9
Zala	261.5	Borsod	197.2	Somogy	76.4
Baranya	189.7	Vas	174.4	Komárom	59.9
Somogy	165.7	Heves	161.2	Csongrád	55.0
Nógrád	149.5	Pest	139.7	Fejér	50.6
Bács	125.0	Somogy	116.1	Hajdú	48.7
Pest	104.4	Fejér	113.9		
The rest	66.0	The rest	78.2	The rest	22.8

Source: A MDP Mezőgazdasági és Szövetkezetpolitikai Osztály feljegyzése a tsz-fejlesztés megyénként eredményeiről, 1954. március. [The HWP Agricultural and Cooperative Policy Department's report on the regional results of the collectivization, March, 1954] MNL OL, M–KS 276. f., 93. cs., 513. ő. e.

as model producer cooperatives, with the intention of using their exemplary practice to convince individually farming peasants of the superiority of the large-scale farm.[94]

RENEWED AGITATION YET A POLICY REVERSAL

It comes as no surprise that, in 1951, the growth of the collective farm sector was greatest in Szolnok county, the general area of Cegléd and Túrkeve. The number of collective farms increased significantly in South Transdanubian (Zala, Baranya, Somogy counties) too, if not to the same extent. A new large-scale land consolidation campaign played a significant role in these increases.[95] But at the same time, results fell far short of planned numbers. In mid-September, 1951, a total of 4,537 producer cooperatives and groups were in operation encompassing 226,063 families. The total territory of producer cooperatives was 1,694,585 kh (965,913 ha), of which 1,425,971 (812,803 ha) was arable land, representing 14.8% of the country's arable land.[96]

In the minds of the Party leadership, the enemies were not just peasants who opposed joining, but in many cases those too who were already members of producer cooperative groups. The operation of Hungarian producer cooperatives and producer cooperative groups in most places bore scant resemblance to that of the idealized Soviet kolkhoz.[97] A good opportunity to emphasize the superiority of Soviet agriculture was offered in the fall of 1951 when a large Soviet agricultural delegation visited Hungary for a month.

We must turn the experience and good advice [*sic*] offered by our guests from the inestimable treasure trove of the Soviet Union's socialist agriculture into a

> public treasure for the widest layers of the working peasantry. We can draw long on these experiences, for long months and years, and, by using them, achieve new results in the consolidation of our producer cooperatives.[98]

Reports on the Soviet delegation's national tour also made mention of labor discipline and labor organizational deficiencies of producer cooperative groups, which were closely connected to the conflict of interests between the producer cooperatives and a government that was trying to maximize revenue-extraction. In the summer of 1951 the system regulating income distribution on independent producer cooperatives and Type III producer cooperative groups was made stricter.[99] The details of this are presented below, but here it is sufficient to stress that the government decree implementing it was the first to spell out that the Soviet Union's kolkhoz income distribution system had to be introduced in Hungary too. Problems in respect of introducing soviet-model collective labor organization became so severe that, in spring 1952, a Council of Ministers decree had to be issued to strengthen labor discipline on producer cooperatives.[100]

An attempt was made to disguise these problems by a noisy propaganda campaign trumpeting success, yet the truth was that, in mid-1952, producer cooperatives still cultivated only 18% of arable land, and the state farm share was 10%. This therefore meant that almost three-quarters of the country's arable area belonged to individual farms.[101] The situation fell so far behind the collectivization plan announced by Rákosi, that, in summer 1952, the original schedule for the socialist reorganization of agriculture had to be modified, a policy correction that is scarcely referenced in the literature. Changes to the Politburo's original decree are justified especially by the following points:

> a) Developing producer cooperatives in leaps and bounds endangers adherence to the principle of voluntary entry into cooperative farms. Compulsion and force, by contrast, can cause a temporary loosening of the alliance between the working class and the working peasantry, which, especially given the international situation, should be avoided by all means.
> b) The increase in agricultural production prescribed by the five-year-plan cannot be guaranteed in parallel with the originally planned dramatic development of the producer cooperative movement. . . .

The new goal was expressed as follows:

> Efforts must be made to increase the share of producer cooperative arable land within total arable land from 22% in fall, 1952, to 25% by spring, 1953, then 38% by spring, 1954, and finally to 45% by that fall. The territorial growth of state farms must be restricted. . . .[102]

A policy shift took place, but the planned schedule indicated that those in charge of system transfer had not understood the causes of failure.

NOTES

1. Iván T. Berend, *Central and Eastern Europe 1944–1993: Detour from the Periphery to the Periphery* (Cambridge: Cambridge University Press, 1996), 3–39; Joseph Rothschild, *Return to Diversity: A Political History of East Central Europe since World War II*. 3rd ed. (Oxford: Oxford University Press, 2000), 125–46; Mark Kramer, "Stalin, Soviet policy, and the consolidation of a communist bloc in Eastern Europe, 1944–1953," in *The Establishment of Communist Regimes in East-Central Europe*, ed. Vladimir Tismăneanu (Budapest: CEU, 2009), 51–102; T. V. Volokitina, ed., *Sovetskii faktor v Vostochnoi Evrope 1944–1953: Dokumenty* [The Soviet factor in Eastern Europe, 1944–1953] 2 vols. (Moskva: Rosspen, 1999).

2. This group of top functionaries (Mátyás Rákosi, Ernő Gerő, József Révai, Mihály Farkas, Imre Nagy) returned to Hungary at the end of the Second World War from Moscow, where they had spent several years as émigrés.

3. Központi Statisztikai Hivatal, *1949. évi népszámlálás* [Census of 1949], vol. 3, Részletes mezőgazdasági eredmények [Detailed agricultural results] (Budapest: KSH, 1950).

4. János M. Rainer, *Imre Nagy: A Political Biography* (London: I.B. Tauris & Co., 2009), 15–32, 79–110.

5. Ibid., 383.

6. At the end of April, 1948, the name of the Village Affairs Committee was changed to Agricultural Policy Committee, but its president remained Imre Nagy. See Jegyzőkönyv az MKP Politikai Bizottság 1948, február 12-i üléséről [Minutes of the HCP Politburo session, February 12, 1948] Politikatörténeti és Szakszervezeti Levéltár [Political History and Labor Union Archive, here on PIL], 274. f., 3. cs., 131. ő. e.

7. Sándor Rákosi and Bálint Szabó, eds., *A Magyar Kommunista Párt* és *a Szociáldemokrata Párt határozatai 1944–1948* [Decrees of the Hungarian Communist Party and the Social Democratic Party, 1944–1948] (Budapest: Kossuth, 1967), 564–76.

8. Sándor Balogh and Lajos Izsák, eds., *Magyarországi pártprogramok, 1944–1988* [The programs of the Hungarian political parties, 1944–1988] (Budapest: ELTE Eötvös Kiadó, 2004), 195–212.

9. Lajos Izsák and Miklós Kun, eds., *Moszkvának jelentjük . . . : Titkos dokumentumok 1944–1948* [Sending our reports to Moscow . . . : Secret documents 1944–1948] (Budapest: Századvég, 1994), 268.

10. *Szabad Föld* [Free Land], August 22, 1948.

11. On September 10, 1948, the HWP Politburo scheduled on its agenda a debate on the decree of the Polish Party's Central Committee, from which it hoped to glean the necessary conclusions for its own use. The body commissioned the Secretariat to prepare a list of mistakes existing within the Hungarian Party, and the Organizing Committee to work out recommendations on the methods to correct them. The plan

was to present the results of the period since party unification to the Central Leadership at its planned meeting in November, to report on mistakes found within the party and the methods of overcoming them. See Jegyzőkönyv az MDP Politikai Bizottság 1948. szeptember 10-i üléséről. [Minutes of the HWP Politburo session, September 10, 1948] MNL OL, M–KS 276. f., 53. cs., 9. ő. e.

12. Magdolna Baráth, "Gerő Ernő és Nagy Imre vitája, 1947–1949" [The debate between Ernő Gerő and Imre Nagy, 1947–1949], in *1956* és *a magyar agrártársadalom* [1956 and the Hungarian agrarian society], ed. János Estók (Budapest: Magyar Mezőgazdasági Múzeum, 2006), 67–80.

13. Jegyzőkönyv az MDP Politikai Bizottság 1948. november 27-i üléséről [Minutes of the HWP Politburo session November 27, 1948] MNL OL, M–KS 276. f., 52. cs., 4. ő. e.

14. *Tartós békéért, népi demokráciáért*, December 7, 1948.

15. Officially, the debate was put to rest about half a year later by not only stating that Imre Nagy, based on his views, was a revisionist with right wing leanings, but further by firing him from the Politburo. Following this he temporarily left politics and taught at both the Hungarian Economics University and the Gödöllő Agricultural Sciences University. In April of 1950 he returned to the Party Headquarters, becoming the director of the Central Committee Administrative Department. Then between December, 1950, and January, 1952, he was Minister of Food Supply, and from January to November, 1952, was Minister of Procurement. In 1951 he was reinstated in the Politburo and the Secretariat of CC. In 1952 he was named Deputy Prime Minister. In 1953, he became prime minister. For more, see Rainer M., *Imre Nagy*, 439–507.

16. András Klenczner, "Az állami gazdaságokról" [About the state farms], in Für, Orosz, and Romány, *Magyarország agrártörténete*, 695–97.

17. "Law no. XXV," in *Törvények és Rendeletek Hivatalos Gyűjteménye 1949* [Official Collection of Laws and Ordinances, here on: TRHGY], vol. 1 (Budapest: Jogi és Államigazgatási Könyv- és Folyóiratkiadó, 1950), 85.

18. István Molnár and Éva Szabóné Medgyesi, *Az állami gazdaságok Magyarországon* [The state farms in Hungary] (Budapest: Mezőgazdasági, 1987), 37–42.

19. Ibid., 285.

20. The author's interview with R. P. May 18, 2010. (Author's files.)

21. Klenczner, "Az állami gazdaságokról," 698.

22. Six months later, effective July 4, 1953, the State Farms and Forests Ministry was again merged with the Ministry of Agriculture, which was headed by András Hegedüs. Later, in April 1955 he became the prime minister of Hungary. He represented Hungary when the Soviet-bloc states entered into the Warsaw Pact in 1955. When the Hungarian uprising began in October 1956, Hegedüs ceded the post of prime minister back to Imre Nagy. József Bölöny, *Magyarország kormányai, 1948–1992* [The governments of Hungary, 1948–1992] (Budapest: Akadémiai, 1992), 217.

23. The construction of the network was for all intents and purposes completed by the end of 1950. They numbered around 360. Later, through mergers beginning in 1952, their number began to decline. Honvári, *A gépállomások*, 83–85.

24. Jegyzőkönyv az MDP Szervező Bizottság 1948. július 23-i üléséről. [Minutes of the HWP Administration Committee session, July 23, 1948] MNL OL, M–KS 276. f., 55. cs., 11. ő. e.

25. Honvári, *A gépállomások*, 143–60.

26. In the first five-year plan period agricultural machinery factories hardly produced small machines and tools required by individual farmers. Ibid., 265–312.

27. Jegyzőkönyv az MDP Titkárságának 1948. október 14-i üléséről. [Minutes of the HWP Secretariat, October 14, 1948] MNL OL, M–KS 276. f., 54. cs., 14. ő. e.

28. See: "228.700/1948. F. M.," *Magyar Közlöny* [Hungarian Gazette, here on: MK], August 25, 1948, 1849–52.

29. Honvári, *A gépállomások*, 389–91.

30. Ibid., 96–102.

31. Honvári, *A gépállomások*, 401–11.

32. Gyöngyi Farkas, "'Gyertek lányok traktorra!' Női traktorosok a gépállomáson és a propagandában" ["Girls, get on the tractor!" Woman Tractor Drivers at the Machine Station and in Propaganda], *Korall* 4, no. 13 (2003): 65–86.

33. Varga Zsuzsanna, ed., *Göröngyös út: Dimény Imre életútja* [The history of the Institute of Agricultural Economics], (Budapest: Kossuth, 2017) 58. This book was based on a series of interviews with Dimény extending over more than a year. He was the Minister of Food and Agriculture between 1967–75.

34. See: "9000/1948. Korm. r.," *MK*, August 29, 1948, 1923–25.

35. Az MDP Mezőgazdasági és Szövetkezetpolitikai Bizottsága 1948. november 17-i ülésének jegyzőkönyve. [Minutes of the HWP Agriculture and Cooperative Policy Committee session, November 17, 1948] MNL OL, M–KS 276. f., 85. cs., 3. ő. e.

36. "After the Party has debated the rules of operation, negotiations must be held with the agricultural and cooperative leaders of the FKGP [Independent Smallholders' Party] and HWP no later than December 1. . . . Following this they wanted to have discussions with 15–20 directors of rural producer groups." They also decided that the governmental decree must be passed by December 5, 1948. Ibid.

37. "14 000/1948. Korm. r.," *MK*, December 20, 1948.

38. Producer cooperative group members could keep one cow, one calf, five sheep or goats, one or two fattening pigs (depending on the size of the family), and an unlimited number of poultry, bees, and rabbits on their household plots.

39. Jegyzőkönyv az MDP Mezőgazdasági és Szövetkezetpolitikai Bizottság 1949. január 21-i üléséről. [Minutes of the HWP Agriculture and Cooperative Policy Committee session, January 21, 1949] MNL OL, M–KS 276. f., 85. cs., 10. ő. e.

40. Ibid.

41. Ibid.

42. Ibid.

43. Pál Germuska, "Socialist Miracle? Hungarian Industrial Development Policy and Economic Growth, 1950–1975." *The Journal of European Economic History*, 42, no. 1 (2013): 87–134.

44. Zsuzsanna Varga, "Wartime Agricultural Policy in Peacetime: A Case Study of Hungary, 1940–1956," in *War, Agriculture, and Food: Rural Europe from the*

1930s to the 1950s, eds. Paul Brassley, Yves Segers, and Leen Van Molle (New York: Routledge, 2012), 96–110.

45. The disproportions in price levels is well illustrated by the following: compared to the 1946 stabilization, free market prices increased sevenfold, but state purchase prices rose only three and a half times, while compulsory delivery prices increased by a factor of only one and a half. Pető and Szakács, *A hazai gazdaság*, 199–203.

46. It is clear from the diagram that the actual investment proportion was less than that planned in every year. This explains why the five-year plan proffered in 1951 only allocated 12.9% of investments for agriculture. The 5 billion forints invested by June 30, 1953, amounted to only 11%.

47. Központi Statisztikai Hivatal, *A szocialista mezőgazdasági üzemek* [The units of the socialist agriculture.] (Budapest: KSH, 1954), 59–60.

48. *Szabad Nép*, January 26, 1950.

49. Magyar Rádió Archívuma [Archive of the Hungarian Radio, here on: MRA] Műsorborítéktár [Collection of program documentation folders] January 28, 1950; January 29, 1950; February 1, 1950.

50. *Szabad Nép*, January 29, 1950.

51. Jegyzőkönyv az MDP Politikai Bizottság 1950. január 26-i üléséről. [Minutes of the HWP Politburo session, January 26, 1950] MNL OL, M–KS 276. f., 53. cs., 44. ő. e.

52. A delegation from the party's Agricultural and Cooperative Policy Committee traveled to Bulgaria for two months prior to the land consolidation of 1949 and collected experiences of land consolidation there. János Keserű, *Parasztsorsfordítók között* [Among Peasant Pioneers] (Budapest: Napvilág, 2007), 42–43.

53. Földművelésügyi Minisztérium, Titkos ügykezelésű iratok. [Ministry of Agriculture, Classified files, here on: FM TÜK] MNL OL, XIX–K–1–c, FM TÜK, 24. d. January 7, 1950. More on the preparations see: MNL OL, M–KS 276. f., 93. cs., 162. ő. e.

54. Jegyzőkönyv az MDP Politikai Bizottság 1950. január 26-án tartott üléséről. [Minutes of the HWP Politburo session, January 26, 1950] MNL OL, M–KS 276. f., 53. cs., 44. ő. e.

55. Jegyzőkönyv az MDP Politikai Bizottság 1950. március 9-én tartott üléséről. [Minutes of the HWP Politburo session, March 9, 1950] MNL OL, M–KS 276. f., 53. cs., 47. ő. e.

56. Initially these were named rules of operation, then model statutes, with the addendum that producer cooperatives could only function in accordance with them.

57. "133/1950. M.T.," in *TRHGY 1950*, 303–4.

58. The text was composed of only four parts: The land and equipment of the producer cooperative; its organs; its tasks; calculating results. Ibid., 304–5.

59. "205/1950. M.T.," in *TRHGY 1950*, 385–87.

60. Both female and male members were required to complete a minimum of 80 work units. Women with small children had to complete 40. Ibid., 386–87. On the problems of labor-day regulation, see Jean Lévesque, "'Part-Time Peasants:' Labour Discipline, Collective Farm Life and the Fate of Soviet Socialized Agriculture after the Second World War, 1945–1953," PhD diss. (University of Toronto, 2003), 86–98.

61. Erdei Ferenc feljegyzése Rákosi részére, 1950. december 6. [Memorandum from Ferenc Erdei to Mátyás Rákosi, December 6, 1950] MNL OL, M–KS 276. f., 93. cs., 236. ő. e.

62. "8.010/1951. F.M.," in *TRHGY 1951*, 619–28.

63. In the cases of independent and Type III producer cooperative groups it was clearly stated that "exploiters, kulak, speculators, profiteers or other persons who are banned from land recipients' cooperatives cannot be accepted as members." Ibid., 619, 623.

64. "A Szovjetunió szocialista mezőgazdasága" c. tananyag feldolgozásának tapasztalatai, 1950. április 26. [Experiences of the elaboration of the teaching material *The socialist agriculture of the Soviet Union*, April 26, 1950] MNL OL, M–KS 276. f., 93. cs., 163. ő. e.

65. A Földművelésügyi Minisztérium Kollégiuma 1950. január 7-i ülésének jegyzőkönyve. [Minutes of the Ministry of Agriculture Steering Committee, January 7, 1950] MNL OL, XIX–K–1–c FM TÜK 24. d.

66. László Cs. Nagy gave a presentation on Labor Day units as agenda point number one at the departmental meeting of February 16, 1950. He dealt with the topic several times a week, generally in the Cooperative News programs. It was also one of the key topics at the departmental meeting of March 29. "Calculating work units cannot be removed from the agenda, we must always present them in a way that explains how to calculate them for daily tasks. We should comment on this three times per week. Person responsible: Tibor Lukács. A Falurádió osztályértekezletei, 1950. [Department meetings at *Village Radio*, 1950] MNL OL, M–KS 276. f., 93. cs., 163. ő. e.

67. A parasztküldöttség feladata és a tanulmányút eredménye. [Goals and results of the peasant delegation] MNL OL, M–KS 276. f., 93. cs., 163. ő. e.

68. Erdei Ferenc miniszteri iratai. Magyar parasztküldöttség a SZ.U.-ban. 1950. [Documents of the Minister Ferenc Erdei. Hungarian peasant delegation in the Soviet Union] MNL OL, XIX–K–1–ah 1. d.

69. Jegyzőkönyv az MDP Titkárság 1950. március 29-i üléséről. [Minutes of the HWP Secretariat session, March 29, 1950] MNL OL, M–KS 276. f., 54. cs. 92. ő. e.

70. Anna Siklósné Kosztricz, "Magyar ösztöndíjasok a Szovjetunióban, 1945–1960" [Hungarians studying in the Soviet Union, 1945–60] (PhD thesis, ELTE, Budapest, 2016).

71. On initial problems see: Kosáry Domokos Könyvtár és Levéltár, Gödöllő [Domokos Kosáyr Library and Archive, Gödöllő], 11/b. 2. d.

72. One of the deputies became responsible for learning-teaching-education affairs, while the other was responsible for personnel, organization, and financial affairs. The Agricultural and Cooperative Policy Committee paid particular attention to the choice of party secretary. "The position of secretary of the Academy's Party body must be filled by a well-trained, preferably industrial worker cadre with experience in Party work. . . ." See Jegyzőkönyv az MDP Mezőgazdasági és Szövetkezetpolitikai Bizottság 1950. június 12-i üléséről. [Minutes of the HWP Agricultural and Cooperative Policy Committee session, June 12, 1950] MNL OL, M–KS 276. f., 85. cs., 53. ő. e.

73. Ibid.

74. Jegyzőkönyv az MDP Mezőgazdasági és Szövetkezetpolitikai Bizottság 1950. június 12-i üléséről. [Minutes of the HWP Agricultural and Cooperative Policy Committee session, June 12, 1950] MNL OL, M–KS 276. f., 85. cs., 53. ő. e.

75. A Földművelésügyi Minisztérium kollégiuma 1950. november 30-i ülésének jegyzőkönyve. [Minutes of the Ministry of Agriculture Steering Committee session, November 30, 1950] MNL OL, XIX–K–1–c FM TÜK 27. d.

76. Jegyzőkönyv az MDP Mezőgazdasági és Szövetkezetpolitikai Bizottság 1950. július 10-i üléséről. [Minutes of the HWP Agricultural and Cooperative Policy Committee session, July 10, 1950] MNL OL, M–KS 276. f., 85. cs., 55. ő. e. The concrete recommendations of the committee were as follows: members who sell their farming equipment, seeds, fodder, ploughing animals, and livestock before joining should where possible immediately pay the price received into the group's communal farm. The minimum of work units for one farming year should not be 60, but 80. For one month each after and before giving birth women must be relieved of group work, and in the last 12 months must be provided the work unit average for one month. The planned decree dealt with the right to retain vineyards and orchards (max: 0.5 kh, 0.3 ha) near the home. These were not included in the calculation of the household plot. The household farm could include 1 cow, 1 calf, 1 sow and her piglets, and 5 sheep or goats. The committee recommended that the quantity of rabbits (20) and bees (5 hives) not be regulated. A social fund was to be set up to provide for the elderly and those unable to work, but its maximum size was set at only 2% of the gross monetary income.

77. Jegyzőkönyv az MDP Mezőgazdasági és Szövetkezetpolitikai Bizottsága 1950. április 28-i üléséről. [Minutes of the HWP Agricultural and Cooperative Policy Committee session, April 28, 1950] MNL OL, M–KS 276. f., 85. cs., 50. ő. e.

78. György Gyarmati, *A Rákosi-korszak: Rendszerváltó fordulatok évtizede Magyarországon, 1945–1956* [The Rákosi-epoch: The decade of system changes, 1945–1956] (Budapest: ÁBTL–Rubicon, 2011), 160–65.

79. Jegyzőkönyv a Politika Bizottság 1950. március 20-i üléséről. [Minutes of the HWP Politburo session, March 20, 1950] MNL OL, M–KS 276. f., 53. cs., 48. ő. e.

80. "15.260/1950. Bk. M.," in *TRHGY 1950*, vol. 2, 512.

81. The Minister of Justice sent fortnightly bulletins to the directors of local courts in which concrete cases were used to illustrate how to execute party policy when passing judgment on agricultural crimes. See MNL OL, M–KS 276. f., 96. cs., 1. ő. e., 2. ő. e., 5. ő. e.

82. "Those who obstruct or frustrate the establishment of a producer cooperative group or obstruct the operations of an existing group or threaten the existence of one through a) agitating against the institution of the group or making slanderous or disparaging remarks against it; b) attempting to keep others from joining the group; c) slander, bringing shame upon or harassing group members or their kin based on their membership in the group; d) obstructing or attempting to obstruct group members or others in their work for the interest of the group are guilty of a crime and are to be punished with two to ten years of imprisonment, loss of office and suspension of political rights." "2.560/1949. Korm. r.," in *TRHGY 1949*, vol. 2, 253–54.

83. Ibolya Horváth et al., ed., *Iratok az igazságszolgáltatás történetéhez* [Documents on the history of jurisdiction], vol. 4 (Budapest: KJK, 1995), 348–49.

84. Kulákgazdaságok 1952. év végén. A KSH jelentése. [Kulak farms at the end of 1952. Report of the Central Statistical Office (KSH)] MG. 1/1953. (March 19, 1953), 5–6.

85. Erdmann, *Begyűjtés, beszolgáltatás*, 106–25; Judit Tóth, "Elimination of the farmer elite in Hungary in the 1950s," in Varga and Halmesvirta, *Agriculture and Rural Life*, 127–37; Judit Tóth, "Kulaks in political cartoons of the Rákosi-Era," in *Countryside and communism in Easter Europe: Perceptions, attitudes, propaganda*, eds. Sorin Radu and Cosmin Budeanca (Berlin: LIT Verlag, 2016), 637–55.

86. "1951. 10. tvr.," in *TRHGY 1951*, 69–78.

87. The fact that all farms of over 5 kh (2.85 ha) were compelled to deliver hay, potatoes, and onions also had a very negative effect. The part of the Council of Ministers decree that en masse categorized as kulak farm holdings under 25 kh (14.25 ha) with an income of less than 350 gold crowns, was particularly harsh. This was also when the multiplier for orchards was set at four and that for vineyards at five.

88. Faced with the resistance of small and middle peasants, the state expected public prosecutors to act more effectively. This change is reflected in the prosecutable bulletins issued by the Minister of Justice over 1950. MNL OL, M–KS 276. f., 96. cs., 5. ő. e.

89. József Ö. Kovács, "The Forced Collectivization of Agriculture in Hungary, 1948–1961," in Iordachi and Bauerkämper, *The Collectivization*, 215–21; Tatjana Thelen, "Violence and social (dis)continuity: comparing collectivization in two East European villages," *Social History* 30, no. 1 (2005): 25–44.

90. György Gyarmati and Mária Palasik, eds., *Big brother's miserable grocery store: Studies on the history of the Hungarian secret services after World War II* (Budapest: ÁBTL and L'Harmattan, 2012).

91. *Szabad Nép*, March 18, 1951.

92. Urbán, *Az első termelőszövetkezeti városok*, 82–98.

93. László Komló and Csaba Kovács, "A közös és egyéni érdek a ceglédi Nagy Sztálin Termelőszövetkezetben" [The common and individual interest in the Great Stalin Collective in Cegléd], *Agrártörténeti Szemle* 21, no. 3–4 (1979): 488.

94. A few months after announcing the 10 model producer cooperatives, the Producer Cooperative Department of the Ministry of Agriculture reported that the inclusion of the Great Stalin farm in Cegléd, the Rákosi farm in Mágocs, and the Dózsa farm in Vaskút was "inappropriate," and instead the Béke farm in Mezőtúr, the Petőfi farm in Tengelic and the Vörös Csillag farm in Baracska were recommended as new model collective farms. See Jegyzőkönyv az FM Kollégium 1952. április 25-i üléséről. [Minutes of the Ministry of Agriculture Steering Committee session, April 25, 1952] MNL OL, XIX–K–l–c FM TÜK 32. d.

95. Over the summer 262 collective farm villages were filled with members, and in the fall another 51 communities were under way. The numbers are as follows: 1,274 collective farm groups and 427 state farms in 716 villages. Jegyzőkönyv az FM Kollégium 1951. augusztus 16-i üléséről. [Minutes of the Ministry of Agriculture Steering Committee session, August 16, 1951]; Jegyzőkönyv az FM Kollégium 1951.

szeptember 27-i üléséről. [Minutes of the Ministry of Agriculture Steering Committee session, September 27, 1951] MNL OL, XIX–K–1–c FM TÜK 30. d.

96. Az MDP Mezőgazdasági és Szövetkezetpolitikai Bizottsága 1951. szeptember 10-i ülésének jegyzőkönyve. [Minutes of the HWP Agricultural and Cooperative Policy Committee session, September 10, 1951] MNL OL, M–KS 276. f., 85. cs., 70. ő. e.

97. Wädekin, "The Soviet Kolkhoz," 95–116.

98. *Szabad Nép*, October 16, 1951.

99. "1.022/1951. M.T. határozat," "18.072/1951. FM rendelet," in *TRHGY 1951*, 398–99, 722.

100. "1.009/1952. M.T. határozat," in *TRHGY 1952*, 231–34.

101. A Földművelésügyi Minisztérium Kollégiuma 1952. július 4-i ülésének jegyzőkönyve. [Minutes of the Ministry of Agriculture Steering Committee session, July 4, 1952] MNL OL, XIX–K–1–c FM TÜK iratok 33. d.

102. Javaslat a Politika Bizottság számára a mezőgazdaság szocialista ütemének átszervezésére, 1952. július 8. [Submission for the HWP Politburo on the socialist reorganization of agriculture, July 8, 1952] MNL OL, M–KS 276. f., 74. cs., 5. ő. e.

Chapter Three

Retrenchment to Private Farming—Twice

DE-STALINIZATION IN AGRARIAN POLICY: THE NEW COURSE OF 1953–54

At the turn of 1952–53, things had reached a stage where there was no section of village society that had not suffered an injury of some sort in the preceding years. At the beginning of 1953, those in power not only saw rich peasants labeled kulaks as the enemy, but also smallholders working just a few acres. What is more, they even found enemies among produce cooperative members and state farm workers as well.

In just a few years the agrarian world in Hungary had been torn apart by the economic, administrative, and physical violence that went with the transfer of the Stalinist kolkhoz system. It says a lot that the quantity of agricultural production in the period of the five-year plan—with the exception of the good harvest of 1951—did not reach the level of the last year of peace (1938). The situation was the same for the production of bread grains, which play such an important role in feeding the population. Only in 1950 did the livestock level rise above prewar figures, by just a few percentage points; and this level, followed by a decline in 1951, was only regained and surpassed in the middle of the decade.[1] Economic problems were accompanied by an accumulation of severe social tensions, and not only in the agrarian sphere.[2] Over the course of a few years the Rákosi leadership had used up the population's reserves of patience. The unrealistically inflated investment sums of the first five-year plan in February, 1951 sunk the living standards of workers and urban dwellers to rock bottom. The purchasing power of the currency collapsed, yet despite this the population's basic demands for food and daily necessities could not be met. In 1952 the gross production of agricultural goods was only 86% of the 1950 level, which was not high to begin with. The per capita level of food consumption had hardly moved from the low level it had been at before the war. The provision of goods was reminiscent of the war years, characterized by queuing, recurring shortages, and poor quality. Agricultural exports were delivered at the expense of meeting domestic needs.[3]

Similar problems also arose in the other socialist countries.[4] The chance to quell the danger of "explosion" came in the spring of 1953 when, after Stalin's death, the soviet party leadership—sensing the signs of crisis in Eastern Europe—committed itself to rapid policy corrections.[5] As a part of this, plans were made to have discussions with the leaders of each country. The most pressing case appeared to be the situation in the GDR, because of its ever-growing flood of emigrants. The more or less open border with the West until 1961 meant that peasants could abandon their farms and migrate to the West. As the statistics of the time show, this path was chosen not only by rich peasants labeled class enemies (*Großbauern*), but also by smaller-scale farmers and those who had received land under the land reform (*Neubauern*).[6] Because of this crisis situation, the leaders of the Socialist Unity Party of Germany were the first to be invited to Moscow, between June 2 and 5. After their return home, they announced a New Course policy, which accurately reflected Soviet advice: the violent collectivization launched in 1952 was halted, the proportion of heavy industry investments was reduced, and so on.[7] Planned changes to work norms were not rescinded, however, and for this reason, on June 15, when workers received their first pay packets following the increase in work norms, demonstrations and protests spread from East Berlin to the entire country. After the uprising was defeated with Soviet military assistance, Walter Ulbricht, the first secretary of the Socialist Unity Party of Germany, was able to hold on to his post. However, in the interest of improving the standard of living, he was forced to execute significant corrections. Under the effect of intense consultations with Soviet advisors, violent collectivization was stopped and peasants who escaped to the territory of the Federal Republic of Germany were invited back, with the promise that their property would be restored.[8]

When the uprising in East Berlin broke out, the Hungarian delegation of party and state leaders was in Moscow, negotiating.[9] The first meeting between members of the soviet party presidium and Hungarian Party and state leaders took place on June 13.[10] The Soviet leaders directed their criticism at Rákosi in particular, since they felt that he had given little evidence of readiness to implement policy corrections. The main elements in their criticism were the following: forced industrialization (in particular the exaggerated development of heavy industry), an inflated army, violent collectivization, decreasing living standards, supply problems, the spread of administrative methods and arbitrary decision-making, show trials, and the cult of personality.

The leaders of the CPSU paid particular attention to the agrarian sector. The new Soviet Prime Minister Malenkov began to list the problems.

> The facts that we are aware of indicate that the situation in agriculture is not good. The level of livestock production is not improving, but, on the contrary, it is getting worse. As far as producer cooperatives are concerned, the situation is not good either. We are aware that 8–10 thousand families have left producer cooperatives in the past year. It is said that the harvest was bad. This cannot explain everything. Compulsory deliveries are over regulated. Procurement of the entire sunflower and rice harvest was a mistake. Many peasants are being brought before the courts because they do not deliver on their commitments to the state. . . . Returning to producer cooperatives, there is data that shows that the income of producer cooperative members is below that of individually farming middle peasants. It is also a mistake to devote such a small amount to investments in the field of agriculture.[11]

Although the agrarian world did not count as one of Beria's areas of expertise, he nevertheless analyzed the components of the agrarian crisis in detail. He also moved on to who was responsible:

> The cooperative sector in Hungary would work much better if the Central Committee and the government paid more attention to agriculture. Then there would not be 750,000 kh [427,500 ha] of abandoned land. There would not be a situation in which peasants leave agriculture and move to industry. There would not be a situation where peasants have large debts to the state. According to our data this debt stands at 400 million forints. There would not be a situation where peasants do not know how much their compulsory delivery will be next year. Comrade Imre Nagy was removed from the Politburo because he recommended that the collective farm movement be developed more slowly. This was incorrect. The comrades who lead the Central Committee and the Council of Ministers have insufficient knowledge of villages, and do not even want to get to know villages sufficiently well.[12]

The diagnosis was thorough; but the Soviet leaders did not provide detailed advice on how to deal with the problem. Only the cornerstones were defined: to redirect investment from heavy industry to the agricultural sector and light industry, to slow down collectivization, and to review the kulak list.[13] It should not be surprising that a more concrete action plan was not provided, because the central factor in Hungarian agriculture remained the individually farming, landed peasantry, a player which had been "eliminated" long before in the Soviet Union. This fact explains the differences between the Soviet and Hungarian crisis management programs in the field of agriculture. Khruschev was to increase production extensively, by incorporating new land for cultivation and increasing investments in agriculture. This took shape first by ploughing virgin soil, and then later in the maize production program. As a consequence of the virgin lands program, total investments in agriculture doubled in 1954 compared to the previous year.[14] In the interest of improving provision for village populations, the burdens placed on household plots were eased. Tax and compulsory delivery burdens on the household plots of kolkhoz members and supplementary plots of sovkhoz employees were reduced. In an important further step, debts accrued over previous years were forgiven.[15]

Mátyás Rákosi reported on the Moscow meeting to the HWP's Secretariat meeting of June 17, where a decision was made to prepare two documents to redress the errors. The first would be addressed to the Central Committee (CC), and the second to the wider public. Rákosi managed to ensure that only an abridged form of the decree passed at the June 27–28 CC meeting was passed on to mid-level party organs, so the party membership, like the rest of the population, only heard of the changes through the speech Imre Nagy gave when he was introduced as prime minister.[16]

The new prime minister's speech on July 4 is well known for introducing the New Course, and it should be emphasized that, although, when compared to the CC decree of June 28, it contained less concrete content concerning mistakes made, and especially on legal violations, it addressed every important set of questions related to agriculture, and in just as much detail.

Imre Nagy spoke openly about the fact that agriculture had in effect become an "internal colony." "Under exaggerated industrialization, especially the overly rapid development of heavy industry and the large-scale investments that accompanied it, insufficient of the country's material resources were available to develop agriculture. As a result, alongside the excessively fast pace of development in industry, but especially, indeed almost exclusively, heavy industry, agricultural production stagnated: it could neither ensure the raw materials necessary for the rapid development of industry, nor meet the increasing food needs of the rapidly increasing industrial workforce and the population in general. The government sees it as one of its most important tasks to reduce industrial investment and simultaneously increase agricultural investment so as to promote as fast and large an upswing in production as is possible."[17]

He also formulated a clear conception of which actors in the agrarian world would serve as the foundation of the program for change:

> It is known that our agricultural production is based mainly on individual farmers; it is not just the case that the country cannot do without their produce, but on the contrary, it is in the country's interest to develop their farming, in land cultivation and animal husbandry alike. The government sees it as a top priority to embrace the production of individual farms and to assist them with produc-

> tion and work equipment, with tools, artificial fertilizer, seed corn and other tools of agro-technology.[18]

The paragraphs on agriculture in the prime minister's speech became law in a matter of weeks. Legislative Decree no. 10, announced on June 12, erased penalties applied that year to individual farms and producer cooperatives for failing to make compulsory grain deliveries in full, and forgave a portion of accumulated delivery arrears.[19] This latter concession was worth a total of 235.5 million forints, while the value of penalties applied for failing make deliveries in full was 445 million forint.[20] Two weeks later, on July 26, a prime ministerial decree regulated tax concessions for the agricultural population.[21] On the same day Legislative Decree no. 11 on amnesties was published, according to which, among other things, hundreds of thousands of villagers who had failed to make compulsory deliveries, or had been condemned because of "ill-considered" expressions of a political nature, or for other reasons were relieved of the burden of their punishments.[22]

A governmental decree of August 2 permitted renting land up to 25 kh (14 ha), and even made it possible to claim back land that had been offered to the state or abandoned after 1951.[23] Two governmental decrees were published the same day: one reduced fees for machine stations and forgave accumulated debts to them,[24] while the other made an important gesture toward producer cooperative members: the upper limit of household plots was raised from 1/2 to 3/4 kh (0.3–0.4 ha) to 1 kh (0.57 ha).[25]

On September 1 a further concession came into force in respect of compulsory deliveries. Farmers who had met their delivery commitments for bread and feed grains in the fall of 1953 could count on a 10% reduction in the amount of corn, sunflowers, and potatoes that had to be delivered.[26] In 1954, in the case of working peasants, the amount to be delivered calculated by size of plot (expressed in wheat kilograms) was 25 to 30% lower than in 1953. From this point on trade restrictions on the more important crops were eliminated. At the end of the month, the delivery price for grapes, partially fermented grape juice, and wine was increased by 50%.[27]

As this list of measures taken already suggests, the workshop where crisis-management measures were elaborated was not the Ministry of Agriculture, but the Secretariat of the Prime Minister, Imre Nagy. Minutes of the steering committees of Ministry of Agriculture in the summer of 1953 confirm that Minister András Hegedüs did not become a committed believer in the New Course.[28]

The government which was called at that time the Council of Ministers issued almost 50 decrees related to agriculture in the second part of 1953. These all indicate that it had recognized that an increase in production and a greater desire to produce could only be achieved if the earlier administrative measures were replaced as far as was possible by economic incentives. The Imre Nagy government strengthened producer security: on one hand by ending land consolidation, on the other by implementing a system of compulsory deliveries fixed for three years.[29] Another novelty was the fact that the government strove to restore the direct market relationship between farmers and consumers. Here is a telling example: before 1953 private farmers' ability to go to market was restricted by a series of regulations on the railway network which placed maximum limits on the amount of hand-luggage that could be carried without incurring an extra charge. Until the new government program had been introduced, passengers were limited to a maximum of 5 liters of wine, 2 liters of milk and sour cream, 2 kg of cottage cheese, 1.5 kg of butter, 1 kg of cheese, etc., if they were to avoid an extra fee. The new recommendation held that all passengers could take without additional charge as much luggage as could fit under and above their seats. In the case of those traveling with season tickets, the earlier regulation limiting hand-luggage only to goods that were unambiguously for personal use was also abolished.[30]

A common feature of the firefighting measures undertaken in the first months of the Imre Nagy government was that producer cooperative groups were granted larger concessions, both in terms of taxation and compulsory delivery, than individual farms.[31] Even these, however, were not enough to make cooperatives sufficiently attractive for landowning farmers to choose to remain in them. Since Imre Nagy made his speech at the beginning of harvest time, the stakes on members immediately exiting from collective farms were enormous, despite the fact that the prime minister had made it clear: "Producer cooperative members who wish to return to individual farming, because they feel they will find prosperity there, may leave producer cooperatives at the end of the farming year."[32] A significant portion of members wanted to give up collective work immediately, and complete the harvest on an individual basis. Reports arrived from many places indicating that, without disbanding officially, producer cooperatives had begun dividing up the livestock and submitting claims for their former land. The general practice, however, was to begin to collect together members' formal statements of intention to leave.[33]

By the end of July, Ministry of Agriculture calculations indicated that 76 independent producer cooperatives, 523 Type III producer cooperative groups, and 60 producer groups of Types I and II, had submitted their intention to dissolve, some 659 of the 5,217 existing producer cooperatives and producer cooperative groups. Estimates suggested that this affected 38,300 families and 302,000 kh (172,140 ha) of land. Dissolution was most intense in the following three counties: 94 of 308 producer cooperative groups (36 from Tabi District, 15 from Kaposvár District) in Somogy County; 187 of 495 producer cooperative groups (53 from Nyírbátor district, 30 producer cooperatives from Kemecse District) in Szabolcs-Szatmár County; and 68 of 401 producer cooperative groups in Borsod-Abaúj-Zemplén County. Reports from Szolnok, Nógrad, Baranya, and Fejér county councils suggested that it seemed that in the near future large-scale exit was likely in 108 independent producer cooperatives, 505 Type III producer cooperative groups, and 38 producer cooperative groups of Types I and II.[34] The responsible leaders in the Ministry of Agriculture viewed the process as follows:

> The producer cooperative members who want to leave are generally those who joined last fall or over the course of the winter. Given that over the past year the economic results of producer cooperatives were exceptionally weak, a large portion of those who joined became producer cooperative members through economic compulsion. Many stressed at the time that they were joining because, after making their compulsory deliveries, they did not have sufficient seeds or feed grain to sow their land. Pressure and violence of a variety of sorts had been used on a significant portion of new members.[35]

It is clear from the discussion so far that it was primarily members of independent producer cooperatives and Type III producer cooperative groups, those organized on the Soviet kolkhoz model, who wanted to dissolve the farm. Members of Type I and II farms were in a wait-and-see mode. They had continued essentially private farming during the previous years, behind the "cooperative shop window," but at the same time had enjoyed various concessions, which, for the time being, they did not want to lose. The national and local organs judged their situation very differently. The latter recommended withdrawing operating permits from 133 lower-type producer cooperative groups, while the Agricultural Department of the party center was of the view that: "This recommendation cannot be accepted, because it betrays a move in the direction of least resistance."[36]

The process of dissolution slowed a little in August. The Ministry of Agriculture report prepared for the September 10 meeting of the Hungarian Workers' Party (HWP) Politburo reported on the following: "In the period from August 10 to September 7 another 159 Type III and 84 Type I producer cooperatives (producer cooperative groups) requested their dissolution in writing. In this period the most requests for dissolution came from Békés County (38), Somogy County (17), Szabolcs County (18), and Vas County (16). According to the latest report, written requests for dissolution were submitted by 761 Type III and 248 Type I, that is a total of 1,009 producer cooperative groups. In addition to this, a significant portion of the membership of a further 700 producer cooperatives wants to leave the producer cooperative at the end of the year."[37]

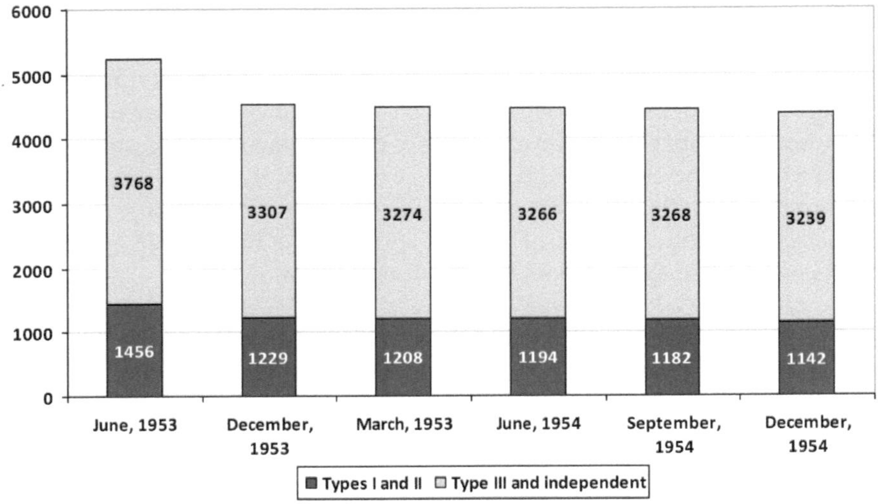

Figure 3.1. Number and Types of Cooperatives, June 30, 1953–December 31, 1954. Source: *A szocialista mezőgazdasági üzemek*, 49.

The New Course was initiated by Moscow, and its future was also determined by Soviet great power interests. In the fall of 1954, after the decision to admit West Germany to NATO, the Soviet leadership felt that, in this new international environment, heavy and military industry development should be accelerated. Prime Minister Malenkov, who had announced the program of improving living standards after Stalin's death, was forced to exercise self-criticism.[38]

Negotiations with Hungarian leaders on this change of direction were held in Moscow in January 1955. This time it was Imre Nagy who was criticized most, and for the very policy that the Soviets had recommended to him as the model to follow in 1953. The key element of the criticism was that the Hungarian government had overprioritized improving living standards, and so had neglected industry, and within that the development of heavy industry; while in villages it had supported strengthening individual peasant farms instead of organizing producer cooperatives. The following excerpt from their minutes well reflects the mood of the talks:

> Voroshilov: . . . It is impermissible to see a country's political and economic issues only from the point of view of peasants. Hungary still has a very high number of petty-commodity-producing peasants. . . . Every day, petty-commodity-producing farms give birth to capitalism. The land in Hungary is not nationalized. Those who do not take all of this into account are clearly wrong

> and represent mistaken views. Comrade Nagy is an intelligent and clever man, but his principles are not sufficiently secure. . . . Neglecting industry is not only incorrect, but dangerous. If there is no heavy industry, and no long-term growth, then we cannot move forward.[39]

Molotov continued as follows:

> In his speech of July, 1953 comrade Nagy took action allowing members to leave producer cooperative farms. (Comrade Nagy interjected: it was not my idea. We were given that advice here. Dobi even argued against it.) True, Beria did give such advice in his comments at that time, but after Beria's arrest we warned you to reconsider the situation and to be cautious. Comrade Nagy spoke with pathos in favor of leaving cooperatives, which especially exacerbated the matter.[40]

Khrushchev's critique of Imre Nagy verged on a threat:

> You have your virtues, but Zinoviev and Rykov had virtues too, in all likelihood no less than you, yet we still took firm action against them when they acted against Party interests. We have to take action against you, too. If others criticize you, it will be more difficult. If we don't take action in time, later the entire Party will step up against you. There is no other way out. . . . Why did you stop building the Sztálinváros steel mills? We criticized you for exaggerated industrialization, but industrialization has to be continued rationally, not stopped.

Khrushchev made clear the correct path to be followed at this meeting in Moscow. "Whether or not there is a war, we must develop industry. There is no point having plenty of bacon if there are no airplanes, that will only lead to trouble."[41]

Once home again in Hungary, Imre Nagy was not willing to exercise self-criticism either, which was understandable given that he had taken on the policy of the New Course not only because this was the direction provided by Moscow, but also because it was in line with the vision he had formulated in 1948–49.[42] Like then, he was once again declared a "right-wing deviationist" and revisionist. The tension within the party leadership became public following the March 2–4, 1955 meeting of the Central Committee.[43] The document released on the meeting stated that the successful implementation of party policy was being obstructed by a growing right-wing threat; at the same time, it condemned Imre Nagy as a representative of right-wing opportunist views. "One of the fundamental features of comrade Imre Nagy's right-wing line was revealed in his denial and underestimation of the great victories achieved by the Party and systematic silence about these results." The CC decree made it unambiguous that, "the main task is to develop industry, and within that above all heavy industry."[44]

At the next meeting of the CC, a decree announced the break with the policies of the "New Course" and with Imre Nagy. According to the verdict, "Comrade Nagy attempted to put the brakes on the motor of socialist construction, socialist industrialization, and within that especially the development of heavy industry, and in villages the producer cooperative movement. . . . In the interest of implementing his right-wing opportunist policy, comrade Nagy resorted to un-Party, anti-Party, and even factional methods."[45]

Following this he was removed from all his party positions, then on April 18, 1955, Parliament relieved him of his post as prime minister, and finally, on December 3, he was expelled from the party.[46] András Hegedüs became the new prime minister, and with this, in the spring of 1955, the Stalinist tendency headed by Rákosi and Gerő gained the upper hand. The prioritization above all else of the development of heavy and military industry was accompanied by a new increase in the rate of accumulation. In the absence of sufficient reserves for such measures, this necessitated restricting the population's consumption.[47]

THE SECOND DRIVE FOR COLLECTIVIZATION IN 1955–56

But it was in agrarian policy that the most conspicuous change was made, because Rákosi and Gerő wanted to put an end as soon as possible to "pro-peasant opportunism." They did not formally revoke the plan for three-year compulsory delivery obligations, but through tiny modifications moved in the direction of increasing burdens and revoking earlier concessions. A tightening of sanctions against those who did not meet their delivery requirements served the same purpose.[48] The kulak issue also returned to the agenda.

As far as the acceleration of collectivization was concerned, at its January 26, 1955 meeting, the Politburo set out the following goal for party organs:

> The results of the producer cooperative movement must be made known to peasants still farming individually and to the population of the country. Forceful agitation must be organized over the month of February, relying primarily on village party organs, with the aim of getting peasants to join existing producer cooperatives; and we must reach the point where, before spring work begins, there is a significant number of new entrants in all regions of the country. With respect to the development of new producer cooperatives, it is not necessary to issue the counties with required targets, either for the spring or the fall, but both county and district party organizations must be required to further develop the cooperative movement numerically too by their dedicated agitation work.[49]

Although the Rákosi group kept the issue of the new collectivization campaign on the agenda from the start of the year, the beginning of actual organization was planned for the end of the summer or fall. At the Politburo session of May 26, 1955, and then at the CC session of June 7–8, 1955, the goal to be achieved was identified numerically: by the end of the year, 50,000 to 60,000 families were to be recruited. By the end of the following five-year plan (1960), they counted on half a million small and middle peasant new entrants and 5 million kh (2,850,000 ha) of producer cooperative cultivated land. A return to previous practice was indicated in the following sentence from the decree: "socialist transformation is taking place in the midst of a sharp and sharpening class struggle."[50]

In the first seven to eight months of 1955, the number of families entering cooperatives was 21,000 to 22,000, while at the same time approximately 7,000 to 8,000 families left or were expelled. The party's central newspaper judged this an "upswing":

> *All signs indicate that after a two-year break and standstill, this year our producer cooperative movement is once again healthily developing further, the socialist sector is winning an ever greater sphere within agriculture.* This change has not been a gift of fate. It is thanks mostly to the fact that the Central Committee's March decree filled the breasts of the memberships of the producer cooperatives with self-confidence, and strengthened them in their conviction that they are following the correct path. . . . Nowadays, the only people who do not acknowledge the superiority of large-scale production are those who do not want to and, like ostriches, deliberately stick their heads in the sand, so that they do not see and do not hear.[51] [Emphasis in original.]

In reality, however, the property-owning peasantry continued to keep its distance from collective farming. The previous campaign had had a strong effect, as had the recent dissolution of cooperative farms. Hostility was particularly strong among those who had left producer cooperatives in 1953 and made great sacrifices in order to restart their individual farms. In addition to this, a role was also probably played by the fact that the apparatus was not as well prepared for struggle as it had been before 1953. On the one hand, an uncertain hesitation was in evidence, because of the criticisms of 1953 and occasional prosecutions consequent on them. On the other, even members of the party apparatus were reluctant to organize producer cooperatives because many of them were themselves involved in farming. All the same, the party leadership expected them to set an example, that is to say, to join.

The numbers referred to above fell far below the requirements of the political leadership, and therefore the August 11 Politburo meeting, taking notice of the slow development of producer cooperatives, obliged party and state organs to redouble their efforts. In addition, it was also stated that "it was desirable" that the development for the whole of 1955 "be reached by the end of September, because this way the communal work could already be ensured by the autumn of this year." There was also a strong expectation that only Type III producer cooperative groups would be formed.[52]

During the first collectivization drive (1949–1953) the Soviet model had been referenced incessantly, but this time greater emphasis was put on the experience of successful producer cooperatives operating at home. This tendency was mirrored not only in the central party newspaper, but also in the local press.

> Individually farming peasants can see all sorts of things from the "outside," but they cannot see into the operation of cooperative farming, they cannot establish precisely how the cooperative membership increases its joint wealth. Only a cooperative member can explain this convincingly. *The producer cooperative farm must be on open book to individually farming peasants*, one they can read and study, so they come to understand that their place too is in the cooperative. But this is only possible if *producer cooperative visits are organized, if the individual farmers are shown how they farm and their results. That is to say: if an opportunity is given for them to see with their own eyes, and feel with their own hands, what a producer cooperative really is*. Visits to producer cooperatives and persistent persuasive words: these are the most important things producer cooperative leaders and members can do to facilitate the transit of individually working peasants to the cooperative path. *One of the most important tasks of county and district party committees is to defeat sectarianism among producer cooperative leaders and members, defeat the underestimation of political conviction, and reach a point where cooperative members become the agitators for and organizers of the development of producer cooperatives*.[53] [Emphasis in original.]

Nor were the earlier methods of administrative compulsion forgotten. Partial and full land consolidation campaigns were restarted with a deadline of the end of summer. A series of administrative measures were taken to cancel peasant rental of state reserve land. At the same time the authorities strove to increase the burdens on individual farmers, harassment over tax and delivery arrears became common place, as did the process, termed "transfers" by the local councils, whereby agricultural and household goods, including furniture and clothing, were seized in lieu of such arrears.[54]

Collectivization campaigns accelerated over the course of September and October in counties east of the Tisza and west of the Danube. Dozens of producer cooperatives were established in Somogy, Zala, and Vas counties. This was achieved by sending waves of people's educators to each village.[55]

The numbers of producer cooperatives and their members grew again in 1955–56 as a result of this rather forceful agitation and coercion, but this increase did not reach pre-1953 levels. The number of producer cooperatives grew by 450 in the second half of 1955, and the number of families who joined by 67,000.[56] What is more, the annual increase-in-area plan had been over fulfilled by 4,000 kh (2,280 ha) by November. This all led the Rákosi leadership to conclude that restructuring could be faster than the original plan for 1956. At the end of 1955, great efforts were made to prepare for the winter campaign.

> Making known cooperative results, making collective farming more popular, and educating individually farming peasants cannot be limited to a few weeks, or months: it is a permanent task. But we must make more intense use of those moments which are *particularly* appropriate for winning over working peasants. One such period is the winter. In the past too, many opted for cooperative farming in December, January or February. It was in the winter and early spring months that the country's first producer cooperative towns were born. That this period is particularly appropriate for developing the movement should come as no surprise. At the beginning of winter, the producer cooperatives' final annual accounts are prepared, and they are of interest not just to cooperative members but also to individual farmers. . . . The final results of these accounts provide plenty of arguments to the people's educators, and make it possible to prove to working peasants in black and white: they can go further in a producer cooperative. Working peasants have more time in the winter months, as do the people's educators working in villages.[57] [Emphasis in original.]

Dissatisfaction and embitterment were exceptionally high among farmers in the first half of 1956. This was reflected in the fact that the number of new members joining producer cooperatives were only just over a tenth of the number for the same period in the previous year. By September 30, 1956, a total of 41 new collective farms had been successfully created, while the number of members grew by 37,000. At this time a total of 4,875 producer cooperatives operated in the country on 1,954,000 kh (1,114,000 ha) of arable land, which accounted for 20.8% of the total. The membership had reached 342,884. The relaunch of collectivization in the autumn of 1955 kept individual farmers in a state of uncertainty, which had an impact on their willingness to produce. All this was compounded by a drought. The annual grain production for 1956 fell 400,000 tons short of what was planned.[58]

Parallel to this, the numbers leaving cooperatives, and indeed of cooperatives breaking up grew ever more quickly. One of the factors in this was that farmers who had been forced into producer cooperatives in the fall had signed up with the proviso that actual joint work would only commence half a year

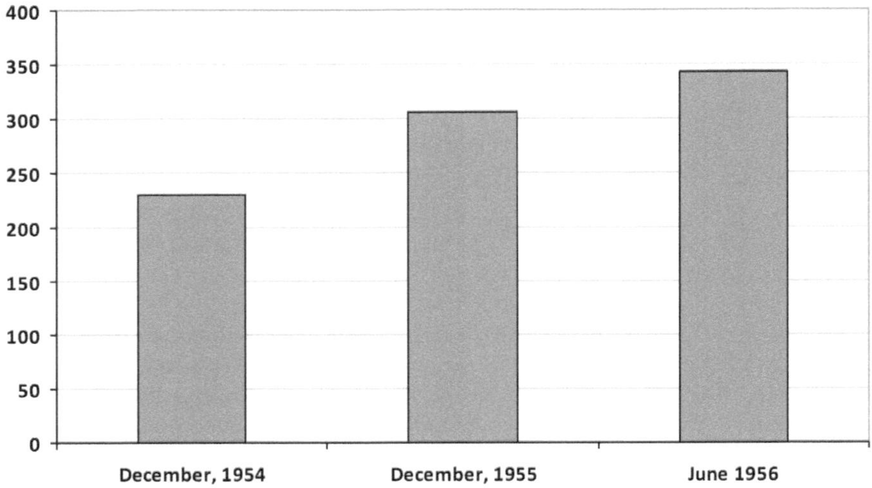

Figure 3.2. Number of Cooperative Members (Thousands of People) December 31, 1954–June 30, 1956. Source: A KSH 5/1956 és 41/1959 sz. mezőgazdasági jelentése.

later, in the spring. Until then, they did not even contribute their equipment or livestock above the household plot limits.

By early fall, 1956, the crisis had become increasingly evident in the spheres of political, social, and economic life. A possible contribution to this was the fact that popular dissatisfaction had intensified in response to the

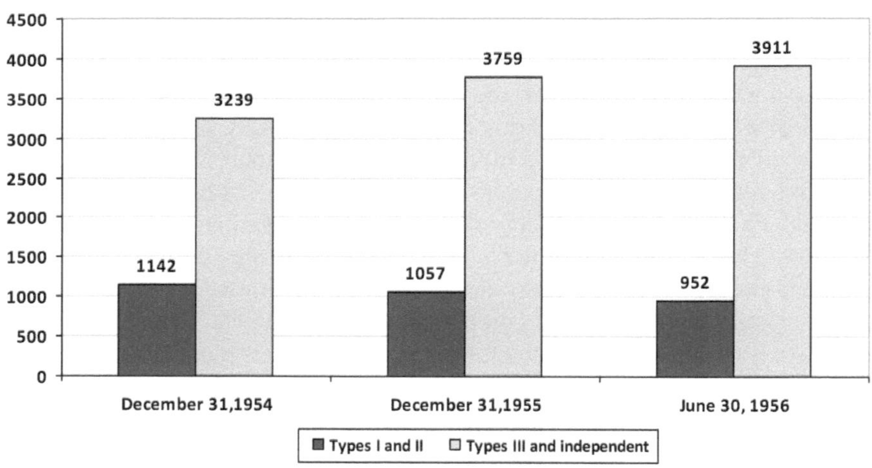

Figure 3.3. Number of Cooperatives December 31, 1954–June 30, 1956. Source: A KSH 5/1956 és 41/1959 sz. mezőgazdasági jelentése.

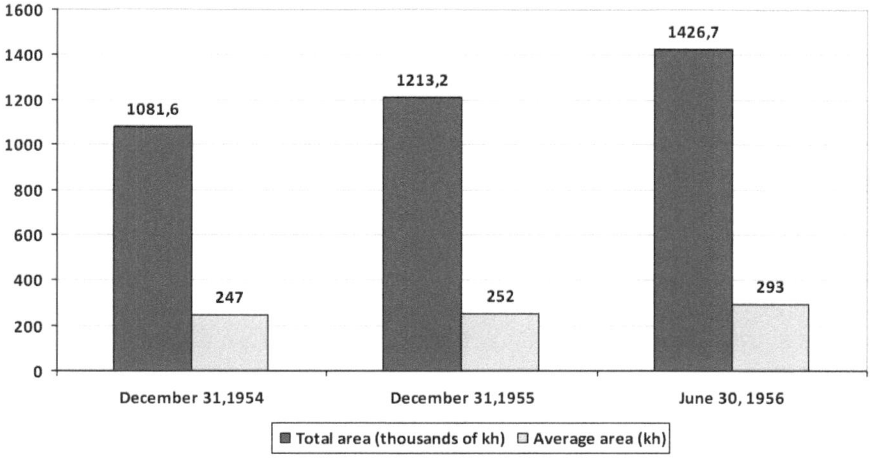

Figure 3.4. Number of Cooperative Members (Thousands of People) December 31, 1954–June 30, 1956. Source: A KSH 5/1956 és 41/1959 sz. mez*ő*gazdasági jelentése.

Party leadership's vacillating policies and undelivered promises following the 20th Congress of the CPSU (February 24–25, 1956) where the idea of multiple roads to socialism had been legitimated. Various layers of Hungarian society felt strengthened by this because, during the year and a half of the "New Course" of Imre Nagy's government, they had themselves experienced that there was indeed another road to the construction of socialism, one that differed from that represented by the Rákosi-Gerő clique. From March 1956, criticism of the leadership became increasingly open, as was well reflected in the public debates of Alliance of Democratic Youth's Petőfi Circle. The flood of information flowing from this forum proved to be a force in shaping public opinion. Political debating circles were established nationwide, from Debrecen to Kaposvár, and in many places agrarian-themed presentations were organized. Prominent in organizing such events were alumni of the people's colleges, which had been established to educate peasant youth immediately before the war, had blossomed in the early postwar year with the support of the Communist Party and Hungarian Peasant Party, but were suddenly closed in 1949 after the arrest of László Rajk.[59]

DEMANDS OF THE PEASANTRY DURING THE 1956 REVOLUTION

The outcome of the second attempt at collectivization launched for 1956 was a severe, multilayered crisis in the agrarian sector. In the autumn of 1956, all action took place amid these tensions; and the village population did take action. However, because the armed struggle was centered primarily on Budapest and the larger provincial cities, a rather simplified picture has emerged according to which the majority of villages remained relatively calm in the revolutionary days of late October and early November. The agrarian population supported the cities with food deliveries, but, "characterized as it was by natural caution, did not take part in the revolutionary events." It is now possible, however, to outline the main characteristics of village behavior in 1956 thanks to better access to ever more provincial archives since regime change in 1989/90, and an increasing number of analyses of their contents.[60]

The above-mentioned general political-economic crisis reached its culmination in October 1956. On October 23 a mass demonstration was organised by university students, which, in the evening hours, turned into armed revolt. As a result of these events, the Presidium of the CPSU—after consultation with the Hungarian party leadership—decided on military intervention.

Between the participants in the mass demonstration and the party leadership, there was only one person who seemed acceptable to both sides: Imre Nagy. On October 24 he was named prime minister, although the composition of the new government differed little from the previous one. In the course of the day production came to a standstill in Budapest and armed clashes broke out all over the city, partly between the revolutionaries and troops loyal to the government, and partly between the revolutionaries and Soviet troops. Demonstrations also took place in several provincial towns and cities (Debrecen, Győr, Kecskemét, Miskolc, Pécs, and Székesfehérvár).[61]

In the days that followed, the clashes, demonstrations and strikes spread throughout the entire country. The change of power in the villages took place three or four days later than in Budapest. It is very significant that, just as in almost every other settlement in the country, self-organization began and new organs of power came into being practically without any central directives. This suggests nothing less than that the whole of the country, including the most remote tiny villages, was ready for change. Otherwise it could not have happened that society was set in motion as if by magic, and everywhere people emerged who took the lead and were ahead of events.

The peasant populations wanted to find solutions to the accumulated tensions and conflicts. On the one hand, this was done through action, by creating their own organs of power. Democratic self-organization was evident in the creation of new organs of administration—national councils, revolutionary committees, national committees, and so on—and in the election of new leaders. On the other hand, a stern message was sent to the government, relaying what immediate actions were expected.[62] The weight of the accumulated tensions is evident in the fact that peasants did not formulate requests or recommendations, but demands.

The election of new governing bodies generally followed a similar script across the country's small settlements. Local action began with demonstrations and marches, during which the masses got rid of the symbols of the Rákosi regime: Red Stars, portraits of Rákosi and Stalin, Walls of Fame and Shame, and memorials to Soviet heroism. In many instances compulsory delivery and tax documents were also destroyed. These actions gave expression to their desire to break with the dictatorship. Following this a village meeting was called, a meeting of the people, where—exercising direct democracy—a new organ of power was elected. In these elections, it was persons known to and respected by the community who gained village trust. At the same time, national guard units were mostly also established.

The immediate establishment of local revolutionary "committees" points to the fact that people retained a vivid memory of the experience of rebuilding local power immediately following the struggles of the Second World War. At the end of 1944 and beginning of 1945, when the front had moved on, people's and national committees, initiatives from below, were formed across the country.[63] In the fall of 1956, self-organization was similarly reborn in the power vacuum created by the collapse of the Soviet-type system of local government.

As far as the national guard is concerned, it can be postulated that memories of the 1848–49 revolution and freedom struggle were at work. Of course, a defining factor in the immediate decisions of the people was that they knew well: without an armed body organized from among themselves, it would be impossible to enforce their own interests. In very many places local police were also drawn into the rapidly organizing national guard, the armed force created by the revolution.

The fact that these two new institutions were called into life spontaneously and exceptionally rapidly, in a matter of days, gives unequivocal evidence of the political maturity of rural society at the time.[64] The newly established bodies strove to take over the running of village life. They set as their most important tasks securing order and calm, protecting private property, and ensuring food supplies.

These new governing organs played a significant role in ensuring that there were only rare examples of scores being settled and vengeance taken for the accumulated tensions of the Rákosi era. Yet there was individual and collective grievance in abundance. The vast majority of the village population nevertheless resolved to wait for the creation of independent courts, which would be entrusted to handle the resolution of their earlier grievances.

A "quiet revolution" was in training in villages at the end of October, whose essence was not armed struggle but multidimensional and multilayered self-organization. Villagers did not wait for central directives but took the organization of life in their own communities into their own hands, while at the same time formulating demands of the government concerning what matters required urgent action on its part.

The new local governments that emerged in provincial cities and villages devoted much attention to questions concerning the peasantry, agriculture, and farming. Interestingly, the peasantry expressed itself surprisingly similarly in settlements very distant from one another and with no communication between them. A common feature of the various proclamations and appeals was that the demands formulated within them were rather uniform. The HWP's desire to sharpen to the utmost class struggle in villages had been in vain; it had not worked. In the fall of 1956, the different groups of peasant society, in differing positions and with differing interests, uniformly demanded remedy for the injuries suffered over the preceding years.

It is instructive to split peasant demands into two groups. In the first can be found demands wherein village people identified with the basic aim of the revolution and freedom struggle. This was expressed through demands for the withdrawal of Soviet troops, the dissolution of the hated State Security Authority and the introduction of a multiparty system. Demands for national independence and an emphasis on national identity can also be noted from the first moment.[65]

The second group of demands consisted of those dictated by peasant grievances. In the light of the analysis above, it is not surprising that among the first places to formulate proposals for improving the situation of the peasantry was Kaposvár, in the center of Somogy County. It is worth noting the most important of the sixteen points compiled on October 25.

> In the interests of a radical change in the situation of the working peasantry, we demand a change in feudal system-type taxation and compulsory deliveries: the abolition of tithes. Let us create a cooperative form which corresponds to Hungarian specificities, on the basis of the greatest possible voluntarism. Let us ensure for our working peasantry the most complete autonomy in interest representation.[66]

Annulment of the system of compulsory deliveries that crippled the peasantry figured not only in Somogy County but as the most general and most forceful demand across the country.[67] Generally, this was closely related to two further demands. The first called for corrections to the price system to take better account of production costs, while the second called for the dissolution of the institutions of the compulsory deliveries system, that is to say the compulsory deliveries ministry and its county, district, and village offices.

Another important node of positions on agricultural topics related to producer cooperatives. Resolute demands were formulated to end violent collectivization, to permit members to leave producer cooperatives freely, and to end land consolidation.[68]

The demands considered so far were essentially aimed at remedying injuries suffered during the Rákosi era. A further examination of the text of rural manifestos and brochures reveals that every element of agricultural policy to date was subjected to critical analysis in the interests of reestablishing the freedom to farm. A demand was formulated for a general reduction in taxes.[69] The moderate tone of peasant demands is reflected in the following addendum issued in Hajdú-Bihar County: "When establishing taxes, a harmony must be found between producer and state interests."[70] Farmers called for the ending of compulsory production contracts as well as compulsory sowing plans.

A striking feature of peasant demands was how surprisingly mature and thought-through they were. Numerous localities in the country worked out true action plans. A good example of the degree of precision with which questions of detail were formulated is the demands of the peasants of Hajdú-Bihar County issued on October 27.

> The compulsory delivery of all items must be cancelled from January 1, 1957, with the exception of deliveries of bread grain and fattened pigs. The delivery of lard from privately owned pigs must be stopped at once. The delivery of bread grain and fattened pigs must be stopped from January 1, 1958.
>
> The need to apply for permission to slaughter livestock—with the exception of cattle—must be terminated. The need to seek authorization for logging must also be terminated.
>
> The compulsory insurance system must be eliminated from January 1, 1957.
>
> . . .
>
> Land consolidation for the year 1956 must be reviewed and justified grievances must be settled by March 15, 1957.[71]

Settling ownership grievances and restoring the inviolability of property that had been taken for nothing in the 1950s were indispensable to the creation of production security. Particular attention was directed toward landownership, because the conflict between the peasantry and those in power was sharpest in this respect. Aspirations pertaining to land focused on remedying the grievances suffered after 1947–48, that is to say, nowhere was there a demand for the restoration of pre-1945 landownership relations. Sorting out property relations was a serious task, as these had become completely chaotic as a consequence of land consolidation and violent land-seizures. The new local administrative bodies generally wanted to begin by first reviewing the land consolidations of 1956. There were some municipalities, of course, where bigger steps were planned. In Makó, for example, it was resolutely demanded that "land and equipment illegally seized from the peasantry immediately be returned!"[72]

In addition to economic grievances, another source of bitterness was the grievous restriction of personal liberty under which human dignity counted for nothing.

In order to restore justice to the peasantry, the new revolutionary bodies encouraged on the one hand, a review of court judgments and, on the other, the reinstatement of rights and freedoms. Alongside freedom of religion, assembly, and "full and injury-free" speech, the demand for a new electoral law was also formulated, the basic principle of which would be: equal, secret, and direct ballots. To this, it was often added that village leaders should be elected secretly and directly by local population. Another general demand was for discredited political and community leaders of past years to be replaced immediately and held to account. As far as the future was concerned, the following standpoint can be found among the demands of the peasantry of Hajdú-Bihar County and is worthy of note:

> In the interest of avoiding daily conflicts between local, state and economic leaders and working people, government organs must stop issuing commands that have been decided internally, without public discussion. All measures regulating people's lives must be published openly in official papers and only these can be implemented.[73]

Another general demand made across the country was for the creation of equal status and equality of opportunity between the actors in agricultural production. This perspective can be well captured in the texts of manifestos and statements formulated in agricultural regions, for space was always found for the demands of the producer cooperative membership alongside those of individual farmers. A recurring element was the demand for producer cooperative independence. What is more, in many places there was pressure for the immediate drafting of a local cooperative law which would make possible the very widest range of producer associations and ensure the financial and production independence of communal farms.[74]

On the basis of the documents reviewed so far it can be established that, beginning on October 25, 1956, the new revolutionary bodies being formed in rural communities examined in turn, although with a certain delay, the most burning questions facing agriculture and the peasantry. October 28, an important caesura in national events too, brought about a significant turnaround for the agrarian population. Ending discrimination against private farmers was put onto the agenda. Prime Minister Imre Nagy announced that the government would put a stop to the serious actions in breach of the law that had taken place over the course of the producer cooperative movement and land consolidation, and would elaborate a large-scale plan to restart much-neglected agricultural production.[75] The words were soon followed by actions: on October 30 the compulsory delivery system, which had so burdened the peasantry, was abolished.[76]

Following this and largely in the name of achieving the fastest possible political consolidation, the local revolutionary councils and national committees enacted measures aimed at maintaining continuity in agricultural work, ensuring public supplies, protecting the property of producer cooperatives and regulating their dissolution. In fact, there were also some revolutionary organs which moved beyond managing daily tasks and formulated their visions of the future of the agrarian sphere.[77]

One day after the policy reversal of October 28, the Revolutionary National Council of Somogy County had already outlined what had to be done, both immediately and long term. "Our county is mainly agricultural in character. For this very reason, one of the most important points in our plan for the future is the prompt elimination of the burning mistakes in Hungarian agriculture and village life by securing the rights of the peasantry in the broadest sense. . . . Individual farmers and producer cooperative members should have equal opportunities. The shameful class struggle in the villages should be ended! The peasantry should freely be able to establish interest-representing organizations in order to defend its rights. Steps should be taken in the near future concerning questions of compulsory deliveries and leaving producer cooperatives. Resolving these burning questions must be executed in an orderly fashion. Because the collapse of order and village peace would result in hatred, as would the reckless pilfering of public property. We know that these are painful and pressing questions, but still we ask every peasant to exercise a little patience and self-restraint until solutions have been worked out. Our most important task now is to restart and secure production immediately. In the interest of doing so we will refrain from all arbitrary measures in respect of both individuals and public property. Debated issues will be handled by the National Revolutionary Council in line with the wishes and the rightful demands of the peasantry."[78]

Makó, a town with a great agricultural past, can serve as an example from the Great Plain. It is remarkable that a manifesto written in another corner of the country at almost the same time is equally as sober and considerate throughout as the one quoted from Somogy County above.

> The National Committee turns to the working peasantry of Makó town with love and asks it to nurture, with all its strength and with the devotion characteristic of the peasantry of Makó town, the land from which next year's bread will be put on the tables of the Hungarian people, until the time comes very soon when their land will be returned. Now is not the moment to look for where boundaries are and in whose name the land is registered, but rather to sow the blessed grain seed in fertile mother earth in time. . . .

> The National Committee of Makó town is convinced that the entire community of our town is aware that everyone must contribute to easing the very serious problems of feeding people, while bearing each other's interests in mind and making noble sacrifices. It is especially important that those who rely on the market have access to important basic food items at reasonable prices. It therefore asks and expects of the community that produces for the market to take these factors into consideration and refrain from raising prices. . . .[79]

Although the peasantry had suffered very great individual and collective hurt over the course of the 1950s, its behavior when formulating its demands, both before and after October 28, was characterized by a sobriety and realism worthy of respect. The various groups within the agrarian population did not simply reject the Stalinist agricultural policy of previous years, but had a determined vision of how to get out of it and normalize. They very consciously elaborated a program for renewal and a return to individual farming.

LESSONS FROM THE 1956 REVOLUTION

The tragic path of the 1956 uprising became a defining experience for both society and those in power. The Hungarian people understood that they could not count on assistance from the West and that the country remained part of the Soviet bloc. At the same time the political decision-makers understood that, not only must they avoid the abuses of the past, but that essential changes were also necessary.[80] One of the most important things recognized by the leaders of the Hungarian Socialist Workers' Party (HSWP) was that the "construction of socialism" could not proceed at the expense of the living standards of wide layers in society. At the December 2, 1956 meeting of the Provisional Central Committee, János Kádár indicated the new direction: "In solving economic questions it is our policy that, in all decisions concerning where to spend produced goods, the first priority must be the gradual increase in the living standards of workers."[81]

From the end of 1956 those in power used the toughest means to eliminate political opponents, but at the same time from the beginning they also sought tools for conciliation with society. The most effective of these turned out to be the standard-of-living policy.[82] Before 1956, keeping consumption levels low had in itself been an important resource for the forced development of heavy and military industry. At the time, and for a long time to come, implementing a standard-of-living policy rested primarily on food supply, for people used the bulk of their income to purchase food.[83] This is not surprising, since wide swathes of Hungarian society had suffered an impoverished, inadequate, and often one-sided diet not only before 1945, but through the

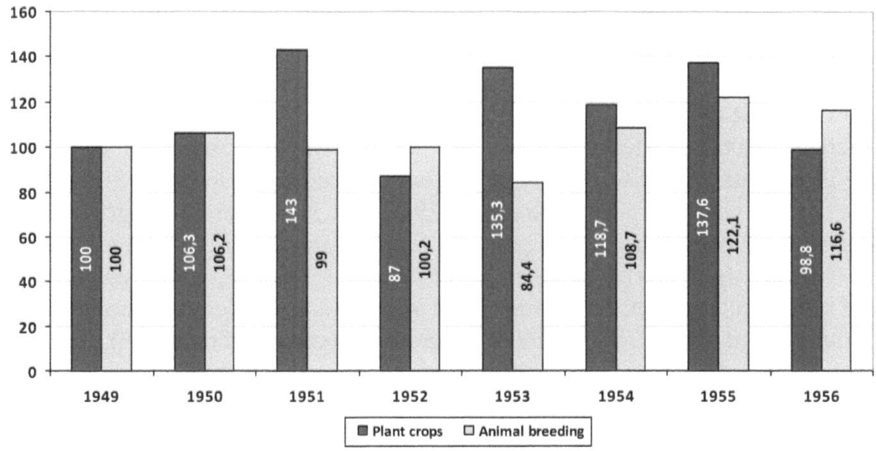

Figure 3.5. Gross Production Ratios in Agriculture 1949–1956. Source: Iván Oros, *A falu és a mezőgazdaság főbb társadalmi és gazdasági jelzőszámai*, 245–47.

1950s as well. Popular demand for a plentiful diet thus presented itself with elemental force in the Kádár era.

After 1956, because of the prioritization of the standard-of-living policy, increasing agricultural production and, related to this, providing incentives for agrarian producers, became of strategic importance. The first step in regularizing relations between those in power and agrarian society was to ease the tensions caused by HWP agrarian policy. The starting point for this was provided by the recommendations elaborated in summer and early fall, 1956, in the Party Center's Agricultural Department, the Ministry of Agriculture and the National Planning Office.[84] In the first half of October, the HWP Central Committee's Agricultural Department had compiled discussion materials on the neuralgic points of agrarian policy. The submission had been debated by county party committee agricultural secretaries and department heads on the day before the revolution broke out, on October 22, 1956.[85] Sharp criticism of agrarian policy to date was voiced at the meeting, as is well illustrated by the excerpts below:

"Unfortunately, when compared to individual peasant farms, the majority of our producer cooperatives produce less, the value of the goods they sell is less, their income is lower, and their hands are tied by more bureaucracy." This comparison was already known from the statistics, but nevertheless its open expression and acknowledgment were very significant. This was accompanied by the following radical observation: "In the future we must not mechanically follow the practice of Soviet kolkhoz building, but take into account our own specific relations . . . the traditions of Hungarian cooperation."[86]

The participants in the meeting agreed that the most important task regarding what had to be done next, was to restore production security and material interest for both producer cooperatives and individual farms. What is more, the three-year compulsory delivery system that had come into force on January 1, 1954 would expire at the end of 1956. The Party Center's Agricultural Department issued the following view regarding the future: "In the interest of ensuring the material interests of farmers, the most important question is the rational change of the current price system, and further, the abolition of compulsory deliveries by means of the gradual abolition of the tax-like nature of deliveries."[87]

In light of the background materials quoted above, it is not surprising that elimination of compulsory deliveries became acceptable to Kádár's Revolutionary Worker-Peasant Government. Kádár and his associates had already promised to end compulsory deliveries in their government program announced on November 4. This significant decision was forced on them by a number of factors. The Imre Nagy government, recognizing this most important demand of the peasantry, had already declared the abolition of compulsory deliveries on October 30. The new Hungarian Revolutionary Worker-Peasant Government did not countermand it. A confrontation with the peasantry, which had control over food stocks, would have had unforeseeable consequences, meanwhile industrial production was at a standstill because of the general strike.[88] In these circumstances, the Kádár government was not only minded to revoke the measure of the Imre Nagy government, but, in the interest of consolidation, it wanted to attribute directly to itself the merit for abolishing compulsory deliveries. This was symbolized by the Presidential Council's legislative decree no. 21 of November 12, which canceled the delivery of agricultural crops and products with retroactive effect from October 25.[89]

In the fall of 1956, therefore, the system of compulsory deliveries was abolished twice, moreover, Hungary was the first socialist country to do so.[90] This burden that the wartime government had placed on the shoulders of the peasantry, and which had been retained in the second half of the 1940s in the interest of maintaining food supplies and meeting reparations obligations, and then, from 1949, made more stringent as an indispensable tool of socialist construction, was abolished. Elimination of the system of compulsory deliveries brought an end to peasants being constantly at the mercy of the authorities, being constantly called to account, having to sweep the hayloft floor, and this resulted in a substantial improvement in the situation of agricultural producers.

This step did away with an element of the Stalinist system of socialist agriculture that had been considered inviolable. In the interest of consolidation, state power gave up use of a tool through which, previously, it had not only gained access to a large stock of produce virtually cost-free, but which was also capable of redirecting significant income from agriculture to industry.

The elimination of the compulsory deliveries system created a situation in which the state could only access produce stocks if it offered realistic purchase prices to producers.[91] As a consequence, purchasing began at a state purchase price which approximated the free market price. Instead of employing the earlier economic tools of coercion, the state structured its relations with the commodity-producing peasantry, the producer cooperatives and the state farms by commercial methods, by striving to ensure that agriculturalists had an interest in producing.

After 1956, therefore, market and commodity-producing activity regained its right to exist, albeit within limits, in one of the fundamental sectors of the Hungarian economy. Over the course of 1957–58 it was confirmed that the population's food supply could be ensured this way at a higher level than previously.[92] But, given that prices were more determined by state price regulation still than the forces of supply and demand, the rehabilitation of the agricultural market could only be limited in nature. Abolition of compulsory deliveries therefore did not mean that the state had given up on controlling agricultural producers. The significance of the measure can be demonstrated rather in the fact that the authorities saw that in the case of various consumer goods (such as vegetables, fruit, eggs, poultry, and so on) space should be provided for an emerging direct, market-based relationship between producers and consumers, and this resulted in an expansion of farmers' autonomy.

The government demonstrated its readiness to remedy the grievances of the peasantry in other respects as well. The key elements of the new agrarian policy were made public by the government on November 27, 1956, in an appeal addressed to the peasantry.

> The Revolutionary Worker-Peasant Government fully condemns the mistaken agricultural policy of past years, the violent organization of producer cooperatives, the use of harassment in land consolidation, all those methods whose employment resulted in the decline of Hungarian agriculture for years. This not only caused moral and material damage to the peasantry, but left insecure basic supplies for industrial workers and the urban population. The government has already put an end to violent land consolidation that made peasant production insecure, and has eliminated compulsory deliveries. . . . It is the government's resolute intent to use all tools at hand to support the peasantry's efforts to bring about an upswing in agricultural production and offer economic support to producer cooperatives and individual peasants alike.[93]

The government statement ensured that there would be undifferentiated support for both cooperative and private farming, and, even more important, that the peasantry could freely choose its mode of farming. This was confirmed by the fact that the Ministry of Agriculture simultaneously issued a decree regulating how members could leave producer cooperatives and how they could be wound up.[94]

The promises expressed in the government appeal were given form by more and more new decrees, which eased the responsibilities of individual farmers. Compulsory sowing plans and mandatory sales were canceled, fire and frost insurance was no longer compulsory, agricultural development supplements (the so-called kulak-tax) were eliminated, and limited sales of land were permitted.[95]

As a result of all of the measures listed above, two-thirds of producer cooperatives were dissolved, and at the same time several hundred thousand peasant farms began work anew. The bulk of landowning peasants left the producer cooperatives, while the majority of the landless and smallholders, in the absence of any other possibility for making a living, decided in favor of staying put.

In the first half of 1957 it appeared that the HSWP, like the Polish Communist Party, was expecting the multisectoral nature of agriculture to continue for the longer term. Emphasis was not on reorganizing for large-production,

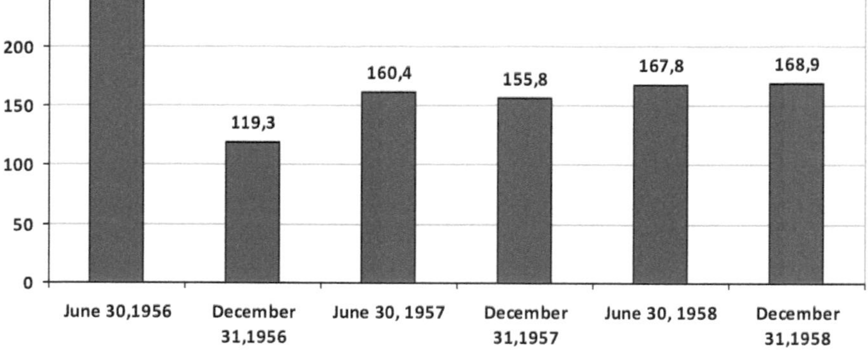

Figure 3.6. Number of Cooperative Members (Thousands of People) June 1956–December 1958. Source: A KSH 53/1959. sz. mezőgazdasági jelentése.

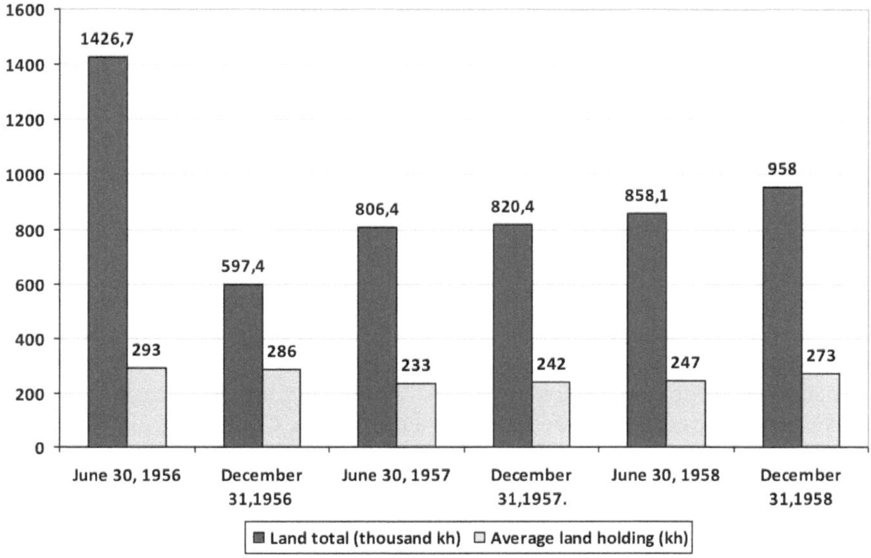

Figure 3.7. Total Area of Cooperative June 1956–December 1958. Source: A KSH 53/1959. sz. mezőgazdasági jelentése.

but on encouraging the will to farm. The big question, of course, was whether it would be a temporary solution, or whether it would define the relationship between the political authorities and agricultural producers in the longer term. The party and state organs of agricultural management were also divided over this dilemma.[96]

The agricultural price system and price policy figured as a separate item for the government meeting of May 30, 1957. The starting point of the submission prepared with the participation of the National Price Office, the Ministry of Agriculture and the Food Affairs Ministry was:

> In past years—especially until 1953—agricultural production and purchasing policy relied too heavily on regulations of coercive administration, at the centre of which was the system of compulsory deliveries and low purchase prices. This system was supplemented by restrictions on marketing and various state monopolies. In this way agricultural economic policy pushed into the background the principle of the planned influence of agriculture through material incentives.[97]

The following statement was formulated regarding the future:

> Planned influence of agriculture via material interests directly requires that—with the exception of monopoly goods—the consumer prices of food be defined

on the basis of production costs with a charge for socially necessary turnover costs.[98]

At this government meeting it also became apparent that the leadership of the Ministry of Agriculture (Minister Imre Dögei and his deputies) found many more negativities in the new purchase price system than the other governing agencies, especially the Agricultural Department of the HSWP CC led by Lajos Fehér.[99] The difference of opinion between the two groups was apparent in almost all important agricultural policy issues, and also precipitated down to the county and district organs of agricultural management. Facing these deep disagreements, Lajos Fehér initiated a wide-ranging discussion about the direction of the post-1956 agrarian policy. By June of 1957 it resulted a special party document, the Agrarian Theses which were accepted by the HSWP conference, but never became a Politburo or CC resolution. The next chapter gives a detailed analysis of the Agrarian Theses.[100]

At a meeting held for the agricultural department heads of county party committees, Lajos Fehér characterized the views of the dogmatic leadership of the ministry, that is too say the Dögei group, as follows:

> People like this want us to put an end to producer interests. I do not think that any responsible Party or state functionary would dare to pledge to end the system of material interests which was created with such difficulty. I think none of us here, not even responsible enterprise functionaries, would take on that responsibility. That is why, in our agricultural policy, we insist that incentives be secured for individuals and producer cooperatives alike . . . what kind of incentives? . . . They fall between two extremes: 1) When with purchase prices I go below or way below actual value. This was the case during compulsory deliveries. In this case there can be no talk of interests, we can only speak of sowing-contract coercion. 2) The other extreme is when we overpay peasants by our pricing. We can't want this, because it would stabilize relations of petty commodity production. . . . Pricing this year is good enough for us to create producer interest and security. . . . We have to have a price system that serves producer interests. The Politburo is united on this question.[101]

With this last sentence, Lajos Fehér wanted to communicate to the HSWP rural apparatus that the party's highest decision-making body had committed itself to an agrarian policy that would organize production by means of market relations and producer interests. The party leadership was decisively influenced in this question by the events of 1957.

The Food Affairs Ministry summarized the experience of the first year of the purchase system for the Politburo as follows:

> After eliminating the system of compulsory deliveries, we must cover the majority of main goods almost completely through commercial methods, via free

> or contract-based purchase. Only the bigger part of bread grains and almost half of feed grains were covered by land tax and payment of fees for state services in kind.[102] In purchases from individually farming peasants and producer cooperatives, the proportion of free and contract purchases for the most important items increased from 38.8% to 86.6%. . . . Using these methods, by October 31 we had completed 92.1% of the purchase plan for the most important items approved for 1957. The expected total purchase for 1957 . . . will mean an 8–12% overfulfillment of the plan originally approved by the Council of Ministers.[103]

A single year had demonstrated that food supply for the population could be ensured at a higher level than before; and this convinced Kádár and his group that this solution, which had been chosen to manage a crisis situation, would be worth sticking to long term.

There was no point therefore in Kádár's left-wing opposition arguing that the peasantry was taking a disproportionate share of national income, to the detriment of the working class, or that capitalist tendencies would gain strength within the peasantry, for the party leadership, the increased desire to produce and booming production following the abolition of compulsory deliveries were more important. In 1957–58, reality had proved that, in a freer economic environment, small farms were capable of ensuring a stable food supply for the urban population.[104] At the same time, experience also showed that while private peasant farmers continued to provide the bulk of produce, market mechanisms could be kept within limits by influencing price and tax policy. This meant, for example, that in 1957, the overwhelming majority of the four million forints that flowed to the peasants through higher purchase prices could be pumped back through a variety of channels.[105]

NOTES

1. Központi Statisztikai Hivatal, *Magyar mezőgazdaság, 1851–2000* [Hungarian agriculture, 1851–2000] (Budapest: KSH, 2000), CD-ROM.
2. Such tensions are analyzed with a new approach by Gyögy Gyarmati in the chapter of his latest monograph with the title "Kettős hadigazdasági túlterhelés és rejtőzködő transzformációs veszteség" [Dual war economy overburdening and hidden transformation costs]. See Gyarmati, *A Rákosi-korszak*, 279–92. Similar problems are discussed in the Eastern European context: Anne Applebaum, *Iron curtain: the crushing of Eastern Europe, 1945–1956* (London: Allen Lane, 2012), 436–83.
3. Szakács, "From Land Reform." 291–93.
4. Mark Pittaway, *Eastern Europe 1939–2000* (London: Bloomsbury Academic, 2004), 55–61; Swain and Swain, *Eastern Europe*, 123–52.
5. Roy Medvedev, *Khruschev: The years in power* (London: Oxford University Press, 1977), 77–105; William Taubman, *Khrushchev: The Man and His Era* (New York: W. W. Norton, 2003), 236–69.

6. Protokoll von der Sitzung des Politburos des ZK der SED. [Minutes of the Politburo session, January 2, 1953] Stiftung Archiv der Parteien und Massenorganisationen der DDR im Bundesarchiv (here on: SAPMO) Bundesarchiv in Berlin (BArchív), DY 30, J IV 2/2–255.

7. Elke Scherstjanoi, "'Wollen wir den Sozialismus?' Dokumente aus der Sitzung des Politbüros des ZK der SED am 6. Juni 1953," *Beiträge zur Geschichte der Arbeiterbewegung* 33, no. 5 (1991): 658–80; Gareth Pritchard, "Workers and the Socialist Unity Party of Germany in the summer of 1953," in *The Workers' and Peasants' State: Communism and Society in East Germany under Ulbricht, 1945–71*, eds. Patrick Major and Jonathan Osmond (Manchester and New York: Manchester University Press, 2002), 112–29.

8. The level of delivery of agricultural goods was lowered. As a result of the corrections the number of agricultural producer cooperatives (in German: LPG) dropped from 5,074 to 4,691 between June and December 1953. This decrease continued into 1954, but at a slower pace. Jens Schöne, *Frühling auf dem Lande? Die Kollektivierung der DDR-Landwirtschaft* (Berlin: Ch. Links Verlag, 2005), 142–53.

9. The members of the delegation were: Mátyás Rákosi, Ernő Gerő, Imre Nagy, András Hegedűs, István Hidas, Béla Szalai, Rudolf Földvári, István Dobi. Also see: Magdolna Baráth, "Szovjet kézi vezérlés az első Nagy Imre-kormány idején" [Direct Soviet control during the first government of Imre Nagy], in *Nagy Imre és kora: Tanulmányok és források* [Imre Nagy and his epoch. Studies and sources], ed. Levente Sipos, vol. 4 (Budapest: Nagy Imre Alapítvány, 2006), 153–80.

10. György T. Varga, "Jegyzőkönyv a szovjet és a magyar párt- és állami vezetők tárgyalásairól (1953. június 13–16.)" [Minutes of the negotiations between the Soviet and Hungarian party- and state leaders, June 13–16, 1953], *Múltunk* [Our Past] 37, no. 2–3 (1992): 234–69.

11. Ibid., 238–39.

12. Ibid., 239.

13. Ibid., 264–69.

14. Starting in 1954, through gradual steps, a total of approximately 40 million hectares was added to the existing ploughed area through including dry steppe land in the south of Siberia and mainly in the north of Kazakhstan. Spring wheat was planted in almost the entire area. This extensive production mode significantly contributed to the growth of state grain reserves. In the short term the campaign was a success, while favorable weather in 1956 and then in 1958 was also a factor. But soon the severely negative consequences of this monocultural mode of production appeared in soil erosion and in ecological effects. Martin McCauley, *Khrushchev and the Development of Soviet Agriculture: The Virgin Land Programme, 1953–1964* (New York: Holmes and Meier, 1976); Richard M. Mills, "The Formation of the Virgin Lands Policy," *Slavic Review* 29, no. 1 (1970): 58–69.

15. Wädekin, *The Private Sector*, 247–56; I. E. Zelenin, *Agrarnaia politika N. S. Khruscheva i sel'skoe khoziaistvo* (Moscow: Institut Istorii Rossiiskoi Akademii Nauk, 2001).

16. T. Varga, "Jegyzőkönyv," 235–37. The June 28, 1953, decree of the HWP Central Committee was only made public 33 years later.

17. "A miniszterelnöki expozé 1953. július 4-én" [The Prime Minister's introductory speech in the Parliament], in *A Nagy Imre vonal: Dokumentumválogatás* [The Imre Nagy-line: Selected documents], ed. Lajos Péter Kovács (Budapest: Reform, 1989), 251–52.
18. Ibid., 253.
19. "1953. évi 10. sz. tvr.," in *TRHGY 1953*, 13–14.
20. János Honvári, *XX. századi magyar gazdaságtörténet: Transzformációk, rendszerek* (Budapest: Aula, 2006), 243–53.
21. "1.033/1953. sz. MT h.," in *TRHGY 1953*, 193.
22. "11. sz. tvr.," in *TRHGY 1953*, 14–15.
23. "42/1953. sz. MT rendelet," in *TRHGY 1953*, 109–10.
24. "1.037/1953. sz. MT h.," in *TRHGY 1953*, 194.
25. "1.038/1953. sz. MT h.," in *TRHGY 1953*, 194.
26. "1953. évi 18. sz. tvr.," in *TRHGY 1953*, 26.
27. "1953. évi 23. sz. tvr.," in *TRHGY 1953*, 28.
28. Jegyzőkönyvek az FM Kollégium üléseiről, 1953. július. 31, augusztus 8, augusztus 22 [Minutes of the Ministry of Agriculture Steering Committee session, July 31., August 8, August 22, 1953], MNL OL, XIX–K–1–c 35. d.
29. "1953. évi 27. sz. tvr.," in *TRHGY 1953*, 37–49.
30. János Honvári, "A klasszikus begyűjtési rendszer változása az 'új szakasz' meghirdetésétől a beadás megszüntetéséig" [Changes in classical system of compulsory deliveries from New Course to the abolition of deliveries], in *Agrártörténet—Agrárpolitika: Tanulmányok Szuhay Miklós Emeritus Professzor tiszteletére* [Agricultural history—agrarian policy], eds. János Buza, János Estók, Ferenc Szávai, and Zsuzsanna Varga (Budapest: Budapesti Corvinus Egyetem and Budapesti Közgazdaságtudományi Egyetem Alapítvány and Miskolci Egyetem Gazdaságtudományi Kara, 2006), 417.
31. Regarding tax breaks, a Council of Ministers decree published on July 26, 1953, for example, forgave all tax arrears for collective farms and collective farm members should they continue to remain members and should they pay their 1953 arrears. In the case of individual farmers only half the tax arrears for 1952 were forgiven for those who paid their 1953 taxes by December 31. "1033/1953. MT h.," in *TRHGY 1953*, 193.
32. "A miniszterelnöki expozé 1953. július 4-én" [The Prime Minister's introductory speech in the Parliament], in Kovács, *A Nagy Imre vonal*, 254.
33. A Mezőgazdasági Osztály feljegyzése a termelőszövetkezeti mozgalomról. 1953. július 28. [Memorandum of the Agricultural Department of the CC on the cooperative movement, July 28, 1953] MNL OL, M–KS 276. f. 93. cs., 508. ő. e.
34. Ibid.
35. Ibid.
36. Ibid.
37. Jegyzőkönyv az MDP Politikai Bizottság 1953. szeptember 10-i üléséről. [Minutes of the HWP Politburo, September 10, 1953] MNL OL, M–KS 276. f., 53. cs., 135. ő. e.

38. Malenkov was finally forced to resign, and was replaced on February 5, 1955 by Marshall Bulganin. János M. Rainer and Károly Urbán, "'Konzultációk:' Dokumentumok a magyar és szovjet pártvezetők két moszkvai találkozójáról 1954–1955-ben" ["Consultations:" Documents of two meetings of the Hungarian and Soviet party leaders in Moscow], *Múltunk* 37, no. 4 (1992): 141–48.

39. Ibid., 142.

40. Ibid., 143.

41. Ibid., 147.

42. Rainer, *Nagy Imre*, vol. 2, 110–24.

43. Jegyzőkönyv az MDP Központi Vezetőség 1955. március 2–4-i üléséről. [Minutes of the HWP Central Committee, March 2–4, 1955] MNL OL, M–KS 276. f., 52. cs., 28. ő. e.

44. Lajos Izsák, ed., *A Magyar Dolgozók Pártja határozatai 1948–1956* [Resolutions of the Hungarian Workers' Party, 1948–1956] (Budapest: Napvilág, 1998), 340.

45. Jegyzőkönyv az MDP Központi Vezetőség 1955. április 14-i üléséről. [Minutes of the HWP Central Committee, April 14, 1955] MNL OL, M–KS 276. f., 52. cs., 29. ő. e.

46. Rainer, *Imre Nagy*, vol. 2, 118–24.

47. Honvári, *XX. századi magyar gazdaságtörténet*, 290–300.

48. Erdmann, *Begyűjtés, beszolgáltatás*, 214–36.

49. Jegyzőkönyv a Politikai Bizottság 1955. január 26-i üléséről. [Minutes of the HWP Politburo, January 26, 1955] MNL OL, M–KS 276. f., 53. cs., 213. ő. e.

50. Jegyzőkönyv a Központi Vezetőség 1955. június 7–8-i üléséről. [Minutes of the HWP Central Committee, June 7–8, 1955] MNL OL, M–KS 276. f., 52. cs., 30. ő. e.

51. *Szabad Nép*, July 31, 1955.

52. Jegyzőkönyv az MDP Politikai Bizottság 1955. augusztus 11-i üléséről. [Minutes of the HWP Politburo, August 11, 1955] MNL OL, M–KS 276. f., 53. cs., 243. ő .e.

53. *Szabad Nép*, August 7, 1955.

54. Orbán, *Két agrárforradalom*, 149.

55. Ö. Kovács, "The Forced Collectivization," 220–21; Szakács, "From Land Reform," 291–95.

56. Up to December 31, 1955, 435 new collectives were established, with the number of members increasing by 75,000.

57. Jegyzőkönyv az MDP Politikai Bizottság 1955. december 1-jei üléséről. [Minutes of the HWP Politburo, December 1, 1955] MNL OL, M–KS 276. f., 53. cs., 259. ő. e.

58. On the state of agriculture in the spring and summer of 1956, see Béla Fazekas, *A mezőgazdasági termelőszövetkezeti mozgalom Magyarországon* [The Hungarian agricultural cooperative movement] (Budapest: Kossuth, 1976), 93–97; Orbán, *Két agrárforradalom*, 143–59; Pető and Szakács, *A hazai gazdaság*, 273–80.

59. Mária Pogány, "Nagy Imre és a (volt) népi kollégisták kapcsolatai" [Imre Nagy's relations with the former people's collegians], in *Nagy Imre és kora: Tanul-*

mányok és források [Imre Nagy and his epoch: Studies, sources], eds. József Sipos and Levente Sipos, vol. 1 (Budapest: Nagy Imre Alapítvány, 2002), 219–40.

60. On the rural events of the 1956 the revolution, see Attila Szakolczai and László Á. Varga, eds. *A vidék forradalma, 1956* [Revolution in the countryside, 1956], vol. 1 (Budapest: 1956-os Intézet and Budapest Főváros Levéltára, 2003); Attila Szakolczai, ed., *A vidék forradalma, 1956* [Revolution in the countryside, 1956], vol. 2 (Budapest: 1956-os Intézet and Budapest Főváros Levéltára, 2006).

61. György Litván, "Imre Nagy's Second Government," in *1956: The Hungarian Revolution and War for Independence*, eds. Lee Congdon, Béla K. Király, and Károly Nagy (New York: Columbia University Press, 2006) 299–310.

62. Zsuzsanna Varga "The Missing Stories from the Rural Hungary in 1956," in *Revolúcia v susedstve: Maďarská revolúcia v roku 1956 a Slovensko*, eds. Attila Simon and Slavomír Michálek (Bratislava and Budapest: Fórum inštitút pre vyskum mensín Vydavatelstvo, 2017), 107–18.

63. From the fall of 1944, thanks to the Red Army's battles in Hungary, the existing political and public administration organs were destroyed. The removal of debris, the organization of food distribution, the launch of production and meeting the needs of the Red Army forced local communities to organize themselves. Under various names—people's, national, operational committees—new governing organs emerged at municipal and urban levels. National committees not only became local forums for politics, but executive and decree-issuing institutions as well, at times fulfilling judicial functions.

64. Gábor Gyáni, "A forradalom társadalomtörténeti paradoxonjai" [Socio-historical paradox of the Revolution of 1956], *Forrás* 38, no. 10 (2006): 27–39.

65. They urged the introduction of the Kossuth-era coat of arms, the marking of March 15, Christmas, Easter, and the second day of Pentecost as holidays, October 6 as a day of national mourning, and October 23 as a national holiday. They stated that the uniforms used in national defense forces should reflect national traditions.

66. "A Hazafias Népfront Somogy Megyei Bizottsága Elnökségének 16 pontos követelése, 1956. október 26." [The 16 points of the Somogy county Presidium of the Patriotic Popular Front, October 25, 1956], in *1956 plakátjai* és *röplapjai* [Posters and handbills from 1956], eds. Lajos Izsák, József Szabó, and Róbert Szabó (Budapest: Zrínyi, 1991), 491.

67. The demand to immediately cancel the delivery system was among those of the university students. The document released by students at the Budapest Technical University on October 22, 1956, stated: "We demand that the delivery system should be placed on a new basis and that produce should be used rationally. We demand equal treatment of peasants farming individually." Ibid., 18–19.

68. Being aware of the precedents, it is not surprising that this demand was made most emphatically in the Trans-Danubian regions.

69. There were differences across regions, of course, regarding which type of tax they found most offensive, and given this there were differing attempts to eradicate various taxes. In some places the tooth tax was in focus, while in others it was the wine tax. This was the case for peasantry in the Szekszárd area, where a demand was

expressed to restore the international reputation of Szekszárd wine. See: Izsák, Szabó, and Szabó, *1956 plakátjai* és *röplapjai*, 533.

70. "A megye dolgozó parasztságának követelése a megújuló kormánytól, 1956. október 27" [Claims of the working peasantry of Hajdú-Bihar county, October 27, 1956], in *1956 vidéki sajtója* [The rural press in 1956], eds. Lajos Izsák, József Szabó, and Róbert Szabó (Budapest: Korona, 1996), 405.

71. Ibid., 405.

72. "Makó Város Dolgozó Népe és Ifjúsága követelései, 1956. október 29." [Claims of the workers and youth of Makó town, October 29, 1956], in Izsák, Szabó, and Szabó, *1956 plakátjai* és *röplapjai*, 366.

73. "A megye dolgozó parasztságának követelése a megújuló kormánytól, 1956. október 27." [Demands of the working peasantry of Hajdú-Bihar county], in Izsák, Szabó, and Szabó, *1956 vidéki sajtója*, 405.

74. It is interesting to note what kinds of demands were expressed in those areas on the Hungarian plains where the proportion of collective farm members in the local agricultural population was high. A good example of such is Karcag, which was granted the status of collective farm town in 1951. The 27 points of the October 27 challenge contained several that pertained to collective farms:

> We support the collective farm movement, but we demand that the working peasantry decide on its own whether it chooses this form of farming. The Party and state should use no force!
>
> Collective farms must be given full independence; this is the foundation of a profitable farm. This absolutely requires that the government immediately forgive the current debts of collective farms—which were caused by improper economic policy. The income of collective farm members must be ensured.
>
> Exit from collective farm membership must be allowed at any time. No demands of any type can be made of workers who choose to leave. Those leaving collective farms must be given land of the same quality as that they proffered to the farm.
>
> The government must ensure that the collective farms receive low-interest loans and be able to buy machinery. Machine and tractor station work should not be mandatory for the collective farms . . . (See Izsák, Szabó, and Szabó, *1956 plakátjai* és *röplapjai*, 515–16)

75. János Kenedi, ed., *A forradalom hangja: Magyarországi rádióadások 1956. október 23.–november 9.* [The voice of the Revolution: Broadcasts in Hungary between October 23 and November 9, 1956], Századvég füzetek 3 (Budapest: Századvég–Nyilvánosság Klub, 1989), 131–32.

76. Ibid., 273–74.

77. The Hungarian National Revolutionary Committee published an article on November 1, 1956, titled "What does the Hungarian farming population demand?" It contained the following: "We support the closure of the delivery system, which oppressed and abused the peasantry, but this was only the first step. . . . We want a delegation to be soon formed of representatives of the peasantry, members of new parties, agricultural experts and journalists who would study the situation of cooperative agriculture in Western Europe (Denmark, the Netherlands, England, etc.) and the northern states (Finland, Sweden) and the United States, and to employ those

experiences here in Hungary." See Lajos Izsák and József Szabó, eds., *1956 a sajtó tükrében. 1956. október 22.–november 5.* [1956 in the mirror of the press, October 22 and November 5, 1956] (Budapest: Kossuth, 1989), 221.

78. "A Somogy Megyei Forradalmi Nemzeti Tanács 1956. október 29-i állásfoglalása" [Standpoint of the Revolutionary National Council of Somogy county, October 29, 1956], in *Az 1956-os forradalom Somogyban: Válogatott dokumentumok* [The revolution of 1956 in the Somogy county: Selected documents], eds. László Szántó–Ferenc Szili (Kaposvár: Somogy Megyei Levéltár, 1995), 123–26.

79. "Makó város Nemzeti Bizottságának kiáltványa, 1956. október 30" [Proclamation of the National Committee of Makó town, October 30, 1956] in Izsák, Szabó, and Szabó, *1956 plakátjai* és *röplapjai*, 367.

80. Bottoni, *Long Awaited West*, 89–130; Mark Kramer, "The Soviet Union and the 1956 Crises in Hungary and Poland: Reassessments and New Findings," *Journal of Contemporary History* 33, no. 2 (1998): 163–214.

81. Sándor Balogh, ed., *A Magyar Szocialista Munkáspárt ideiglenes vezető testületeinek jegyzőkönyvei* [Minutes of the Provisional Leadership Bodies of the HSWP], vol. 1 *(1956. november 11–1957. január 14.)* (Budapest: Intera, 1993), 151.

82. György Földes, "The Characteristics of the Kádár-Era," in *Regimes and transformations: Hungary in the twentieth century*, eds. István Feitl and Balázs Sipos (Budapest: Napvilág, 2005), 297–324.

83. Béla Tomka, "Fogyasztás a második világháború utáni Kelet-Közép-Európában: politikai meghatározók és transznacionális hatások" [Consumption in East-Central Europe after World War II: political determinants and transnational effects], *Aetas* 34, no. 4 (2019): 62–74; Tibor Valuch, "Changes in the Structure and Lifestyle of the Hungarian Society in the Second Half of the XXth Century," in Gyáni, Kövér, and Valuch, *Social history of Hungary*, 651–57.

84. Ferenc Erdei, the deputy prime minister, supervised agriculture and in the first half of 1956 had several initiatives aimed at improving the situation of the sector. Facing ever more apparent signs of the collapse of the collective farm system, in the summer of 1956 he commissioned the writing of an Act on collectives. Another long-term task was to work out what to do with the three-year delivery plan worked out in 1954 after 1956. Varga, *Göröngyös út*, 89–90.

85. A KV Mezőgazdasági Osztályának előterjesztése az MSZMP Politikai Bizottsághoz a mezőgazdasági politikában szükséges főbb változásokra. 1956. október 22. [Submission of the Agricultural Department of the HSWP CC to the Politburo, October 22, 1956] MNL OL, M–KS 288. f., 28. cs., (1957) 5. ő. e.

86. Ibid.

87. Ibid.

88. Also see: István Papp, "A Begyűjtési Minisztérium az 1956-os forradalom idején és a beszolgáltatási rendszer felszámolása 1956–57-ben" [The Ministry of Delivery during the revolution of 1956 and the abolition of the compulsory delivery system], in *1956 okai, jelentősége* és *következményei* [Reasons, importance and consequences of the revolution of 1956], eds. Lajos Pál and Ignác Romsics (Budapest: Magyar Történelmi Társulat, 2006), 267–89.

89. *TRHGY 1956*, 62.

90. Wädekin, *Agrarian Policies*, 65.

91. Központi Statisztikai Hivatal, *A mezőgazdasági termékek felvásárlása 1960* [The state purchase of the agricultural products], Statisztikai Időszaki Közlemények 43 (Budapest: KSH, 1961), 83–84.

92. Az Élelmezésügyi Minisztérium előterjesztése az MSZMP Politikai Bizottságához az új felvásárlási rendszer eredményeiről és tapasztalatairól. [Food Ministry submission to the HSWP Politburo on the achievements and experiences with the new central purchasing system] November 19, 1957. MNL OL, M–KS 288. f. 28 cs., 13. ő. e.

93. "A Magyar Forradalmi Munkás-Paraszt Kormány felhívása a parasztsághoz!" [The Revolutionary Worker-Peasant Government's proclamation to the peasantry], *MK*, November 27, 1956, 579–80.

94. *TRHGY 1956*, 263.

95. Ibid., 68–69, 263–65.

96. Zsuzsanna Varga "The Impact of 1956 on the Relationship between the Kádár Regime and the peasantry, 1956–66," *Hungarian Studies Review* 34, no. 1–2 (2007): 155–76. http://epa.oszk.hu/00000/00010/00041/pdf/HSR_2007_1-2_155-176.pdf

97. Magdolna Baráth, ed., *Kádár János első kormányának jegyzőkönyvei, 1956. november 7.–1958. január 25.* [Minutes of the first Kádár-government, November 7, 1956–January 25, 1958] (Budapest: MOL, 2009), 490.

98. Ibid., 490–91.

99. Lajos Fehér (1917–1981) started his career as journalist, and in 1942 he became a member of the illegal Communist Party of Hungary. After the World War II, from 1947 to 1954 he was responsible editor of *Szabad Föld* which was the peasant weekly of HCP. He supported Imre Nagy agricultural politics consequently Fehér was appointed to the editor of *Szabad Nép*, the daily of the HWP in 1954. After the fall of Imre Nagy, he had to leave Budapest in 1955 and directed a state-farm in Somogy county. In first days of revolution of 1956 he opposed the new political line, did not accept the radical aims of revolution. After the Soviet invasion he became the editor-in-chief of *Népszabadság*, the new daily newspaper of HSWP, and later the head of the Agricultural Department of the Central Committee. From 1962 his task was to supervise agriculture as a vice prime minister, thereby becoming one of the leaders of the agrarian lobby. He was a member of the Central Committee until his death, and a member of Politburo between 1956 and 1975. After his political fall in 1974, he started to write his memoirs, and he published the first volume in 1979.

100. Bianca L. Adair, "The Agrarian Theses and Rapid Collectivization: Accommodation in Hungarian Agriculture, 1956–1960," *Journal of Communist Studies and Transition Politics* 17, no. 2 (2001): 131–47; Levente Sipos, "Reform és megtorpanás: Viták az MSZMP agrárpolitikájáról (1956–1958)" [Reform and Baulking: Debates on the Agrarian Policy of the HSWP, 1956–1958], *Múltunk* 36, no. 2–3, (1991): 188–97.

101. Jegyzőkönyv az 1957. október 28-án a Magyar Szocialista Munkáspárt megyei pártbizottságainak mezőgazdasági osztályvezetőivel folytatott értekezletről. [Minutes of the meeting of the agricultural leaders of the county HSWP committees, October 28, 1957] MNL OL, M–KS 288. f., 17. cs., 9. ő. e.

102. In 1957 more than 90% of the state grain reserve was covered by the land tax applied to cereal farmers with holdings of over four acres, threshing machine and mill customs, and the produce of state farms.

103. Az Élelmezésügyi Minisztérium előterjesztése az MSZMP Politikai Bizottságához az új felvásárlási rendszer eredményeiről és tapasztalatairól. (1957. november 19.) [Food Ministry submission to the HSWP Politburo on the achievements and experiences with the new central purchasing system. November 19, 1957] MNL OL, M–KS 288. f., 28. cs., (1957) 13. ő. e.

104. Tibor Valuch, "Agrárkérdések és a magyar falu 1956–57-ben" [Agrarian questions and the Hungarian village in 1956–57], *1956-os Intézet Évkönyv* 8 (2000): 286–302.

105. Honvári, "A klasszikus begyűjtési rendszer változása," 426–30.

Chapter Four

The Final Drive for Collectivization

A NEW MEDIATOR BETWEEN THE PARTY AND THE PEASANTS—THE AGRARIAN LOBBY

After the initial "firefighting" measures, clarification was awaited concerning what kind of agricultural policy the Hungarian Socialists Workers' Party (HSWP) might follow in the future. Views on this were deeply divided. As 1956 turned to 1957, the situation that developed was one in which the HSWP's Village Department—later renamed Agricultural Department—became the clearing post for all those who were deeply critical of the Rákosi agrarian policy.[1] This did not happen by chance, because Lajos Fehér had been entrusted with leading this department at the beginning of 1957. As it was mentioned in the previous chapter, he had been a committed believer in the new agrarian policy that had been the backbone of the New Course in 1953. It is important to note that the Soviets had serious reservations about him, and he got into debates with János Kádár many times over November and December, 1956. Kádár voted confidence in Fehér all the same, because he had known him from the illegal interwar communist movement.[2]

While Lajos Fehér was still serving as the government commissioner for coal, management of the operations of the Village Department fell to his deputy, János Keserű. He characterized Fehér in his memoirs as follows:

> As one of the highest-level leaders of the HSWP, he was a dedicated representative of the agrarian issue. He had very strong ties to agriculture and the peasantry. He had a clear conception of what party agrarian policy should be. The essence of it was that there was *a need for a far better understanding of the situation and problems of the peasant population and of the role of agricultural policy* than that of the HWP before 1956. . . . He was extraordinarily consistent

with respect to eliminating the mistakes and crimes of agrarian policy before 1956.[3] [Emphasis in original.]

A completely different position was represented by the leaders of the Ministry of Agriculture: Minister Imre Dögei and his deputies: Mihály Keresztes, András Magyari, Antal Márczis, and Mátyás Szőke. They strove to minimize the mistakes of Rákosism and amplify those of Imre Nagy's policy.[4]

Excising dogmatic views was one of the goals of the monumental task that Lajos Fehér initiated in December 1956 with the aim of elaborating the main directions of the party's agrarian program for the following years. It is worth noting that it was in December 1956 too that the Kádár government decided to review the entire system of economic management.[5] What we know about the operations led by the non-party economics professor István Varga is that they essentially remained within the confines of expert committees and were removed from the agenda before wider public opinion could become familiar with them.[6] In contrast, the HSWP's future agrarian policy was debated in many kinds of forums across the whole country.[7] This proved a good occasion for Lajos Fehér to activate the relations that he had established with alumni of the people's colleges during the New Course.

Learning from Imre Nagy's mistake (in 1953 he had begun to work out his agriculture policy outside the aegis of the party), Lajos Fehér immediately asked the HSWP Organizing Committee at the beginning of 1957 to authorize the establishment of an expert committee. Thus, on the basis of the January 24, 1957 decree of the HSWP Organizing Committee, the Agrarian Policy Committee, working alongside the Village (later Agricultural) Department of the Central Committee, came into being under the leadership of Lajos Fehér. Its task was defined as follows: "To debate submissions addressed to the party's leading organs concerning agriculture and participate in the elaboration of important political and economic questions affecting agriculture."[8] The Agrarian Policy Committee held its first meeting on February 20, 1957, at which the main agenda item was to debate the Agrarian Theses.[9]

While Lajos Fehér entered into the force-field of high politics, Ferenc Erdei did not accept a formal political position after 1956. It is known that when Erdei was freed from Soviet captivity in December 1956—in István Bíbó's words, "as a worn-out man"—he made a vow to retreat from active politics.[10] However, he did not want to stand aside entirely, and therefore accepted a role in the field of scientific research. On January 1, 1957, he was commissioned to head the Agricultural Administrative Science Institute of the Hungarian Academy of Sciences. (In Hungarian: Mezőgazdasági Üzemtani Intézet, later: Agrárgazdasági Kutató Intézet, in short form: AKI.) It was very significant that the Administrative Science Institute came under the supervision of the Hungarian Academy of Sciences, because this gave it independence from the then dogmatically led Ministry of Agriculture.

Erdei also took part in the elaboration of the Agrarian Theses, sending written comments to János Keserű, the deputy director of the Agricultural Department, who forwarded them to Lajos Fehér, noting that they should definitely be taken into consideration when reworking the theses. Ferenc Erdei partly called their attention to problems with statistical data, and partly made comments on the land issue and operational structure. He emphasized that unless realities on the ground were taken into account agricultural policies would be misguided again. His chief criticism was expressed in his final paragraph:

> In summary, there is not enough emphasis in the material on nailing down the importance of agriculture in our current circumstances. In terms of both the entire people's economy and the employment of the whole population, it is much more important than the way it has been handled by the Party so far. The basis of the question is, where do we stand now that the country has become industrial? We cannot avoid putting down an unambiguous statement on this. I therefore suggest that the material be supplemented by this theme.[11]

The Dögei position clashed sharply with that of the group centered around Lajos Fehér as early as the debate of the first draft of the Agrarian Theses. The difference in opinions can be best sensed in relation to the perspective for agriculture:

> The whole material led me to conclude that we cannot knowingly bring about the socialist reorganization of agriculture in a way that allows the income from their tiny plots to rise upwards . . . on the contrary, the peasants must be told that the state cannot take on the burden of saving them from the difficulties of farming small plots.

Dögei supported his argument by reference to Lenin's position "without economic compulsion peasants will not abandon their plots, and they will only abandon them when they do not meet their expectations." Lajos Fehér entered the debate with him with the following words:

> That was our policy in 1945–53 and we saw what the results were. This point of view cannot be accepted, because if the peasantry has no hope of ever increasing its income, it will not produce and so the production of commodities will not be bigger. . . . It is natural thing for a section of the peasantry to get to the stage of expanded reproduction. There is nothing to be frightened of in this, it should not be treated as dogmatically as it was in spring, 1955. The fact that the government made possible the purchase of land up to 5 kh [2.85 ha] also in itself made expanded reproduction possible.[12]

The second draft of the Agrarian Theses was debated at the HSWP Provisional Executive Committee session of March 12.[13] In his closing statement Lajos Fehér responded as follows to attacks from hard-liners:

> We are not infected at all by a kind of worship of the peasantry, but exclusively by the interests of the people's economy: 1. the raw material basis for industry should be bigger, 2. the people should live even better, 3. the people's economy should help increase exports and from this point of view let's admit that agricultural investments were never fulfilled.[14]

In the end the Executive Committee accepted the draft theses.

By July 1957 the final version of the Agrarian Theses had been completed.[15] Although it was not published as a party decree, its significance was still enormous. On the one hand, condemnation of the Rákosi–Gerő-era Stalinist agrarian policy was made public, on the other, continuity with the New Course's agrarian program was made clear, although no mention was made of Imre Nagy's name at the time.[16] The 1953 goals were rearticulated: eliminating disadvantaged treatment in relation to industry, improving the standard of living of the peasantry, evolving a structure farming entities that was appropriate to Hungarian circumstances, partial rehabilitation of the market, and so on. A number of my interviewees confirmed that throughout the Kádár period the agrarian lobby viewed the Agrarian Theses as the official, still-in-force agrarian policy program. For this reason, it is worth quoting some of its strategic points.

HWP agrarian policy was severely criticized particularly in relation to collectivization practice.

> Although the "dual task" was consistently proclaimed, raising the level of agricultural production was in practice subordinated to socialist reorganization. And yet the transformation to large-scale farms is not an end in itself but a tool or chief method for the permanent development of production forces in agriculture. . . . Along with the many occurrences of violence when organizing producer cooperatives and the frequent land consolidations, many places experienced the mistake of not ensuring appropriate property in exchange for, or not restituting for, the crops or investments on consolidated land, which caused unwillingness and production insecurity on the part of the peasants affected. Individually farming peasants in particular did not feel themselves secure and therefore did not bother to fertilize properly, did not plant perennial crops, neglected their vines and fruit trees, and so on. Mistakes were multiplied in that bread-grain production was forced on farmers with no consideration for such basic tasks as ensuring fodder needs for the animal stock. While the animal stock increased when compared with pre-war years, the area devoted to fodder, mainly land producing fibrous fodder, fell. The state and other organs interfered excessively

with peasant but especially cooperative farming. It was a grave mistake too that little progress was made in the area of modernizing agricultural production.[17]

The following crucially important sentences also found their way into the Agrarian Theses, and they signified nothing less than a critique of the Stalinist economic policy that had been forced on Hungary since the end of the 1940s. We can add too that it was this very thought that constituted one of the main pillars of the program of the agrarian lobby:

> Because of industrialization that did not reflect sufficiently the endowments of the country, sufficient material resource did not get to the development of agriculture. Because of this, it is still the case that Hungarian agriculture uses insufficient fertilizer, that its machinery is impossibly outdated, with poor capacity and made of weak materials, that there is too little modern mechanized equipment, possibilities for irrigation are not exploited, and so on. As a consequence of all of this, we have made only little progress compared with the pre-war situation in respect of average yields per kh and animal output.

As far as the future was concerned, it was unambiguously formulated that the agrarian lobby identified, as tokens of the successful transformation of agriculture, on the one hand, the assurance of material conditions, and, on the other, the expansion of transitional cooperative forms suited to Hungarian conditions.

The arguments between the Lajos Fehér and Dögei groups did not calm down after the summer of 1957. As indicated above, their opinions differed in practically every question of substance.[18] This is well illustrated in the case of the producer cooperatives that survived the liquidation wave in 1956. The membership of producer cooperatives that continued in operation wanted in fact to order the life of their cooperative in ways that differed from earlier operational and organizational regulations. This was the equivalent of abandoning the soviet-modeled, compulsory model charter.[19]

This desire was in no way surprising, given that the peasant demands of the fall of 1956 had included the call for independence for producer cooperatives. The Kádár government supported these producer cooperative initiatives, as is reflected in the following passage from the November 27 manifesto. "The government deems it necessary to draft a cooperative law that establishes that peasants should themselves choose their form of collective, determine themselves cooperative operational regulations, and decide themselves on the mode of income distribution. The government will tolerate no interference in cooperative affairs."[20]

In this climate, the producer cooperatives therefore set to it to change relations that had hindered the realization of both member and cooperative interests. On the one hand, the producer cooperatives wanted to achieve independence from those organs (the party, the council, the banks, the machine and tractor stations) that had previously interfered in their farming, while, on the other, they wanted to regulate their internal affairs in accordance with their own capacities.[21]

The main goal of the producer cooperative membership, however, was directed at obtaining a regular income throughout the year, and at an appropriate level. Instead of the Labor Day unit with its uncertain value, the majority of producer cooperatives moved to a system of in-kind shares, in the form of either share-cropping or various types of bonus.[22]

The common thread in these local initiatives was that they permitted the membership to receive an income throughout the year (whether in the form of money or a share in kind); that is to say, realizing the interests of the membership preceded state and other commitments. Conservative members of the political leadership, primarily the leaders of the Ministry of Agriculture, strongly attacked these grassroots producer cooperative initiatives.[23] The following passage from a contemporary speech of Imre Dögei, the Minister of Agriculture, illustrates their views.

> There is a lot of talk and chatter nowadays about every cooperative writing its own model rules and distributing income as it pleases, and that we should not interfere because that would injure the principle of voluntarism. This, comrades, is nothing less than the purposeful, subversive work of the enemy. We are not going to stand for it. We say there is no point you chattering about Hungarian uniqueness this and Hungarian uniqueness that, you have brought nothing new to the table, you have not created anything better than the model rules, you have not come up with a better model of income distribution than the labor day unit, only something worse, and we therefore stand by it.[24]

At the same time, another group in the leadership, led by Lajos Fehér, argued that use of the new approaches to incentives would make members interested in improving the quality of production, in increasing yields and reducing costs and that this served the interests of the state.[25]

> Producer cooperative peasants, like others, do not like their every step to be regulated in advance, to be "spoon fed." That is why the opportunity must be provided for producer cooperatives, while maintaining fundamental socialist principles, to modify their operating rules to local circumstances, to make them more flexible, so that the membership has a better sense that it is the true owner of their producer cooperative.[26]

This debate also signaled that the two groups judged the methods for future collectivization differently. The leaders of the Ministry of Agriculture stuck unconditionally to Stalinist agrarian policy, holding that its main elements could not be changed. The group centered around Lajos Fehér however wanted the main directions of HSWP agrarian policy to take Hungarian conditions and peasant interest into account, so avoiding the mistakes of the past. The exceptionally tense situation between the two groups is well illustrated in a memorandum prepared by the Agricultural Department in early 1958.

> Certain leaders in the Ministry of Agriculture do not believe in establishing the advantages of producer cooperative large-scale production. . . . They can only conceive of collectivization at the cost of essentially impoverishing individual peasants, in the soil of poverty. They strive to develop and have accepted, verbally and in writing, all kinds of theories in favour of this. Comrade Dögei . . . in his memorandum to the Secretariat expounded as follows, "for years we have been conducting economic policy that artificially sustained small peasant private property," that is, we stabilized individual farms. . . . The aforementioned comrades hold that this was the main mistake in peasant policy over the last eight years. (Following this logic, the main problem was not that it resulted in one million kh of reserve land, but that it was not three million.)[27]

This debate took place within a rather wide circle, activating not only upper level leaders but also economic actors and scientific researchers. Rezső Nyers, who would become an influential ally of the agrarian lobby and the "father" of the New Economic Mechanism, reflected on the period in an interview:

> I was already against a restrictive policy against the peasants when I was president of the National Alliance of Cooperatives, so I belonged to the Lajos Fehér group. Ferenc Erdei was already participating in my conversations at this time. András Gyenes,[28] Imre Dimény, Ernő Csizmadia and János Márton figured too. I was part of it. The Institute of Agricultural Economics (of the Hungarian Academy of Sciences) was the base. Of course the whole group was under the aegis of Lajos Fehér. Although I was one of them, I only got involved in the matter directly, personally, when I became Minister of Finance.[29]

The research institute led by Ferenc Erdei did indeed become the background institute for the Agricultural Department led by Lajos Fehér. However small it was in the beginning, about a dozen worked there, it quickly gained significant influence. Erdei played a decisive role in this: his confrontation with pre-1956 agrarian policy motivated him to seek out possible ways for correcting mistakes.[30] Erdei held that the first step in seeking a way out was to get to know the real economic and social relations. It was for this reason that, from the start, he paid great attention to constructing his own database, especially because there were hardly any statistical data available on themes that he held to be of key importance (budget and income calculations for example). The institute developed permanent contacts with various actors in Hungarian agricultural production: not only with producer cooperatives, but with individual peasant farmers too.[31]

Contact with the countryside in practice was also served by the regular trips to rural areas embarked on by both Erdei and his colleagues. Erdei's network of contacts was especially worthy of note, as it included one-time peasant party activists, alumni of the people's colleges, and of course the economic experts and producer cooperative and state farm leaders whom he had got to know during his periods as minister in the first half of the fifties.[32]

In Ferenc Erdei's view, the other direction for finding a way out was to get to know the developments that had taken place in the agrarian world of the West. It is well known that in the 1930s Erdei traveled to many Western European countries in order to study developed agricultural cultures and seek a modernization model for Hungary.[33] After the war too he made efforts to follow the results of Western agrarian development, which, in the years of the Cold War, became an ever more difficult task, even for a minister. The thaw that followed Stalin's death made gathering information about the West easier, and it quickly got moving in the fields of science and culture. Steps were taken in the direction of establishing East–West relations in the field of the economy, including agriculture.[34] Few are aware that Khrushchev sent an agricultural delegation to the USA as early as 1955; and Hungary followed this example.[35] As noted at the beginning of the Introduction, in December 1955, a three-person delegation traveled from Hungary to the USA with the aim of studying corn production and purchasing hybrid corn seed.[36]

After 1956, establishing contacts with the Western world became difficult again because of Hungary's partial international isolation. Ferenc Erdei and Lajos Fehér were in agreement that the only way out of the situation they found themselves in was to promote the exchange of scientific experience.[37] The agricultural lobby's room for maneuver in the field of international relations was increased by the fact that Erdei became general secretary of the Hungarian Academy of Sciences in December, 1957.[38]

THE INTERNATIONAL CONTEXT—LEARNING FROM FRATERNAL PARTIES

The Polish crisis of 1956, but especially the Hungarian uprising of the same year, triggered a shock whose impact extended to fellow bloc countries and the Soviet Union.[39] Criticism of Khrushchev's policies—de-Stalinization, attempts at liberalization—strengthened among the Stalinist leaders in Eastern

Europe. This came just at the right time for the Chinese leadership, which was dissatisfied with Soviet monopolization of leadership of the socialist camp.[40] Retaining the support of the Eastern European parties thus became a question of survival for Khrushchev. The leaders of the Communist and workers parties met in Moscow in November 1957, on the occasion of the fortieth anniversary of the Russian (Great October Socialist) Revolution, so offering an opportune moment at which to reestablish Socialist bloc unity. The statement accepted by the meeting indicated that the dogmatic line had prevailed. The most visible manifestation of the ideological offensive determined at the Moscow conference was a renewed effort to collectivize agriculture in the countries of Eastern Europe.[41] It was a repeat attempt, since the Communist parties had already addressed the task as part of Sovietization in the first half of the 1950s.

As 1957 turned into 1958, an acceleration in the pace of "restructuring" could be observed within the socialist camp.[42] Pressure to conform was considerable, but at the same time this task represented a serious risk for the Hungarian leadership. As earlier chapters have demonstrated, collectivization in Hungary had failed twice in the first half of the 1950s. Restarting "restructuring" required not only addressing the failures of the past, but might also undermine the results of the post-1956 consolidation. For the standard-of-living policy that substituted for legitimacy was largely premised at this time on the food supply, and the vast majority of agricultural production came from peasant farms.[43] Despite these risk factors, it was also clear to the communist leaders that they had to complete the task in order to prove to Moscow not only that they were loyal, but, not least, that they were able.

This is well reflected in the end-of-year speech given by the first secretary of the party at the Barcs producer cooperative in mid-December, 1957, which was published a few days later by the party daily *Népszabadság* on the front page of its Sunday edition. In his speech, János Kádár made it clear: "We are for socialist large-scale production." Referring to the example of the other socialist countries, he added that the time was right for the completion of the "socialist restructuring" of agriculture. "We cannot fool people, *we are not going to beat people with sticks into joining cooperatives, because we have learned that it cannot be done that way. Please choose, which is better: cooperatization or going back to the old capitalist penury?*"[44] [Emphasis in original.] The topic continued to be on the agenda. From the beginning of 1958, it is noticeable that not a month passed without a high-ranking party leader making a statement on collectivization. These speeches and interviews all emphasized that the time was ripe for "restructuring."[45]

All this represented a great challenge for the agricultural lobby, because, as indicated in the Agrarian Theses, Lajos Fehér and his followers envisioned a long-term, economically based, gradual transition. News arriving from other socialist countries, however, indicated that almost all fraternal countries were further ahead in the process, and some of them (China, Bulgaria) were preparing to complete agricultural collectivization. In this situation, an obvious solution, which would also win time, was to exchange experiences. The evidence suggests that this process was consciously undertaken, despite the fact that the historical situation had forced the leaders of the HSWP into a "learner driver" role. Kádár characterized their situation at the end of 1957 as follows: "Our party is the youngest collective of all the fraternal parties. We conceive of our task as follows: we have two critics who are also our helpers: the Hungarian working class, and the community of fraternal parties."[46] Later too the Hungarian leadership was at pains to emphasize its willingness to learn, even when, in reality, it had shunned this role.[47]

Over the course of 1958, Hungarian Party and state leaders visited practically all of the "fraternal parties." In February, they travelled to Romania, then to the GDR in March, to Bulgaria in June and to Czechoslovakia in December. The Soviet Union and Poland were left out because high-level delegations from those countries visited Hungary that year.[48] The unusually high number of foreign trips can be explained by many factors. On one hand, after the Moscow summit meeting, the HSWP leaders might have felt that they were beginning to be accepted into the socialist camp, and wanted to speed up the process by their visits. On the other, they wanted to inform themselves directly on the state of development of "restructuring towards large-scale" agriculture.

Embassies also acted as important channels for exchanging of information and experience, in addition to fraternal parties. Reports sent to the Ministry of Foreign Affairs on the economic situation of the countries in which embassies were located regularly included agriculture. What is more, the ministry regularly commissioned embassies to examine a concrete group of questions in each country.[49] It is also worth noting in addition the role of the Hungarian News Agency, which, on one hand, had an extensive network of correspondents abroad, and, on the other, had a large and well-trained staff in Hungary that monitored the foreign press, from which it regularly prepared confidential publications for the highest level party leadership.

The structure of Hungarian agriculture at the time exhibited most similarly with that of Poland (among the socialist countries).[50] The vast majority of producer cooperatives in Poland had also dissolved in the fall of 1956, yet, even in 1958, the Gomulka leadership had no plans to relaunch collectivization. Their rationale was that the preconditions for mass "restructuring" had not yet been created in Poland.[51] The Hungarian side, however, felt that the central problem in Polish agrarian policy was that the creation of socialist agriculture was the Polish goal too, albeit in the long term, but that they had no concrete plans for how to do it.[52]

The Romanian case signaled caution to the Hungarian Party leadership. There, over 1957, a number of provinces were collectivized quickly, but so much violence had been employed that the party was ultimately obliged to suspend the campaign.[53] The Hungarian ambassador in Bucharest, Ferenc Keleti, wrote a number of reports in 1957 on the problems of collectivizing agriculture in Romania. In his report of October 26, 1957, supported by data, he described how wheat harvest yields in Constanta fell far below the average for other provinces, even though Constanta was the country's first and only fully collectivized, and coincidentally most mechanized, province.[54] The Romania expert of the Ministry of Foreign Affairs and the HSWP's Foreign Affairs Department prepared several summary reports on the situation of agriculture before the visit of the Hungarian Party and government delegation in 1958. The material prepared by the Hungarian specialist on Romanian agriculture state the following.

> Although the acceleration in the construction of socialist agriculture in 1957 brought serious results in terms of numbers . . . in practice—thanks to neglect of voluntarism and gradualism—there were abuses and violence, which in many areas, for example Constanta and Galati provinces, provoked extreme revulsion, to such an extent that the Party and government ordered special measures to stop compulsion when creating cooperatives.[55]

Experiences in Bulgaria and Czechoslovakia appeared to be much more positive. Collectivization in Bulgaria was completed in the spring of 1958. The process was coming to a close in Czechoslovakia too: at the end of 1958, the socialist sector extended to 82% of agricultural land.[56] While the majority of information on Czechoslovakia in 1958 flowed through the embassy,[57] a number of high-level delegations visited Bulgaria. The first opportunity was provided by the 7th Congress of the Bulgarian Communist Party, which celebrated the victory of the collectivization of agriculture. The leader of the Hungarian delegation was Lajos Fehér, who felt that one of the decisive factors in the success of Bulgarian collectivization had been the fact that, in producer cooperatives, land remained in individual ownership, and members were paid a rental for its use. In his travel report he emphasized: "The land rent is a new economic category, which, however, has no exploitative connotations. The existence of the land rent does not affect the socialist nature of the producer cooperative. Producer cooperatives are flexible economic forms, in constant development."[58] After the delegation returned to Hungary, Lajos

Fehér commissioned his deputy János Keserű to assemble a team of specialists to travel to Bulgaria as soon as possible to study producer cooperatives.[59] János Keserű remembered their 1958 study tour to Bulgaria as follows:

> The delegation familiarized itself with many good and bad experiences of Bulgarian mass collectivization and reported these in its findings. . . . They successfully utilized . . . recalling respected experts who had left the village . . . and agitation work carried out in entire villages (this, for example, was an important method from the point of view of avoiding land consolidation) . . . ensuring significant startup capital for each producer cooperative to begin its operations, flexible handling household plot size, etc. In addition to identifying the many good methods used, the Bulgarian leaders also reported honestly on mistakes made. They considered the occasional use of violence (the compulsory deliveries press, etc.) as damaging and cautioned Hungarian organizers to avoid it. In addition to all of this, the delegation called attention in its report to differences between Bulgarian and Hungarian circumstances, to the fact that the party had a much greater weight in the population in Bulgaria than in Hungary. . . . Another difference was that Bulgaria had a deep historical tradition of village communities engaging in communal work.[60]

Like Janos Keserű, others who prepared reports on their visit, stressed that the experience of fraternal countries had been very useful, but could not be adopted automatically, because in many respects Hungary's circumstances were very different. This kind of argument might appear quite logical nowadays, but at the time this was far from self-evident, because previously all socialist countries had been under an obligation to follow the Soviet (until 1953, Stalinist) model. The change had begun at 20th Congress of the CPSU in February 1956, when it was officially recognized that there could be national roads to socialism and national characteristics.[61]

TOP-LEVEL DEBATES ON THE EVE OF FULL COLLECTIVIZATION

HSWP leaders could sense, therefore, the requirement to keep step with the other socialist countries, but, at the same time, every foreign study visit had confirmed the importance of detailed preparation. At the end of April, 1958, the Central Committee decided to grant a relatively long time period, four months, in which a detailed plan for "socialist restructuring" might be drafted.[62] János Kádár gave the Agricultural Department clear guidelines for this phase of the work, which included the following:

> *Reference should certainly be given and by name to the best results and experience of international development (Bulgarian and Czechoslovak experiences at least)* because we do not live in isolation and we deal with these issues in the world. . . . *When should we make use of them, if not now?*[63] [Author's emphasis]

The level of intensity of consultations taking place in these months within the "inner circle" of the Agricultural Department can be well traced from Lajos Fehér's secretarial materials.[64] The relationship between the two central figures of the agrarian lobby—Lajos Fehér and Ferenc Erdei—became even more intense than before. Fehér sent the plan of his memorandum on the development of the producer cooperative movement for comment to Erdei, who attached the following notes to the material:

> My general observation is that, in terms of development strategy, the concept has changed in comparison to the Agrarian Theses, and this should give us food for thought. The Agrarian Theses are about the general development of agriculture, and the "main method" in this is large-scale restructuring, but it is not a goal in itself. . . . This point of view is obscured in the plan. . . . Another grave danger is hidden within the way in which, in the line of the apparatus, the development of production has been pushed into the background. If this is not emphasized to the same extent as it was in the Agrarian Theses, then, in practice, it will sink to the background, as happened before. A further danger is that the development of producer cooperatives will not expand by relying on peasants within and outside producer cooperatives, but in opposition to them. This position is already evident in the current text of the plan. . . . Based on these thoughts, my proposal is that the entire decree plan be placed unambiguously on the foundational principles of the Agrarian Theses and that the organization of cooperatives be placed into a framework of general agricultural development. . . .[65]

A week later, Erdei sent more comments to Lajos Fehér. He had reported on his trips to the countryside to Fehér previously, and so this was a tried and tested communication channel. His reflections on the producer cooperative day in Nagykőrös nevertheless merit particular attention, not only because of the date, but mainly because of its expressive and direct style.

> On September 21, at the invitation of Nagykőrös town leaders, I participated in the 10th anniversary celebrations of the town's two producer cooperatives and spoke at the meeting organized for the occasion. At the event, I had long conversations with many town and county leaders on the situation of producer cooperatives there and on opportunities for development. Both the producer cooperative day and my conversations brought up many very serious problems, and I therefore think I ought to share them with you. . . .
>
> I pay constant attention to the situation of producer cooperatives in Nagykőrös, and have therefore made several visits this past year, and have dealt with issues

faced by both land recipients' cooperatives and producer cooperatives. Adding yesterday's experiences to these, it is my uniform impression that cooperative development is incapable of moving forward in the town, and the main reason for this is that neither the land recipients' cooperative nor the producer cooperative operate in ways that bring esteem to the producer cooperative movement. They can point to certain results, but these are too meager to merit the respect of realistic and indeed strictly judgmental common peasant opinion. . . .

The situation is made worse by the fact that those who are familiar with the situation in Pest County and Bács County paint a similar picture, and, for the most part, the opinion of county leaders is in agreement too. . . .

The consequence of all of this, which is both sharply apparent and exceptionally dangerous, is that, when the apparatus experiences difficulty achieving the prescribed pace for development, it will be susceptible to using administrative coercion in its dealing with cooperatives. . . . It is not just my conviction, but ten years' experience, that this cannot be done successfully."[66]

Following this, Erdei summarized his recommendations in three points:

a) We must make it possible for producer cooperatives to use new supplementary forms alongside the fossilized, hackneyed and outdated labor day unit accounting and income distribution system, or to have the apparatus support such measures, as happens in Bulgaria and above all in the Soviet Union.

b) It is vital to find new methods in the administration of producer cooperatives. . . . I feel obliged to put onto the agenda, in some form or other, my old hobby horse, the question of a producer cooperative center or alliance. The political judgment on how this is possible, you know better than I.

c) Finally, the situation is made inflexible by the exclusively agrarian-proletarian nature of existing producer cooperatives and the complete separation from them of small and middle peasants. Now, when determining producer cooperative questions, serious thought must be given to being more courageous about providing space for separate cooperative organizational structures for the small and middle peasantry, whether of lower or higher types.[67]

The documents quoted above clearly illustrate two important dimensions of Erdei's lobbying activity. On one hand, his role as a mediator is clear, which he fulfills between local actors in the agrarian sphere (economic managers and functionaries) and Lajos Fehér, who was a political decision-maker. On the other, Erdei did not remain at the level of merely signaling problems that arose in practice, but rather made recommendations (for example on forms of remuneration that differed from the work unit system, on lower-type cooperative forms, and so on), and he supported these with expert arguments and evidence, including foreign examples.

When the Politburo debated the prepared material on September 23, it was decided to wait one or two months before finalizing it.[68] The background to this indecision was the fact that the Hungarian leadership was neither unified on preparation for collectivization nor its timing and methods. The Soviet Embassy in Budapest was also aware of the problem. On the day after the Politiburo meeting, Károly Kiss provided Ambassador Gromov with a detailed report on the debate that had taken place. Károly Kiss strongly criticized the Agricultural Department's memorandum, which, in his opinion

> paid a great deal of attention to the lower forms of the cooperative movement, emphasized needlessly often the principle of voluntarism when creating new cooperatives, and proposed the purchase or rental of land from individual peasants as a means of increasing cooperative land. The plan orients the Party to accepting that only 50% of the peasantry need be cooperative members by 1965.[69]

Károly Kiss also reported:

> The solution to agricultural questions . . . to a certain degree is made difficult by comrade Fehér on one hand, and comrade Dögei, the Minister of Agriculture, on the other, and the abnormal relationship that has developed between them. Comrade Fehér takes every action possible to replace comrade Dögei in the post of Minister of Agriculture with comrade Tömpe (the current deputy Minister of Agriculture), who, for his part, supports comrade Fehér's positions on every question.[70]

As discussed above, the leaders of the Ministry of Agriculture—Minister Imre Dögei, as well as deputy ministers Mihály Keresztes, András Magyari, Antal Márczis, and Mátyás Szőke—all represented rather dogmatic views, and on every issue insisted on the pre-1956 principles. Thus, for example, they insisted on strict enforcement of the Soviet kolkhoz model statute, the work unit system, brigade-based labor organization, and so on. In contrast, the party's Agricultural Department strongly criticized numerous elements of pre-1956 agrarian policy, citing the earlier failures, and wanted to develop HSWP agrarian policy in the direction of respecting peasant interests and avoiding the mistakes of the past.[71] Lajos Fehér took every opportunity to convince the members of the political leadership that a fall back in production could only be avoided by a restructuring that was gradual, strengthened existing producer cooperatives, and supported simpler cooperative forms. He consistently stressed the importance of an appropriate quantity and quality of agricultural investment. It is important to note that it was at this time that the foundations were laid (decree no. 3004) for the support system for producer cooperatives that remained in force for close to a decade.[72] Lajos Fehér and his followers initiated several important practical measures based on the experiences of other socialist countries, which they wanted to incorporate in the new operating rules. Not only did they want to make payment of land rent compulsory, they also wanted to bring into producer cooperatives those formerly labeled as kulaks, so that they could be included in the leadership.[73]

The representatives of the two positions sought to bolster their arguments in the debates with international examples. This is well illustrated by the fact that there was even a difference of emphasis in their assessments of Soviet agriculture. The success of Soviet agriculture and the need to follow it was, naturally, not questioned, nor could it have been. But, while the dogmatic orientation stressed that the success of Soviet agriculture lay in strict adherence to kolkhoz forms, the Lajos Fehér group's interpretation held: "The loosening of rigid restrictions, the increase in kolkhoz planning independence, the creation of their own operating rules, mechanization and the realization of material incentives in production have become important factors in the rapid development of Soviet agriculture."[74]

China also served as a great example, in addition to the Soviet Union, because collectivization had neared completion there at the end of 1956 and beginning of 1957. Dögei's group stressed that one of the key reasons for Chinese success was that they had leaned on poor peasants, while the middle peasantry had been squeezed into producer cooperatives via the tax press. However, it kept silent about the fact that China had introduced a wide array of simple cooperative forms, which ensured a more gradual transition. On its return from a study tour to China, the National Association of Cooperatives delegation led by Rezső Nyers called attention to the following lessons.

> A mode of collectivization whereby the vast majority of the peasant masses are organized into lower-stage cooperatives, and then, following that, are all moved together, and at once, to higher-stage cooperatives seems worth taking into consideration. By doing this, there was no need for land consolidation because whole villages joined both the lower and higher cooperatives. . . . It is noteworthy that in the entire period of collectivization and today cooperatives are ensured an extraordinarily wide-reaching degree of independence.[75]

In the fall of 1958, international pressure had become so strong that Hungary too could no longer postpone relaunching collectivization any longer. János Kádár, when negotiating with Ambassador Gromov at the end of October, was quick to clarify that the next Central Committee meeting would debate the situation of agriculture, because "this is the most important question in all the Party's work."[76] He also added that there was a need to clarify the difference of opinion between Lajos Fehér and Dögei, which was obstructing progress.[77]

At the Central Committee meeting held between December 5 and 7, 1958, Kádár referred many times to the requirement for international alignment.

> The entire international working class is running ahead within the socialist camp. . . . Both on the paths of socialist transformation and the development of agricultural production. Compared to our pace, the Soviet Union, China, Bulgaria, Czechoslovakia and all the fraternal countries with the exception of the Poles are rushing ahead. They are all ahead of us, even the Albanians are far ahead of us. This is true. So, what are we to do now? Under the heel of this pressure, should we make decisions that in the end do not move us forward, but throw us back? I think this is not permissible.[78]

Kádár also stressed many times that the latest, now third, attempt at the socialist restructuring of agriculture brought with it great dangers, and for this reason he felt it all the more important to put an end to diverging conceptions within the party leadership. According to Tibor Huszár: "The views of Dögei and Fehér embodied two orientations that existed in reality, but the way in which Kádár pitted the one against the other from 1957 was part of the political game, the first 'classic' appearance of the construction, which he himself was happy to call a 'struggle on two fronts.' It is a technique adapted from the Machiavellian political tool-box. . . ."[79]

Kádár used the technique at the December 1958 Central Committee meeting in the following manner.

> There is a duality in the conduct of agricultural policy. I believe at least three shades of opinion can be distinguished in practical work: there is a right-wing deviation, there is a sectarian, left-wing deviation, but as well these, let us not forget that there is also the proper conduct of Party policy. . . . In my opinion, there is a very serious gap between published principle and everyday acts, even among leading party functionaries. In my opinion, it is the task of our meeting now to analyze and abolish them. . . . In the Party's agricultural department, and in comrade Lajos Fehér, since he has been working there—November, 1956, by my calculation—the ruling viewpoint has long been to make reparation for past injury and to tremble in the face of old mistakes. In terms of actions, they deviated to the right of the Party's leading line for a long time, and to a degree they still deviate to the right today in their practice. This is the truth. . . . We always rambled on about cooperatives, socialism, about this, about that; and comrade Fehér and his circle responded with voluntarism, avoiding sectarianism; and this is all correct, but it was a little one-sided, that is my opinion. . . . I have known comrade Fehér since Second World War times. As a person, I do not just respect him and honor him, I also like comrade Fehér, because of what he was in the Second World War period, in the period of the struggle for power. . . . But this does not save him from criticism, or us from our duty to say what we think. . . . I know enough about comrade Fehér, and in my view his Marxism stands on weak legs. I think he is an honorable man, he has worked for the village his whole life, he lives and dies for the peasants, he seeks their rights,

> but, in my view, not in the way a Marxist-Leninist should. *I think the person who loves the peasant most is the person who gets workers to lead peasants, and not someone who never thinks about the other side of the matter for years, that is to say, what does this look like from the workers' side, comrade Fehér's Marxism is limping in this matter and requires strengthening*. . . . If he gets used to class struggle, thinks always of workers first, and then peasants . . . we do good for peasants when we succeed—I am speaking of the Party—in leading them to socialism. . . . I have a very poor opinion of the work of the Ministry of Agriculture, including comrade Dögei—forgive my candor, I should add that I have also known comrade Dögei for a few years, and since then I know that he has loyally stood by the Party, and never betrayed the village poor, but this in no way excludes the possibility of his working badly. . . . Fehér's group worked for the good of individual peasants, but with a talent that I have always respected, they are practical people, they knew how to take action. Dögei's group sighed for socialism in the Ministry of Agriculture and did not know how to take action. . . . Comrade Dögei took into his head the idea of removing "surplus income" . . . I think the Central Committee needs to take a position on these questions of principle. And then everyone is duty bound to implement it without exception.[80] [Author's emphasis.]

The decree that was accepted on December 7, at the end of the three-day session, indicated that the conception submitted by the Agricultural Department, which counted on a transition that kept pace with material possibilities and gave preference to lower forms of cooperative, had suffered a defeat.

The restructuring, which took place between January and March 1959, brought unexpected results.[81] By the end of March, a total of 1,000 producer cooperatives were established, as a result of which the number of cooperative members was three times, and total territory two and a half times, greater than at the end of 1958.[82]

Over the course of the campaign launched in the winter of 1958–59, earlier individual and family survival and accommodation strategies were therefore reborn.[83] Those who were unable to accept communal farming sought work in industry or construction, often by changing jobs as well as places of residence. "I saw no future in the producer cooperative. I saw servitude. I deserved more. I was afraid my fate would be like that of farm servants in the past. I did not even start working, I went to a factory."[84]

The party leadership was particularly irritated by the behavior of "dual income" workers (in Hungarian: *kétlaki*), who took on industrial jobs but maintained homes and farms in villages.[85] At the beginning of the 1950s, it again became apparent that dual income workers, when presented with the crossroads, rarely parted from their land, that is to say they did not give their land to the state either for free or in return for some recompense. The party leadership's interpretation was that despite the fact that dual income work-

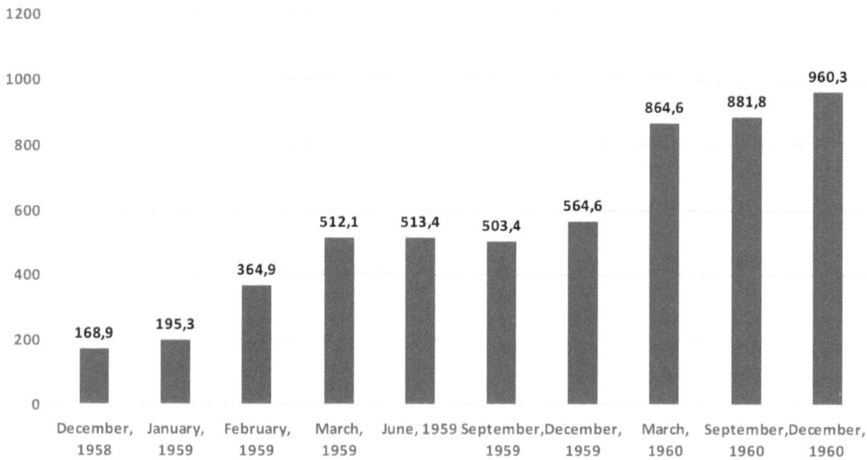

Figure 4.1. Number of Cooperative Members (Thousands of People) December 1958–March 1961. Source: Központi Statisztikai Hivatal, *Mezőgazdaságunk a szocialista átszervezés idején, 1958–1962*, 150, 173.

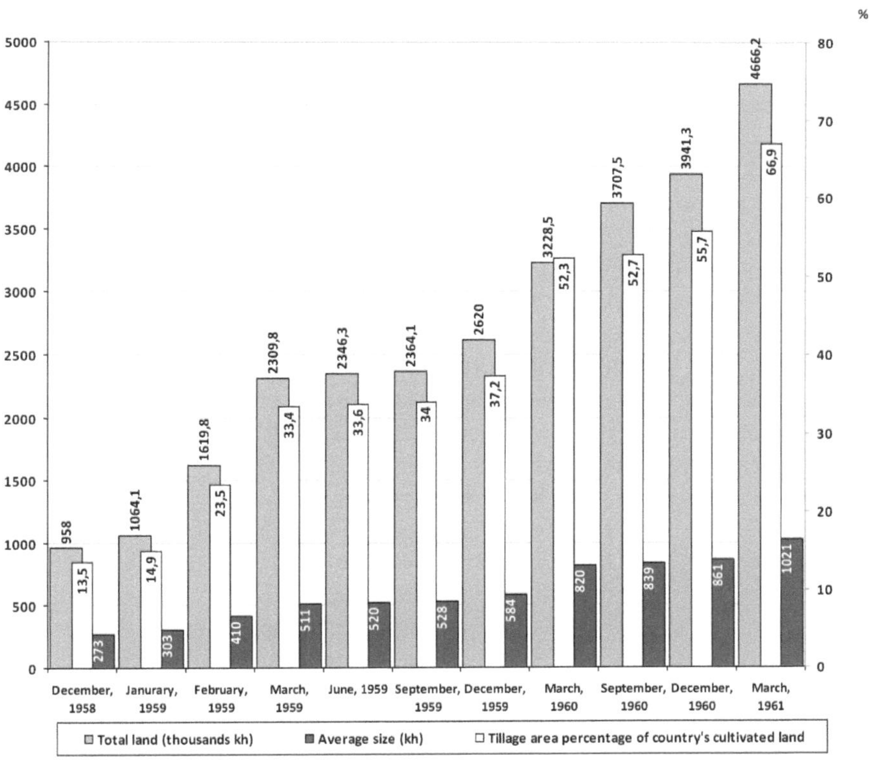

Figure 4.2. Development of the Cooperatives' Area in the Final Phase of Collectivization December 31, 1958–March 31, 1961. Source: *Mezőgazdaságunk a szocialista átszervezés idején, 1958–1962*, 150, 173.

Table 4.1. Migration Affecting the Village Population 1958–66

Year	*Town migration balance, towns vis-à-vis villages*	*Town migration balance per 1,000 residents*
1958	–36,777	–6.1
1959	–43,025	–7.2
1960	–52,285	–8.7
1961	–44,996	–7.6
1962	–49,701	–8.4
1963	–44,968	–7.7
1964	–40,825	–7.0
1965	–42,170	–7.3
1966	–38,203	–6.7

Source: Oros, A falu és a mezőgazdaság, 147.

ers spent years within the working class, the latter had little effect on them: they remained committed to privately owned land and developed a strategy whereby the head of family who worked as a worker kept his workplace, while another family member, such as the wife, joined the producer cooperative with their land.

Furthermore, over the course of the latest campaign, the authorities had to face the fact that, in many places, peasant families with larger holdings began to follow the example of the dual income workers. That is to say, the family's most valuable source of labor power did not join the producer cooperative but instead moved into a branch of production where a steady monthly wage could be relied on, as well as rights to other (for example, social security) benefits. Taking advantage of the acceleration of industrialization and an increasing labor shortage, male peasant family members in many places sought and found work outside agriculture. The new workplace might be a state farm, or state forest, but also an industrial plant or construction site, which brought with it embracing the burden of daily or weekly commuting. In 1959 the number of agricultural earners fell by 51,000. The following year this number had increased by a factor of three.[86]

Over the course 1959, it became increasingly clear that the Ministry of Agriculture led by Imre Dögei was incapable of handling these problems, and, in this situation, the value of the proposals from Lajos Fehér's Agricultural Department increased. Their essence was to make use of the experience of old, "survivor" producer cooperatives, by which was meant producer cooperatives that had survived and ridden out the dissolution waves of both 1953 and 1956. These farms had been able to stay afloat, among other reasons, because they adjusted their internal lives to local circumstances and the needs of the membership, even if this meant diverging from the compulsory Soviet kolkhoz form.

The Lajos Fehér group emphasized too that the landowning peasant groups within peasant society that were now being targeted had a different work culture and a different value system from former estate servants and day-laborers. The power-holders in Hungary still did not dare nationalize land, and so the ownership rights to land that entered cooperative use did not formally change.[87] However, there were strong restrictions on the private property of cooperative members: owners could not sell their land, and the use to which the land was put was determined by the producer cooperative's rules of operation. For all practical purposes, the owner's rights of disposal (with the exception of inheritance) were ended, although, as a recognition of property rights in principle, they could claim land rent.[88]

It was particularly significant that the new rules of operation clearly established entitlement to land rent, however, the level of the cooperative share was low, and its payment was irregular. The modest amount paid as land rent fell far below a realistic fee for land rental. The income that could be expected from the producer cooperative therefore bore no relation to income from land rented earlier, and it was decisively linked to communal labor. The other pillar of producer cooperative income, besides a share in cash or kind from joint farming, was the household plot.

Pensions were introduced to producer cooperative to win over older groups of peasants. Previously, only farm servants and wage-laborers within the agrarian population had received a modest old-age benefit after reaching 65.[89] According to the system introduced in 1958, men working on producer cooperatives aged 65 could retire, as could women aged 60. The basic pension of 315 forint per month was supplemented by 3.15 forint (or 1%) for every year spent in the system. Those who, because of their advanced age, were unable to complete the necessary 10 years' employment on the producer cooperative to qualify for a pension were given an old-age benefit of 260 forint per month.[90]

During the third collectivization campaign launched in the winter of 1958–59, unlike the earlier ones, the main basis was considered to be small and medium peasants with greater experience of farming, and not poor peasants or the landless. The organizers strove first to convince the most respected farmers in a village to join, in the hope that others would follow their example, hence accelerating the organization of villages into producer cooperatives. This method also served the goal of preventing such peasants from experiencing a loss of their position in the village hierarchy when joining the producer cooperative.[91] While in the fifties it was mostly urban "cadres" who were placed at the head of producer cooperatives, between 1959 and 1961, in many places, local farmers had already become producer cooperative presidents. Another important novelty was that farmers previously labeled kulaks could join producer cooperatives, and indeed could later enter their leadership.[92]

Table 4.2. The Comparison of Kolkhoz Model Charter (1935) and Model Charter for Agricultural Cooperatives (1959)

Kolkhoz Model Charter, 1935	*Model Charter for Agricultural Cooperatives, 1959*
Kulaks can only be accepted as members under certain conditions.	Kulaks and other exploiters can be members, and after two years exemplary work can be elected into management positions.
Members cannot freely leave the kolkhoz (domestic passport system). Exit and exclusion: based on agreement of two-thirds of the members.	Three-year ban on exit.
In theory the general meeting elects the leadership for two years.	The general meeting elects the leadership for four years.
Land is owned by the state.	The land stays in private hands, but is used collectively, for which a land rent is paid by the collective farm to the landowner.
Mandatory submission of farming equipment, yokes, and livestock.	Mandatory submission of tools, livestock.
Household plot: area of 1/4–1/2 ha	Household plot: 1/2 to 1 kh (0.28–0.57 ha).
Permitted animals: 1 cow, 1 calf, 1 pig, 1 piglet, 4 sheep, unlimited number of poultry and rabbits.	Permitted animals: 1 cow, 1–2 young cattle, 1–2 sows with piglets, 5 sheep or goats, unlimited number of poultry, rabbits, bees, further 3–4 fattening pigs. Rights granted not to members but households.
Sphere of activity: crops, livestock, household plot	Sphere of activity: crops, livestock, processing and selling of own produce, construction industry.
Compulsory planting plans.	Compulsory planting plan only for bread grains.
Delivery system.	Cancelled in 1956.
Residue principle remuneration.	Residue principle remuneration.
Remuneration based on work unit system, payment once per year at the end of agricultural year. Advance payments paid under certain conditions.	Remuneration based on work unit system, which the general assembly can "further develop," i.e., modify. Advance payments paid under certain conditions.
Collective labor organization (brigade, labor team).	Collective labor organization (brigade, labor team).
Disciplinary punishment (admonishment, warnings, reprimand, reduction of work units, fines, exclusion).	Annual labor minimum (120 work units).
–	Introduction of collective farm pension.

All these considerations were realized, if only partially, in the preparation of legislative decree no. 7 of 1959 on agricultural producer cooperatives and producer cooperative groups, which established new operating rules for producer cooperatives. The changes are presented in table 4.2.

MIDTERM MODIFICATIONS TO THE KOLKHOZ MODEL—LEARNING FROM THE PEASANTRY

While it can be said that restructuring at the beginning of 1959 took village society by surprise, there was ample time to prepare before the next campaign. In the autumn months, individual farmers on the one hand attempted to sell their more valuable animals and even a part of their farming equipment, and on the other they built up reserves of harvested produce.[93] In a report from November 1959, the following can be read: "As a result of malicious rumors, in Csongrád County, for example, only 30 wagons [300 metric tons] of a planned purchase of 829 wagons [8,290 metric tons] of maize, could be acquired by November 1."[94]

Individual farmers prepared for the next campaign in other ways as well. They got together on occasion and in some places agreed that no one would join, because then the state would not know what to do with them. In other places it was the exact opposite: they discussed what conditions they should impose on joining, who among them should be elected as leaders, how large household plots should be, and so on. Maintaining intense contact with family members living in neighboring villages served to strengthen solidarity and common resolve.[95] This flow of information also helped families keep themselves informed about local or even distant workplaces. Because incomes from producer cooperatives were low, it was not worth the entire family joining.

No matter how circumspect village families had been in their endeavors to establish self-defense and survival strategies, the start of actual restructuring nevertheless brought about an unexpected turn. Learning from the spring 1959 campaign, the party leadership issued the following order: it is not permissible to allow new entrants to postpone to a later time the organization of joint farming or the beginning of joint labor.

> Experience shows that it is neither expedient nor correct to allow a form of organization in which long months stretch between the establishment of the cooperative and the commencement of joint activity, and during this period the cooperative members essentially continue to farm individually. In reality cooperatives of this type have to be organized twice.[96]

This amendment to collectivization tactics prompted changes in peasant opposition and accommodation. It is immediately striking that opposition to the agitation tactics of the producer cooperative organizers strengthened, because the stakes of signing an intention-to-join document had increased. This feature received more intense attention in the reports of the local organs of state security.

> It was generally observable that at the time of the fall and winter producer cooperative development, the opposition elements were better prepared in their actions than during the spring 1959 development. This is demonstrated by the fact that the Ministry of the Interior's county organs engaged in extraordinary measures 103 times in October, 109 times in November and 159 times in January of 1960. By contrast, during the spring 1959 development, the number of extraordinary anti-producer cooperative events was roughly 10–15 per month. . . . Threats and actual harassment of producer cooperative leaders and agitators increased. We were informed of eight such incidents in October, 30 in November, and 29 in January.[97]

Further, provincial security organs reported a growing number of threatening letters, graffiti, and pamphlets.

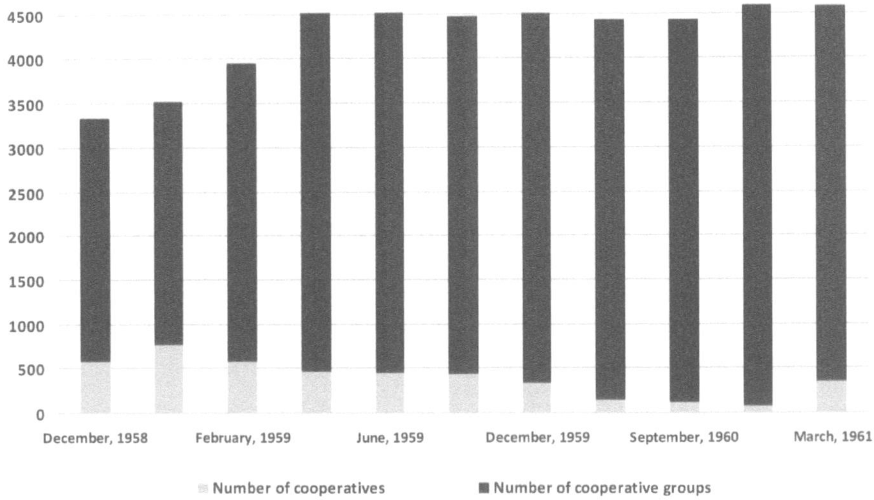

Figure 4.3. Number of Cooperatives and Cooperative Groups December 31, 1958–March 31, 1961. Source: ***Mezőgadaságunk a szocialista átszervezés idején, 1958–1962,*** **150, 173.**

The resolve of farmers coerced into joining is reflected in the fact that, while restructuring was taking place or immediately following it, they organized demonstrations, in an attempt to get their intention-to-join documents back. In the first three months of 1960, state security organs reported 13 antiproducer cooperative incidents, which were concentrated in Pest, Szolnok, and Szabolcs-Szatmár counties. According to the public prosecutor, in February of 1960, there were five open antiproducer cooperative demonstrations in Szabolcs-Szatmár County.[98] One of these, the women's demonstration in Nyírcsaholy, has been analyzed in fine detail by Gyöngyi Farkas.[99]

Given the impossibility of postponing the commencement of communal work, peasants also took stronger actions to preserve their movable property. Taking stock of tools and equipment prior to joining could occasion tough conflicts. It was common for new members to put their poor-quality, low-yielding and often unhealthy animals into the cooperative, keeping the better ones for their household plots.[100]

The presentation above gives adequate support to the claim that relaunched collectivization based on Dögei's dogmatic tendency had in its first year already caused such serious economic and social problems that the party leadership was forced to correct its course midstream. This step, however, was preceded by multilateral negotiations. The approach to solving the problem recommended by the Lajos Fehér group carried with it considerable political risk. For it essentially questioned one of the fundamental pillars of socialist agriculture, including many elements of the kolkhoz model, and wanted to introduce in its place a cooperative form that was appropriate to Hungarian conditions.

The staff of the Agricultural Department of the Central Committee were at pains to pull together as many arguments as possible for policy correction from "fraternal countries," Czechoslovakia being the main source.[101] In parallel, an attempt was made to soften the opinion of the Soviet side. Several opportunities arose for this in 1959. Khrushchev visited Hungary from June 4 to 6, met the leaders of socialist countries in Bucharest in the last week of June, and then visited Hungary again in late November to participate in the 7th Congress of the HSWP.[102] The series of consultations continued at the beginning of 1960: on February 2–3 representatives of Communist and labor parties of European socialist countries met in Moscow to discuss the development of agriculture.

For reasons of space, this account concentrates primarily on the February 1960 meeting in Moscow, or more precisely, on its consequences for Hungary. One of the most important messages of the meeting was relayed to the members of the Politburo by Kádár thus.

Comrade Khrushchev expressed it in this way . . . the masses measure socialism and communism by whether their lives are better or not. . . . If we cannot satisfy

> *these endeavors and requirements of the masses appropriately, then for them the importance of socialism and communism themselves is lost too.*[103] [Author's emphasis]

Moving to the neuralgic questions of food supply, Kádár continued:

> In this respect, the opinion was expressed there, and there was agreement on it, that, *for all socialist countries . . . the first duty is to produce the country's bread grain needs*. In fact, in the name of the Soviet delegation, comrade Khrushchev unequivocally stated that they are not willing to take on indefinitely the role of being the only grain producer, with everyone coming to them for grain.[104] [Author's emphasis]

This last statement of Khrushchev's touched a raw nerve on the part of the Hungarian leadership, because it was well known that Hungary had been a famous grain exporter before 1945, but during restructuring had been obliged to import significant quantities of grain.[105]

The HSWP was therefore in a difficult situation. Despite numerical successes in collectivization, those in power had to face the fact that, although they could force agricultural producers into producer cooperatives, they could not get them to work there conscientiously and diligently. In addition, the labor power of those flooding out of agriculture in hundreds of thousands could not be replaced by mechanization in the foreseeable future. In these conditions, what was needed to increase agricultural production was the Hungarian peasant's diligence and love of labor, just as much as the farming tools and buildings to be found in household plots.

The first agenda item of the next Politburo session reflected the political leadership's search for a solution. The material presented by the Agricultural Department was titled "Recommendation for a decree concerning various methods of remuneration and income distribution designed to increase the degree to which the material interests of the producer cooperative membership are represented." The complex formulation of the title was sufficient to conceal the essence, but those speaking to it soon made it clear what was at stake.

Kádár formulated his position with particular candor.

> We have certain time-honored principles which constitute the essence of the producer cooperative movement. One of these is the work unit. . . .That is why I do not agree with the starting point of the material, that the income distribution system based on the traditional work unit does not ensure sufficiently the individual material interests of cooperative members. . . . If we were to issue this, people will say: that is the end of the work unit. But if, by contrast, we say that in many respects it needs to be further developed, or its further development is possible, then that is a different starting point. . . .[106]

The first secretary of the party, therefore, defended a fundamental principle of the classic kolkhoz model—payment based on work units—but at the same time adopted a position that allowed a little room for maneuver. With this he essentially tolerated forms of remuneration that deviated from the Soviet model, and indeed in reality were known from the capitalist era; but their greatest positive feature was that they resulted in higher yields with no significant expenditure of capital.[107] This pragmatic turnaround in agrarian policy, however, represented such a huge risk in the field of ideology that Kádár wanted guarantees, and he tried to get them from the highest level. In December of 1959, Kádár made mention of the incentive systems that had been formed in the everyday practice of Hungarian producer cooperatives to Khrushchev, who was taking part in the 7th Congress of the HSWP. In his response, the First Secretary of the CPSU said: "[P]rofit shares and bonuses too share common ground. They encourage individuals to hope that the plan is as low as possible. If we can discover how to raise individual shares while inducing people to fight for a higher plan, then we have won the battle."[108]

It was precisely this latter point that rendered sharecropping "acceptable in polite society." Because this form of remuneration—which previously communist ideology had stamped as a vestige of either feudalism or capitalism—had consistently made members interested in achieving higher production. In contrast to this, under a bonus system linked to plan completion, the member really was interested in low plans because they could easily be over fulfilled. A further problem was that if, because of the weather, completion of the plan seemed unachievable in advance, this had a negative effect on the membership's future labor. After long debate the following decree finally emerged:

> The Politburo considers it necessary to extend more widely, as most appropriate to local conditions, time-honored methods of remuneration and income distribution that further develop the work unit system. In every case, the introduction of forms most appropriate to local conditions should be decided by the cooperative general assembly.[109]

A turnaround in cooperative policy took place, therefore, that promoted, at the level of producer cooperatives, locally already tried and tested solutions, which in practice related to the activation of material interests; and it had been adopted at the very highest level.

The party leadership took the position that the decree need only be sent to county-level party committees, and added: it is not necessary "in the current situation for the press and the radio to concern themselves with the new methods of income distribution." The fact, though, that, at the beginning of 1960, the dogmatic Minister of Agriculture Imre Dögei was dismissed and replaced, in the person of Pál Losonczi, by a reform-minded producer cooperative president signaled to the public at large: an important correction has taken place in agrarian policy.[110]

The agricultural lobby was also in a hurry to make the changes known because news arriving from year-end closing accounts at the beginning of 1960 bore witness to huge dissatisfaction because of low incomes, and the expectation that, despite the ban, many would abandon producer cooperatives over the course of the year.[111] The income of producer cooperative members was considerably lower than it had been in 1959. In 1959 the average income from communal farming was 11,400 forint, but the following year it decreased to 8,400 forint.[112]

The statistical data also revealed that there was wide variation behind the national average. There were significant differences, on the one hand, within producer cooperatives, between work places, and, on the other, between regions.[113]

On the eve of the final push, fewer than 500 of the country's 3,373 villages did not have a producer cooperative. It was no accident that these municipalities had been left to last. They were places where either the hilly terrain did not favor large-scale mechanization, or they were vine and fruit-growing regions where the intensity of labor demand did not fit well with large-scale labor organization. In these areas, in the end, partly thanks to peasant resistance and partly thanks to those in power recognizing reality, in many cases producer cooperative groups or specialist cooperatives were established instead of producer cooperatives.[114] These were registered as lower-type cooperatives. It had been possible in principle to establish them previously, but the Ministry of Agriculture under Imre Dögei gave absolutely no support to the idea. The reasoning was that it had been so difficult in the first half of the 1950s to develop them into higher, that is kolkhoz-type cooperatives. After

Table 4.3. The Average Annual Income of Cooperative Families 1958–66

Year	*Communal*	*Household plot*	*Total cooperative income*
	Income within the cooperative		
1958	11,870	9,200	20,870
1959	11,400	9,200	20,600
1960	8,400	8,600	17,000
1961	7,800	9,300	17,100
1962	9,000	9,600	18,600
1963	10,000	10,100	20,100
1964	10,400	11,430	21,830
1965	10,600	10,300	20,900
1966	12,300	12,600	24,900

Source: Iván Oros, *A falu és a mezőgazdaság*, 147.

Table 4.4. The Distribution of Cooperative Members According to the Size of Their Total Cooperative Income (%), 1960–66

	1960	*1961*	*1962*	*1963*	*1964*	*1965*	*1966*
6,000 HUF or lower	41.1	51.4	45.3	40.6	39.1	35.8	31.5
6,001–8,000 HUF	17.4	13.0	13.1	11.9	10.6	10.4	9.3
8,001–10,000 HUF	14.5	10.2	10.6	9.9	9.5	9.6	8.8
10,001–12,000 HUF	10.0	8.1	8.6	8.8	8.4	8.7	8.4
12,001–15,000 HUF	8.5	7.4	8.6	9.4	9.6	10.0	9.9
15,001–20,000 HUF	5.3	6.0	7.7	9.8	10.7	11.4	12.1
Higher than 20,000 HUF	2.9	3.9	6.1	9.6	12.1	14.1	20.2
Total	100	100	100	100	100	100	100

Source: Központi Statisztikai Hivatal, *Mezőgazdasági statisztikai zsebkönyv* (Budapest: KSH, 1967), 247.

Dögei was removed, more space was proffered for such forms, all the more so because the Lajos Fehér group pushed for their formation.[115]

Rather intense conflicts took place in locations where the agitators insisted on organizing producer cooperatives. It was not only the case that the most stubborn and most resistant farmers were left until last, but also that the behavior of both parties was influenced significantly by tensions that had accumulated over a restructuring that was now in its third year. During the campaign carried out as 1960 turned into 1961, there was a strengthening in the verbal and physical abuse of people's educators taking part in producer cooperative organization. There were places where they were attacked with kitchen knives, others where people tried to pour boiling water over them. These and similar incidents were reported in Baranya, Bács, Borsod, Hajdú, Pest, Somogy, Szabolcs, Veszprém, and Zala counties, that is to say, almost throughout the whole country. It was no accident that in the course of only a month and a half, between December 1, 1960, and January 15, 1961, 153 cases of antiproducer cooperative incitement were registered.[116]

The majority of village families coerced into joining producer cooperatives in 1959–1961 had to face lost certainties in relation to their livelihoods and existence, although at different income levels. Those who were not satisfied with the income from communal work asked for permission to leave, on the grounds that the cooperative could not ensure their livelihood. Such cases were reported by county organs in Borsod, Fejér, Győr, Heves, Somogy, Szolnok, Vas, and Veszprém counties.[117]

Thus, while the HSWP Central Committee announced on February 17, 1961, that "we have reached a milestone in the transformation of Hungarian agriculture: following industry, socialist relations have become dominant in agriculture too,"[118] the reality was that formal success in restructuring had not been accompanied by the rapid consolidation of cooperative farming.

NOTES

1. Pál Romány, "A 'Nagy Imre-tanszék' és utóélete" [The so-called Imre Nagy's department and its aftermath], in *1956* és *a magyar agrártársadalom* [1956 and the Hungarian agrarian society], ed. János Estók (Budapest: Magyar Mezőgazdasági Múzeum, 2006), 120–22.

2. Papp, *Fehér Lajos*, 185–202.

3. Keserű, *Parasztsorsfordítók*, 85–86.

4. Levente Sipos, "Kolhozosítás vagy szövetkezetesítés: Dögei Imre és Fehér Lajos vitái 1957-ben" [Organizing a kolhoz or a cooperative: Debates between Imre Dögei and Lajos Fehér in 1957], in Buza, Estók, Szávai, and Varga, *Agrártörténet—Agrárpolitika*, 443–58.

5. György Péteri, "The field of economic research in Hungary after Stalin, 1953–56," in *Life and the First Crisis of State Socialism in East Central Europe, 1953–1956*, ed. György Péteri (Trondheim: Programme on East European Cultures and Societies, 2001), 47–79; László Szamuely, ed., *A magyar közgazdasági gondolat fejlődése, 1954–1978: A szocialista gazdaság mechanizmusának kutatása* [Development of Hungarian economic thinking, 1954–1978: Research into the mechanism of the socialist economy] (Budapest: KJK, 1986), 189–92.

6. Credit received from the Soviet Union played a decisive role in this. A. N. Artizov and György Földes eds., *Sovetsko-vengerszkie ekonomicheskie otnoseniia 1948–1973: Dokumenty* (Moskva: Mezhdunarodnyi Fond Demokratiia, 2012), 129–138; György Földes, *Kádár János külpolitikája* és *nemzetközi tárgyalásai 1956–1988* [The foreign policy of János Kádár and his international negotiations] (Budapest: Napvilág, 2015), 1:17–35.

7. In his memoirs Lajos Fehér's deputy János Keserű wrote: "In total we debated the plan with close to ten thousand people and incorporated the opinions of 1,500 people in the unified guideline program." See: Keserű, *Parasztsorsfordítók*, 81.

8. Javaslat az Agrárpolitikai Bizottság létrehozására. [Proposal on the establishment of the Agrarian Policy Committee] MNL OL, M–KS 288. f., 6. cs., 9. ő. e. 9.

9. Az Agrárpolitikai Bizottság anyagai. [Documents of the Agrarian Policy Committee] MNL OL, M–KS 288. f., 28. cs., (1957) 18. ő. e.

10. Erdei was arrested on November 3, 1956, as a member of the Hungarian delegation sent to Tököl to negotiate the withdrawal of Soviet troops. He was commissioned by Imre Nagy and served as the civic leader of the delegation. István Nagy, *Nagy Imre* és *Erdei Ferenc 1956-ban* [Imre Nagy and Ferenc Erdei in 1956], Az Erdei Ferenc Társaság füzetei 16 (Makó: Erdei Ferenc Társaság, 2003), 50–59.

11. Erdei Ferenc: Hozzászólás az agrárpolitikai tézisekhez. 1957. február 21. [Ferenc Erdei's contribution to the Agrarian Theses, February 21, 1957] MNL OL, M–KS 288. f., 28. cs., (1957) 3. ő. e.

12. Az Agrárpolitikai Bizottság anyagai. [Documents of the Agrarian Policy Committee] MNL OL, M–KS 288. f., 28. cs., (1957) 18. ő. e.

13. Jegyzőkönyv az MSZMP Ideiglenes Intéző Bizottság 1957. március 12-i üléséről. [Minutes of HSWP Provisional Politburo, March 12, 1957] MNL OL, M–KS 288. f., 5. cs., 18. ő. e.

14. Ibid.

15. Henrik Vass and Ágnes Ságvári, eds., *A Magyar Szocialista Munkáspárt határozatai* és *dokumentumai 1956–1962* [The resolutions and documents of the HSWP, 1956–1962, here on The resolutions of the HSWP, 1956–1962], 2nd ed. (Budapest: Kossuth, 1973), 102–22.

16. Utilizing his contacts in journalism Lajos Fehér strove to publicize the Agrarian Theses as much as possible. *Szabad Föld*, for example, dealt with the topic over an entire month. See: "Milyen irányban fejlődik a magyar mezőgazdaság?" [In which direction is our agriculture going?], 4 parts, *Szabad Föld*, August 11, 18, 25, September 1, 1957.

17. Ibid., 104.

18. The following pieces offer detailed descriptions of these debates: Pál Romány, Az Agrárpolitikai Tézisektől a Nemzeti Agrárprogramig" [The Completion and Partial Dismantling of Collective Agriculture], in Gunst, *A magyar agrártársadalom*, 357–65.

19. This is supported by materials dealing with early 1957 collective farms by the HSWP Central Committee Village Department (later Agricultural Department). Feljegyzés a tsz-ek helyzetéről és legfontosabb problémáiról. (1957. január 10.) [Memo on the situation of the producer cooperatives and their problems, January 10, 1957]; Jelentés a mezőgazdaság helyzetéről. (1957. január 26.) [Report on the situation of the agriculture, January 26, 1957]; Jelentés a parasztság különböző rétegeinek problémáiról és a falusi pártmunkáról. (1957. február 18.) [Report on the problems of different peasant strata and the village party work, February 18, 1957.] MNL OL, M–KS 288. f., 28. cs., (1957) 1. ő. e.

20. *MK*, November 27, 1956, 580. This approach was reflected in state affairs in the Minister of Agriculture's command 65/1956, which established that the membership of the collective farm has exclusive rights in organizing farming and sales and in managing the collective. See: *MK*, November 27, 1956, 580–81.

21. A tsz-ek törvényes és alapszabályszerű működésének vizsgálata. (A Legfőbb Ügyészség összefoglaló jelentése). [.Summary report made by the General Prosecutor's Office on the investigation on the functioning of the cooperatives functioning lawfully and in accordance with the statutory rules] MNL OL, M–KS 288. f., 28. cs., (1958) 14. ő. e.

22. Megyei jelentések a termelőszövetkezeti mozgalom helyzetéről [County reports on the situation of the cooperative movement, 1957] MNL OL, M–KS 288. f., 28. cs., (1957) 17. ő. e.

23. Dögei Imre feljegyzése a mezőgazdaság szocialista átszervezésének néhány problémájáról. 1957. április 16. [Memorandum of Imre Dögei on the certain problems of the socialist transformation of agriculture, April 18, 1957.] MNL OL, M–KS 288. f., 17 cs., 2. ő. e.

24. Jegyzőkönyv az MSZMP Zala Megyei Nagyaktíva üléséről 1957. május 29. [Minutes of the HSWP activists'general meeting in Zala county] MNL ZML, 1. f., 1957. 2. ő. e.

25. On debates between the two orientations: Sipos, *Reform* és *megtorpanás*, 188–97.

26. Lajos Fehér, *A magyar mezőgazdaság fejlődésének* útja*: Előadás az MSZMP KB Politikai Akadémiáján* [The road of the Hungarian agriculture's development: A lecture given at the Political Academy of the HSWP CC] (Budapest: Kossuth, 1957), 36.

27. Ibid.

28. It is most likely that Rezső Nyers meant to refer not to András Gyenes, but to Antal Gyenes.

29. Tibor Huszár, *Beszélgetések Nyers Rezsővel* [Conversations with Rezső Nyers] (Budapest: Kossuth, 2004), 227.

30. This process can be traced in Erdei's notes from 1957. Pál Romány has published two of these. See: Pál Romány, "'Feljegyzés a falusi helyzetről': Erdei Ferenc a szövetkezeti átalakításról, 1957–58" [Memorandum on the village situation: Ferenc Erdei's views on the cooperative transformation, 1957–58.], *História* 17, no. 9–10. (1995): 32–35.

31. Data that served as raw material to launch theoretical economics research was collected in 120 collective farms and 150 peasant farms. Operations statistics and then quantitative data collection was consistently continued in the future. See: Agrárgazdasági Kutató Intézet, *Az Agrárgazdasági Kutató Intézet története, 1954–1969* [The history of the Institute of Agricultural Economics] (Budapest: AKI, 1970), 15–16.

32. Erdei's statement is widely quoted in various contexts: "I can learn more about the actual situation of Hungarian agriculture by talking with three smart collective farm presidents than a dozen academics!," Gyula Varga, "A 'tudományos munkás'" [The "scientific worker"], in *Erdei Ferenc emlékezete: Válogatott* írások*, tanulmányok* és *visszaemlékezések* [Remembrance of Ferenc Erdei: Selected writings, studies and memories] (Szeged: Bába Kiadó. 2010), 338.

33. Mihály Tamasi, "A nyugati tanulmányút hatása Erdei Ferenc gondolatvilágára" [Effects of a Western Study Trip on the Thoughts of Ferenc Erdei], in *Erdei Ferenc levelesládájából: Müncheni levelek* [From Ferenc Erdei's Letter Box: Letters from Munich], ed. Ferenc Tóth, Az Erdei Ferenc Társaság füzetei 8 (Makó: Erdei Ferenc Társaság, 1997), 19–35.

34. For more on economic relations moving beyond the "Iron Curtain" and initiated by the Soviet Union see: Philip Hanson, *Trade and Technology in Soviet–Western Relations* (New York: Palgrave Macmillan, 1981); Philip Hanson, „The Soviet Union's acquisition of Western Technology after Stalin: Some thoughts on people and connections," in Autio-Sarasmo and Miklóssy, *Reassessing Cold War Europe*, 16–32; Ethan Pollock, "From 'Partiinost' to 'Nauchnost' and Not Quite Back Again: Revisiting the Lessons of the Lysenko Affair," *Slavic Review* 68, no. 1 (2009): 95–115.

35. Sándor Rajki, who at this time was the director of the Agricultural Research Institute in Martonvásár, reflected on the preparations for the trip as follows: In October of 1955 Roswell Garst, an American trader in hybrid seeds, visited Hungary, and Erdei arranged for him to visit Martonvásár, where, through Endre Pap's research, hybrid production was advanced. Of course this was secret, because hybridization clashed with the Michurin approach to genetics. Hale-Dorrell, *Corn crusade*, 167–96; Lowitt–Lee, *Letters from an American Farmer,* xx–xxvi.

36. The study visit, which lasted a month and a half and was tied in with a business trip, is reported in the memoirs of another members of the delegation. See: Keserű, *Parasztsorsfordítók*, 61–63.

37. Erdei had smuggled references to Western examples in his notes written in early 1957, and later on this feature became increasingly emphasized. For documentation of this, see: Erdei Ferenc hagyatéka. [Bequest of Ferenc Erdei] MTA Könyvtára, Kézirattár, [Manuscript Collection of the Hungarian Academy of Science, hereafter: MTAK] Ms 5875/1–2, 5878/2–4, 5883/4, 5884/5.

38. From 1964 he served as the vice president of the Academy of Sciences and the general secretary of the Patriotic People's Front. In 1969 he took over the presidency of the National Council of Collectives, and then in 1971 once again became the general secretary of the Academy. Tibor Huszár, *Erdei Ferenc 1910–1970: Politikai életrajz* [Ferenc Erdei 1910–1970: Political biography] (Budapest: Corvina, 2012), 386–96.

39. Swain and Swain, *Eastern Europe*, 134–36.

40. John K. Fairbank, *China: A New History* (Cambridge: Belknap Press of Harvard University Press, 1994), 352–57; Peter Nolan, "The collectivization in China: some comparisons with the USSR," *Journal of Peasant Studies* 3, no. 2 (1976): 192–220.

41. The Moscow statement contained only general ideological guiding principles, and none of them called directly for the acceleration of collectivization. At the same time there was an unambiguous statement on property relations: the work of constructing socialism was obstructed by the fact that socialist property relations had not become dominant in rural areas. The difference between industry and agriculture, or city and village, was seen as very damaging, and the statement called for the elimination of these differences. See: *Az emberiség békéjéért, jövőjéért: A szocialista országok kommunista és munkáspártjainak nyilatkozata, Moszkva, 1957. november 14–16.* [For mankind's peace and future: A declaration of communist and workers' parties of socialist countries, Moscow, November 14–16, 1957] (Budapest: Kossuth Kiadó, 1957), 22–24; Taubman, *Khrushchev*, 325–360.

42. Pittaway, *Eastern Europe*, 87–108; Wädekin, *Agrarian Policies*, 63–82.

43. Központi Statisztikai Hivatal, *A mezőgazdaság eredményei 1958-ban* [The agricultural results of 1958], Statisztikai Időszaki Közlemények 26 (Budapest: KSH, 1959).

44. "Fejlesszük az egész mezőgazdaságot—a falun is a szocializmus a végcél," ["Let us develop the entire agriculture—socialism is the ultimate goal in the villages, too"], *Népszabadság*, [People's Freedom] December 15, 1957. This speech was published one week later on the front page of the biggest rural weekly *Szabad Föld*.

45. On the role of the press in preparing collectivization see: Varga, *Politika, paraszti érdekérvényesítés*, 58–66.

46. Jegyzőkönyv az MSZMP Központi Bizottság 1957. november 29-i üléséről. [Minutes of the HSWP Central Committee, 29 November 1957] MNL OL, M–KS 288. f., 4. cs., 14. ő. e.

47. Kádár and Khrushchev's unusual relationship helped. Initially this relationship was characterized by an acknowledgment of mutual dependence, but later it can be

said to have been characterized by a special sympathy and perhaps even friendship. See more on this: Roger Gough, *A good comrade: János Kádár: Communism and Hungary* (London and New York: I. B. Tauris, 2006), 119–21, 146–49.

48. Miklós Nagy, ed., *A magyar külpolitika, 1956–1989: Történeti kronológia* [The foreign policy of Hungary, 1956–1989: Chronology] (Budapest: MTA Jelenkorkutató Bizottság, 1993), 28–34.

49. The most valuable diplomatic materials are those that not only collected officially released information on the given topic, but which also contained evaluative-critical sections. This of course required a wide array of knowledge and an expanded network of contacts. The operation of the party-state mechanism is well reflected in the fact that ambassadors sent their reports not only to the Ministry of Foreign Affairs, but also forwarded agriculture-related materials deemed important to the Central Committee's Agricultural Department, the Ministry of Agriculture, the Political Committee and functionaries responsible for this sector in the Central Committee. It was mostly Lajos Fehér, János Keserű, Rezső Nyers, Károly Németh, Imre Dögei, and later Pál Losonczi who received such materials.

50. Dariusz Jarosz, "The Collectivization of Agriculture in Poland: Causes of Defeat," in Iordachi and Bauerkämper, *The Collectivization*, 113–46.

51. Jelentés a lengyel mezőgazdaság jelenlegi helyzetéről, 1958. április. [Report on the actual situation of Polish agriculture. April 1958] MNL OL, M–KS 288. f., 32. cs., (1958) 14. ő. e.; A Külügyminisztérium visszaminősített titkos ügykezelésű iratai [Ministry for Foreign Affairs, Classified Documents, hereafter KÜM TÜK] MNL OL, XIX–J–1–j Lengyelország 1945–64. 8. d. [Poland, 1945–64, Box No. 8]

52. Jegyzőkönyv az MSZMP Politikai Bizottság 1958. május 13-i üléséről. [Minutes of the HSWP Politburo, 13 May 1958] MNL OL, M–KS 288. f., 5. cs., 78. ő. e.

53. For more on this phase of the collectivization of Romanian agriculture: Constantin Iordachi, "'Constanta, the First Collectivized Region': Soviet Geopolitical Interests and National and Regional Factors in the Collectivization of Dobrogea (1949–62)," in *Transforming Peasants, Property and Power: The Collectivization of Agriculture in Romania, 1949–1962*, eds. Constantin Iordachi and Dorin Dobrincu (Budapest: CEU Press, 2009), 103–39; Gail Kligman and Katherine Verdery, eds., *Peasants under siege: the Collectivization of Romanian Agriculture, 1949–1962* (Princeton and Oxford: Princeton University Press, 2011).

54. MNL OL, XIX–J–1–j KÜM TÜK Románia 1945–1964. 27. d. [Romania, 1945–1964, Box No. 27]

55. Politikai és gazdasági helyzetkép a Román Népköztársaságról, 1958. január. [Political and economical overview on the People's Republic of Romania. January, 1958] MNL OL, M–KS 288. f., 32. cs., (1958) 15. ő. e.

56. Mihail Gruev, "Collectivization and Social Change in Bulgaria, 1940s–1950s," in Iordachi and Bauerkämper, *The Collectivization*, 329–68; Jan Rychlik, "Collectivization in Czechoslovakia in Comparative Perspective," in Iordachi and Bauerkämper, *The Collectivization*, 181–210.

57. While preparing the work plan for the year for the embassy in Prague, the Ministry of Foreign Affairs paid particular attention to ensuring the embassy closely follow the situation of the collectivized agriculture, with special focus on the price

system, the problems of mechanization and the social insurance of the collective farm membership. MNL OL, XIX–J–1–j KÜM TÜK Csehszlovákia, 1945–1964. 2. d. [Czechoslovakia, 1945–1964, Box No. 2]

58. Tájékoztató jelentés a Bolgár Kommunista Párt VII. kongresszusának lefolyásáról. [Report on the events of the 7th congress of the Bulgarian Communist Party] MNL OL, M–KS 288. f., 28. cs., (1958) 3. ő. e.

59. Lajos Fehér also counted on Erdei's institute. On the experiences of the delegation to Bulgaria see: László Csete and Ferenc Erdei, eds., *A szocialista mezőgazdaság fejlődése Bulgáriában: Három tanulmányút 1959–1960-ban* [The development of the socialist agriculture in Bulgaria: Three study-tours in 1959–1960] (Budapest: Mezőgazdasági Üzemtani Intézet, 1961).

60. Keserű, *Parasztsorsfordítók*, 88–89.

61. Ferenc Fejtő, *A népi demokráciák története* [The history of people's democracies], vol. 2 (Budapest and Párizs: Magvető, 1991), 46–56.

62. Jegyzőkönyv az MSZMP Központi Bizottság 1958. április 25-i üléséről. [Minutes of the HSWP Central Committee, 25 April 1958] MNL OL, M–KS 288. f., 4. cs., 16. ő. e.

63. Kádár János levele a Mezőgazdasági Osztálynak, 1958. július 23. [A letter from János Kádár to the Agricultural Department, July 23, 1958] MNL OL, M–KS 288. f., 17. cs., 7. ő. e.

64. Fehér Lajos 1958. évi anyagai. [Documents of Lajos Fehér] MNL OL, M–KS 288. f., 17. cs., 3. ő. e.

65. Feljegyzés Fehér Lajos elvtárs részére a termelőszövetkezeti határozattervezet tárgyában. 1958. szeptember 15. [Memo for Lajos Fehér on the draft on the HSWP Politburo resolution on cooperatives] MNL OL, M–KS 288. f., 28. cs., (1958) 12. ő. e.

66. Feljegyzés Fehér Lajos elvtárs részére a nagykőrösi szövetkezeti napról. 1958. szeptember 22. [Ferenc Erdei's memo to Lajos Fehér on the collective farm day in Nagykőrös] MNL OL, M–KS 288. f., 28. cs., (1958) 14. ő. e.

67. Ibid.

68. Jegyzőkönyv az MSZMP Politikai Bizottság 1958. szeptember 23-i üléséről. [Minutes of the HSWP Politburo, September 23, 1958] MNL OL, M–KS 288. f., 5. cs., 95–96. ő. e.

69. Magdolna Baráth, ed., *Szovjet diplomáciai jelentések Magyarországról a Hruscsov-korszakban* [Reports of the Soviet diplomacy on Hungary during the Khruschev-era] (Budapest: Napvilág–Politikatörténeti Intézet, 2012), 119.

70. Ibid., 120.

71. For more on the conflict between the two orientations see: Sipos, *Reform* és *megtorpanás*, 188–97.

72. *A termelőszövetkezetek megszilárdításáért és fejlesztéséért: Részletes magyarázat a Magyar Forradalmi Munkás-Paraszt Kormány 3004/1958. sz. határozatához* [Strengthening and further boosting the collective farms: A detailed explanation on the governmental decree no. 3004/1958] (Budapest: Kossuth, 1958).

73. They hoped to make the payment of land rent compulsory based on the Bulgarian model. Developments in Czechoslovak collectivization convinced the Hungarians

that it was not worth pushing for the highest order of collective farms in areas with poor quality land, or mountainous areas.

74. Jelentés a Szovjetunióban járt pártmunkás küldöttség tapasztalatairól. [Report on the experience gathered by the party delegation during their trip to the Soviet Union] MNL OL, M–KS 288. f., 21. cs., (1959) 28. ő. e.

75. Jelentés a SZÖVOSZ delegáció kínai útjáról, 1958. március. [Report on the trip of the delegation of the National Association of Cooperatives to China, March 1958] MNL OL, M–KS 288. f., 32. cs., (1958) 15. ő. e.

76. The ambassador's notes recorded Kádár's text as follows: "Comrade Fehér (member of the Political Committee, director of the Central Committee Agricultural Department) is unnecessarily cautious, indecisive, and even fearful of the execution of restructuring, which from time to time can lead to diversions from the party's general orientation. Dögei (Central Committee member, Minister of Agriculture) has many leftist leanings. In his words everything is revolutionary, but in terms of acts his Ministry does bad work and appears fully irresponsible. We have to put an end to this situation, we have to end the incomprehensible debate between Fehér and Dögei, we have to work out solid and precise commands and publish them, on how to move the issue of the collectivization of our agriculture forward." Baráth, *Szovjet diplomáciai jelentések*, 122.

77. Ibid., 122.

78. Jegyzőkönyv az MSZMP Központi Bizottság 1958. december 5–7-i üléséről. [Minutes of the HSWP Central Committee, December 5–7, 1958] MNL OL, M–KS 288. f., 4. cs., 20–21. ő. e.

79. Tibor Huszár, *Kádár János politikai életrajza* [Political biography of János Kádár], vol. 2 (Budapest: Szabad Tér–Kossuth, 2003), 134.

80. Jegyzőkönyv az MSZMP Központi Bizottság 1958 december 5–7-i üléséről. [Minutes of the HSWP Central Committee, December 5–7, 1958] MNL OL, M–KS 288. f. 4. cs. 20–21. ő. e.

81. "A parasztokkal együtt, egy akarattal. Kádár János elvtárs nyilatkozata a termelőszövetkezeti mozgalom néhány kérdéséről" [Together with the peasants, in agreement. A statement of János Kádár on certain questions of the collective farm movement], *Szabad Föld*, April 12, 1959.

82. The numbers were as follows: Between January 31, and March 31, 1959, the number of members grew by close to 316,000 persons, while the total of joint land increased by 1.2 million hectares. Központi Statisztikai Hivatal, *Mezőgazdaságunk a szocialista* átszervezés *idején, 1958–1962* [Our Agriculture in the Time of Socialist Reorganization, 1958–1962] (Budapest: KSH, 1963), 151, 173.

83. A Központi Bizottság 1958. decemberi határozatának végrehajtása a megyékben. [Implementation of the "December resolution" of the HSWP Central Committee in the counties] MNL OL, M–KS 288. f., 28. cs., (1959) 3. ő. e.

84. Author's interview with L. Sz., July 25, 2004. (Author's files.)

85. See more on this Mark Pittaway, *The workers' state: industrial labor and the making of socialist Hungary, 1944–1958* (Pittsburgh: University of Pittsburgh Press, 2012).

86. *Mezőgazdaságunk a szocialista átszervezés idején, 1958–1962*, 147.

87. Three-quarters of the total of collective farm land was in private hands, and one-quarter was state land. *Mezőgazdaságunk a szocialista átszervezés idején,* 45.

88. The level of the land rent (annuity) was defined as follows in the Minister of Agriculture's decree no. 19/1959 (VII. 12.): "The level of land rent is established by the general meeting of the collective farm, uniformly in monetary terms at the annual closing of accounts; its lower limit is the forint equivalent of the state purchase price of 5 kg of wheat as established in the decree for every gold crown of cadastral net income of own land in communal use; its maximum limit is the forint value of 10 kg of wheat." At the same the regulation established "the total sum payable as land rent cannot exceed 25 per cent of the share divided among the members in proportion to the land they contributed to the cooperative." *A mezőgazdasági termelőszövetkezetekre vonatkozó jogszabályok: 1958. január 1.–1959. május 31.* [Legal regulation of collective farms: January 1, 1958–May 31, 1959] (Budapest: KJK, 1959), 22.

89. On the situation between the two World Wars: Monika Kozári, *A nyugdíjrendszer Magyarországon Mária Teréziától a második világháborúig* [The pension system in Hungary from Maria Theresia to the World War II] (Budapest: Gondolat, 2012), 319–31; Béla Tomka, *Welfare in East and West: Hungarian Social Security in an International Comparison 1918–1990* (Berlin: Akademie Verlag, 2004).

90. Ferenc Virágh, "A mezőgazdasági termelőszövetkezeti tagság szociális ellátása" [The social insurance of the collective farm membership], in *Tanulmányok a szocialista mezőgazdaság kialakulásáról* [Studies on the rise of the socialist agriculture], eds. Sándor Orbán and Ferenc Pölöskei (Budapest: MSZMP KB Társadalomtudományi Intézete–ELTE BTK, 1988), 453–506.

91. Also see: Ferenc Kunszabó, *Elnöktípusok a termelőszövetkezetekben* [The types of the presidents on the collective farms] (Budapest: Akadémiai, 1974); Swain, *Collective Farms*, 114–32.

92. § 11 pt. 2 of Act number 7 of 1959 read as follows: "Collective farm members who were earlier an exploiter can only be elected to an office, or retain their office, if they have proven at least two continuous years of exemplary work in the producer cooperative deserving the respect of the membership. Exceptions to this rule can be authorized in some cases by the president of the county council executive committee." *A mezőgazdasági termelőszövetkezetekre vonatkozó jogszabályok*, 8.

93. Jegyzőkönyv az MSZMP Politikai Bizottság 1959. szeptember 15-i üléséről. [Minutes of the HSWP Politburo, September 15, 1959] MNL OL, M–KS 288. f., 5. cs., 149. ő. e.

94. Jelentés a tsz-ek ellen irányuló ellenséges tevékenységről. [State-security summary report on anti-cooperative activities] November 19, 1959. ÁBTL, 1.6. 67–2782/1959.

95. Author's interview with Mrs. L. F. January 23, 2002. (Author's files.)

96. Jegyzőkönyv az MSZMP Politikai Bizottság 1959. október 6-i üléséről. [Minutes of the HSWP Politburo, October 6, 1959] MNL OL, M–KS 288. f., 5. cs., 151. ő. e.

97. Jelentés a tsz-ek ellen irányuló ellenséges tevékenység tapasztalatairól. [State-security summary report on anti-cooperative activities] February 11, 1960. ÁBTL, 1.6. sz. n.

98. A Legfőbb Ügyészség összefoglaló jelentése a termelőszövetkezetek törvényes és alapszabályszerű működésének, valamit a termelőszövetkezeti mozgalom ellen irányuló bűncselekmények felderítési, nyomozási, vádemelési, ítélkezési gyakorlatának vizsgálatáról. [Summary report by the Public Prosecutor's Office on the investigation on the lawful functioning of cooperatives in accordance with the statutory rules as well as on the discovery, investigative, prosecuting and judgmental practice of anti-cooperative crimes] July 2, 1960. MNL OL, M–KS 288. f., 28. cs., (1960) 22. ő. e.

99. Farkas, *Lázadó falvak*, 239–84.

100. Considering the chaotic conditions in stock-farming (lack of space and fodder, etc.) it is no wonder that 1960 saw significant livestock deaths. Compared to the first six months of 1959, the number of perished animals grew 2.5-fold, which means 400,000 animals. In horse- and pig-stock, the increase was threefold. Előterjesztés az MSZMP Államgazdasági Bizottsága részére a sertés és szarvasmarha-tenyésztés és árutermelés helyzetéről, valamint a szükséges intézkedésekről. [Submission to the HSWP Economic Committee on the situation of pig- and cattle-breeding and produce as well as the measures required] MNL OL, M–KS 288. f., 28. cs., (1960) 25. ő. e.

101. In 1959 mostly county and district level delegations visited Czechoslovakia. Reading the travel reports it is clear that most information was gathered in the area of material incentives. *Delegációkkal kapcsolatos anyagok.* [Materials related to the delegations' reports] MNL OL, M–KS 288. f., 21. cs., (1959) 28. ő. e.

102. Nagy, *A magyar külpolitika, 1956–1989*, 35–39.

103. Jegyzőkönyv az MSZMP Központi Bizottság 1960. február 12-i üléséről. [Minutes of the HSWP Central Committee session, February 12, 1960] MNL OL, M–KS 288. f., 4. cs., 29. ő. e.

104. Ibid.

105. In the years 1934–38 on average the surplus for export was more than half a million metric tons. Under collectivization, however, grain imports had to be increased despite decreasing consumption. Between 1959 and 1962 on average 227,000 metric tons of bread grain had to be imported annually. See: Honvári, *XX. századi magyar gazdaságtörténet*, 290–300.

106. Jegyzőkönyv az MSZMP Politikai Bizottság 1960. február 16-ai üléséről. [Minutes of the HSWP Politburo, February 12, 1960] MNL OL, M–KS 288. f., 5. cs., 170. ő. e.

107. For more on the practice of incentives for collective farms, see: Varga, *Politika, paraszti érdekérvényesítés*, 51–57.

108. Jegyzőkönyv az MSZMP Politikai Bizottság 1960. február 16-i üléséről. [Minutes of the HSWP Politburo, February 12, 1960] MNL OL, M–KS 288. f., 5. cs., 170. ő. e.

109. Ibid.

110. For more on the background of the cabinet reshuffle see: Huszár, *Kádár János*, vol. 2, 128–40.

111. Csaba Kovács, "Panaszok a kollektivizálás befejező hullámának időszakából: az egyéni és a szövetkezeti gazdálkodás problémáinak sajátosságai" [Complaints from the final phase of the collectivization], Múltunk 58, no. 3 (2013), 207–51.

112. The decrease was visible mostly in income from collective farming itself. Household farms played a stabilizing, income-supplementing role, which is illustrated in the fact that between 1960 and 1963 over half of collective income came from this sector. *Mezőgazdaságunk a szocialista átszervezés idején*, 202.

113. Központi Statisztikai Hivatal, *Mezőgazdasági statisztikai zsebkönyv* (Budapest: KSH, 1967), 247.

114. "Over the winter there developed in addition to the agricultural producer cooperatives, producer cooperative groups, specialist groups, specialist cooperatives, producer associations and mountain communities. Currently producer cooperative groups are in operation, of which 291 were established over the winter. The number of specialist groups and other lower forms of cooperative is 168, of which 68 were founded over the winter." Az FM Szövetkezetpolitikai Főosztály jelentése az FM Kollégiumához a termelőszövetkezeti mozgalom és megszilárdítás helyzetéről. 1961. március 10. [Report of the Collective Farm Policy Department to the Ministry of Agriculture steering committee on the situation of collective farms, March 10, 1961] MNL OL, M–KS 288. f., 28. cs., (1961) 5. ő. e.

115. Hann, *Tázlár*, 84–98.

116. Jelentés az MSZMP KB október 29-i határozatának végrehajtása során tapasztalt ellenséges tevékenységről, megnyilvánulásról. 1961. január 30. [State-security report on oppositional activities since the October 29, 1960 HSWP Central Committee resolution. January 30, 1961] ÁBTL, 1.6. 67–312/1961.

117. A Mezőgazdasági Osztály jelentése a PB számára a tsz-ek zárszámadásáról. 1961. április 15. [Report of the Agricultural Department to the HSWP Politburo on the year-end accounts of the collective farms] MN OL, M–KS 288. f., 28. cs., (1961) 6. ő. e.

118. Vass and Ságvári, Az MSZMP határozatai és dokumentumai, 497.

Chapter Five

Convergence or Divergence?

MEMBERS ON PAPER BUT NOT IN SPIRIT

The final collectivization campaign brought a major turnaround, which is well reflected in the following data: in 1961, 271 state farms, approximately 4,200 producer cooperatives and close to 165,000 individual farms operated in Hungary. At the beginning of the collectivization campaign, in the winter of 1958/1959, a total of 13% of the country's arable land was used by producer cooperatives: by the end of March, 1961, it was already almost 70%. Parallel to this, the number of cooperative members rose from 169,000 to 1.2 million; therefore, while at the beginning of the restructuring, 80% of those making a living from agriculture worked in the private economy, by the end of the campaign, 75% were already active in producer cooperatives.[1] Formally, therefore, collectivization had been a success; yet, even as the restructuring was taking place, and also after it, severe problems emerged. Restructuring meant that agriculture's need for equipment increased substantially. Despite agriculture receiving ever more investment, it was to little avail: for a decade, the majority of investment resources served to substitute for the small-scale farms that had fallen out of production.[2] At the same time, the higher operating costs of the newly formed large-scale units had to be ensured.

Another group of problems arose from the fact that the nearly complete destruction of individual farming did not mean that the majority of peasants had accepted producer cooperatives.[3] The rejection behavior of earlier years did not end when intention-to-join documents were signed. Alongside out-migration and commuting, there were examples of every form of passive opposition that can be observed anywhere in the world where subjugated labor hopes to improve its situation.

Over the period of restructuring, the number of agricultural earners decreased by 350,000. The effect of this was an unfavorable development in the age and gender composition of the producer cooperative. In 1958, more than half of the members were still under 40, by contrast, at the end of 1961, three-quarters of the membership was older than 40, indeed, 36% was over 60. It is no surprise, then, that while the average age of producer cooperative members in 1958 was 41, by 1961 it was already 52. Since the majority of earners leaving agriculture were men, the proportion of women among agricultural earners also increased at the time of restructuring: from 26% in 1958 to 38% at the end of 1961.[4]

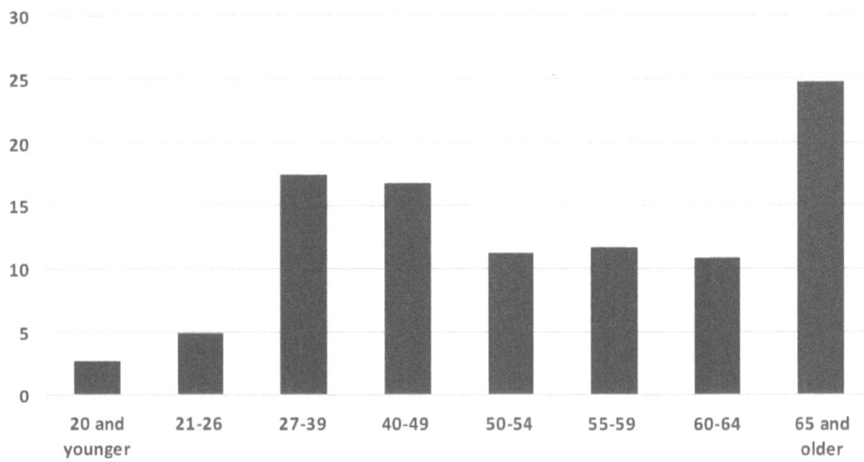

Figure 5.1. Distribution of Cooperative Members by Age (1961). Source: Oros, *A falu és a mezőgazdaság*, 276.

Mechanization could not replace in a couple of years the labor force of many hundreds of thousands that left agriculture.[5] There was a further problem, namely that, contrary to prior expectations, producer cooperative members did not feel a moral obligation to work on communal farms with the care of the good farmer. Quite the reverse happened: in many places the women and elderly who stayed in producer cooperatives only worked on the communal farm for the minimum number of work units required to have the right to a household plot. They focused their concentration to the maximum extent on the household plot, rightly feeling that this was the only sphere in the producer cooperative where there was a direct relationship between labor invested and income derived. They hoped that their plots would compensate to a degree the meager income that could be derived from communal work.

Table 5.1. The Average Annual Income of Producer Cooperative Families 1958–66

	Communal	*Household plot*	
	Income within the cooperative		*Total cooperative income*
1958	11,870	9,000	20,870
1959	11,400	9,200	20,600
1960	8,400	8,600	17,000
1961	7,800	9,300	17,100
1962	9,000	9,600	18,600
1963	10,000	10,100	20,100
1964	10,400	11,430	21,830
1965	10,600	10,300	20,900
1966	12,300	12,600	24,900

Source: Oros, *A falu és a mezőgazdaság*, 273.

They were at pains to, first, use more land than was permitted for their household plot, second, prioritize household plot work over current work for the communal economy, and third, transfer to their household plots, goods, such as fodder, from the communal economy. This euphemistic formulation meant theft pure and simple.[6]

Contemporary producer cooperative and party documents bear witness to massive occurrences of these forms of peasant resistance; weak labor discipline and passive behavior on the part of members is their constant theme. A few indicative examples: "A significant portion of the membership displays a lack of participation towards collective work." "Unfortunately, not every member comes to work regularly." "A part of the members was absent from communal work for longer than is justified, because of individual work." It became a common occurrence for brigade leaders to run from house to house every morning to gather the members together for the work of the day, otherwise work started late, because the brigade members waited for everyone to arrive. The members would not even hear of carrying out urgent fieldwork on a Sunday. The quality of work performed left a lot to be desired: "they put black onto green," that is to say, they did not hoe properly, and so weeds often grew higher than the planted crop. Problems did not only occur with crop care but also harvest. Produce was not harvested in time, because, for example, "there were members who prioritized their own grape harvest," or "harvesting the household plot, over lifting communal sugar beet."[7] This situation was aptly characterized by a district council leader: "When the agitators were here, fellow members joined the producer cooperative all right, but they left their hearts outside, and this can generally be seen in their work."[8]

These phenomena were reflected at the national level too, in statistics, which show that a considerable portion of registered members (20–25%)

Table 5.2. The Participation of Cooperative Members in Communal Labor (%) 1958–62

	1958	*1959*	*1960*	*1961*	*1962*
Executing no work units	3	20.6	21.3	21.4	20.3
Executing 1–150 work units	21	22.3	25.3	27.4	26.7
Executing 151–350 work units	42.7	23.1	28.8	26.9	27.4
Executing more than 350 work units	33.3	34	24.6	24.3	25.6

Source: Központi Statisztikai Hivatal, *Mezőgazdasági statisztikai zsebkönyv* [Agricultural statistical pocketbook] (Budapest: KSH, 1966), 246.

either did not work at all or did not work satisfactorily on the communal farm. This is supported by the fact that the average quantity of work performed on the communal farm fell from year to year. The number of work units per producer cooperative family in 1958 was 390, then 301 in 1959 and 169 in 1960.[9] The number of family members participating also fell short of expectations.

To anyone familiar with traditional peasant labor morale, sight of the statistical indicators in the above table would come as a shock. Labor discipline issues were previously unknown in Hungarian agriculture. Individual peasant farms operated as well-adapted and disciplined labor organizations, because peasant families that did not work with the uttermost strength and discipline would soon fall behind in the ceaseless struggle to survive.[10] Furthermore, farmers were respected in the village not only on the basis of how much land they had, but also on their industry and conscientiousness as farmers. Reading the documents cited here gives us the sense that the Hungarian peasant's well-known discipline and love of work had died out in one or two years. The reality though was that, in the spirit of passive resistance and waiting to see what happened, they divided their efforts between their household plots and communal farming. They developed a "dual labor morale," and one in which they learned to "work badly" in communal farming.

The overwhelming majority of producer cooperatives struggled with start-up difficulties, with shortages of equipment, labor, and willingness to work, and with dissatisfaction; and so, for years, they could not justify the expectations of those in power in respect of the advantages of large-scale farming. In the first half of the 1960s, the level of agricultural production only just reached the average for 1958–59. During collectivization, the country's animal stock had fallen dramatically, with the exception of sheep, and its quality had declined, occasioning supply problems which lasted for years.[11]

In these circumstances, there was an ever-growing need to import foodstuffs if the welfare pact of the Kádár group was to be assured. There is, for example, among Deputy Prime Minister Antal Apró's files, a separate dossier

Table 5.3. The Soviet Union's Grain Exports to Hungary (Thousands of Metric Tons)

	1953	*1957*	*1958*	*1959*	*1960*	*1961*	*1962*
Total	120	436	152	224	195	416	294
Wheat	20	301	80	224	195	386	40

Source: Az SZKP Központi Bizottság levele az MSZZMP Központi Bizottságának kenyérgabona-ügyben. 1964. február 5. [A letter from the Central Committee of the CPSU to the Central Committee of the HSWP in the matter of grain export, February 5, 1964] MNL OL, M–KS 288. f., 23. cs., (1964) 2. ő. e.

of "bread grain letters," in which the Hungarian government asked the Soviet Union for help.[12]

What is more, it proved impossible to fulfill the agricultural export plan, even though agricultural exports might have played a serious role in hard currency acquisition, and thus maintaining the balance of payments.[13] This led to the question: how can an increase in production be ensured that at least makes the country self-sufficient again? How can collective farms be made to work? Should producer cooperatives be pushed back into the contours of the kolkhoz model, or should space be given for local initiatives?

KHRUSHCHEV'S AGRICULTURAL REFORMS

The dilemmas of the Hungarian leadership were aggravated all the more by the fact that in the Soviet Union at this time, Khrushchev was initiating ever-newer agricultural reforms. He addressed two pillars of the Stalinist system in addition to the virgin lands program mentioned above. Over 1958, the machine and tractor station system began to be dismantled, and the machines were bought by the kolkhozes. This represented a significant financial burden for them, but it improved their level of mechanization. According to the original plan, the restructuring of machine and tractor stations was to have taken place over many years; however, a substantial proportion of kolkhozes—responding to pressure from above—undertook to pay the full price for the machinery in a single year rather than in installments over three to five years. Thanks to this, the majority of kolkhozes were obliged to give up on all other plans for years, in fact they even had to reduce salaries.[14]

At the same time, the compulsory delivery and price systems were restructured by the decrees of June 18 and 30, 1958.[15] Compulsory deliveries were abolished and various other types of deliveries united. The latter were classified henceforth as state purchase. Of course, the purchase quotas remained just as compulsory as the deliveries had been previously.[16]

Khrushchev's belief that large-scale farms would achieve the monumental production goals set before them was so great that he did not even take small-scale farming on household plots into account, in fact a series of measures restricted this sector.[17] On the one hand, citing various administrative factors, the permitted area of household plots was decreased, on the other, limits were placed on the amount of fodder given to kolkhoz members as an element of payment in kind. After 1957, similar measures were implemented throughout the country, the effect of which was that, by 1959–60, household plot production began to stagnate. This had a negative effect on the living standards not only of kolkhoz and sovkhoz workers, but also of rural commuting workers, many of whom were also engaged in small-scale production.[18]

Restrictions on household plot farming also had negative consequences for the socialized sector: labor morale decreased, as did food supplies for the urban population via kolkhoz markets. It also had an impact on livestock production, because a form of cooperation had previously evolved between household plots and kolkhozes. Kolkhoz members reared young livestock on their household plots, which were then sold by the kolkhoz, or sold to state purchasing companies or cooperatives. This was a way of making use of the marginal labor time of many family members (such as wives, the elderly, and the young) whose labor power could not otherwise be accessed by the kolkhoz.[19]

The situation was worsened even further by the fact that, in 1959–60, a campaign was launched to turn kolkhozes into sovkhozes in the spirit of the long-emphasized ideological tenet regarding the superior status of state property.[20]

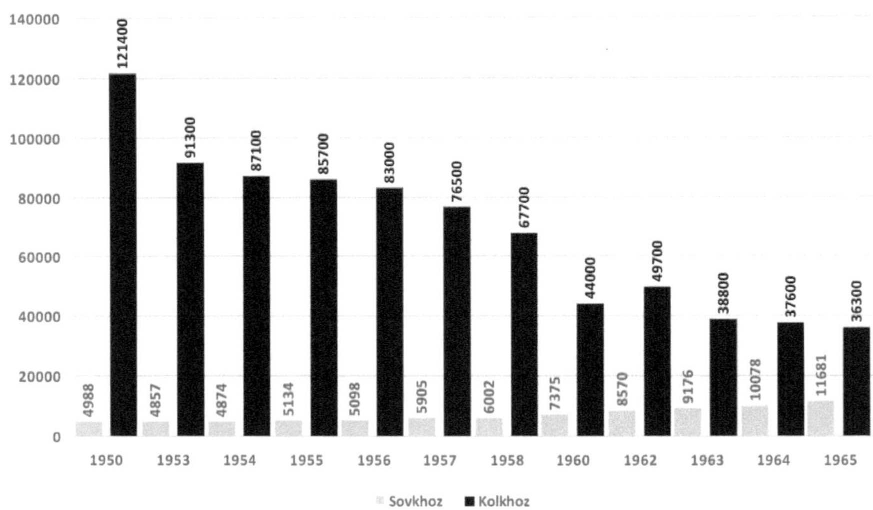

Figure 5.2. Number of Sovkhoz and Kolkhoz 1950–1965. Source: Ciepielewski, *A Szovjetunió gazdaságtörténete*, 279.

Meanwhile, a forceful increase in production remained a priority, especially as the party program had just announced the project of catching up and overtaking the USA.

> The CPSU has set the task in the next 20 years of raising people's living standards to a level higher than that of any capitalist country. . . . Situations whereby citizens suffer shortage of any kind will, for the first time in history, completely and permanently cease. . . . The Party has set out as its task in the next ten years the development of our homeland as the world's foremost industrial power, to surpass the United States both in terms of the absolute measure of industrial production and industrial production per capita. . . . But this is merely the first step, we will not stop here. In the second decade—up to 1980—our homeland will leave the United States of America far behind in terms of industrial and agricultural production per capita.[21]

The results from 1961 did not vindicate this audacious plan: total agricultural production grew by a mere 2.5%, while product output increased by only 0.7%. Less meat was supplied to the population than in 1959.[22] This, however, only inspired Khrushchev to take further action. First, federal and republican ministries were reorganized, and the tasks of production planning, operational management and finance were taken from them. From then on, their sphere of authority included only the scientific administration of agriculture and administering experimentation and professional training. Throughout 1962, centrally administered kolkhoz-sovkhoz production and purchasing directorates were established, covering larger areas than in the past—usually the territory of two or three districts—which were independent of local council organizations. Production and purchase ministries were organized in the federal republics. Agricultural committees were created at both federal and republican levels in order to coordinate the work of the various organs dealing with agriculture.[23]

Czechoslovakia and the GDR implemented changes similar to those in the Soviet Union, while Romania and Bulgaria created production directorates or agricultural councils under the control of local councils. The general pattern in these countries was twofold: to bring producer cooperatives and state farms under a unitary administration, and to establish administrative units which covered larger areas than before.[24]

THE AGRARIAN LOBBY IN ACTION

Within the socialist camp, therefore, there was a wealth of examples of dealing administratively with agricultural problems from above. Lajos Fehér and his followers also planned corrections to administrative system, but they did not expect them to solve agriculture's problems. Their emphasis was on material incentives and the finance-policy and legal changes that they necessitated. In order to do this, they initiated a complex program of work on agricultural reform at the end of 1961 and beginning of 1962. Part of the agricultural reform package consisted of the elaboration of new price, tax, and financial systems, a review of the administrative structure, and drafting a new producer cooperative law. One of the important goals of the new law was to harmonize legal regulation with practice on the ground, which would strengthen further the process of distancing Hungary from the Soviet kolkhoz form.[25] Gaining political support to handle this problem was not easy, because the majority of the party leadership considered that the concessions granted during collectivization had only been a temporary measure.

The agricultural reform measures and restructurings taking place within the socialist camp were subjected to deep examination by the Hungarian Party leadership. János Kádár reported on them as follows at the February 9, 1962 Central Committee meeting:

> We can see the various experiences of fraternal Parties, and, without gloating, we have to see and know, and be pleased, that we did not get into a mess like the Bulgarian comrades. . . . And the problems were no fewer in the GDR, or for the Czechs. . . . *The experiences of the Soviet Union are much more positive than those of other fraternal parties, but the biggest problem is that we can use so few of them in our conditions, because the conditions are completely different, comrades.*[26] [Author's emphasis]

This decision represented an important crossroads in the formation of the HSWP's agrarian policy. Not only because it spared the Hungarian agrarian world the sort of unsuccessful administrative reorganization that took place in the majority of socialist countries and also in Hungarian industry at around this time, but also because it created a chance for handling problems according to Hungarian conditions.

The reform package put together by the agrarian lobby was on the agenda of a Central Committee session at the end of March 1962.[27] Lajos Fehér tried to get everyone battle-ready before the Central Committee session. He even brought in Ferenc Erdei, who participated as a guest and representative of scientific research. It is instructive to quote how, and using what arguments, Erdei entered the debate:

> There are many questions that the cooperatives have solved for themselves, in areas such as organizational structure, work organization, income distribution and management. It is especially interesting that, in recent years, producer cooperatives have made progress in this area without really any direct instructions.

> Model charter and the act that regulated them have, by and large, become outdated, yet the official organs did not prescribe any mandatory methods. I think it is correct that things happened this way, because it facilitated the evolution of appropriate relations within changing conditions. What is more, regarding the question of remuneration, producer cooperatives received reassurance, from all organs beginning with the Central Committee, to find the best solution appropriate to their conditions. This was facilitated by the widespread diffusion of very many original, interesting, successful and proven management, organizational and payment solutions in our cooperatives. These are well known, and cooperatives learn from them . . . in many cases they developed original and interesting solutions that were even interesting theoretically. There is in fact much more interest in them than in the entire literature on the subject, because research and literature on this topic is just beginning.[28]

The decree accepted at the Central Committee session gave the green light to work on a new producer cooperative law, but it was clear at the same time that elaborating it would take a year and a half. As a consequence, the first third of the 1960s was a period when, because cooperative regulation still conformed to Stalinist norms, measures designed to promote incentives for the membership counted as illegal. In these circumstances, much depended on the readiness of local party and state organs to make concessions. But the vast majority of the HSWP apparatus was made up of former HWP members, many of whom stuck to the dogmatic tenets of the 1950s,[29] such as, for example, that the dominant form of socialist labor organization in producer cooperatives was the brigade, while that of socialist distribution was the work unit. These forms were identified with socialism itself, that is to say, they did not recognize the right of any solutions other than these to exist. Because of this type of dogmatism, in many places the party and council leaders adopted the position that "everything is banned that is not expressly permitted," and, with this as their starting point, endeavored to force producer cooperatives back into the framework of mandatory model rules based on the Soviet model statute. At the same time, the leaders of the agrarian lobby represented the position that, "what is not expressly banned, is permitted."

Research for this book has revealed very wide differences in the implementation of agrarian policy, not just between counties, but also between districts. This confirms Tibor Huszár's findings concerning the spatial distribution of the Kádár-era nomenclature. The agrarian lobby tried a variety of ways to get around this problem. For example, it subjected local party and council organs to intensive "enlightening" in the form of dedicated conferences and study courses.

> One of the most important tasks of our Party is to teach local leaders how to lead in a communist manner. The most valuable characteristic of a communist leader

> is never losing sight of the noble goal of building socialism and communism, always starting from things as they are, and, having analyzed them, drawing conclusions about what to do . . . not holding what has emerged, current relations to be valid for ever. . . . Replacing outdated methods and organizational frameworks that hold back development with new methods and progressive forms. . . .[30]

In addition to special courses, an important role also devolved to the press in the domain of "reorienting" the local apparatus. The national leaders of the agrarian lobby regularly published articles in which they called attention to supporting incentive solutions that had become accepted in producer cooperative practice. A series of articles published in the party's official daily *Népszabadság* starting in March, 1961, titled *Ezer tsz-elnök véleménye* [The opinions of one thousand producer cooperative presidents] was of symbolic significance.

The following article appeared in the party's theoretical journal *Társadalmi Szemle* [Social Review] at the beginning of 1961. The author was the head of the Agricultural Cooperative Policy Department in the Ministry of Agriculture.

> The task of our producer cooperative leaders and Party organizations is to . . . defeat the narrow-mindedness that can be met in more than one place, a narrow-mindedness that is fearful of exposing socialism to these solutions, and, for this reason, shuts itself off from them, or forbids their use. It is not difficult to decide what serves socialism: is it to ignore the slow pace of change in the way that the new producer cooperative peasantry thinks, and to encourage measures which do not motivate it sufficiently to communal work, which results in parts of production being lost and damage to the people's economy and the producer cooperative membership; or, by contrast, if we avoid all this, to accelerate development?[31]

Half a year later, Gáspár Nádas, a staff member at the Central Committee Agricultural Department, argued in the journal *Pártélet* [Party Life] in favor of the need for a new way of handling the problem as follows.

> Material incentives are an important motive force in socialist industry too, where the socialist consciousness of the workers is higher than in producer cooperatives. There is even more need for material incentives in producer cooperatives, because people only broke free from small-plot farming a short time ago, and there the only motive for production is individual material interest. Properly used material incentives do not contradict the principle of socialist distribution. . . .[32]

In this field too, Lajos Fehér leaned to a great extent on Ferenc Erdei, who was widely known to be a good speaker as well as a good writer. He also had another special skill, one that Pál Romány recalled: "Erdei had a special magic which he could use to activate people, to get them to join up to things. It should also be emphasized that while he could be simple, he could exchange words too with the greatest expert authorities."[33] It is no accident that from the beginning of the 1960s, Erdei's annual lectures at the National Association of Hungarian Journalists became regular events, at which he informed participants of current questions of agrarian policy.[34]

At the same time, attempts to embolden the producer cooperatives continued, partly in the press and partly on the radio. Reports from producer cooperatives regularly appeared in *Népszabadság*, and in them, journalists—István Almási, Ferenc Cserkúti, Benedek Tóth—often notified readers of locally adopted initiatives to promote incentives. In 1961, these were summarized in a brochure, which *Népszabadság* published as part of its Producer Cooperative Advisor series. Village Radio also called the attention of its listeners to the publication.[35] The program promoting better methods of corn farming in the Village Radio also played an important role in broadcasting the views of the agrarian lobby. The focus in the third week of March 1961, for example, was on the following message:

> Even now, our experience is that in many places, cooperative leaders are not trying hard enough to increase household plot commodity production at the same time as strengthening the communal farm as quickly as possible. It is sometimes the case they are not even aware of official actions launched in this respect. Yet it is a peremptory requirement of the interests of the people's economy that, from the point of view of commodity production, every cooperative leader consider the communal farm and household plots as a unified whole.[36]

Throughout 1961, many solutions were formulated in the areas of remuneration and household plot farming. At the end of the year, the Ministry of Agriculture and the editors of *Népszabadság* jointly organized a conference on the experiences that had emerged in practice.[37] It emerged from the speeches of the invited cooperative leaders and agrarian experts, that 1961 was felt to be a significant turning point, because by that time more than 80% of cooperatives used bonus systems based on plan-fulfillment. This was explained by the fact that the Minister of Agriculture had made public his suggestions for forms of producer cooperative income distribution and remuneration at the beginning of the year,[38] suggestions which offered concrete remuneration and work-organization solutions that, though not defined in statute, could be used in practice from then on. The conference covered problems as well as positive results. The biggest difficulty was caused by the "opposition" of local administrative organs.[39] The speeches were replete with sharp judgment and condemnation as it was to be expected that the sources of these conflicts would have to be taken into account over the course of 1962 too. The following section of a speech by a leader of the Ministry of Agriculture's Cooperative Policy Department gives a sense of them.

> In many counties and districts a certain inflexibility and incorrect position could be experienced in relation to the forms of income distribution and bonus systems proposed by the Ministry of Agriculture. In many cases, the district and county organs obstructed the use of the best solutions by the producer cooperatives . . . in the future we cannot allow various organs to ignore the proposals of the Ministry and obstruct producer cooperatives in their choice of forms of remuneration and bonus that are most appropriate to their circumstances.[40]

Forceful criticism was directed at party organizations as well as council organs of agrarian management. This is reflected in the lecture that Lajos Fehér's gave at the HSWP Political Academy on December 20, 1961.

> Initiatives with regard to the further development of income distribution on producer cooperatives warrant close attention and deep study on the part of party organs. They should promote the fastest possible dispersal of forms of income distribution that conform to socialist principles and better reflect material incentives. . . . We must stand against inflexibility, ignorance and all endeavors too that fear for the "prestige" of the work unit because of these incentives systems, against conservatism that hinders the dispersal of the correct methods for further developing the work unit system.[41]

The leaders of the agrarian lobby often traveled to the countryside to discuss the experiences of 1961 with those involved and used this as a foundation for working out proposals for 1962.[42] An intensive exchange of information and experience between the country's national and local actors became a permanent feature of those years. Pál Losonczi and István Dobi fulfilled important roles in this respect, in addition to Ferenc Erdei and Lajos Fehér.[43] They had different pasts, which meant they could each make connections with different groups. They were able to call upon cooperative and state farm leaders from Peasant Party or even Smallholder Party backgrounds, as easily as alumni from the people's colleges who had entered various posts in the district and party apparatus, yet they could also communicate with producer cooperative presidents from former "bare-foot," poor peasant stock.

Year after year, ever more local initiatives moved from being "prohibited" or "tolerated" to being "supported" as a result of this unique dialogue, and, with this, there was a constant expansion in producer cooperative room for maneuver.[44] All of this represented an important message for those who had been forced into producer cooperatives in the final phase of collectivization. A situation had developed in which producer cooperatives made ever more widespread use of forms of remuneration that were acceptable to the membership because it could predict how much income it would get from what sort of work. Cooperative life therefore became more predictable than before, and the stabilization of the situation of household plots contributed to this. The agrarian lobby hoped that these incentive-based solutions could reduce the numbers leaving collective farms. And that is what happened.[45]

Table 5.4. Change in the Number of Active Earners in Agriculture 1961–65

Year	*Active earners in agriculture*	*Change in number of active earners in agriculture over the given year*
1961	1,779.000	–81,000
1962	1,697.000	–68,000
1963	1,629.000	–85,000
1964	1,544.000	–33,000
1965	1,511.000	–13,000

Source: Mezőgazdasági statisztikai zsebkönyv, 1966, 248.

But at the same time, the effectiveness of these local initiatives was limited because the legal and economic environment of producer cooperatives still conformed to the Soviet model. The far-reaching reform operations launched at the end of 1961 and beginning of 1962 sought to remedy every aspect of this very problem.

The Institute of Agrarian Economics led by Erdei, involved itself in the reforms, first by preparing expert background materials on restructuring the state administration of producer cooperatives.[46] The increased weight and influence of the institute is well reflected in the fact that the Agrarian Work Science Research Institute under the direction of the Ministry of Agriculture was merged into it. The name of unified institute remained the Institute of Agrarian Economics, but its supervisory body became the Ministry of Agriculture rather than the Academy of Sciences. The reflections of Erdei's close colleague Gyula Varga reveal much about the atmosphere in the institute at the time:

> The AKI was unique in terms of its staff too. . . . In the AKI there were some old estate bailiffs, who represented the older generations, but there were lots of economists, the majority of whom belonged to the younger generation. It should also be said that the AKI was a kind of political refuge and a chance for a new beginning for a number of outstanding people, primarily the "fifty-sixers."[47]

It also included a former landowner and the son of a wartime prime minister.

> This "medley of approaches" greatly assisted the multifaceted work that the AKI carried out in the 1960s, and one particular characteristic of this work

> was its close cooperation with people from outside the institute. The strongest feature in maintaining these links was almost daily meetings with agricultural enterprises.[48]

The agrarian lobby's three major blocks of reform proposals had been prepared by the end of 1963.[49] But severe balance of payment problems appeared in the economy at this time: the country's debt on both capitalist and socialist accounts was growing at an accelerating pace.[50] Given these circumstances, introduction of the reform package was postponed to late 1963, early 1964.[51] Rezső Nyers also involved himself in the agricultural reform work, partly as Minister of Finance, partly as Economic Policy Secretary of the Central Committee. In an interview on precursors to the 1968 reform, he indicated that the material prepared in 1963 for the review of agricultural price, tax, and finance systems "had already addressed the questions of the economic mechanism from the agricultural perspective . . . *in essence it posed the 'age-old' mechanism question from the agrarian perspective.*"[52] [Emphasis by author.] A conception had taken shape, therefore, for positioning agriculture on a growth path by the partial rehabilitation of the market.

Work on reforms also helped consolidate the agrarian lobby's network building. It created a good opportunity for consultations with various authorities, where potential allies might be discovered. And here it was not just a question of those who linked themselves to the lobby because of their rural origins or as alumni of the people's colleges. Contacts were created on the basis of a desire to represent specific Hungarian interests. Learning from 1956, many, even in the party center and the ministries, thought that the interests of the country and the Hungarian Party should not always be subordinated to Soviet ambitions. Later, the increased expert knowledge and the professionalization of various parts of the apparatus itself created a common platform.[53]

The agrarian lobby gradually established a horizontal network of influence within the socialist economy's hierarchical structures. At its pinnacle stood the National Planning Office and it was therefore hugely significant who headed its agriculture department. Between 1955 and 1962, the department director was prominent agrarian lobby member Imre Dimény, who from 1960 was also one of its vice presidents. In 1962, he took over heading the Party Center's Agricultural Department, his successors in the Planning Office were the like-minded Vilmos Sághy, and János Hont in 1967. In the Ministry of Finance, Károly Garamvölgyi and until 1962 the minister himself, Rezső Nyers, counted as agrarian lobby allies; after 1962 Nyers could be relied upon as Secretary of the Central Committee. In the first half of the sixties the lobby included the director of the agricultural department at the Hungarian National Bank (Gyula Páles, followed by Pál Kiss); while in the National Materials and Price Office, the sympathetic Pál Vallus oversaw agricultural matters.

There were even allies in the Ministry of Heavy Industry, in the person of the former People's College student Gyula Szekér, who, as deputy minister, oversaw the chemical industry. As János Keserű recalled, ". . .agriculture at the time was well served with artificial fertilizer and pesticides by the domestic chemical industry."[54] The Central Statistical Office under the leadership of György Péter also became a valuable ally. Béla Fazekas, head of the Office's Agricultural Statistics Department and also a People's College alumnus with a past in the Peasant Party deserves special mention.[55] It would be worth examining too how the members of the lobby used hunting to strengthen and develop their network. A recent study has examined changing networks within the *Egyetértés Vadásztársaság* [Concord Hunting Society] (founded for party and state leaders) through its trophy presentations.[56] It is well known that Lajos Fehér himself was a passionate hunter, but when possible, he preferred the company of a close circle of friends over the *Egyetértés* society, whose members included many hard-liners.[57]

Another important characteristic of the network was the fact that certain members of the lobby that might be called "liaison officers" (e.g., Ernő Csizmadia, Imre Dimény, Pál Romány, János Keserű, and so on) nurtured intense contacts with representatives of scientific research, education, and the media. Cooperation with research institutes and representatives of the press and radio have been considered above, but the area of higher education deserves special attention. From the lobby's point of view this was a down-payment on their plans for the future, for a modern training system could ensure a pool of experts that could make the most of the opportunities that the lobby had fought for.

In sum, the significance of the network that came into being in the first third of the 1960s can be seen to lie in the way that it created horizontal permeability in a party-state hierarchy built on decidedly vertical relations of super- and subordination. It would be interesting to continue to examine how the members of the lobby made use of their hunting network at national and local levels to expand and potentially fortify their network.

In his position as deputy prime minister, Lajos Fehér sought to institutionalize this horizontal network of contacts. He created an advisory committee as part of this process, at which all important questions could be discussed with leaders and experts concerned.[58] The fact that he was responsible for many other areas (for example national defense, popular control, water affairs, food industry, and so on) in addition to agriculture created the official basis for this. The fact that agricultural affairs were handled by two ministries and numerous authorities indicates well how great was the need to coordinate agrarian matters. The head of the Party Center's Agricultural Department always participated in the coordination sessions, because this department represented the professional base for Fehér as deputy prime minister. The ministries of Agriculture and the Food Industry were represented either by the ministers themselves or their first deputies. Permanent participants also included the relevant department heads from the National Planning Office, the Ministry of Finance, the Ministry of Domestic Commerce, the National Material and Price Office as well as the National Bank of Hungary. Ferenc Erdei too often participated in the coordination discussions, as representative of scientific research.

BÁBOLNA: THE FIRST ATTEMPT AT MODEL TRANSFER FROM THE WEST

The problem-management activities of the agrarian lobby in the first third of the 1960s were complemented by a further important dimension, which is usually called opening to the West. Following the defeat of the 1956 revolution, the Soviet leadership had granted its Hungarian counterparts more room to maneuver in certain questions in order to ensure the superiority and viability of the socialist system,[59] and this is how the Kádár government's very rapid embrace of measures to establish contacts with the West can be explained. Hungary's relations with Western countries deteriorated following the events of 1956, yet official diplomatic isolation was not accompanied by a break in cultural and economic relations.[60] The Kádár government consciously sought to exploit these channels.

Attention should be paid to two features of how the country's "image" was constructed at the time, features which built on traditions from the Hungarian agrarian sphere which facilitated establishing contacts with Western partners. The Kádár government was quick to recognize the opportunities offered by "hunting diplomacy."[61] Hungary's game stock was famous across Europe, but earlier hunting relations had been "frozen" in the early 1950s. The Hungarian government changed this as early as 1957 by opening up the possibility of commercial hunting.[62] The fact that, for example, from 1957 an annual exhibition of trophies bagged in Hungary was organized in Cologne, West Germany bears testament to its favorable reception in the West.[63]

The other possibility for improving the country's "image" resided in "equestrian diplomacy." Hungarian equestrian sports and horse breeding had a long and successful history, and, as a result, had a wide system of international contacts. After 1956, efforts were made to bring it back to life.[64] First, spectacular horse shows were organized abroad, such as the tour organized in the Netherlands in 1958.[65] Following this, more invitations arrived, which resulted in Hungarian equestrian shows being organized in West Germany,

Denmark and Austria. Later, the emphasis shifted ever more to equestrian sports and thoroughbred sales. Dezső Fehér, who was president of the Hungarian Horse-Racing Company from 1971, played an outstanding role in the constant expansion of Western relations.[66]

As mentioned above, the Institute of Agricultural Economics led by Ferenc Erdei played a definitive role from the beginning in the dissemination of the results of Western agricultural science, also referred to as the "green revolution."[67] On the one hand, institute staff closely followed up-to-date research literature, and, when possible, took part in the work of international organizations; on the other, Erdei, as general secretary of the Hungarian Academy of Sciences, communicated information from other research institutes to the party center, primarily to Lajos Fehér. By this process, a channel was formed through which the results of scientific research reached the level of decision-makers.[68]

The information that most interested the party leadership was that which reported on methods to effect a spectacular increase in production, especially meat production, which was why most expert delegations were sent to European countries which were leaders in this field. Western experience showed that poultry and egg production had developed at an exceptionally fast pace since the Second World War. This branch of production was the first to employ "industrial" solutions by combining the results of biological and technical sciences with systems theory. As the term indicates, a closed system was created in which all factors influencing production—light, air, water supply, hygienic conditions, and so on—were regulated automatically. By regulating light and temperature, the animals' biological rhythms could be separated from the change of seasons. As a result, the branch became capable of producing mass quantities of meat year on year.

This was exactly what was needed by a Hungarian leadership that had adopted a standard-of-living policy but was confronting the production difficulties of collectivized agriculture. The political decision to initiate the poultry program, that is to say to adopt the Western model of poultry and egg production, was made, therefore, at the highest level.[69] First it had to be decided, which of the three market-leading Western firms should Hungary buy from: Canada's Shawer, Austria's Landersmann or West Germany's Lohmann.

In the end, the West German company was chosen. At the time it was not only the leading poultry and egg production and marketing company in the West Germany, but it also had a significant share in the poultry markets of other Western European countries. In May 1960, a three-person Hungarian delegation (consisting of Gyula Dabronkai, first deputy Minister of Food Industry, György Láng, executive director of Baromfiipari Tröszt [Poultry Industry Trust] and János Keserű, the deputy director of the Central Committee's Agricultural Department) visited the Lohmann company in Cuxhaven.

In the report on their study visit, much emphasis was placed on the fact that the Lohmann company not only provided chicken hybrids which were capable of exceptionally high performance, but it had also developed a complex system that stabilized the continuous utilization of that capacity.[70] The German owner told the Hungarian delegation that, after several unsuccessful attempts, he had decided to purchase patents from American companies both for producing broiler chickens and breeds of hen with high laying capacity. The patents for both breeds of animal held for the whole of Europe. The Lohmann company had thus established relations with global companies that had twenty years of experience in poultry breeding and poultry-meat and egg production by these two American contracts. One kilogram, of poultry meat could be produced from 2.30–2.50 kilograms of feed, while the egg-laying hens that they produced laid an average of 250 eggs per year.[71] The analysis of the Lohmann company continued as follows:

> With this leap the company essentially managed to surpass the results of its largest competitors in Europe, Danish and Dutch breeders. The owner is very proud of the fact that, in his opinion, he has taken a significant step forward in the interest of all of Europe, not just West Germany. In addition, he recognized that he had done good business. In his view, he had to put up a big fight against those who opposed the new activity, who opposed his initiatives in the interest of defending traditional German poultry breeds. He had also been strongly opposed by the Alliance of German Poultry Breeders. He took the position that German poultry breeding based on traditional methods was uncompetitive, as confirmed by year-on-year increases in poultry and poultry meat imports. In his account, despite the debate being exceptionally intense, he was still able to win easily. For as long as the traditional breeds of German producers reached yields of approximately 100 eggs, and 1 kilogram of poultry meat required approximately 4 kilograms of feed, his arguments (250 eggs, 2.5 kg of feed) were irrefutable.[72]

The writers of the report also stressed that the plant in Cuxhaven "has patented not only the eggs it produces, its breeders and baby chicks, but also the end product it produces, the slaughtered poultry. The price of Cuxhaven slaughtered poultry, branded "golden chicken," is 20–25% higher than that of other slaughtered poultry found on the German market, whether imported or from the domestic breeders."[73]This brand was so good that it could be sold even more expensively, making even more profit.

The delegation was authorized to purchase 2,000 to 3,000 eggs that could be used for breeding stock, or to buy baby chicks.

> We were not a little surprised when the owner announced that he had no intention, either now or in the future, of selling either day-old chicks or breeding eggs abroad. Explaining his decision, he said that he had experienced with his

> own skin the fact that these eggs and day-old chicks could not be transported without significant losses. In any case, these animals could only be reared successfully with exceptional care, with specially composed feed, in housing that had been appropriately constructed and equipped. He had sold small quantities for export before on a few occasions, mainly in order to share experiences, but had not achieved satisfactory results, and in the end he had received only was rebuke from the purchasers.[74]

Nevertheless, within a few months, the German owner was persuaded. The agreement was signed at the end of October 1960, with the condition that the Hungarian partner guarantees to use it in a consequential manner. To this end, the Lohmann company ensured not only the provision of breeding animals and complete poultry sheds but also the training in West Germany of Hungarian experts (architects, mechanical engineers, veterinarians, chemists, animal breeders, feed providers).[75]

The next step was to find an appropriate Hungarian partner farm. The choice for the site for the experimental program was Bábolna, a former royal stud-farm established in 1789.[76] At first glance, it might seem a little odd to entrust this task to a significant historical state farm, which specialized in horse breeding. Furthermore, in the chaotic conditions of the 1950s, the Bábolna State Farm had been characterized by low-level and loss-making farming.[77] Nevertheless, the decisive factor was that the old horse stables appeared to be appropriate for testing the new breeding technology.

The majority of the Bábolna management, however, considered that, after horse-breeding, it was beneath its dignity to retrain for chickens and hens.[78] It came as no surprise then that a new director was appointed to head the farm. The choice fell to Róbert Burgert.[79] In him they found a young manager, but one who already had farming experience, was brimming with ambition and the drive to prove himself, and proud of the task that the party had entrusted him with. In addition, he had been granted broad decision-making powers to achieve this task, far beyond those of other state farm directors at the time. His preferential treatment was not restricted to moral support: the farm was granted start-up capital and a relatively free hand (though not entirely free) in establishing international contacts.

Lajos Fehér was the main supporter of the poultry program within the political leadership. He also played a role in convincing the higher authorities to allocate an investment fund of 50 million HUF at the end of 1960 for the three-year program.[80] Not only this imposing investment sum, but also his authorization to import the necessary technology from the West, indicated that political support came from the highest level. Bábolna in this way was recipient of one of the state's most important concessions, because Hungary, like the other socialist countries, consistently faced a shortage of convertible currency; only truly privileged enterprises could purchase Western technology.[81]

At this time, it was exceptionally complicated to import tools and production procedures from Western companies. Resorting to semilegal methods was often the only possible way to overcome the many foreign trade monopolies, fiscal restrictions, and hard currency rules. This also turned out to be the case when the first complete Lohmann system barn was imported. The Lohmann company put a barn complex, fitted with the necessary equipment, on display at the 1962 National Agricultural Exhibition; but it was not taken home, instead it was left in Hungary for the Bábolna State Farm. János Keserű, Deputy Minister of Agriculture responsible for production affairs, took responsibility for this unusual procedure in his capacity as president of the exhibition's board.[82]

First the huge, old horse and cattle stables were restructured, then construction of the new poultry sheds began. Space had to be found for approximately 100,000–130,000 hens by 1963. The cropping structure was adjusted to fit the new profile. Only three remained of the 40 different crops grown previously: wheat, autumn barley, and corn.

The German production system strictly separated out three phases of production for both poultry meat and egg production: breeding, propagation, and production.[83] Róbert Burgert also restructured the work organization system on the farm: district management was replaced by branch management, and, further, new skills were introduced, such as, hatcher, feed mixer, poultry keeper, and so on.

Western technology also required a new kind of labor morale.[84] Creating strict labor discipline and attention to detail was not easy. Many workers were sacked, which resulted in frequent conflicts between the enterprise management and local party organs. Burgert was able to smooth over these conflicts with the help of the support he received from the highest level.[85]

The farm completed the three-year poultry program with great success. By 1963, the farm's hen breeding branch produced 18.8 million eggs and hatched 2.3 million day-old chicks. In 1963, each egg-laying hybrid laid an average of 262 eggs, with each egg requiring 192 grams of feed. A broiler chicken gained 1.31 kg in 63 days, and every kilogram, of increased weight utilized 2.79 kilograms of feed. Fifty-two percent of the farm's poultry stock was breeders, the increase in which, in 1964, resulted in a production capacity of approximately 7,710 metric tons of poultry meat and 250 million eggs. In 1963, the branch made a profit of 18,175 million HUF.[86]

By 1963, and with the help of state support, Bábolna was the first farm in Hungary and Eastern Europe to lay the foundation for industrialized poultry meat and egg production. The next step was for the Bábolna State Farm, as owner and administrator of the system, to transfer this technology of modern poultry production. The less capital-rich farms that became Bábolna's partners undertook to follow precisely the production procedures determined by the system center.

Bábolna offered its partner farms a variety of cooperation possibilities: selling partners day-old chicks and ensuring feed, maintenance system, and a market at the poultry-processing plant in Győr; selling them egg-laying hybrids; and selling them meat hybrid breeding pairs and buying back hatching eggs.[87]

Bábolna, therefore, dealt not only with breeding, but also production technology, machinery, materials, feed seed acquisition, various forms of examination, professional advice, worker training, and organizing a servicing network. The only role of the partner farms, on the other hand, was to produce commodities following the guidelines of the system owner. This division of labor proved to be mutually advantageous, and therefore quickly spread. In 1964, there were 63 partner farms, but in 1966 the number was 158, and in 1967 as many as 217.

This new, emerging horizontal integration allowed weaker, capital-poor cooperatives and state farms access to developed technology, and in a way that allowed the costs incurred by new production equipment to be covered from production costs rather than their development fund. The results of science and technology were dispersed faster than ever before, without the partner farms needing to worry about questions of technical development. It should also be noted that the partner farms shared their production experiences with the system center and in doing so helped its research work.[88]

The Bábolna program was of exceptional importance to the agrarian lobby, because it proved that Western technology could be made operable in a socialist economic environment. It is important to point out that Bábolna's example also prompted other state farms to act. In 1962, the Bóly State Farm purchased egg-laying hybrid breeding material from the Canadian competitor to Lohmann, Shaver Poultry Breeding Farms Ltd.[89] Following this the farm specialized in breeding outstanding egg-capacity Shaver hybrids. As system owner, the Bóly State Farm provided partner farms with feed supply, livestock health services and professional advice.[90]

EXPANDING INFORMAL AND FORMAL RELATIONS WITH THE WEST

The above examples draw attention to the need to rethink the periodization of various dimensions of relations across the Iron Curtain. In line with the common stance of the Socialist bloc, Hungary did not officially recognize the West German state. At the same time, Hungary's economic interests forced it to seek possibilities to normalize relations. Acquiring West German investment goods was necessary for the development of the Hungarian economy, and Hungarian agricultural goods also needed the West German consumer market. At the beginning of the 1960s, West Germany was only Hungary's fourth-largest economic partner, but it was its top capitalist partner, with a share fluctuating between 18–20%.[91]

Various West German economic groups also had an interest in expanding relations, as was reflected, for example, by the visit of Berthold Beitz, head of the Krupp company, and his delegation to Hungary between September 9 and 16, 1959.[92] This visit constituted an integral part of the Krupp company's opening to the east. Beitz visited Poland in February 1958, the Soviet Union in May 1958, and Bulgaria in December 1958. The Hungarian negotiations in 1959 brought not only economic returns, but also opened up important informal communication channels. The "hunting diplomacy" mentioned earlier created especially good possibilities in this regard.[93]

While the GDR viewed burgeoning relations between West Germany and Hungary with disapproval, and even gave voice to it, the Soviet leadership was considerably more tolerant. As mentioned above, the Soviet leadership hoped to reach the point where the fraternal countries could finally stand on their own feet, and stop expecting their "big brother" to, for example, plug the gaps in their food supply. It emphatically reminded the leaders of the socialist camp of this fact from time to time. Finally, at the beginning of 1964, the CPSU Central Committee informed all fraternal countries that, in the future, it would not be able to meet their grain needs. It is appropriate to quote a few lines from the letter.

> Weather conditions during the last two years were particularly unfavorable for agriculture in the Soviet Union. Harvests were insufficient for our needs in the cases of grains and other agricultural products. This obliged us to buy wheat from abroad, mostly from Canada and Australia and partly from the United States of America. We also bought certain amounts of grain from other capitalist countries. . . . It is well known that the Soviet Union has always supported its fraternal countries by satisfying their needs for grain, cotton and other agricultural products. In recent years, exports to Comecon countries from our grain-exporting country were considerable, as demonstrated in the following table [see table 5.5].
>
> Over just the last seven years, we have delivered 27,850 thousand tons of grain to the fraternal countries in this way, and in 1963, despite a bad production and significant difficulties related to it, we essentially fulfilled the commitments of our commercial agreements in respect of fraternal countries. At the same time, the situation that has developed forces us seriously to consider the creation

Table 5.5. The Grains and Wheat Production of the Comecon, 1953–62 (Thousand Metric Tons)

	1953	*1957*	*1958*	*1959*	*1960*	*1961*	*1962*
GDR total	924	1,861	1,747	1,689	1,848	1,787	2,186
of this wheat	301	1,095	1,298	1,366	1,489	1,227	1,251
Czechoslovakia total	875	1,632	1,176	1,829	1,661	1,176	1,451
of this wheat	504	1,298	956	1,649	1,399	768	903
Poland total	107	1,215	328	852	847	604	862
of this wheat	–	1,124	236	852	749	303	505
Hungary total	120	436	152	224	195	416	294
of this wheat	20	301	80	224	195	386	40
Bulgaria total	–	170	23	140	135	5	108
of this wheat	–	170	23	140	132	5	94
Romania total	–	508	193	–	101	–	–
of this wheat	–	456	193	–	101	–	–
Grains total	2,026	5,822	3,619	4,734	4,787	3,988	4,901
of this wheat	825	4,444	2,786	4,231	4,065	2,689	2,793

> of adequate grain reserves, and this cannot be achieved if we deliver large quantities of agricultural products abroad . . . in the next 3–4 years we cannot commit to delivering grains and animal products to the fraternal socialist countries, because we must take extremely strict measures in order to create reserves.[94]

The severity of this problem indicated by the Soviet leadership has to be understood in light of the fact that, as noted above, the CPSU had announced its program to catch up to and overtake the USA in twenty years, and this applied not only to industrial, but also agricultural production. It is precisely this that explains why Khrushchev devoted exceptional attention to stimulating agricultural production, and the great interest he showed in the results of agricultural research in both socialist and capitalist countries.[95]

Research for this book has confirmed that possibilities for the exchange of professional views already existed, even when, in official forums, Hungary's international isolation had scarcely thawed.[96] From the beginning of the sixties, an increasing number of Western European countries demonstrated a readiness to welcome Hungarian delegations visiting for business or scientific purposes.[97] The intense and wide-ranging nature of this process is well reflected in the following list. In spring 1960, a Hungarian delegation was invited to Denmark to study the food industry there. In November, Hungarian experts traveled to England to purchase cows and pigs for breeding. In the summer of 1961, a delegation visited Sweden to purchase breeder pigs. In addition to visiting numerous plants of various sizes the delegation was given the opportunity to visit some scientific research institutions (such as a station that studied weight-gain, a pig breeding supervision station, and so on). In 1961 Danish experimental and animal breeding organizations hosted a Hungarian group, and in the same year Pál Losonczi, the Minister of Agriculture, led a group of experts in a visit to Denmark. In 1961 two agricultural delegations visited neighboring Austria. One made a study of grape and fruit growing, while the other examined characteristics of the meat and poultry market. In the fall of 1961 and the summer of 1962 Hungarian experts went to Italy to study the latest results in mixed feed production. In September of 1962, Ferenc Erdei, as the president of the Scientific Council of Cooperatives, traveled to Vienna, where he was received by the Austrian Minister of Agriculture.[98]

Initially, these professional visits to Western Europe were only reported in papers that addressed professional audiences (*Baromfiipar*, *Szőlészet*, *Magyar Állatorvosok Lapja*, *Borgazdaság* [Poultry Industry, Viticulture, Paper of Hungarian Veterinarians, Wine Culture, and so on]), but they were later given wider publicity. Thanks to the activities of Pál Sárkány and Sándor Horváth, the Mezőgadasági Kiadó [Agricultural Press] took on a pioneering role in this area. In 1963, it published the first book that tried to summarize, for specialists in agriculture, "the experiences of travels to capitalist countries with high levels of production."[99] János Keserű, the deputy minister responsible for production in the Ministry of Agriculture, formulated the essence of the opening to the West in the forward to the volume.

> The book is about experiences gained in agricultural units in Western, capitalist countries! About agricultural units in capitalist countries which currently produce at a generally higher rate than here. Peaceful economic competition, which we would like to have with these countries, forces us to study deeply developed capitalist agricultural units, to get to know all those methods which can move our production forward, and which can be carried out here. If we were not to do this, we would be artificially putting a break on our own development, which would ruin our prospects in this competition. If, as a result of reading this text, we turn out a little more meat, milk, eggs, fruit or other agricultural products, then the collection and publication of the materials will have been useful, of this I am already convinced.[100]

More books followed this initiative in subsequent years.[101] One of the best West German scientists to visit Hungary was Georg Blohm, professor in agrarian economics at Kiel University. Hungarian agrarian economists had read Blohm's famous 1963 book with great interest. A review of the German language edition summarized the book's virtues as follows:

> Rarely can we read a more interesting text than Professor Blohm's recently published book. This is partly because it informs us about questions of the latest research in Western business administration, and some methodology that is

> important for us too, but partly too because we get a glimpse of the . . . current problems and expected prospects of the main branches of West German agriculture.[102]

An abridged version of the book was published in Hungary in 1967.[103]

At the same time, agricultural periodicals also regularly reported on news about capitalist agriculture. The journal *Gazdálkodás* [Farming], established by Ferenc Erdei, had three regular columns which effectively promoted the communication of up-to-date professional results and scientific debates. The column titled *Figyelő* [Observer] was devoted to longer summary reports. The column titled *Hírek* [News] gave information in short, telegramic style about conferences organized by various important international organizations (CIGR, CIOSTA, EAAE, IAAE), or the features of specific countries. It is also important to mention the column *Szakirodalom* [Specialist Literature], which is worthy of note not only for listing works that had appeared but also foreign publications that the National Agricultural Library had already translated. Copies of these could be obtained at little cost.

A further initiative to transmit international experiences was an international book show and fair organized in 1964 as part of the annually held agricultural exhibition. Reputable publishing houses from nine capitalist countries represented themselves at the fair, as well as publishers from socialist countries. The greatest success of the event was the fact that the domestic and foreign books on display could be purchased. "Above all, sale of foreign books exceeded all expectations, even though, compared to our book prices, they were stiffly priced," emphasized the press release about the exhibition.[104]

In addition to information about Western Europe, since the late 1950s, Hungarian experts had been paying attention to agrarian developments in overseas agrarian producing countries, especially agrarian development in the USA. An impulse for this was given by the fact that the Soviet Party leader Khrushchev was also very interested in the results of agricultural research in capitalist countries, especially the USA. In September 1959, during his visit to the United States, he spent two days in the state of Iowa, which is famous for its corn production.[105] It is an interesting and perhaps not chance coincidence that 1959 saw the Hungarian language publication of *The Agriculture of the United States of America*. In its forward Ferenc Erdei wrote: "George S. Wheeler's book fills a tangible gap in Hungarian book publishing, and in a wider sense, in Hungarian public opinion." Erdei identified the key goal of the Hungarian edition to be to ". . . help dispel the ill-informed, overly one-sided and simplified judgment that reigned in this respect in earlier years."[106]

At the beginning of the 1960s, Hungarian diplomacy—supported by leaders of Soviet foreign affairs—took several steps to normalize Hungarian–American relations. The Soviet side too had a particular interest in this because keeping the "Hungarian question" on the UN agenda meant a continuing loss of prestige not just for the Soviet Union but for the international communist movement.[107] As is well known, after long negotiations, an agreement was reached in late 1962. The Hungarian government accepted that it would grant a wide-ranging amnesty to those condemned because for the 1956 revolution, and, in exchange, at an American initiative, the "Hungarian question" was taken off the UN agenda at the end of 1962.[108]

The atmosphere of normalization was reflected in the visit to Hungary a few months earlier of a famous American professor, Earl O. Heady, a teacher at the University of Iowa and an internationally recognized representative of agrarian economics. The invitation came from Hungarian Academy of Sciences, and it was clear that General Secretary Ferenc Erdei had initiated it. During Heady's weeklong stay in Hungary, he visited a number of producer cooperative and state farms, visited the Agricultural Exhibition and gave a lecture at the academy. In this, he emphasized that, under socialist relations, there was a very great significance to the planned and wide-scale utilization of linear programming and other mathematical models, especially in planning. The report that was made on his visit praised the American guest extremely highly. "In Professor Heady we recognize a modest, conscientious, serious scientist, who exhibits a great interest in Hungarian socialist agriculture, and, in his own field, honestly tries to offer assistance to his Hungarian colleagues."[109]

The exchange of experiences was such a success that Professor Heady promised to return soon. This took place in 1964, when he was elected an honorary member of the Hungarian Academy of Sciences. This was also a year when important changes took place in international relations, when President Johnson announced his policy of "bridge-building" toward East European states.[110] Thanks to fruitful negotiations between the Ford Foundation and the State Department, he had ambitions to build relations with East European states, or East European intellectual elites, in the field of scientific research. In 1964, a cultural and scientific exchange program was established between the Ford Foundation and Hungary's Institute of Cultural Relations.[111] Professor Heady helped chose the Hungarian scientists who would travel to the United States in the framework of the Ford Foundation exchange program. Later too, he nurtured intense contacts with workshops of Hungarian agricultural research and higher education. He established particularly close collaboration with the agrarian economist Ferenc Fekete, who was one of the leading figures in Erdei's institute.[112]

In parallel with all of this, and through different channels, Hungarian experts were beginning to familiarize themselves with the achievements of American agriculture. Hungarian agricultural experts visiting Yugoslavia could be convinced with their own eyes of how much higher than domestic ones were the yields on *kombinát*, which made use of American technology.[113] István Szabó, the president of the Red Star Producer Cooperative in Nádudvar, recalled the experience he gained of Yugoslav agriculture as follows: "I was really pole-axed by what I saw and heard there. Till then, I thought that we should be truly proud of what we were doing in Nádudvar. In Tito's Yugoslavia, though, I suddenly realized that we are not top dogs, not by a long shot. Indeed, despite all our results, we had been left behind."[114]

Study visit experiences of this kind motivated the leaders of the agrarian lobby to introduce the achievements of industrialized agricultural production into domestic crop farming too, and as quickly as possible. It was as hard to create the necessary material conditions for this as it was to change the mentality of cadres, because throughout the 1950s the position had been that there was nothing in the world more advanced than Soviet agriculture. Through his contacts in the media, Lajos Fehér did much to ensure that as many factual reports as possible be prepared on agricultural production in capitalist countries. In this respect, role of the radio is worthy of note. Béla Burján, Mihály Kovács, and Ferenc Simon regularly prepared very interesting news reports for the programs *Gazdaszemmel a nagyvilág mezőgazdaságáról*, and *Vita a korszerű mezőgazdaságró*l [The world's agriculture through the eyes of a farmer, and Debates on modern agriculture].[115]

The image of a business and professional partner emerged in place of that of the enemy, which had been prevalent in the 1950s. This all had to be made acceptable to the Soviet leadership, which, after the side-lining of Khrushchev, did not always go smoothly. Béla Marosi, the Hungarian agricultural attaché in Moscow, played an important role in clarifying questions which emerged in the sphere of agrarian affairs and getting Hungarian initiatives accepted.[116]

NOTES

1. *Mezőgazdaságunk a szocialista átszervezés idején*, 150.
2. Pető and Szakács, *A hazai gazdaság*, 478–89.
3. This is evident in the fact that when collectivization was completed in spring, 1961, the end of the three-year ban on leaving farms applied to those who entered in the first wave, in early 1959, was approaching. At the end of summer, 1961, waves of exit requests arrived from regions west of the Danube. See: Havi jelentések: a tsz-fejlesztéssel és megszilárdítással kapcsolatos anyagok, 1961. június–1962. január. [Monthly reports on the development and stabilization of the cooperatives, June 1960–January 1962] MNL OL, M–KS 288. f., 28. cs., (1961) 11. ő. e.
4. Ibid., 152.

5. Another serious problem for Hungarian agriculture, which was still based on human and animal labor, was that the stock of horses in this period fell from 720,000 to 460,000. The pace of the development of mechanization was not fast enough to cause this level of decrease. The horse was a symbol of farming independence, for this reason sending horses to slaughterhouses demonstrated there was no path back to independent farming by decimating the horse stock.

6. This latter strategy was characteristic nationwide, but at the same time was a taboo topic in both political and professional discourse. For more on the peasants' defense and survival strategies in general, see: James C. Scott, *Weapons of the Weak: Everyday Forms of Peasant Resistance* (New Haven, CT: Yale University Press, 1985).

7. The above-mentioned forms of "everyday resistance" were easy to trace in the weekly and monthly reports that were sent from both the HSWP district committees and the agricultural departments of local councils to the HSWP Central Committee Agricultural Department. MNL OL, M–KS 288. f., 28. cs., (1961) 10. ő. e.; 28. cs. (1962) 7., 8., 9. ő. e.; 28. cs. (1963) 11., 12. ő. e.

8. Péter Halász, *A termelőszövetkezeti mozgalom története Apátfalván* [The history of the producer cooperative movement in Apátfalva] (Budapest: Akadémiai, 1975), 47.

9. *Mezőgazdasági statisztikai zsebkönyv,* 1961, 272–73.

10. Edit Fél and Tamás Hofer, *Proper Peasants: Traditional Life in a Hungarian Village* (Chicago: Aldine Publ. Co., 1969), 40–58, 144–50, 184–90; Lampland, *The Object of Labor*, 35–88.

11. Pető and Szakács, *A hazai gazdaság*, 466–74.

12. MNL OL, XIX–A–2–gg. 147. d.

13. The decrease of the agricultural surplus in the years 1960–62 was caused by the fact that imports, which increased yearly, could not be balanced by the incremental increase in exports. Between 1960 and 1962 the growth of imports was 550 million hard currency or convertible forints, in which the growth of feed and bread grain imports was most significant. A KSH jelentése a külkereskedelmi forgalom alakulásáról, 1960–1963. [Report of the Central Statistical Office on the volume of foreign trade, 1960–1963] MNL OL, M–KS 288. f., 23. cs., (1963) 43. ő. e.

14. In 1959 the proportion of investments in the gross income of kolkhoz reached 23–24% compared to the earlier 17–18%. S. N. Andreenkov, "Prichiny i alt'ernativy reorganizacii mashinno-traktornyh stantsii 1958 g," *Gumanitarnye nauki v Sibiri* 20, no. 4 (2013): 42–46; Hale-Dorrell, *Corn crusade*, 27–54; Sydney Ploss, *Conflict and decision-making in Soviet Russia: A case study of agricultural policy, 1953–1963* (Princeton: Princeton University Press, 1965), 113–53.

15. Smith, *Works in Progress*, 158–235; Karl-Eugen Wädekin, "A New Deal for Soviet Agriculture: The Khrushchev Era," in *Agrarian Policies*, 61–62.

16. After the record harvest of 1958 the quotas were increased and prices were lowered, which became rather unfavorable in later years with poorer production. This was especially problematic in weak kolkhozes, especially where climate conditions did not favor bread grain crops. Dronin and Bellinger, *Climate Dependence*, 173–82; Hale-Dorrell, *Corn crusade*, 55–86.

17. The decree of August 27, 1956, limited the livestock holdings of urban residents through taxation. Another decree released on the same day banned peasants from purchasing potatoes, bread, or other foods from state shops for the purpose of feeding their animals. A decree published on July 4, 1957, stated that from 1958 no delivery would be required of household plots. This is often interpreted as the liberalization of household plots, but it actually meant that the state hoped that through increasing its own production there would no longer be a need for household plots, and as such there was no need to deal with the requirements of this sector. D. N. Konyshev, "Gosudarstvennaia politika ogranicheniia lichnogo podsobnogo khoziaistva (konets 1950-kh—nachalo 1960-kh gg.)," *Rossiyskaya istoriya* 55, no. 3 (2011): 102–11; Wädekin, *The Private Sector*, 274–315; Zelenin, *Agrarnaia politika*, 134–39.

18. Markevich, "Finding additional income."

19. Wädekin, *The Private Sector*, 274–315.

20. This was a significant step forward for kolkhoz members, given that their unstable-valued work unit payments were replaced by fixed monthly salaries. The value of such salaries was not high, but it was at least secure. At the same time this move dramatically increased the deficit of the sovkhoz sector. It is no surprise that mass reorganization was stopped in 1969. Hale-Dorrell, *Corn crusade*, 137–66; Roy D. Laird, "Khrushchev's Administrative Reforms in Agriculture: An Appraisal," in *Soviet and East European Agriculture*, ed. Jerzy F. Karz (Berkeley–Los Angeles: University of California Press, 1967), 29–50.

21. *A kommunizmus* építőinek *kongresszusa, 1961. október 17–31: Részlet az SZKP XXII. kongresszusának anyagaiból* [Selections from the materials of the 22nd Congress of the Communist Party of the Soviet Union] (Budapest: Kossuth, 1961), 213–14; See more on this: Susan E. Reid, "Who will beat whom? Soviet popular reception of the American National Exhibition in Moscow, 1959," *Kritika: Explorations in Russian and Eurasian History* 9, no. 4 (2008): 855–904; Jutta Schrerrer, "'To catch up and overtake' the West: Soviet discourse on socialist competition," in *Competition in socialist society*, eds. Katalin Miklóssy and Melanie Ilič (New York: Routledge, 2014), 10–23.

22. SSSR v cifrakh v 1965 godu., Moskva, 1966, 69. For a discussion of source critical problems with contemporary Soviet statistics see: Dronin and Bellinger, *Climate Dependence*, 15–30; Nove, *An Economic History*, 333–35.

23. Natalia Kibita, *Soviet Economic Management under Khrushchev: The Sovnarkhoz Reform* (London and New York: Routledge, 2013).

24. Jerzy F. Karcz, ed., *Soviet and East European Agriculture* (Berkeley and Los Angeles: University of California Press, 1962), 1–21, 29–50; Wädekin, *Agrarian Policies*, 44–62.

25. Also see: Zsuzsanna Varga, "Mezőgazdasági reformmunkálatok (1961–1964)" [Agricultural reform efforts 1961–1964], *Múltunk* 45, no. 2 (2000): 253–82.

26. Jegyzőkönyv az MSZMP Központi Bizottság 1962. február 9-i üléséről. [Minutes of the HSWP Central Committee session, February 9, 1962] MNL OL, M–KS 288. f., 4. cs., 45. ő. e.

27. Jegyzőkönyv az MSZMP Központi Bizottság 1962. március 28–30-i üléséről. [Minutes of the HSWP Central Committee session, March 28–30, 1962] MNL OL, M–KS 288. f., 4. cs., 46–47. ő. e.

28. Ibid.

29. Földes, *Hatalom és mozgalom,* 60–61, 68.

30. Jelentés az Egyéves Mezőgazdasági Pártiskola 1961–1962-es tanfolyamának tapasztalatairól. [Report on the experiences of the 1961–1962 courses of the One-Year Agricultural Party School (training county and district party leaders)] MNL OL, M–KS 288. f., 28. cs., (1962) 16. ő. e.

31. *Társadalmi Szemle* 16, no. 2 (1961): 71–84.

32. *Pártélet* 5, no. 6 (1961): 31–36.

33. The author's interview with R. P. May 18, 2010. (Author's files.)

34. Ferenc Erdei, "A szocialista magyar mezőgazdaság sikereinek és nehézségeinek forrásairól" [About the sources of the successes and problems of Hungarian socialist agriculture], in *Erdei Ferenc* összegyűjtött *művei: Agrárproblémák* [Selected works of Ferenc Erdei: Agrarian problems], eds. Ferenc Fekete and Magdolna Dzúr, vol. 2 (Budapest: Akadémiai, 1986), 163.

35. MRA Műsorboríték-tár [Collection of program documentation folders], January 5, 1961.

36. MRA Műsorboríték-tár, March 21, 1961.

37. *Népszabadság*, December 7, 8, 1961.

38. The first such document was published by the minister in early 1961. *Mezőgazdasági* Értesítő, January 11, 1961, 9–14.

39. A case study analyses the conflict between the local party-apparatus and the Nádudvar Red Star Collective Farm over the above-mentioned family farming method. Zsuzsanna Varga, "A Hajdú-Bihar megyei mezőgazdasági termelőszövetkezetek érdekérvényesítési küzdelmei a korai Kádár-korszakban" [Hajdú-Bihar County agricultural producer cooperative struggles to assert their interests in the early Kádár era], in *A Hajdú-Bihar Megyei Levéltár Évkönyve* [The yearbook of the Hajdú-Bihar County Archive], vol. 24 (Debrecen: Hajdú-Bihar Megyei Levéltár, 1997), 239–68.

40. *Népszabadság*, December 8, 1961.

41. *Társadalmi Szemle* 16, no. 2 (1961): 18–31.

42. A KB Mezőgazdasági Osztály tájékoztató jelentése a PB számára a termelőszövetkezetek 1961. évi zárszámadásáról. [Report of the HSWP Agricultural Department to the Politburo on the end-of-year accounts of the agricultural producer cooperatives in 1961] MNL OL, M–KS 288. f., 28. cs., (1962) 3. ő. e.

43. Varga, *Göröngyös út,* 108.

44. In Hungarian, the words "prohibited," "tolerated," and "supported" happen to begin with the letter "T" (*tiltott, tűrt, támogatott*), so these three official categories of censorship policy developed a wider resonance.

45. Zsuzsanna Varga, "'Földindulás után': A hatalom és a parasztság Magyarországon az 1960-as évek első felében" ["After the earthquake": Power and the peasantry in Hungary in the first half of the 1960s], *Történelmi Szemle* 51, no. 2 (2009): 231–58.

46. Erdei Ferenc feljegyzése a mezőgazdasági irányító szervezet kérdéséhez, 1963. március 11. [Memo of Ferenc Erdei on the question of the agricultural administration, March 11, 1963] MNL OL, M–KS 288 f., 28. cs., (1963) 42. ő. e.

47. Varga, "A 'tudományos munkás,'" 338.

48. Ibid.

49. Jegyzőkönyv az MSZMP Politikai Bizottság 1963. december 10-ei üléséről. [Minutes of the HSWP Politburo session, December 10, 1963] MNL OL, M–KS 288. f., 5. cs., 322. ő. e.

50. The emergence of economic and plan issues, as well as the facing of an increasingly critical situation, can be traced in the following meetings of the HSWP Politburo. MNL OL, M–KS 288. f., 5. cs., 312. ő. e., 337. ő. e., 352. ő. e., 363. ő. e.

51. Jegyzőkönyv az MSZMP Politikai Bizottság 1964. február 4-én megtartott üléséről. [Minutes of the HSWP Politburo session, February 4, 1964] MNL OL, M–KS 288. f., 5. cs., 326. ő. e.

52. Katalin Ferber and Gábor Rejtő, *Reform(év)fordulón* [Reform anniversary] (Budapest: KJK, 1988), 20.

53. György Péteri, "Controlling the Field of Academic Economics in Hungary, 1953–1976," in György Péteri, *Academia and State Socialism: Essays on the Political History of Academic Life in Post-1945 Hungary and Eastern Europe* (New York: Columbia University Press, 1998), 209–16; *Éva Sztárayné Kézdi*, "Az 1963 és 1989 közötti káderkinevezések elemzése" [Analysis of the cadre appointments between 1963 and 1989], in *Nómenklatúra Magyarországon (1957–1989)* [The Nomenclature in Hungary (1957–1989)], ed. László Kiss (Budapest: ELTE Társadalomtudományi Kar, 2005), 151–98.

54. Keserű, *Parasztsorsfordítók*, 119.

55. István Csahók, ed., *Fazekas Béla (1922–1994) műveinek válogatott bibliográfiája* [The selected bibliography of the works of Béla Fazekas] (Budapest: KSH Könyvtár és Dokumentációs Szolgálat, 1998), 7–14.

56. Károly Bozsonyi, Zsolt Horváth, and Zoltán Kmetty, "The Power Grid: The Social Network of the Hungarian Elite in the Socialist Era Based on Hunting Habits," in *Historische Netzwerkanalysen: Österreichische Zeitschridt für Geschichtwissensschaften*, eds. Albert Müller and Wolfgang Neurath (Innsbruck, Wien, and Bozen: Studien Verlag, 2012), 186–228.; György Péteri, "Nomenklatura with Smoking Guns: Hunting in Communist Hungary's Party-State Elite," in *Pleasures in Socialism: Leisure and Luxury in the Eastern Bloc*, eds. David Crowley and Susan Reid (Evanston: Northwestern University Press, 2010), 311–43.

57. Fehér called such occasions "narodnik hunting." In the Soviet Union the term narodnik was associated with peasant politics in the 19th century. Author's interview with T. S. June 20, 2009. (Author's files.)

58. Fehér Lajos miniszterelnök-helyettesi iratai. Koordinációs emlékeztetők 1964–1973. [Documents of Lajos Fehér, as deputy Prime Minister. Records of the coordination committee meetings, 1964–1973] MNL OL, XIX–A–2–ll 38. d.

59. János M. Rainer, "Magyarország a Szovjetunió árnyékában, 1944–1989" [Hungary in the shadow of the Soviet Union, 1944–1989], in János M. Rainer, *Bevezetés a kádárizmusba* [Introduction into the Kadarism] (Budapest: L'Harmattan, 2011), 30–34; Swain and Swain, *Eastern Europe*.

60. Csaba Békés, "A kádári külpolitika, 1956–1968: Látványos sikerek—'láthatatlan' konfliktusok" [The foreign policy of Kádár, 1956–1968: Visible successes—invisible conflicts], in Csaba Békés, *Európából Európába: Magyarország*

konfliktusok kereszttüzében, 1945–1990 [From Europe to Europe: Hungary in the cross-fire of conflicts] (Budapest: Gondolat, 2004), 237–56.

61. Author's interview with T. S. June 20, 2009. (Author's files.)

62. The precedents reach back to 1954, when, in the thaw following the death of Stalin it became possible for a three-person Hungarian delegation to participate in the hunting exhibition in Düsseldorf. The delegation drew the conclusion that Hungary should open itself to hunters from the West, because this could provide a significant source of hard currency for the Hungarian economy. The first West German commercial hunters arrived in 1956. György Majtényi, *K-vonal: Uralmi elit* és *luxus a szocializmusban* [Party elite and luxury in the socialism] (Budapest: Nyitott Könyvműhely, 2009), 84–85.

63. Ibid.

64. In this case too, precedents are visible in the new course period of 1953–54. The program of the 1954 National Agriculture Exhibition was supplemented (for the first time) by an equestrian exhibit that to a large degree was based on "bourgeois" traditions from before 1945. Sándor Kecskés et al., eds., *Az Országos mezőgazdasági kiállítások* és *vásárok története, 1881–1990* [The history of agricultural fairs and exhibitions in Hungary, 1881–1990] (Budapest: Magyar Mezőgazdasági Múzeum–Agroinform, 1996), 37–39.

65. Author's interview with P. J. October 3, 2009. (Author's files.)

66. Dezső Fehér played an exceptional role in the continuous expansion of Western ties: from 1971 he was the director of the Hungarian Horse Racing Company. Dezső Fehér, "A magyar lótenyésztés, lóversenyzés és lovassport Széchenyi korától napjainkig" [The Hungarian horse-sport from the Szechenyi's epoch to present days], in *Személyiségek a magyar agráriumban* [Important Personalities in Agrarian Life], eds. János Nagy and János Kovács, vol. 1 (Debrecen: Debreceni Egyetem Agrártudományi Centrum, 2005), 59–68.

67. It is also important to mention the periodical *Gazdálkodás* [Farming], which Erdei established in 1957. He was inspired by two goals: on one hand he sought to connect agricultural economics with farming practice, while on the other hand he hoped to communicate novelties from international literature. Two columns were dedicated to such in the journal: *Figyelő and Szakirodalom* [Observer and Literature].

68. Zsuzsanna Varga, "Agricultural Economics and the Agrarian Lobby in Hungary under State Socialism," *East Central Europe* 44, no. 2–3 (2017): 234–308.

69. Jegyzőkönyv az HSWP Politikai Bizottság 1960. szeptember 13-i üléséről. [Minutes of the HSWP Politburo session, September 13, 1960] MNL OL, M–KS 288. f., 5. cs., 200. ő. e.

70. The Cuxhaven poultry combine was comprised of the following sections: an incubator station with a capacity for 10 million eggs; a site capable of raising 600,000 animals; an egg factory working with 63,000 laying-hens; a pedigree unit with 4,000 laying-hens; a fattening unit for 600,000 chickens at a time; a poultry feed-concentrate factory capable of producing 100 metric tons per day; a poultry slaughter and processing unit capable of handling 10,000 animals every 8 hours; a freezer plant capable of freezing 70 metric tons of produce; a veterinary laboratory with a dissecting area for parasite, bacteria, and histology examination.

71. Keserű János feljegyzés Fehér Lajos részére a nyugat-németországi tanulmányútról. 1960. május 17. [Memo from János Keserű to Lajos Fehér on his study trip in West Germany, May 17, 1960] MNL OL, M–KS 288. f., 17. cs., 5. ő. e.

72. Ibid.

73. Ibid.

74. Ibid.

75. Keserű, *Parasztsorsfordítók*, 111–12.

76. Péter Gunst and Imre Wellmann, *A 200 éves Bábolna múltjából, 1789–1945* [Two hundred years of history of Bábolna, 1789–1945] (Bábolna: Bábolnai Mezőgazdasági Kombinát, 1989), 13–14.

77. Schlett, *Sziget a szárazföldön*, 35–45.

78. József Dancs, *Ez történt a kulisszák mögött* [This happened behind the scenes] (Bábolna, 1983), 8–10.

79. Róbert Burgert was born on August 20, 1924, in Baranya county (Ivánbattya). In the period 1942–1945 he worked as an apprentice on the estate in Fürged, and after 1945 he participated in organizing farmers' collectives in Baranya. From 1950 to 1960 he worked in the Pécs State Farm, initially as an agronomist, then later as director. This was followed by three decades at the Bábolna State Farm (later Combine) as executive director. His name is associated with developing the Industrial Corn Production System, which he helped spread widely in Hungary. From 1978 he was a titular Full Professor at the Gödöllő Agricultural Sciences University. Later he was president of the Industrial Corn Production System directorate, and in the period 1985–90 served as president of the Executive Board of the National Alliance of State Farms. He passed away on January 12, 1999, in Budapest.

80. This sum was twice that marked for the development of the poultry branch for all state farms the previous year.

81. Bábolnai Mezőgazdasági Kombinát, *Bábolna: Tények és adatok, 1945–1989* [Facts and Data, 1945–1989], vol. 1 (Bábolna: Bábolnai Mezőgazdasági Kombinát, 1989), 12–17.

82. Keserű, *Parasztsorsfordítók*, 113.

83. The state farm did not conduct independent breeding until 1969. Up to that point the Lohmann company transported breeding materials. Schlett, *Sziget a szárazföldön*, 44–45.

84. Visitors were not allowed to enter the poultry barns. Only those employed there could enter the animal stalls. They were given work clothes and footwear, which could only be worn on-site. In the interest of eliminating infection the farm banned workers from keeping poultry stocks at home in 1962. To compensate, the farm paid workers a monthly indemnity. Ibid., 39–42.

85. Initially the solving of these conflicts was heavily influenced by Burgert's supporters in the HSWP Politburo Committee (e.g., Lajos Fehér). Later he himself took a position in the highest level of political leadership. The first such step was his election to membership in the HSWP Central Committee on December 3, 1966, at the 9th Congress. Ibid., 107–117.

86. *Bábolna: Tények* és *adatok*, 12–15.

87. Róbert Burgert, *Iparszerű termelési rendszerek szervezése a mezőgazdaságban: Bábolna* [Organizing industrial-style production in agriculture] (Budapest: Országos Vezetőképző Központ, 1985).

88. Pál Sárkány, ed., *Termelési rendszerek az* állattartásban [Closed production systems in the animal husbandry] (Budapest: Mezőgazdasági, 1975), 159–65.

89. In his memoir János Keserű wrote that he introduced the world famous Canadian geneticist Shaver to Lőrinc Grünfelder, who successfully established consumer egg-laying Shaver hybrids in Bóly. Keserű, *Parasztsorsfordítók*, 114.

90. Sárkány, *Termelési rendszerek az állattartásban*, 173–79.

91. Az NSZK-val folytatott kereskedelmi forgalom alakulása, 1958–1963. 1964. március. 10. [The development of the trade between Hungary and FRG, 1958–1963, March 10, 1964] MNL OL, M–KS 288. f., 32. cs., (1964) 42. ő. e.

92. Mihály Ruff, "A magyar–NSZK kapcsolatok (1960–1963): Útkeresés a doktrínák útvesztőjében" [The Hungarian–FRG relations, 1960–1963: Seeking ways and means in the labyrinth of Doctrines], *Múltunk* 44, no. 3 (1999): 7–8.

93. Beitz made a return trip to Hungary in 1960, from September 5 to 14. This time he was not on a business trip, but came hunting. He requested and was granted a meeting with János Kádár, to whom he gifted a hunting rifle. Ibid., 11.

94. Az SZKP Központi Bizottság levele az MSZMP Központi Bizottságának kenyérgabona-ügyben. 1964. február 5. [The letter of the Central Committee of the CPSU to the Central Committee of the HSWP on the bread-grain problem, February 5, 1964] MNL OL, M–KS 288. f., 23. cs., (1964) 2. ő. e.

95. It is no coincidence when in spring 1964 N. S. Khrushchev visited Hungary the first agricultural plant he was taken to was Bábolna, where director Róbert Burgert proudly reported the results of the three-year poultry program and how the farm as system manager had taken to spreading industrial poultry meat and egg production throughout the collective farm system. *Magyar Mezőgazdaság,* 19 (1964): 15.

96. Csaba Békés, "A kádári külpolitika 1956–1968" [The foreign policy of Kádár, 1956–1968], *Rubicon* 9, no. 1 (1998): 19–22; János M. Rainer, "The Sixties in Hungary: some historical and political approaches," in *Muddling Through in the Long 1960s: Ideas and Everyday Life in High Politics and Lower Classes of Communist Hungary*, ed. György Péteri (Trondheim: Norwegian University of Science and Technology, 2005), 2–26.

97. For more on the Finnish political initiative and its effects on Hungary see: Anssi Halmesvirta, ed., *Kádár's Hungary—Kekkonen's Finland*, Hungarologische Beiträge 14 (Kopi-Jyvä: Jyväskylä, 2002).

98. Lajos Gecsényi, *Iratok Magyarország és Ausztria kapcsolatainak történetéhez, 1956–1964* [Documents on the history of Hungarian–Austrian relations, 1956–1964] (Budapest: Magyar Országos Levéltár, 2000), 229–33; Maximilian Graf et al., "A Masterpiece of European Détente? Austrian–Hungarian Relations from 1964 until the Peaceful End of the Cold War," *Zeitgeschichte* 41, no. 5 (2014): 311–38.

99. Pál Romány, ed., *Mezőgazdasági üzemekben Skandináviától Itáliáig* [Visiting farms from Scandinavia to Italy] (Budapest: Mezőgazdasági, 1963).

100. Ibid., 6.

101. See: László Komló, *Ipari mezőgazdaság felé* [Toward the industrialized agriculture] (Budapest: Közgazdasági és Jogi Könyvkiadó, 1964); Aladár Sipos, *Agrárviszonyok Nyugat-Európában* [Agriculture in Western Europe] (Budapest: Kossuth, 1967).

102. *Gazdálkodás* 8, no. 1 (1964): 93.

103. Georg Blohm, Új irányzatok a nyugat-német mezőgazdaságban [New Trends in West German Agriculture] (Budapest: Mezőgazdasági, 1967).

104. *Gazdálkodás* 8, no. 6 (1964): 81.

105. Medvegyev, *Hruscsov,* 189–201.

106. George S. Wheeler, *Az Amerikai Egyesült Államok mezőgazdasága* [The Agriculture of the United States of America] (Budapest: Kossuth, 1959), 5.

107. Magdolna Baráth, "Magyarország a szovjet diplomáciai iratokban, 1957–1964" [Hungary in the documents of the Soviet diplomacy], in *Múlt századi hétköznapok: Tanulmányok a Kádár-rendszer kialakulásának időszakáról* [Everyday life in the 20th century: Studies on the formation of the Kádár-system], ed. János M. Rainer (Budapest: 1956-os Intézet, 2003), 79–82.

108. For more on the details of the process see: László Borhi, *Dealing with dictators: The United States, Hungary, and East Central Europe, 1942–1989* (Bloomington: Indiana University Press, 2016), 138–83.

109. *Gazdálkodás* 6, no. 4 (1962): 83–84.

110. Borhi, *Dealing with dictators*, 138–83.

111. A Ford Alapítvánnyal kapcsolatos tapasztalatokról. [Report on the experiences regarding the Ford Foundation] ÁBTL, 2.7.2. 1. d. 41–9/58/64.

112. Interview with Ferenc Fekete. Conducted by Gyula Nagy. OHA, 13. sz. 214–220. The Oral History Archive contains interviews that can be researched but not cited and others that can be both researched and cited. All interviews used in this book come from the latter category. During the American study visit Ferenc Erdei had regular letter correspondence with Ferenc Fekete. This material was placed in the Erdei collection files. MTA Könyvtára, Kézirattár [Library of the Hungarian Academy of Sciences, Manuscript collection] Ms 5823/41–54.

113. After Stalin's death the party leadership in Yugoslavia deemed collectivization a mistake and stopped it. The more than 2.5 million peasant farms operated alongside several hundred large-scale plants (combines) that on average cultivated 20–25,000 hectares.

114. Ignác Romsics, *Szabó István életútja Nádudvartól Nádudvarig* (Budapest: Osiris, 2012), 132.

115. *Gazdaszemmel a nagyvilág mezőgazdaságáról 1966–1968: Vita a korszerű mezőgazdaságról, 1966–1969.* [The world's agriculture through the eyes of a farmer: Debates on modern agriculture] MRA Műsorboríték-tár.

116. Author's interview with M. B. January 15, 2003. (Author's files)

Chapter Six

American Model Transfer

POLITICAL, ECONOMIC, AND INSTITUTIONAL CONTEXT

In the first third of the 1960s, Comecon member states began to suffer from general problems of a slowdown in economic growth, unsatisfactory production in agriculture, technical and scientific backwardness, and increasing debt.[1] These combined to create a particularly tense situation, because, since 1961, as mentioned above, catching and overtaking the developed capitalist countries was on the agenda. The amassed tensions and contradictions obliged changes to take place. In September 1965, the Soviet Union launched an economic reform which is generally referred to as the "Kosygin reform," after the Soviet prime minister at the time who initiated it.[2] The GDR initiated the "New Economic System" [Das Neue Ökonomische System, NÖS] in 1963.[3] In Czechoslovakia, the party leadership decided in favor of reforming the economic management system in January 1965.[4]

The Hungarian leadership was also facing serious economic problems and difficulties fulfilling plans at this time. The leadership wanted to keep the promises of its standard-of-living policy, but concerns were caused by the fact that, beginning in 1961, Soviet loans taken out in 1957 had to be paid back. Furthermore, Hungarian commitments within the Warsaw Pact also increased. As a consequence of these accumulated tasks, signs of exhaustion appeared very quickly over the course of the second five-year plan (1961–1965).[5] Quantitative growth in production was not in harmony with either quality or efficiency requirements; the stock of unsalable goods grew ever larger. The growth in national income slowed, balance of payment problems arose, and debt to both capitalist and socialist lenders grew at an accelerating rate.[6] Tensions like this in the economic sphere were of particular significance in Hungary, because they endangered the successes in domestic and foreign policy consolidation that had started to pay dividends at precisely this time.

An expert committee of economic leaders and economists was formed over the course of 1964 and entrusted with the task of elaborating a comprehensive reform package to be implemented later. In December 1964, the HSWP Central Committee decided that critical evaluation of the current economic mechanism must be completed in two years, and then, on the basis of this, a comprehensive concept for modernizing the economic mechanism must be developed.[7] This would eventually become Hungary's New Economic Mechanism which was introduced at the beginning of 1968.

In this environment, the agricultural reform package discussed in the previous chapter, which had previously been set aside, became realistic again. The most pressing problems began to be addressed as early as 1965. For example, the liquidation of the machine stations, which had been underway for years, was completed, and their machinery was purchased by the producer cooperatives.[8] Processes of forgiving or restructuring accumulated producer cooperative debt were begun. In essence, debts that had arisen in connection with collectivization were forgiven, such as the costs of paying for equipment and animals, and constructing the necessary buildings for large-scale farming.[9]

At the end of 1965, in the interests of preparing further measures and acquiring political support, the Agricultural Department led by Imre Dimény prepared a 35-page summary report on current problems and proposed solutions. The strength of the agrarian lobby is well illustrated by the fact that, at the beginning of January 1966, with the help of Rezső Nyers, the department's report was submitted to the Politburo.[10] There was heated debate at the session, because the submitted material wanted to solve the disadvantageous situation of agriculture and producer cooperative memberships as soon as possible, and this had serious financial consequences. Several Politburo members expressed their opposition, including István Szirmai, Dezső Nemes, Mihály Korom, Béla Biszku, and Zoltán Komócsin. The latter directly accused the Agricultural Department and the Ministry of Agriculture of being excessively biased toward producer cooperatives and their memberships. He had the following to say about peasant living standards: "I think that the leaders of the Ministry of Agriculture are following a particularly biased line on this question. There is no point in competing over who holds the peasants closer to their hearts. Our obligation of communist objectivity demands a different judgment on this question."[11] In the end, no final decisions on any of the questions were made at this Politburo session, but the themes remained on the agenda throughout the year as a part of preparations for the next party congress.[12] With the support of János Kádár and Rezső Nyers, the agrarian lobby managed to have its proposals included in the decrees of the 9th Congress of the HSWP. It is no accident that this party congress was referred to as the "peasant congress" at the time. Two factors influenced decisively János Kádár's openness to the proposals of the agricultural lobby. First, he had none of the visceral anti-agriculture and anti-peasant sentiment that was characteristic of, for example, party leaders like Rákosi and Gerő. Second, in numerous areas, including agrarian policy, he evaluated Hungary's specific national interests differently from the Rákosi group. As most of those interviewed for this book expressed it, Kádár took responsibility for Hungary's specific agrarian policy, which he defended both in Hungary and in Moscow.

It is worth quoting verbatim the part of the decree passed at the Congress that dealt with agriculture:

> We have gradually developed a situation in relation to agricultural enterprises which makes it possible for the vast majority of them to cover the costs of personnel and equipment necessary to increase production from their own income. We must make it possible for producer cooperatives to move to guaranteed monthly remuneration, in all branches of production. In the future too, increased care should be devoted to exploiting, alongside the forceful development of communal farming, the greatest possible opportunities concealed in household plot farming.
>
> If the desired pace of agricultural development in the current plan period is to be assured, it is necessary to work out a system of producer cooperative credit, investment, state support and taxation that is appropriate for the new economic farming system.
>
> We propose that over the coming year, the first national congress of producer cooperatives should be convened, which should debate the main questions concerning the operation and farming of producer cooperatives, elect a National Council of Producer Cooperatives and take a position on the establishment and operation of regional producer cooperative associations.[13]

Political approval in hand, on Lajos Fehér's initiative and under his presidency, the Central Committee Cooperative Policy Working Group was established in December 1966, which, by including the inner circle of the agrarian lobby (Ferenc Erdei, Pál Losonczi, Sándor K. Nagy, and Imre Dimény in addition to Fehér), represented its quasi-institutionalization at the center of power.[14]

NEW LEGITIMACY FOR COOPERATIVES

The background to these developments was that, as part of the preparations for reforming the economic mechanism, the socialist property hierarchy, which held that state property was of the highest order and truly socialist, while all other forms of ownership, including cooperative ownership, were lower order, had been modified. Official ideology had previously stressed that the role of cooperatives in the socialist system could only be temporary: as schools for communism, they would help the former propertied classes integrate into the socialist economy, and then, after some time, cooperatives too would transmogrify into higher order, state, all-people's ownership.

It was in May 1966 that the significant ideological correction in this respect took place, when the Central Committee recognized the multisectoral nature of the economy as one of the guiding principles of the reforms necessary for the New Economic Mechanism. "Our planned economy is based on the joint development of both forms of socialist ownership, state and cooperative ownership (including the household plots of cooperative members). Alongside the decisive superiority of the socialist sector, the private sector is to be maintained in the future too in a complementary role, including small-scale industry, petty commerce, producers' markets and the auxiliary plots of non-peasants."[15] But a significant portion of the party apparatus did not give up easily its previously held Stalinist positions on producer cooperatives and household plots. As part of the preparation for the New Economic Mechanism, a great deal of attention was paid to communicating these ideological changes in both party education and the press. The debate that unfolded in the pages of the party's theoretical journal *Társadalmi Szemle* [Social Review] in 1968 could be seen to signal this change.[16] The "father of reform," Rezső Nyers (economic policy secretary of the Central Committee), contributed to the debate, arguing in favor of the idea that cooperatives had a long-term place too in "the construction of socialism." He summarized the advantages of the cooperative sector as follows:

> The cooperative sector in the people's economy is not there only because certain groups of people find it more acceptable to do their work, or to secure their consumption, as members of cooperatives, but also because it is more advantageous, rational and cheaper for the whole society if certain activities are carried out by cooperatives and not state enterprises. Economic efficiency is thus greater, and society's sense of ownership more direct in cooperatives that work together, and this represents a great motive force in small and medium-scale economic activity.[17]

There was also a hierarchical dimension to the sphere of interest relations. The previous socialist axiom had held that individual and group interests (enterprise and cooperative interests) had to be subordinated to social (all people's, people's economy) interests. With the introduction of the New Economic Mechanism, the conception gradually began to take hold that the existence of social groups with various interests was a natural characteristic of socialist society too, so making the idea of group interests acceptable to "polite society."[18] It was, in fact, development on producer cooperatives that proved that cooperative enterprises were a stage on which individual and group interests could be brought into harmony.

Rezső Nyers characterized the change at a fall 1966 session of the Central Committee as follows: "At the Csepel Works, and in Ózd and in many other areas, it is the interest of society as a whole that dominates, and there, all-society ownership is essential. But just as the cooperativization of the Csepel Works would lead to an inconsequential socialism, a similarly inconsequential socialism would arise from the nationalization of small scale activities. If I might express myself colloquially, we would lose our shirts if we did so, which cannot be in the interest of the people."[19]

Why did these ideological corrections take place, and why, in turn, did measures aimed at improving the situation of agriculture and agricultural producers take place? How was the agrarian lobby able to get its ideas accepted? The explanation lies unambiguously in the fact that, in the mid-1960s, the group held a trump card. Ferenc Erdei expressed it as follows, in a memorandum to Imre Dimény, head of the Agricultural Department: "Agriculture can stand, with a certain self-consciousness, at the front of the country and the Party."[20] What did this sentence mean? By that time, the point had been reached where Hungary was self-sufficient in bread grains and its meat imports were declining.[21] The results, therefore, appeared to justify the separate-path policy that Lajos Fehér and his group had initiated, and which the majority of the party leadership had initially only tolerated as a necessary but forced concession.

THE MINISTRY OF AGRICULTURE AND FOOD AND THE NATIONAL COUNCIL OF PRODUCER COOPERATIVES

From the middle of the decade, therefore, the agrarian lobby recorded success upon success, a trend which reached its peak in 1967. Legislative decree no. 8 of 1967 saw the establishment on April 14 of the Ministry of Agriculture and Food (here after MAF), which came into being from the merger of two ministries (the Ministry of Agriculture and the Ministry of Food Affairs) and two directorates (National Forestry Directorate and the Stater Land Surveying and Cartographic).[22] The former Minister of Agriculture, Pál Losonczi, was appointed president of the Presidential Council. By breaking with the branch administrative structure and creating an umbrella over horizontally connected institutions, the new ministry embraced much of the spirit of the New Economic Mechanism before it had actually been introduced.

The unified ministry was entrusted to the leadership of Imre Dimény, who recalled this period as follows:

> This was the most exciting task of my life, and the one where I took on the most responsibility. I did not get any special economic or political-type "direction" for it. Political-type agreements were provided by Lajos Fehér and Rezső Nyers. This was the first ministerial institution in Hungary to adapt to the new system of the economic mechanism launched in the mid-1960s. Instead of earlier direct control activities, the new ministry fulfilled tasks of a mainly administrative, bureaucratic, economic-regulatory and technical development nature. This was a wholly new task. A small group of us was able to work out the structure, thanks to its "secret" nature. The structural and operational order of the ministry and its personnel were accepted on the basis of my proposals for the most part, and in April 1967 I was named minister to head the Ministry. . . . We started work, as you might say, in the cross-fire of strong political dogma, and we constantly worked "close to the flames." Our motto was professional preparation, love of the profession, knowledge, and a sense of calling. But every day, the result was strengthening political antipathy. We could only struggle against this strong dogmatic political pressure because we had the trust of Lajos Fehér and Rezső Nyers, who held a political "umbrella" over our heads.[23]

As Imre Dimény indicated, one of the important new features in the restructuring of the system of economic management was the prominence given to economic regulators. The central task of the ministry became the following: while taking account of branch and sectoral specificities, to work out proposals for the elaboration and, where necessary, modification of economic tools (price system, credit policy, product marketing system, wage and income regulations, investment system, and so on) which would ensure the realization of national economy goals. In addition to laying out the direction and proportions of product development, and material and technical conditions related to them, the ministry naturally also had tasks as a state authority. These included regulating specialized administrative (state authority) activity pertaining to production, effective management, marketing and the operational units (enterprises, producer cooperatives, farms, institutions), as well as directing organizations that executed policy.

The structure of MAF was complex. On the one hand it organized departments covering the breadth of the ministry's activities. On the other, it created branch offices (with their own departments and subdepartments) within the structure to bring together specific tasks (economic, technical development and administrative): the Office of Food Affairs, the Forestry Office, and the National Land Affairs and Cartography Office. In addition, corporate organizations and councils were set up to coordinate economic and technical-development and scientific activities: the National Animal Health Council, the

Agricultural Standards Council, the National Game Management and Hunting Council, the Scientific Council, and the Technical Development Council and Economics Council. The latter acted as an advisory, opinion-forming and proposal-making organ for the Minister of Agriculture and Food. Its task became to assist, using economic measures, the execution of government economic policy in agriculture, forestry, the food industry, and the lumber industry, and land affairs administration (land surveying and cartography). This ministerial structure naturally changed from time to time in response to challenges arriving from the agrarian economy, but only minor internal restructuring took place, and over the next two decades it did not undo the integration of the agricultural and food industry portfolios.

The establishment of the MAF represented an important innovation in another respect. By welding together the agricultural and food affairs portfolios, a new structure came into being in which a single hand was responsible for agricultural production, purchasing, commerce, and industrial processing; that is to say, the management of everything, from planting to industrial processing, was focused on a single portfolio. This represented much more than a pragmatic restructuring of the governmental structure, and it ran counter to Soviet practice. An important change in conceptions stood behind it: acceptance of principle of the food economy, rather than simply the production of food.[24] The importance of this conceptual modernization remains relevant to this day. What is more, acceptance of the necessity of vertical integration appeared not only at the macro level, but at the micro level as well.[25]

The other major innovation in organizational and institutional changes within the agrarian sphere was the establishment of interest-group bodies to represent the interests of producer cooperatives separate from party structures. The agrarian lobby turned a network of interests into a structure of institutions. Preparatory work took place in the HSWP Central Committee Cooperative Policy Working Group. In the first months of 1967, producer cooperative delegates across the country elected regional associations, and these then appointed delegates to the first national congress of producer cooperatives. The congress was held on April 20–22, 1967, in the former upper-house chamber of Hungary's Parliament building.[26] Here, the National Council of Producer Cooperatives came into being, and it elected as president István Szabó of the Red Star Producer Cooperative (Nádudvar), and as general secretary Sándor K. Nagy.

István Szabó remembered the creation of this interest group as follows:

> The National Council of Producer Cooperatives . . . in all of its strength and power was the invention of Lajos Fehér and Erdei. . . . Fehér initiated it with the goal of ensuring that cooperatives, and through them the entire agrarian branch, have a permanent organ defending their interests. The idea fitted in well with

> the [New Economic M]echanism concept of Rezső Nyers and his colleagues, which, over and above a reform in economic management narrowly conceived, originally included the institutionalization of the appearance of interests as a component. . . .[27]

Another important success of the agrarian lobby was that it was able to win more investment for the actors in the agrarian branch. The third five-year plan, which became law in June of 1966, continued to reflect the prioritization of heavy industry (basic materials industry) in development. However, as the plan was implemented, the branch distribution of investments changed considerably, and, from 1968, the share of industry, and within it primarily heavy industry, began to fall, while that of agriculture, and from 1969 non-producing branches (and within them communal areas), began to increase. The guidelines for the fourth five-year plan for 1971–1975 reflected a further shift toward agriculture.[28] Ágnes Ungvárszki is right in her verdict on this reorganization; "two-decade-old magical borders" collapsed: the share of industry in investments in the socialist sector decreased below 40%, with heavy industry falling below 30%, while that of agriculture and nonmaterial areas rose above 20%.[29]

NEW LAWS TO CREATE INDEPENDENTLY FUNCTIONING COOPERATIVE ENTERPRISES

In the fall of 1967, Parliament accepted two laws that defined the economic and social relations of producer cooperatives for the next twenty years. Law III on agricultural producer cooperatives aimed to resolve the duality that had arisen from the discrepancy between producer cooperative practice and the legal regulations in force. The local initiatives that had become common producer cooperative practice, especially in the areas of remuneration, work organization and household plot farming were successfully included in the APC Law.[30] The intention to maintain a distance from the kolkhoz model was also reflected in another important law (Law IV of 1967), which dealt with landownership and land use.

The 1967 cooperative law built on the concepts of self-management and legal equality to include the following innovations. The law granted producer cooperatives the right to decide on their income; producer cooperatives were no longer subject to plan obligations, and could, therefore, independently decide on their production and their operating plans; the material consequences of producer cooperatives' economic decisions had to be borne by the farms themselves. The law also specified not only that producer cooperatives were independent legal persons, but that they had no economic superior (trust or territorial or production directorate), and therefore that they were legal persons that represented themselves in every respect.

Restructuring toward this independent enterprise economic activity required, first of all, securing the financial background. The agrarian lobby's starting point was to recognize that difficulties of material incentives, on the part of the members or the producer cooperative itself, would not disappear until the price system accurately reflected expenditure and results. The joint goal of the price increases and credit concessions that took place in 1966–67, therefore, was to lay the foundations for the ability to self-finance, that is for the majority of producer cooperatives to become capable of independent enterprise-like farming. The essence of this was that the producer cooperatives were able, from their sales receipts, to: guarantee the regular payment of profit shares to the membership; maintain funds to ensure working capital and replace worn-out equipment; and to cover a portion of equipment needed to increase production and repay loans taken out for this purpose. Their investments, however, could not yet be financed fully from income. One of the most important and consciously maintained restrictions on the independent enterprise-like of producer cooperatives was investment policy.[31]

The membership too was affected by these changes, because, in the name of independent enterprise-like farming, many changes were introduced in the area of income distribution, the most important or which was the ending the residue-principle. This was of tremendous significance because, however much the producer cooperatives endeavored in the first half of the 1960s to find ever-better incentive solutions for their memberships, in the ever-widening room for maneuver provided by the party and state leadership, the efficacy of local solutions remained restricted within the frame of residue-principle income distribution. Law III of 1967 prescribed that the wages paid to members over the course of the year should count as cooperative production costs, and it also specified that their payment preceded the demands of the state and replacing material expenditure.[32] These measures brought about a new situation in respect of incentivizing members, for the preparation of a wage fund validated the position that cooperative members, like all other workers, deserved a guaranteed wage, fixed in advance, which was regularly and continually paid in proportion to the amount worked. The unambiguous formulation of the ACP Law met the interests of the producer cooperative membership in full: "The primary purpose of the new regulation is to express those basic features of the operation of producer cooperatives that have taken shape following developments in the past years. . . ."[33] The decree which implemented Law III of 1967 also passed measures in relation to remuneration, allowing producer cooperatives to make use of any form of remuneration that conformed to socialist distribution. "The producer cooperative establishes how labor is measured and remunerated, whether on the basis of meeting requirements (work norm), the amount of time spent, or a share of production (yield) or its value."[34]

In the name of independent enterprise-like farming, a series of economic decision rights had to be transferred from the state administration to the producer cooperatives, because previously self-management of producer cooperatives had been in form only. In practice, their activities had been administratively directed, by district councils, contracting enterprises, and bank branches, using partly political pressure but mainly economic tools, granting or revoking credit and support.

> Although, in theory, it is not permitted to subject producer cooperatives to plan directives, the consequence of their high degree of dependence on the council apparatus and state support, is that their plans in practice are built on framework numbers broken down from above, which has resulted more than once in measures contrary to the cooperative's characteristics and long-term interests.[35]

One of the basic principles the Producer Cooperative Law was that producer cooperatives would independently choose their production structure and direction of development.[36] Similarly, they would use their farming equipment and sell their products independently. It was still compulsory to prepare a plan and farm according to it, but the plan was not submitted for official approval.[37] Numerous other steps were necessary in order to realize these declared principles. For example, the distribution of production equipment (machinery, chemical fertilizer, and so on) by state authorities was replaced by free-market sales.[38] The precondition of independence was free right of disposal over the products that they produced, and the possibility of selling them freely. From this moment on, purchasing and processing enterprises stood in direct contact with producer cooperatives, and the "mediating" task of councils disappeared. Producer cooperatives could sell products, from either the communal farm or household plots, not only to purchasing enterprises, but also to petty commerce, the hospitality industry, public bodies, industrial users, and foreign trade enterprises. Furthermore, producer cooperatives could open their own shops in which to sell their produce.

One of the consequences of recognizing independent, enterprise-like farming was that Law III of 1967 abolished the earlier narrow limits placed on their sphere of activity. The limitations of the Soviet kolkhoz model had long prevented producer cooperatives from engaging in supplementary activity beyond crop cultivation and animal husbandry, despite the fact that in earlier times there had been traditions of this in Hungary, both within the structure of former noble estates and peasant farms. Reference can be made to the extent of village household industry, woodworking, carting and food processing.[39]

The new regulations defined the activities of producer cooperatives to permit processing, procurement, sales, and services in addition to agricultural production. They could use their facilities and equipment not only for the needs of the communal farm and household plots, but also for work or services on behalf of state enterprises, institutions, associations, and the population.[40]

Law III of 1967, then, established the equal legal status of producer cooperatives, but other difficulties remained. The state bank continued in a monopolistic position in that cooperatives could only access significant credit via the bank's district branches. The main problem with state purchasing enterprises was that they were in almost exclusive possession of the facilities and qualified labor necessary for getting agricultural products onto the market. This situation changed only gradually as the processing and sales activities of producer cooperatives expanded.

Outdated legislation had to be repealed if producer cooperative self-management was to be achieved. The framework offered by Law III of 1967 made it possible for producer cooperatives to regulate their organizational structure and modes of operation in accordance to their own specific situations.[41] Before 1967, the administrative order of producer cooperatives was not given by a law of the land, but merely local operating rules. In 1967, by contrast, the rights and duties of the membership, together with the sphere of authority and legal status of the president, the leadership, and cooperatives' various committees were all established in law.[42] As far as these matters were concerned, Law III of 1967 essentially just repeated everything that the 1963 draft of the producer cooperative act had contained. However, there was an important innovation in that the producer cooperative membership elected the cooperative president, leadership, and committee members by secret ballot. Furthermore, it was the general assembly that determined the size of, and ratio between, personal income and capital accumulation, the methods of work organization and remuneration.

The aim of the agrarian lobby was not just to win equality for the cooperative sector economically, but also in terms of social policy. Its first result in this respect was to end disadvantage of producer cooperative members in terms of social provision.[43] Beginning in 1949, the social security system had been gradually extended to producer cooperative members in order to increase their "attractiveness." The level of provision, however, fell significantly below that of workers and employees.[44] Producer cooperative members felt, with reason, that this differential treatment was not only disadvantageous, but offensive. It was as though they only counted as second-class citizens. Everyday speech of the time included the terms "industrial pension" and "producer cooperative pension." This differentiation was no coincidence. It was because, on the one hand, producer cooperative members could only

Table 6.1. The Comparison of Operating Rules for Agricultural Producer Cooperatives (1967) and Kolkhoz Model Standard Charters (1969)

Operating rules for agricultural producer cooperatives (1967)	*Kolkhoz model standard charter (1969)*
Kulak and other former exploiters can be members, and after 2 years of exemplary work can be elected into leadership positions.	Kulak can only become members after fulfilling certain conditions. Priests and their children excluded.
Cancellation of 3-year ban on exit.	The member cannot freely leave the kolkhoz (domestic passport system). Exit equals exclusion: based on 2/3 majority agreement of members.
Leadership elected by general assembly for 2 years.	Leadership elected by general assembly for 2 years.
Producer cooperative can own land.	Land under state ownership.
Further existence of limited private land ownership for producer cooperative members, for which cooperative pays a land rent.	
Duty to contribute farming equipment, animals.	Duty to contribute farming equipment, ploughing animals and livestock.
Area of household farm: 1/2 to 1 ha.	Area of household farm: 1/4–1/2 hectare
Number of animals allowed: 1 cow, 1–2 fattening calves, 1–2 sows with piglets, 5 sheep or goats, unlimited number of poultry, rabbits and bees, further 3–4 fattening pigs.	Number of animals allowed: 1 cow, 1 calf, 1 pig, 1 piglet, 2 sheep, unlimited number of poultry and rabbits. Rights held by kolkhoz household.
All members allowed to have household plot. Household plot committee.	
Exceptional expansion in sphere of activities.	Sphere of activities: crop production, animal husbandry, household plots.
No compulsory planting plans.	Compulsory planting plans.
No compulsory deliveries.	Duty to make some deliveries.
Cancellation of residue-principle income distribution	Residue-principle income distribution.
System for remuneration established by producer cooperative.	Remuneration based on work unit system, paid once per year and the end of the farming year. Advances paid under certain conditions.
Labor organization determined by producer cooperative.	Collective labor organization (brigade, labor team).
Annual labor minimum (men: 150; women; 100 ten-hour workdays).	Disciplinary action (monition, warning, reprimand, work unit revoked, fine, exclusion).
Introduction of producer cooperative pension.	
Introduction of paid vacation.	
National Council of Producer Cooperatives, a producer cooperative interest group (territorial alliances, TOT).	

Source: Fóris, *Mezőgazdasági termelőszövetkezeti törvény*, 16–49.

retire five years later than industrial workers, and, on the other, the level of the pension was not based on actual income but was based on a uniform income of 900 forints per month. As a result, the amount paid in pensions was about 350 forints per month (compared to an average of 862 forints per month for industrial workers). The size of the old age disability benefit pension was only 260 forints per month.[45]

The Lajos Fehér group wanted to remedy these tensions too.[46] Their efforts can be interpreted as a kind of "civil rights movement." The guiding principle in working out the new pension system was to ensure a pension provision for produce cooperative members that, in principle, approximated the pensions of those who lived from wages and salaries.[47] The retirement age remained at 65 for men and 60 for women, as before. The pension sum was determined depending on members' incomes, and its lower limit (the legal minimum) was set at 400 forint per month. The equalization of the previous system was ended, in that the pension fund set at between 900 and 5,000 forint per month, depending on members' income, professional training and sphere of work.[48] Eligibility for pension was tied to ten years of producer cooperative membership. Pension years were based on every calendar year in which contributions were paid and the member contributed labor equivalent to 150 10-hour workdays (100 days for women). In the new system, the producer cooperatives paid a uniform 7.5% of distributable income as social security payments (which comprised sickness benefit fees and accident insurance contributions), while the members paid a progressive pension contribution related to their income, identical to that of those living from wages or salaries (with a 3% minimum). Family allowance was extended to families with two children, but the amount remained at 70 forint (compared to 120 forint for industrial workers).[49]

A NEW FOCUS ON TRADE WITH THE WEST

The development of the Hungarian economy reached a point by the mid-1960s where it needed significant additional resources, whether they came from international cooperation in the fields of technical development, or cost reduction, or selective development. Because cooperation within Comecon was incapable of meeting this need,[50] the Hungarian economic policy leadership attached great importance to organic integration into the system of East–West relations when preparing for the New Economic Mechanism.

The most important economic policy body of the HSWP, the Economic Policy Committee that worked next to the Central Committee, dealt with the possibility of expanding relations with capitalist countries several times over the course of 1966. A joint submission from the Foreign Trade Ministry and Finance Ministry summarized the reasons obliging integration into international division of labor as follows:

> The only markets where we can obtain numerous important raw materials and semi-manufactured goods are foreign markets; for many branches of industry, especially those that are developing dynamically, it is from them that the machines necessary for industrial development have to be assured, and a significant portion of the investment credit to accelerate economic development comes from there; our export capacities in many areas exceed the absorption capacity that can effectively be met on socialist markets, and we certainly need markets; we have significant imports from capitalist countries.[51]

In the atmosphere of international detente and the economic conjunction of dynamic Western growth, it seemed realistic to count on the long-term intensification of East–West relations. The purchase of machines and facilities, licenses and know-how, which had emerged almost spontaneously in the 1960s, became accepted significant sources of further technical-economic development.

Another possible means of acquiring intellectual products was international cooperation, which meant long-term, contractual production relations for the preparation of certain products, based on a division of labor and a community of interests between enterprises from various countries. Cooperation often extended to research, market research, market acquisition, sales, technological transfer, and training activities. Its concrete form might be a joint venture or a company of mixed ownership. In 1967, before the New Economic Mechanism was even introduced, those preparing decisions engaged in intensive study of questions of cooperation with the companies from capitalist countries.[52]

The capitalist partner was generally motivated by the possibility of breaking into new markets and expanding capacity, as well as the fact it could end manufacture of products that were becoming dated and supply them via its new partner. As a small country with an open economy, Hungary was motivated primarily to acquire modern technology and improve its export structure. It was hoped that knowledge gained through manufacturing cooperation would facilitate the satisfaction of domestic needs at higher level.

As noted above, the opportunity to establish such cooperation had already presented itself in the first half of the 1960s, but hopes in that respect had not been realized in the circumstances of the centralized planning system. A good example of this is the activity of the Cooperation Office of the Ministry of Metallurgy and Machine Industry. In the years before the New Economic Mechanism, it had worked on 127 cooperation projects, but only 27 produced a contract, and not one resulted in actual cooperation before the end of 1967. The economic policy decision-makers expected the New Economic Mechanism to provide solutions here too:

> We must build on the principle of enterprise interest. Enterprises too can be initiators; the focus of work related to cooperation will shift into manufacturing companies' own spheres of authority, and it will be automatically permitted, provided that the activity is in accordance with the commercial and industrial policy interests of the people's economy.[53]

The tasks of the ministries and the National Bank of Hungary were identified as creating favorable conditions, primarily in respect of official authorization and financing.

Over the course of 1968, the possibility of turning to capitalist investment credit, as a means of acquiring the material resources necessary for structural transformation, gained currency, given the inability to obtain goods through socialist imports. According to a memorandum debated by the Economic Policy Committee in March, "To realize our economic policy goals, we must take on foreign long-term loans, to a larger degree and in a more organized manner than before."[54] There was nothing new in itself in taking out loans from Western countries, but what was new, was the intention to use them to replace socialist equipment and installations of inadequate quality. Great expectations of a different sort were also attached to them: the long-term loans were to be spent on investments which would primarily make possible an increase in capitalist exports and the acquisition of convertible currency. The Economic Policy Committee stressed that "the primary goal in taking on loans is to equip the investments prescribed in the plan with up-to-date installations and machinery, and to contribute to the improvement of our international financial liquidity."[55] The environment appeared favorable for taking out loans, because "on the side of the capitalist countries, there is a supply of credit, and in this area there are possibilities for acquisition and expansion."[56]

The question of credits came before the Economic Policy Committee again in December 1968 in the form of making use of foreign working capital needed to accelerate economic development. The situation report put it as follows: "In the world economy, simple forms of commercial activity are turning into forms of cooperation whereby, in addition to the exchange of material goods, great weight is placed on the exchange of intellectual goods (know-how, licenses); the experiences of technical development are assured by cooperation on the market." The conclusion drawn was:

> Nowadays it is no longer enough for a partner to participate by just offering loan-capital, rather, mutual interest in lasting optimal development and the

> building of lasting commercial ties require both partners to take part with working capital. Our political and economic policy goals require that, in conformance with our economic interests, on capitalist markets too we adjust to the requirements of world market trends.[57]

Following the introduction of the New Economic Mechanism, therefore, opening to the West was raised to the rank of official policy. Improvement in the country's competitiveness was unambiguously linked to integrating into the world economy, the exchange of intellectual products and the need for cooperation. It became acceptable that "expanding commercial relations is justified with every capitalist country that brings us economic advantage and which does not create a politically undesirable level of dependence."[58] This latter aspect, however, was increasingly squeezed into the background in comparison to expected economic benefits. After 1968, for example, ever-greater emphasis was placed on the idea that adjustment to the high standards of developed capitalist countries would promote developing the domestic market into a discerning one.

> We must create a social and economic climate in which producers are obliged to manufacture high quality goods that adapt to the changing needs of consumers, while consumers have the ability to choose between goods offered by a variety of producers. This is why it is necessary to loosen the current excessive centralization of production and sales, and liquidate economically undesirable monopolies. . . .[59]

The West took assiduous care that there was not even an accidental possibility of the technical content (know-how) of its exports being adapted for the military industry. But if Hungary's import requirements did not figure on the Comecon list, that is to say, were not embargoed, then the only limit on purchases was its ability to pay. In terms of concrete partners, first consideration was understandably given to the Federal Republic of Germany. In both European and world relations, it was Hungary's largest capitalist trading partner, and in many areas it had the world's most developed technology. The guiding principles formulated above emphasized how advantageous it would be to sign long-term economic agreements with West German companies, both in terms of concrete equipment acquisition and technical and technological cooperation. From the Hungarian side, it gave the possibility of ending import restrictions in the interest of ever-wider partnership. In this spirit, long-term economic, industrial, and technical agreements were authorized to the extent that they contained concrete steps in respect of efficiently supporting technical development and contributing to export growth.[60]

Hungary ended up establishing economic relations with the United States of America too, despite the fact that official policy considered it to be undesirable partner.[61] The rationale underpinning these economic relations was that they would be useful supplements for all socialist countries, but they also signaled caution: the USA's commercial goals also served its political plans, that is to say, the country was trying to enter socialist markets, while striving to maintain its own restrictive measures regarding trade with socialist countries.[62]

As part of the New Economic Mechanism, the Hungarian leadership wanted to move forward opening to the West not only by bilateral relations but also within the framework of international organizations. An important stage in this would be accession to the International Monetary Fund and the World Bank.[63] Over the course of 1967, representatives of the Hungarian government initiated negotiations for admission. In a question of such significance, the Hungarian side naturally had to consult with the Soviet leadership, which was strongly opposed membership of the IMF. They argued that "the IMF is a United Nations institution in form only, in fact it is under American influence."[64] This stance frustrated Hungary's accession ambitions.

In 1967 too, Hungary tried to join UN Food and Agriculture Organization (FAO), and this provides an interesting parallel.[65] The FAO is one of the UN's most important economically specialized institutions, which promotes international cooperation in the areas of food supply, the food supply industry, and agriculture. Its key aims can be summarized as: promoting growth in agricultural and food production, agricultural scientific research, developing technology, training experts, disseminating the latest results in these fields, practical implementation, providing material, technical and expert assistance in the execution of large scale technological, research, and education programs aimed at increasing production.[66] The body also tracks the world food situation and the production, consumption and trade of the most important agricultural and food industry goods. It prepares orientation materials on expected tendencies of development, economic reviews, and statistics. The FAO's activity extends to agriculture in the wide sense, that is to say, it covers the food industry, water management, forestry, and fishing as well.

Hungary had been a member of the organization between 1946 and 1951, but under Soviet pressure, and after Poland and Czechoslovakia had ended their membership, the Hungarian leadership decided to quit too, leaving behind a debt of 89,000 dollars.[67] The idea of rejoining had resurfaced several times in Hungary before 1967, and in the meantime "unofficial" requests to rejoin had come from the FAO itself. Although the Soviet Union, which was not a member of the organization, had reservations about Hungary's request to renew membership in 1967, the attempt was successful nevertheless.[68] On March 23, 1967, the Hungarian government passed a decree on accession (3077/1967), and in May it submitted its application, followed by final acceptance at the FAO Conference in November.[69] At this time, Poland, Yugoslavia, and Romania were the only socialist countries to be members of the FAO.

In 1968, Hungarian representation at the FAO headquarters in Rome was established, although it consisted of one person at the time, who operated with the help of the ambassador in Rome and professional direction from the National Committee. Further, accession made it possible for Hungary to send delegates to the FAO apparatus, in proportion to its membership-fee contribution.

Participation in FAO conferences made it easier to establish relationships with agricultural politicians and experts from Western countries. This is well illustrated by the fact that over the course of 1968, the Hungarian delegation participated in 35 committee sessions, conferences, study visits, and so on, and 10 FAO delegations visited Hungary in that same year.[70] FAO Director-General A. H. Boerma's five-day visit to Hungary in 1969 was especially significant.[71] In 1970, the FAO European Conference was held in Budapest.[72]

Besides sharing information on experience and new developments, the FAO supported various projects from member state funding and from the framework of the UNDP.[73] In 1968, it was agreed as part of negotiations on this, that "in addition to direct contribution to development taking place in the Hungarian people's economy, it could ensure the development of technical-scientific and economic cooperation relations . . . with developed capitalist countries and . . . the UNDP would purchase a license for Hungary, together with export rights."[74] The organization offered developing countries technical assistance, by sending international experts, providing equipment, organizing scholarships and study visits, and further tried to increase production possibilities for these countries by identifying investment opportunities and ensuring an appropriate investment environment. The first support for Hungary of this kind was sum of 1.14 million dollars.[75]

Another international success in the second half of the sixties was the reestablishment of membership for Hungarian cooperative organizations in the International Cooperative Alliance (ICA). Much like the FAO, relations in this case had been broken in 1948 in the atmosphere of the Cold War. This was a particularly significant loss because the relationship of Hungarian cooperative movements and organizations with the ICA stretched back to its founding year of 1895. Representatives of the Hungarian cooperative movement were involved in the establishment of the international organization, and in fact, the Alliance held its 6th World Congress in Budapest in 1904. There were several steps to the rebuilding of the official relationship in the second half of the 1960s. In 1966, the National Council of Consumer Cooperatives [Fogyasztási Szövetkezetek Országos Tanácsa] joined successfully, followed by the National Council of Industrial Cooperatives [Ipari Szövetkezetek Országos Tanácsa] in 1968, the National Cooperative Council [Országos Szövetkezeti Tanács] in 1970, and then the National Council of

Producer Cooperatives [Termelőszövetkezetek Országos Tanácsa] in 1971.[76] It should be stressed in relation to this process, that prior to each body joining, the ICA had a team of international experts study the organization concerned to ascertain whether it operated in accordance with the values and principles of the world organization.

INTERMEDIARIES AND TRANSFER CHANNELS IN THE EMERGENCE OF HYBRID AGRICULTURE

In addition to the positive features listed above, it should be noted too that membership of the FAO offered a new possibility for building relations with the United States. In terms of average farm size, the Hungarian large-scale system at the time had much more in common with American agriculture than that of Western Europe. Furthermore, as far as the application of complex technologies and systems was concerned, American agriculture was in advance of the otherwise well-developed Western European agriculture.[77] This explains why professional interest in the United States had already begun to grow in the first half of the 1960s. Unresolved questions in Hungarian-American diplomatic relations obstructed their expansion for years.[78] As mentioned above, the agricultural reforms predated the New Economic Mechanism, and as a consequence they capitalized on the opportunities offered by the NEM too. Especially in the field of technical cooperation with capitalist countries, especially the United States.

The first foreign visit of a high-level agricultural delegation only took place in 1969. Its leader was István Gergely, deputy minister responsible for production matters,[79] and other delegation members were Lajos Tóth, also a member of the MAF, Lajos Lada from the Ministry of Foreign Trade, András Klenczner from the National Centre of State Farms, Róbert Burgert, the director of the Bábolna State Farm, and Professor Péter Sárközy. Although the delegation was invited to the United States by American companies, the trip had a semiofficial character because the U.S. Department of Agriculture worked out the delegation's detailed program, and the delegation was received by the Secretary of State and the Deputy Secretary of Agriculture.[80] The aim of the visit was to gain familiarity with the scientific, technical, and practical achievements of the previous five years, and further to obtain information about animal and plant types, production methods, and tools that could be used in Hungarian conditions.

An examination of the channels through which the experiences gained in the USA were shared in Hungary could be the subject of a separate study. For example, two films were produced, along with two books and several newspaper articles. The members of the delegation gave several lectures across the country. Numerous newspaper articles about the trip were published, and a book authored by one of the delegation members, Péter Sárközy, was published under the title *Face to Face with American Agriculture*. The book was an easy-to-read travel journal in which the author shared the American lifestyle with the reader. Sárközy also covered the achievements of the American agricultural economy, introducing new technologies, methods, and research/education modes.[81] Transmitting scientific results was more important in another 1970 publication, György Enyedi's summary of his one-year stay and study visit in the USA through a Ford Foundation grant titled *Farms and Farmers: American Agriculture*. His goal was to provide news of the general developmental characteristics of agriculture and its problems, given that experiences in America were important to Hungary. The author emphasized "in Hungary we are trying to construct a developed socialist food economy system comparable to the best—and elements of the American model can be used to do so." Enyedi paid a great deal of attention to the high level of facility and territorial specialization characteristics of American agriculture. He held the other secret to success was that new technical achievements were very quickly utilized by masses in American agriculture.[82]

The companies that were visited by the 1969 delegation showed the Hungarian guests numerous new breeds of corn, sugar beet, soybean and vegetable types, cultivation technology, and equipment.[83] The delegation visited among other locations, Roswell Garst's farm, and the following companies: FMC, Northrup King, Ralston Purina, De Kalb, and John Deere.[84] Most of the companies visited were at the cutting edge of agricultural technology development, and, significantly, the presidents, managing directors, and owners of these companies received the Hungarian delegation. Experts were provided to implement the program and provide information. Over the course of the American negotiations, it proved possible to agree on some deals in principle for future cooperation, while more leaders promised to visit Hungary very soon in order to agree on concrete cooperation.[85]

The delegation members, including Róbert Burgert, director of the Bábolna State Farm, paid particular attention to corn production. The USA was a truly great power in this field, not only because it provided 49% of the world production, but also because it had doubled its corn yields between 1955 and 1969.[86] At the same time, Hungary was struggling with serious problems in assuring a fodder basis for its livestock farming. At the end of the study visit, the Bábolna State Farm was able to purchase John Deere machinery complexes capable of producing 6,000 hectares of corn.[87] The Hungarian Foreign Trade Bank made the purchase possible with a hard currency loan construction, repayable over three years. Bábolna wanted to cover payments through the extra produce it would achieve using the modern technology it had bought, and in fact the new machinery complexes realized the hopes attached to them so well that the farm was able to pay back the entire loan in 1970.[88]

On the basis of his experience of the first year of industrial-type corn production, Róbert Burgert prepared a proposal for Hungarian–American cooperation. In his letter to Lajos Fehér he wrote:

> The corn production system can only be developed at a high level, in the framework of wide-ranging cooperation and education, like the poultry system. The chief task is to find the most suitable foreign and domestic partners. A joint venture to be established with Corn Production System (CPS), the pre-conditions for which are under negotiation, would complete the close cooperation with foreign, mostly American, companies that have joined the corn production system in the Bábolna State Farm so far, and the organization and development of the whole cooperation. An opportunity is opening, therefore, to judge objectively the potential possibilities of various companies and continuously to integrate the best production elements into the system. In this way we want to commit ourselves, not to individual companies, but continuously to the constantly changing best machines, materials and procedures. The aim of the joint venture is to organize cooperation between the foreign and domestic partners participating in the industrial-type corn production system.
>
> The aim of the cooperation is that, long term (7 to 10 years), the domestic partners taking part in the cooperation will achieve a growth in average production sufficient for them to *be able to repay their expenditure from the increment*. In this cooperation, therefore, we seek not only to adapt domestically foreign intellectual knowledge and rapidly increase development, but to pay for the necessary hard currency with the extra production (above current yields) that will derive from the establishment of the closed production system.[89] [Emphasis in original]

The proposal won the support of Rezső Nyers as well as Lajos Fehér. By involving 11 farms in the project, Bábolna's industrial-type corn production extended to almost 30,000 hectares. In 1971, the Hungarian–American joint venture CPS-ZugAg (Corn Production System) was established, with Bábolna State Farm owning 30% of the total, Inter-cooperation Ltd. owning 20%, and CPS-USA owning 50%. Later, in 1973, 71 farms (35 state farms and 36 producer cooperatives) participated in founding the Industrial Corn Production CPS Joint Venture [Iparszerű Kukoricatermelő CPS Közös Vállalat], which from 1975 was named the IKR Joint Venture.

From 1972, two other state farms initiated their own CPSs, indicating that state farms had achieved an advantage over producer cooperatives in the dispersal of Western technology. The Baja Corn Production System (BKR) started to organize production on 11,000 hectares as a venture of the Baja State Farm,[90] and the Szekszárd State Farm began the Corn Production Socialist Cooperation (KSZE) in cooperation with the Gödöllő Machine Experimentation Institute, on 14,000 hectares.[91]

Every one of the three above-mentioned production systems was organized by a state farm, in conformity with the expectation that only state enterprises can be development centers. Driven by the spirit of competition, the president of the Nádudvar producer cooperative, István Szabó, who was also president of the National Council of Producer Cooperatives, fought, with the help of Lajos Fehér and Imre Dimény, for access to hard currency loans, like Bábolna. The essence of the transaction was that, with the help of a state hard currency loan, the enterprise could purchase up-to-date, modern machines, technology, and know-how from the West, and only had to repay the loan later from the export of extra product.[92] The Nádudvar Red Star Producer Cooperative also established contact with the world famous John Deere Company, but it soon became apparent that the farm was too small to make this kind of deal alone. For this reason, in 1972, it and eight neighboring producer cooperatives established the Corn and Industrial Plant Production Cooperation (KITE), which continues to function to this day. Production began in 1973 with 16 complete machinery complexes and 10,300 hectares of corn, and later 5,500 hectares of sugar beet.[93] The closed production system, however, did not only include the machinery, but seeds and the highly effective herbicides as well. The prescribed high plant numbers aroused the biggest doubts concerning the technology. It was unimaginable to plant corn as densely as the new technology demanded using traditional methods. In the first year, average production of corn in Nádudvar was 6.2–6.3 metric tons, which was almost 40% more than the average before the project started.[94]

In 1974, the number of member cooperatives in KITE grew to almost 200. The increase in production achieved was so great that the hard currency loan was paid back in four years instead of the planned five. Csaba Balogh, who played a key role in the organization of the production system, summarized the advantages of the hard currency loan construction as follows:

> We were given the right to export corn directly through Agrimpex, and we received the export price differential as a surcharge. In this way, the units were given an interest in exporting: the more they could export, the cheaper, in relative terms, each unit could access technology. The construction was a dazzling success, because it gave farms hard currency with which they could buy up-to-date equipment. It was profitable for the farms too in that the price of their products was upgraded to world market prices, because they were world market goods, purchased at world market prices.[95]

Reflecting the ambitions of the New Economic Mechanism to perhaps a greater extent than elsewhere in the economy, intense competition developed between the first production systems from the moment that they were established. Farms faced a real choice of provider offering to increase their production dramatically. A few examples follow. The CPS production unit was based on 790 hectares of corn, and a machinery complex based on International Harvester Company (IHC) tractors and Claas combines. The joint venture purchased the machines on credit and then rented them for five years to the producers for an annual 536 kilograms of export-quality corn per hectare. The center asked for 20% of the extra production. Farms did not pay on joining, but only took ownership of the machinery complex after five years of rental. The BKR machinery complex was designed for 400 hectares. The system center supplied only Hungarian and socialist machinery: D4K-B tractors and E 512 combines. The machinery became the property of the farm, but 30% had to come from their own resources at the time of payment. Fifteen percent of additional production in export-quality corn was paid for expert advice and other services. The KSZE machinery complex was planned for 500 hectares of corn using John Deere tractors and John Deere adapted E 512 combines. A deposit of 30% was required to buy the machines, and the hard-currency loan had to be paid from extra corn. For expert advice and services, there was a basic fee of 150 forint per hectare plus 4% of extra production of export quality corn up to a threshold of 40 quintals per hectare, and 5% above that.

When KITE was set up, it established the principle that all extra production went to the farm and the system center received no share in it, because it did not have to pay for any losses either. The own resources necessary for purchasing machinery came from the farms, while the system manager secured hard currency loans. The machinery became farm property, so the production risk and its full income devolved to the farm. KITE was maintained as a development and service apparatus by the members who paid a lump sum of 150 forint per hectare for services and advice. The system center kept its services attractive by concessionary pricing and also because the KITE constructed an apparatus which, in addition to acquiring machines, undertook to service them, even after their warranties had expired.[96] Furthermore, Nádudvar did not stick to the two crops that it had started out with, but constantly added new branches so that it quickly included within the system the production of sugar beets, sunflowers, fall wheat, soya beans, rice and so on, and, as a result, was able to quickly increase its level of arable crop production.

While, in the case of closed systems for poultry and egg production, the member farms were required to do nothing beyond sticking point by point to the directions of the system manager, with CPSs, the system managers were able to adapt the framework technologies that they had developed to local conditions. Csaba Balogh, one of the directors of KITE, explained the process in an interview:

> For example, KITE technology was different for areas with saline soil, from mountainous areas, or again black earth regions. Corn cannot be grown in the same way everywhere. There is of course a basic KITE offer for machinery and technology, but, for example, it is only with local knowledge that we can decide whether the technology can handle 50,000, or even up to 80,000, depending on the soil, the strain and many other factors. In the end, the KITE consultant makes this decision jointly with the experts of the farm concerned.
>
> Climatic conditions vary too. Hungary is a small country, but temperature and levels of precipitation differ, even between regions which are relatively close to one another, what is more, local observation can reveal that individual valleys and gullies can be storm zones, hail stone collection points or even dry crevices.[97]

Adapting the framework technology on the one hand required continuous consultation between the system center and farms that joined the system, on the other, it was necessary to reshape the organizational structure of the member farms. Modern, expensive machinery complexes required the precise organization of arable work, the efficient utilization of machines and secure operations. The former rigidly hierarchical, pyramidical management structure was replaced by a branch system of management that was empowered with decision-making authority, so that it could make possible the delivery of work on an optimal schedule from the point of view of agronomy, and the coordination of internal organizational tasks.

Consultations between system manager farms and member farms also meant the accumulation of a previously never experienced mass of reliable data.[98] Foreign manufacturers were interested in this too.[99] For them, experiments and studies of Hungarian, large-scale, large-field farming represented new bases of information, which could help their general market growth. Agronomic experiments, demonstrations of machinery, regular expert training, with hundreds, more realistically thousands of participants, brought a true sparkle to the sector. This was one factor among others that resulted in a boom in Hungarian seed production supply, the development of seed-corn producers and the creation of new producers; corn hybrids were produced in the biggest volumes (Pioneer, Dekalb, and so on). Researchers in Martonvásár and Szeged contributed to success by breeding new strains with greater productive capacity: hybrid corn, intensive wheat strains. Universities and colleges also participated alongside research and development institutions in this horizontally structured transfer of knowledge.

One of the defining characteristics of Western model transfer was that the development and dissemination of new production procedures, or generally the role of innovation centers, operated horizontally rather than vertically. It was not provided by a state authority, but rather by state farms and a few innovative, capital-rich producer cooperatives, which then, as system managers, extended horizontally to partner farms the radius of their modernizing capacities. Another unique characteristic was that the producer cooperatives and state farms could decide entirely freely whether or not to join a production system, or how many systems to join. As voluntary associations based on economic interests, these types of operational cooperation quickly spread. This was the case not only in arable cropping, but also in animal husbandry and horticulture.[100]

When the amount of territory integrated into systems grew from tens to hundreds of thousands of hectares, and when the value of this developmental method was justified by results, the Hungarian machine industry, chemical industry and commercial sector, which had lost good customers, began to mobilize themselves. *Mezőgéptröszt* [Agricultural Machinery Trust] and its companies signed a whole series of manufacturing cooperation contracts and cooperation agreements with Western machinery producers (Claas, Heston, JD). Large companies in the chemical industry imported the effective agents for pesticides and herbicides and developed local formulas, which they then introduced to the market. There were positive examples of cooperation between industry and agriculture too. The Bábolna State Farm played an important mediating role in developing cooperation between the Rába Vagon és Gépgyár [the Rába Wagon and Machinery Factory] and the Steiger company of the USA to produce powerful tractors.[101]

The Western model transfer was organically related to the New Economic Mechanism. It could not have happened without that mechanism's focus on East–West trade, and the mechanism's commitment to competition and horizontal relationships meant that there was real choice for farms and a genuine stimulus for constant improvement on the part of the systems managers, their foreign suppliers, and domestic competitors.

THE DEVELOPMENT OF HYBRID AGRICULTURE AND ITS RECEPTION IN EAST AND WEST

The agricultural sector was quickest to adapt to the New Economic Mechanism, because its reforms removed numerous ideological, legal, organizational, and material obstacles from the path of agricultural development. Within the agricultural sector, it was producer cooperatives that adjusted most quickly and most successfully to the changed political and economic environment. Following the reforms, the annual growth of agricultural production was 5.5% overall, but for producer cooperatives it rose to 9.4%.[102] The main explanation for this dynamic development was that the share of agricultural investments increased to a higher level than ever before. Not only did their quantity change in a way that benefited producer cooperatives, but so too did their sectoral distribution. Previously, reference to the higher status of state property had placed state farms in a privileged position.

By this time, for the most part, investments served real development and no longer replaced the equipment of individual peasants lost through collectivization. A turnaround took place in the structure of investments too: emphasis moved from investment in buildings to investment in machinery.[103] In the first half of the 1970s, truck capacity increased most strongly, while from 1976 the expansion of powerful tractors accelerated. As a result, by the mid-1970s, the level of mechanization for wheat harvesting and threshing, as for corn harvesting, reached 100%, while that for sugar beet and potato harvesting was 89% and 98% respectively; and both approached 100% by the end of the decade.[104]

In this period too, the use of herbicides and pesticides became general. The main means for soil replenishment was chemical fertilizer: its use grew by a factor of 3.5 between 1967 and 1975, by which time, 1.5 million metric tons of it (224 kg per hectare) was used in agriculture. The first complex artificial fertilizers were introduced. At the same time as use of chemical fertilizers grew, that of organic manure declined, because the entire strategy of mass production was based on chemicals (and mechanization), and these squeezed out natural processes of soil replenishment.[105]

The process of technological renewal became dominant as a result of reforms. Ever more producer cooperatives expressed an interest in industrial-like production systems,[106] and an important precondition for integrating and adapting them was the emergence, by the beginning of the 1970s, of a staff of suitable producer cooperative leaders and experts, which was made possible by mass middle and higher agricultural education.[107] Imre Dimény, the minister of agriculture and food, developed a concept for technical development in agriculture in which training and knowledge were just as important as new breeds, artificial fertilizers, chemicals, or mechanization.[108]

> Many people have debated whether the development of human resources is part of technical development. Dogmatic-sectarian attitudes held that this question was not relevant. My colleagues and I were of the opinion that, without the human factor, everything that we think about development cannot be realized, because people are the creators and instigators of the whole of technical development. Harmony must be found between technical development and the level of expertise of workers in agriculture, the development of their knowledge. . . .

> Recognition of this fact contributed greatly to a spotlight being shone, from as early as the mid-1960s, on moral and material support for the whole system of specialist agricultural (middle, higher and adult) education. . . .

One important dimension to this was the fact that, by keeping agricultural educational institutions under the control of the MAF, the curriculum at both middle and higher level could be adjusted to the needs of American technology transfer. Textbooks reflected the very latest developments as a "40,000 strong body of qualified agrarian experts" was trained.[109] Dimény too stressed this point.

> The leadership of the Ministry of Education at the time tried, on several occasions, to have the administration of agricultural universities and high schools changed so that they came under its wing. But their attempts were always unsuccessful, mainly because the directors and professors of our universities and colleges valued the work of the MAF highly, and they felt fine and secure. . . . All of our institutions underwent significant modernization in terms of buildings and equipment, and increasing the number of beds in halls of residence. Their material and moral esteem was assured. They also valued positively the fact that they could operate as research universities, that they could become centres of expert advice on developing production, that their voices could be heard in the formation of agrarian policy.[110]

These developments in the technical and intellectual background of agrarian production quickly became apparent in results. Cereal production, mainly wheat and corn was the most successful area of crop farming.

In addition to restructured material and technical conditions of production, a further contributory factor to the crop production results was a change in biological fundamentals. Over the course of the 1970s, a complete change of wheat variety took place, while the choice of corn hybrid changed twice. The effect of these changes was that the average annual wheat yield grew from 2 to 3 metric tons per hectare at the beginning of the 1970s to over 4 metric tons by the end of the decade, that for corn (maize) in the same period rose from 3.4 to 5.3 metric tons.[111]

Increases in leaps and bounds of average yields for wheat and corn provided the foundation for a rapid upswing in livestock levels and meat production. At the same time, these sectors too underwent technological renewal. Elaboration of a cattle-breeding program in state farms had begun when they put into practice their experiences gained on the 1969 American study trip. The program gained further momentum after an official link was established in 1972 between the Hungarian and American agricultural ministries. A new link was established with the Holstein-Friz and the Hereford Society as the result of negotiations led by Deputy Minister Kálmán Kazareczki, while, over

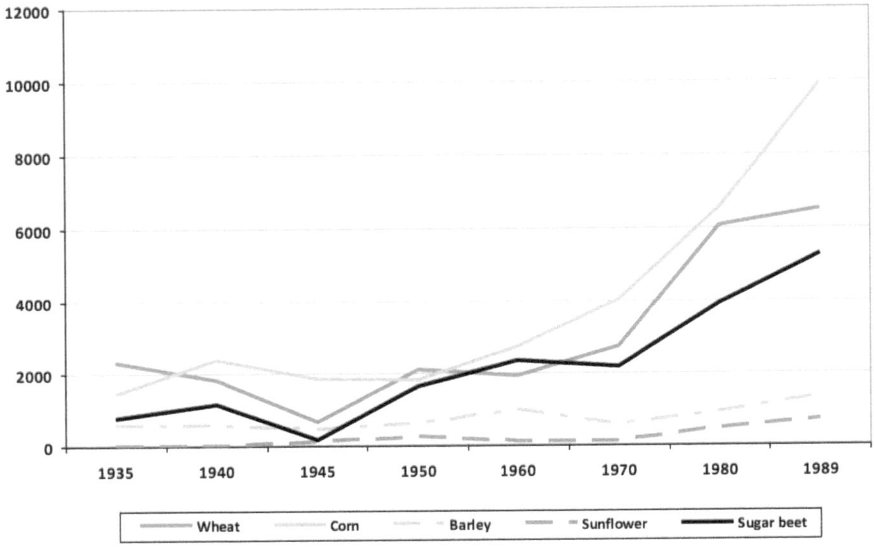

Figure 6.1. Produced Quantity of Key Crops in Hungary (Thousands of Metric Tons). Source: *Magyar mezőgazdaság 1851–2000*, CD-ROM.

the course of negotiations with Secretary of Agriculture Butz, purchase of breeding stock was successfully included in the Concessionary Commodity Purchase Program (CCC). This made it possible to set in motion an expansion of Hungarian cattle breeding with new breeds, and, through this, specialization in milk and meat had become a government priority.[112]

A further success in the 1970s was achieved in the field of poultry breeding, when the further development by Hungarian enterprises of technology purchased from the West began to bear fruit. Bábolna, again, is worthy of note. As discussed above, it had bought an industrial poultry production system from the Lohmann company. After eight years of cooperation, the link was broken and Bábolna started its independent poultry program.[113] This was so successful that Bábolna-developed hybrids became cutting-edge products. In 1973, the TETRA-SL egg-laying hybrid produced the best results in international test studies. In the same year, according to a comparative study of broilers carried out in West Germany, the TETRA-B meat hybrid won first place. By achieving results at the pinnacle of international poultry production, Hungarian farms were able to break into new markets. The best example of this was the Middle East. In 1968, Hungary began to export hatching eggs, poultry and even complete production systems to rich, oil-producing countries (Saudi Arabia, Iraq, and so on).[114] Later, having taken stock of local requirements, an industrial system for sheep rearing was also developed. The

Table 6.2. The Average Yield of Key Crops in Hungary (Kg/Ha)

Year	*Wheat*	*Corn*	*Barley*	*Sunflower*	*Sugar beet*
1945	1,340	1,200	1,270	810	16,100
1945	870	1,440	810	720	8,930
1950	1,520	1,570	1,260	850	14,600
1953	1,650	2,240	1,860	1,180	20,220
1960	1,910	2,030	1,890	820	18,120
1970	2,130	3,380	1,950	1,010	28,730
1980	4,760	5,320	3,770	1,660	37,640
1989	5,240	6,440	4,690	1,950	43,980

Source: Magyar mezőgazdaság 1851–2000, CD-ROM

example of Bábolna and several other cases made it possible to demonstrate that Hungarian companies did not merely adopt Western technology, but developed it further so that they could appear on the market with products that they had developed themselves. The development of turkey production by the Nádudvar producer cooperative illustrates this process well.[115]

Thanks to all these efforts, by the midseventies, total meat production had increased by 44% compared to 1960: from 730,000 metric tons to 1,300,000 metric tons. This was attributable mostly to the growth in pork and poultry meat production: while beef production essentially stagnated, that of pork meat doubled, while that of poultry meat grew two and a half times. All in all, the results reached in grain and meat production made it possible for Hungarian agricultural exports to triple between 1965 and 1975.[116]

Hungarian agriculture built its export policy from the 1960s around three main markets. First, it expanded from year to year its foreign trade relations with socialist countries, primarily the Soviet Union, Czechoslovakia, the GDR, and Poland. Second, in the interest of developing exports to capitalist markets and developing independent breeding, cooperation was established with European capitalist companies. Third, mention must be made of relations with the very dynamically developing markets of the Middle East, which became increasingly significant from the 1970s, because of the volume of hard currency involved.

Naturally, the biggest export markets in terms of volume were the socialist countries. At this time, given the attractive exchange ratios, the Comecon region absorbed Hungarian agricultural products without limit. It is important to emphasize that the commodities concerned were ones that the partners had such great need of that they were even willing to pay in dollars. As a result, on the one hand, the agrarian sphere placed a trump card in the hands of the economic policy leadership when it came to negotiating import conditions for fuels and raw materials.[117] On the other, however, despite the restrictions of common market agrarian regulations, Hungary was able to export foodstuffs to Western Europe, and, in doing so, "produced" significant quantities of convertible currency, so ensuring resources to provide a basic cover for importing the Western materials, equipment, and intellectual property necessary for Hungarian industrial and agricultural development.

From the end of the sixties and beginning of the seventies, Hungary's agricultural production results attracted an increasing number of visiting delegations. After delegations from Sweden, England, and West Germany, in the mid-1970s the American Secretary of Agriculture visited Budapest. In the following year, his Hungarian counterpart traveled to the United States to study agriculture, farmers' associations, and the work of research networks there.[118]

An analysis of the visits of delegations from capitalist countries reveals that in reality they were curious about a potential future competitor. This feature came up repeatedly during the visits. This is indicated in a sentence from the press release on the 1972 visit of the Danish agricultural minister: "While visiting Hungarian large-scale farms and producer cooperatives, the minister gained experiences that prompted him to urge Danish farmers to increase their competition and perfect their work."[119]

NOTES

1. Peter G. Hare, H. K. Radice, and Nigel Swain, eds., *Hungary: A Decade of Economic Reform* (London: Unwin Hyman, 1981), 3–22; Christoph Boyer, ed., *Zur Physiognomie sozialistischer Wirtschaftsreformen: Die Sowjetunion, Polen, die Tschechoslowakei, Ungarn, die DDR und Jugoslawien im Vergleich* (Frankfurt/Main: Max-Planck-Institut für Europäische Rechtsgeschichte, 2007).

2. Alec Nove, *The Soviet Economic System* (London: Routledge, 1977), 307–16.

3. André Steiner, *Von Plan zu Plan: eine Wirtschaftsgeschichte der DDR* (München: Deutsche Verlags-Anstalt, 2004), 123–64.

4. Ota Šik, *A szocialista áruviszonyok* [The commodity relations in the socialism] (Budapest: Kossuth–KJK, 1968), 46–110.

5. Iván T. Berend, *Gazdasági útkeresés 1956–1965* [Search for an economic path 1956–1965] (Budapest: Magvető, 1983), 414–47; György Földes, *Az eladósodás politikatörténete, 1957–1986* [The political history of indebtedness, 1957–1986] (Budapest: Maecenas, 1995), 27–38; Pető and Szakács, *A hazai gazdaság*, 414–47.

6. The emergence of problems in executing the plan, and acknowledgment of the increasingly severe crisis can be traced in the minutes of Politburo meetings of the HSWP. MNL OL, M–KS 288. f., 5. cs., 312., 337., 352., 363. ő. e.

7. Jegyzőkönyv az MSZMP Központi Bizottság 1964. december 8–10-i kibővített üléséről. [Minutes of the HSWP Central Committee extended session, December 8–10, 1964] MNL OL, M–KS 288. f., 4. cs., 71–72. ő. e.

8. This was an enormous financial burden on producer cooperatives, however, the advantages dominated. The idea of the farm-owned machinery moved them from being customers to being owners in accordance with their own economic interests and needs. Honvári, *A gépállomások*, 547–57.

9. Pető and Szakács, *A hazai gazdaság*, 523–31.

10. Jegyzőkönyv az MSZMP Politikai Bizottság 1966. január 4-i üléséről. [Minutes of the HSWP Politburo session, January 4, 1966] MNL OL, M–KS 288. f., 5. cs., 384. ő. e.

11. Ibid.

12. Jegyzőkönyv az MSZMP Politikai Bizottság 1966. szeptember 20-i üléséről. [Minutes of the HSWP Politburo session, September 20, 1966] MNL OL, M–KS 288. f., 5. cs., 405. ő. e.

13. *A Magyar Szocialista Munkáspárt IX. kongresszusának jegyzőkönyve, 1966. november 28.–december 3.* [Minutes of the 9th congress of the HSWP, November 28–December 3, 1966] (Budapest: Kossuth, 1967), 466.

14. Jegyzőkönyv az MSZMP Központi Bizottság 1966. december 3-i üléséről. [Minutes of the HSWP Central Committee session, December 3, 1966] MNL OL, M–KS 288. f., 4. cs., 85. ő. e.

15. Henrik Vass, ed., *A Magyar Szocialista Munkáspárt határozatai* és *dokumentumai, 1963–1966* [Resolutions and Documents of the HSWP, 1963–1966] (Budapest: Kossuth, 1968), 305.

16. The significance of the debate is clear in the fact that two years later the HSWP Central Committee Party College included a summary of the debate in a dedicated chapter of its agricultural policy textbook. See: Emil Gulyás, ed., *Az MSZMP agrárpolitikájának fő vonásai* [The main features of the HSWP's agrarian policy] (Budapest: Kossuth and Mezőgazdasági, 1970), 295–355.

17. *Társadalmi Szemle* 23, no. 10 (1968): 73.

18. Vass, *Az MSZMP határozatai, 1963–1966*, 402–9.

19. Jegyzőkönyv az MSZMP Központi Bizottság 1966. október 13-i üléséről. [Minutes of the HSWP Central Committee session, October 13, 1966] MNL OL, M–KS 288. f., 4. cs., 83. ő. e.

20. Erdei Ferenc feljegyzése Dimény Imre elvtárs részére a KB elé készített mezőgazdasági jelentéshez. 1964. január 15. [Memo of Ferenc Erdei to Imre Dimény on the agricultural submission draft to the HSWP Central Committee, January 15, 1964] MNL OL, M–KS 288. f., 28. cs., (1964) 1. ő. e.

21. A Belkereskedelmi Minisztérium jelentése a közellátás helyzetéről. 1965. december 10. [Report of the Ministry of Domestic Trade on the state of public supply. December 10, 1965] MNL OL, M–KS 288. f., 28. cs., (1965) 14. ő. e.

22. See: Beatrix Boreczky, ed., *Központi szervek, 1950–1970: A magyar* állam *szervei* [Central organs of the Hungarian state 1950–1970] (Budapest: MOL, 1993), 323–26.

23. Ferenc Kovács, ed., *A Magyar Tudományos Akadémia Agrártudományok Osztálya 50* éve [50 years in history of the Department of Agricultural Science of HAS] (Budapest: MTA Agrártudományok Osztálya, 1999), 467.

24. Ernő Csizmadia, *Bevezetés az élelmiszergazdaságtanba* [Introduction into the food economy] (Budapest: Akadémiai, 1973), 39–55.

25. It became possible for producer cooperatives to deal with food processing and sales beyond basic agricultural activities. This circle of activity was called simply ancillary activity. Holger Fischer, "The non-agricultural activities of the agricultural production cooperatives and state-owned farms in socialist Hungary 1967–1989," in *Agriculture and Rural Life in Finland and Hungary*, eds. Zsuzsanna Varga and Anssi Halmesvirta (Loimaa: Sarka, 2018), 113–25; Ervin Zsuffa, *A termelőszövetkezetek kiegészítő tevékenységének továbbfejlesztése* [The expansion of non-agricultural activities of collective farms], Új falu könyvek (Budapest: Kossuth, 1972).

26. Producer cooperatives joined the associations voluntarily, based on the decision of the general assembly of the farm; then through their delegates every member farm participated in the work and management of the territorial association; the associations were not hierarchical, i.e., the member farms were not subservient to their associations, nor was there a hierarchical relationship between the territorial associations and the national headquarters. See: Lajos Szemes, *A mezőgazdasági termelőszövetkezetek* érdekképviselete [Interest representation for agricultural producer cooperatives], (Budapest: Akadémiai, 1970).

27. Romsics, *Szabó István*, 98.

28. Pető and Szakács, *A hazai gazdaság*, 531–34.

29. *Ágnes Ungvárszki, Gazdaságpolitikai ciklusok Magyarországon (1948–1988)* [Economic policy cycles in Hungary, 1948–1988] (Budapest: KJK, 1989), 48.

30. Imre Fóris, ed., *Mezőgazdasági termelőszövetkezeti törvény: Földjogi törvény* [Law on collective farms: Law on land rights] (Budapest: KJK, 1968); K. Eu. Wädekin, "The re-emergence of the kolkhoz principle," *Soviet Studies* 41, no. 1 (1989): 20–38.

31. Also see: András Schlett, "Success and Failure of the Hungarian Agrarian Model," *Arhivele Totalitarismului* [Totalitarianism Archives] 20, no. 1–2 (2012).

32. Fóris, *Mezőgazdasági termelőszövetkezeti törvény*, 68–69.

33. Ibid., 172.

34. Ibid., 110.

35. Jegyzőkönyv az MSZMP Politikai Bizottság 1965. szeptember 21-i üléséről. [Minutes of the HSWP Politburo, September 21, 1965] MNL OL, M–KS 288. f., 5. cs., 375. ő. e.

36. In this way, for example, beginning in 1966, with the exception of cultivation land for bread grain, the breakdown of plan indicators for council organs was stopped. At the same time the council function of approving plans was also halted. János Keserű, "A termelőszövetkezetek gazdaságirányítási reformjának alapelveiről" [Basic principles of the economic management reform of the collective farms], *Társadalmi Szemle* 21, no. 4 (1966): 3–13.

37. Előterjesztés az új termelőszövetkezeti törvény irányelveiről. [Submission on the guidelines of the new law on cooperatives] MNL OL, M–KS 288. f., 28. cs., (1966) 8. ő. e.

38. János László, "A gazdaságirányítási reform és a szövetkezetek gazdasági önállósága" [The economic management reform and the economic independence of the collective farms], *Tudomány* és *Mezőgazdaság* 5, no. 5 (1967): 71–76.

39. Pál Juhász, "Agrárpiac, kisüzem, nagyüzem: Agrárszociológiai tanulmányok" [Agrarian market, small-scale and large-scale farms], in *Medvetánc: Magyar gazdaság és szociológia a 80-as években* [Bear's dance: Hungarian economy and sociology in the 1980s], ed. Tamás Miklós (Budapest: Minerva, 1988), 24–50.

40. Fóris, *Mezőgazdasági termelőszövetkezeti törvény*, 56.

41. Ernő Csizmadia, "A vállalati önállóság szervezeti alapjai a termelőszövetkezetekben" [The organizational bases of enterprise independence on producer cooperatives], *Közgazdasági Szemle* 13, no. 7–8 (1967): 844–50.

42. Fóris, *Mezőgazdasági termelőszövetkezeti törvény*, 16–49.

43. To the end of the 1940s, within the agricultural population, only servants and wage laborers could access minimal care by a doctor, while those past 65 had a modest elderly benefit. For more on the situation between the two World Wars see: Kozári, *A nyugdíjrendszer Magyarországon*, 319–31.

44. Membership was given access to the following services from the following dates: care for the sick since April, 1949; family allowance since March, 1953; maternal allowance since October, 1953; accident compensation since June, 1957; mandatory mutual retirement insurance since January 1, 1958; the institution of age or disability benefit since February, 1960. See Virágh, "A mezőgazdasági termelőszövetkezeti tagság," 453–506.

45. A tsz-ek tagságának szociális helyzete és a fejlesztés érdekében szükségesnek tartott intézkedések. [The social situation of the collective farm membership and suggestions for its improvement] MNL OL, M–KS 288. f., 28. cs., (1964) 2. ő. e.

46. Interview with Antal Gyenes. Conducted by István Hegedűs. 1986. OHA, 4.sz. 194.

47. Előterjesztés az MSZMP PB számára a termelőszövetkezeti nyugdíjrendszer továbbfejlesztésére. [Submission to the HSWP Politburo on the improvement of the pension system of collective farms] MNL OL, M–KS 288. f., 5. cs., 405. ő. e.

48. See "1966/31. sz. Tvr,;" "30/1966. (XII. 20.) Korm. sz. rendelet" [Legislative decree 1966/31 and the government decree on its execution 30/1966 (December, 20)], in *TRHGY 1966*, 143–48, 206–10.

49. See also: "16/1966. Korm. sz. rendeletet," in *TRHGY 1966*, 193–97.

50. István Feitl, "Hungarian Plans to Reform the Council for Mutual Economic Assistance, 1967–1970," in *Influences, Pressures Pro and Con, and Opportunities: Studies on Political Interactions in and Involving Hungary in the Twentieth Century*, ed. Zoltán Ripp (Budapest: Napvilág Kiadó, 2014), 239–71; Pál Germuska, "Failed Eastern integration and a partly successful opening up to the West: the economic re-orientation of Hungary during the 1970s," *European Review of History: Revue européenne d'histoire* 21, no. 2 (2014): 271–91.

51. Gazdasági kapcsolataink alakulása a fejlett tőkés országokkal. [Hungary's economic relations with the developed capitalist countries] MNL OL, M–KS 288. f., 15. cs., (1966) 115. ő. e.

52. A termelési kooperáció kérdései a tőkés országok vállalataival. [Cooperation in production with the enterprises of capitalist countries] MNL OL, M–KS 288. f., 15. cs., (1967) 128. ő. e.

53. Ibid.

54. Beruházási hitelek igénybevételének lehetősége a tőkés országoktól. [The Possibilities for Making Use of Investment Credit from Capitalist Countries] MNL OL, M–KS 288. f., 15. cs., (1968) 142. ő. e.

55. Ibid.

56. Ibid.

57. Külföldi működő tőke igénybevétele fejlődésünk meggyorsításához. [To accelerate our development towards making use of foreign working capital] MNL OL, M–KS 288. f., 15. cs., (1968) 155. ő. e.

58. A nemzetközi gazdasági kapcsolatok fejlesztésének kérdései a nem szocialista országokkal. [The questions of the expansion of international economic relations with non-socialist countries] MNL OL, M–KS 288. f., 15. cs., (1970) 182. ő. e.

59. Ibid.

60. A magyar–NSZK gazdasági kapcsolatok néhány főbb problémája. [Some major problems of the Hungary–FRG relations] MNL OL, M–KS 288. f., 15. cs., (1970) 178. ő. e.

61. Analyzing the Hungarian case could contribute considerably also to the wider topic of the Americanization of European economies after 1945. For recent overviews, see: Konrad Jarausch and Hannes Siegrist, *Amerikanisierung und Sowjetisierung In Deutschland, 1945–1970*, (Frankfurt/Main and New York: Campus Verlag, 1997); Matthias Kipping and Ove Bjarnar, *The Americanisation of European Business: the Marshall Plan and the transfer of the US management models* (New York and Oxford: Routledge, 1998); Jonathan Zeitlin and Gary Herrigel, *Americanization and its limits: reworking US technology and management in post-war Europe and Japan* (Oxford and New York: Oxford University Press, 2000).

62. Gazdasági kapcsolataink az Egyesült Államokkal. [Hungary's economic relations with the US] MNL OL, M and KS 288. f., 15. cs., (1969) 159. ő. e.

63. János Honvári–Csaba Torda, "Magyarország csatlakozása az IMF-hez és a Világbankhoz" [Hungary's accession to the IMF and the World Bank], *Archívnet* 9, no. 1 (2009), http://www.archivnet.hu/gazdasag/magyarorszag_csatlakozasa_az_imf-hez_es_a_vilagbankhoz_i._resz.html

64. Földes, *Az eladósodás politikatörténete*, 52–53.

65. The decision to establish the institution came in 1943, during the first Conference on Food and Agriculture in Hot Springs, USA. The organization was founded on October 16, 1945, in Quebec, Canada, with 44 members. The headquarters was based in Washington until 1951, whereupon it moved to Rome. The number of members grew steadily: by 1965 there were 110 members, including all the states of Western Europe and the USA. During the period in question all members of the FAO contributed to the institution's operation and projects. The level of support was established according to various criteria, with the most important being GDP per capita and total population. Based on this, the United States of America was the key funder, given that it provided for 31.91% of the full budget for 1966–67. This was followed by West Germany at 9.74% and the UK at 9.48%. The minimum contribution at this time was 0.04%, which was the quota for 47 developing countries. Ralph W. Phillips, *FAO: its origins, formation and evolution, 1945–1981* (Rome: FAO, 1981).

66. A FAO alapokmányai. [The foundation documents of the FAO] MNL OL, XIX–K–9–ae 24. d.

67. It is not widely known that in early 1957 Hungary made efforts to rejoin, but the Hungarian government demanded the canceling or restructuring of membership fees and other payments accrued since 1951. See the minutes of the government meeting of January 24, 1957: Baráth, *Kádár János első kormányának jegyzőkönyvei*, 187–88.

68. A significant role in the preparation of rejoining was played in Rome by Andrew de Vajda, who was of Hungarian origin, and who later, as an expert commissioned by FAO, directed the construction of the irrigation system in the Tisza River valley. I am grateful to Dr. Péter Vándor for this information.

69. Information related to the FAO membership of the Hungarian People's Republic. MNL OL, XIX–K–9–ae 24. d.

70. A FAO MNB 1968. évi kiutazási és meghívási terve és költségvetése. [The 1968. travel plan and budget of the Hungarian National Committee of the FAO] MNL OL, XIX–K–9–e 133. d.

71. A FAO vezérigazgatójának magyarországi látogatása. [The visit of the Director-General of the FAO in Hungary] MNL OL, XIX–K–9-ae 24.d.

72. Zsuzsanna Varga, "Agrarian Development from 1945 to the Present Day," in *History of Hungarian Agriculture and Rural Life, 1848–2004*, ed. János Estók (Budapest: Magyar Mezőgazdasági Múzeum, 2004).

73. The UNDP (United Nations Development Program) was a program of the UN Development Organization. It was established on November 22, 1965, by merging the EPTA (Extended Program of Technical Assistance, founded in 1950) with the UN Special Fund (founded in 1959). Within the UNDP these two areas remained separated. A FAO működése, szervezete és programja. [The functioning, organization and programs of the FAO] MNL OL, XIX–K–9–ac 82. d.

74. Tájékoztató a FAO küldöttség magyarországi látogatásáról, 1986. [Information on the visit of the FAO delegation in Hungary] MNL OL, XIX–K–9–e 36. d.

75. This was used to establish the Tisza II experimental model farms project in the 1970s (Irrigational agriculture in the valley of the Tisza River), and it was decided that an experimental fishing hot water station would be established and the Fishing Research Station in Szarvas would be further developed as a fishing research and education institution. The latter two projects were completed in the 1980s. Andrew de Vajda, *Adventure, achievements, altruism: The story of my life* (Rome: Bonte-Friedheim, 1983), 140–45.

76. János Gyenis, *A nemzetközi szövetkezeti mozgalom története és mai helyzete* [The past and present of the international cooperative movement] (Budapest: Erdei Ferenc Szövetkezeti Alapítvány, 1993).

77. Deborah Fitzerald, *Every Farm a Factory: The Industrial Ideal in American Agriculture* (New Haven, CT: Yale University Press, 2003); Noël Kingsbury, *Hybrid: The History and Science of Plant Breeding* (Chicago: University of Chicago Press, 2009); John H. Perkins, *Geopolitics and the Green Revolution: Wheat, Genes, and the Cold War* (New York: Oxford University Press, 1997).

78. Borhi, *Dealing with dictators*, 265–322.

79. Tájékoztató jelentés a Magyar Forradalmi Munkás-Paraszt Kormány részére a mezőgazdasági szakdelegáció tanulmányútjáról, 1969. [Report to the Revolutionary Workers-Peasants Government on the study trip of the agricultural specialists' delegation, 1969] MNL OL, XIX–K–9–ab 34. d.

80. Úti beszámoló Amerika mezőgazdaságáról. [Travel report on the agriculture of the US] MNL OL, XIX–K–9–ab 34. d.

81. See: Péter Sárközy, *Szemtől szembe Amerika mezőgazdaságával* [Face to face with the American agriculture] (Budapest: Mezőgazdasági, 1970).

82. See: György Enyedi, *Farmok és farmerek: Az amerikai mezőgazdaság* [Farms and Farmers: American agriculture] (Budapest: Mezőgazdasági, 1970).

83. István Gergely, "Az amerikai tanulmányút tapasztalatai" [The experiences of the American study trip], *Magyar Mezőgazdaság* 21, no. 49 (1969): 5–7.

84. It was not the first time that Roswell Garst hosted Hungarian guests. The expert delegation visiting the USA in December 1955, also visited his farm with the goal of purchasing hybrid corn seed and a hybrid corn processing plant.

85. Gergely István feljegyzése Fehér Lajos részére az USA kapcsolatok alakulásáról. 1970. május 8. [Memo of István Gergey to Lajos Fehér on the development of relations with the US], MNL OL, XIX–A–2–ll 13. d.

86. Burgert, *Iparszerű termelési rendszerek*, 32–38.

87. Each complex consisted of, among other things, tractors, deep ploughs, disc machines, 12-row seeding machines equipped with photocells and seeding control monitors, row cultivators, insecticide spraying machines, and combines. Ibid., 32–33.

88. Paul Marer, *East-West Technology Transfer: Study on Hungary 1968–1984* (Paris: OECD, 1986), 159–160.

89. Burgert Róbert javaslata Fehér Lajosnak a bábolnai iparszerű kukoricatermesztési rendszer kifejlesztésére, 1970. december 5. [Proposal of Róbert Burgert to Lajos Fehér on the development of industrial-style corn production at Bábolna State Farm, December 5, 1970.] MNL OL, XIX–A–2-ll 13. d.

90. Sárkány, *Termelési rendszerek az állattartásban*, 103–19.

91. Ibid., 87–102.

92. Ibid., 120–21.

93. A Nádudvari "Vörös Csillag" Mezőgazdasági Termelőszövetkezet iratai, 1952–1975. [Documents of the "Red Star" Collective Farm, Nádudvar, 1952–1975] MNL HBML, XXX. 421.

94. Ibid.

95. Csaba Balogh, "Szántóföldi növénytermesztési rendszerek" [Closed production systems in crop farming], in *A mezőgazdaság szolgálatában: Emlékkönyv Dimény Imre tiszteletére 90. születésnapja alkalmából* [In attendance on agriculture: Memorial volume in honor of Imre Dimény on the occasion of his 90th birthday], eds. Judit Dimény and Péter Szendrő (Budapest and Gödöllő: SZIE, 2012), 99.

96. As long as the technology was in working order the service network assisted with repairs, the delivery of parts and special repairs that the local facility could not carry out. The technological and service contract was renewed every year. The basic contract was for an undisclosed period of time, for which the new member received basic services and technology. The member could purchase any further machinery or

services. The level of farm satisfaction with the work could be measured by looking at whether contracts were renewed for the same areas. Documents of the "Red Star" Producer Cooperative, Nádudvar 1952–1975. MNL HBML, XXX. 421.

97. Gábor Csontos, *A Hortobágy szélén: nádudvari beszélgetések* [At the edge of Hortobágy: conversations in Nádudvar] (Budapest: Hét Krajcár, 2005), 232.

98. The scale of this data is reflected in the fact that the KITE database contained data on 800–1000 sunflowers, 1,000–1,500 wheat, and 1,500–2,000 corn plots per year. Vera Garai and András Meszticzky, *Tapasztalatok* és *gondolatok a szántóföldi növénytermelési rendszerekről* [Experiences and ideas on the closed production systems in crop farming] (Budapest: AKI, 1977), 55–59.

99. The annual 2,500–3,000 operational hours squeezed out of large tractors provided manufacturers with accelerated operational experience data for future development. It would have taken family farms several years to produce such large quantities of data.

100. Sárkány, *Termelési rendszerek az állattartásban*; Imre Dimény, ed., *Kertészeti termelési rendszerek ökonómiai jellemzői* [Special economic features of the closed production systems in horticulture] (Budapest: Mezőgazdasági, 1980).

101. Schlett, *Sziget a szárazföldön*, 76.

102. Iván Oros, ed., *A falu és a mezőgazdaság főbb társadalmi és gazdasági jelzőszámai* [Main economic and social indicators of village and agricultural development] (Budapest: KSH, 1994), 246–47.

103. Fazekas, *A mezőgazdasági termelőszövetkezeti mozgalom*, 248–49, 266.

104. Központi Statisztikai Hivatal, *Mezőgazdasági statisztikai zsebkönyv* [Agricultural statistical pocketbook] (Budapest: KSH, 1980), 136–37.

105. Ibid., 97–99.

106. On the long-term effects of the process see: Ferenc Glatz, *Új vidékpolitika* [The new rural development policy] (Budapest: MTA Társadalomkutató Központ, 2008), 15–27.

107. László Bosznay, "Az agrárszakoktatás 50 éve" [50 years of the agricultural special training], in Orosz, Für, and Romány, *Magyarország agrártörténete*, 616–23; Pál Juhász, "Az agrárértelmiség szerepe és a mezőgazdasági szövetkezetek" [The role of the agricultural intelligentsia and agricultural cooperatives], *Medvetánc* 2–3, no. 4 (1982) / no. 1 (1983): 191–224; András Meszticzky, "Elnökök, szakvezetők, munkavezetők a termelőszövetkezetekben" [Presidents, Managers and Professional Leaders in Agricultural Cooperatives], in *Szövetkezeti Kutató Intézet Évkönyve 1975* [Yearbook of the Cooperative Research Institute, 1975] (1976): 279–333.

108. Imre Dimény, *Mezőgazdaságunk* és *a műszaki fejlesztés* [Our agriculture and technical development] (Budapest: Kossuth, 1972).

109. The figure of 40,000 professionally qualified agrarian experts was repeated in many interviews conducted for this project.

110. Imre Dimény, "A magyar mezőgazdaság sikeressége a 60-as, 70-es években" [The successfulness of Hungarian agriculture in the 1960–70s], in Nagy–Kovács, *Személyiségek a magyar agráriumban*, vol. 1, 89–90.

111. *Mezőgazdasági statisztikai zsebkönyv, 1980*, 73–76.

112. János Pék, "Ötven év a magyar állattenyésztésben—ami száz évet jelentett" [Fifty years in the Hungarian animal husbandry], in *Falvak, földek, földművesek: Agrárpolitikai, agrártörténeti, településfejlesztési tanulmányok* [Village, land, peasantry: Studies on agrarian policy, agricultural history and rural development], ed. Gyula Pócs (Budapest: Agroinform, 2004), 221–22.

113. Schlett, *Sziget a szárazföldön*, 63–66.

114. In the 1970s almost 30% of all Hungarian poultry meat exports went to the Middle East. Központi Statisztikai Hivatal, *Mezőgazdasági statisztikai zsebkönyv* (Budapest: KSH, 1976), 18.

115. Sárkány, *Termelési rendszerek az állattartásban*, 180–85.

116. *Mezőgazdasági statisztikai zsebkönyv 1976*, 18.

117. György Földes, "A magyar–szovjet gazdasági kapcsolatok 1948–1973" [Hungarian–Soviet economic relations, 1948–1973], *Századok* 147, no. 6 (2013): 1349–76.

118. Varga, "Agrarian development from 1945," 284–85.

119. *Magyar Mezőgazdaság* 22, no. 30 (1971): 11.

Chapter Seven

Contextualizing the "Hungarian Agricultural Miracle"

HUNGARIAN SPECIFICITIES UNDER ATTACK

Success within the Eastern bloc was noticed worldwide, and it is no coincidence that the Western press increasingly used the term "Hungarian model."[1] This term is not used in this monograph, not because it accepts the official line of the time that denied the existence of the model out of deference to Soviet superiority (see below), but in the belief that proper use of "Hungarian model" requires a systematic comparative study of the other socialist countries. It is appropriate nevertheless to pull together the initiatives through which Hungarian agricultural cooperatives emerged as independent entities by comparison with the kolkhoz form. It was precisely these characteristics that were in the sights of the forces that, in the following years, tried, sometimes overtly, sometimes covertly, to put the brakes on economic reform.

The first point to make is that producer cooperatives became independent farming undertakings. The producer cooperative disposed of the equipment necessary for farming, and it could use with security both the land that had become its own property and that which formally remained property of members, for which it paid a rent. It owned an ever-increasing quantity of livestock and machinery, storage facilities, and means of transportation. It enjoyed a very wide freedom to conduct various industrial and construction activities. It could sell its produce through a choice of channels. It built up an ever-closer relationship with household plots, and developed a rational division of labor with them. The historic debate, over whether small-scale or large-scale agriculture was better or more efficient, was settled (for the time being). The Hungarian answer was: a combination of the two. But it must immediately be added that this was not made possible by the discernment of those in power, in and of itself, but by the strength of the producer cooperative memberships in defending their interests, and by the agrarian lobby, which was able to transmit that strength wisely to those in power.

Second, it is worth emphasizing that, through the local initiatives of producer cooperatives, an unbelievable variety of incentive systems had emerged in place of the previously imposed work-unit system which was totally alien to the Hungarian peasantry. Forms of incentive, that were adjusted to the work-culture and habits of the memberships, had already broken free of plan indicators and were tied to results.[2] It is understandable that when income and later property differences appeared in villages, the majority saw them as just. Basic social security was guaranteed; producer cooperatives could not abandon the elderly, and they strove to keep the young in villages by grants for house-building and scholarships for study. An increasing number of trained experts were attracted through production systems that adapted developed Western knowledge and technology transfer: they formed a university-educated agrarian intelligentsia. Not only was the basis of the agrarian lobby strengthened by this, but this modern intelligentsia acted as a role-model in village societies in flux.

To summarize, therefore, it can be said that, while the kolkhoz model disintegrated the Hungarian village by divesting members of their property, and further in the main assuring state interests over those of the producer cooperative membership, by the second half of the 1960s, through grassroots initiatives, the producer cooperative provided a framework for the realization of individual and collective life goals. All these "unplanned" phenomena were as repugnant to the dogmatic thinkers in the Hungarian political leadership as they were to the Soviet leadership. It is not surprising that, at the beginning of the 1970s, debate sharpened over the direction of future development. The debates and their consequences are presented in the next two sections. They betray a great deal about the "fundamental nature" of the party-state system.

As is also indicated above, not all branches of the Hungarian economy were able to take advantage to the same degree of the opportunities opening from 1968. In the decade and a half from 1960 to 1975, a rapid push forward took place in the agricultural and food sectors. The following data illustrate this clearly: Hungarian agricultural production grew faster than the world average and the Comecon average.

Transition to the new system of economic management was more difficult for industrial enterprises, despite the fact that they benefited temporarily from numerous concessions and discounts,[3] and, in fact, the values of the main economic regulators in 1968 were tailored so that they would not immediately make it impossible for low level, inefficient enterprises to operate.

Meanwhile, agriculture, thanks to the flexible and successful adaptation of producer cooperatives, became ever more the "star performer." Agriculture

Table 7.1. Gross Agricultural Production Index, 1975

	Gross agricultural production index for the year 1975 (1960 = 100%)	*Gross agricultural production index per capita for the year 1975 (1960 = 100%)*
Comecon level	145	125
Hungarian level	155	147

Source: Ernő Csizmadia, "Élelmiszertermelésünk és a külgazdaság," in A *mezőgazdaság fejlődésének szocialista útja a legutóbbi két évtized magyarországi tapasztalatai tükrében*, ed. Károly Girus and Péter Simon, kézirat gyanánt (Budapest: Tudományos Szocializmus Információs és Továbbképzési Intézet–ELTE BTK, 1982), 53.

and the food industry were praised not only for the improving level of domestic food supply, but also for the results that they achieved in the areas of both ruble and dollar exports. By contrast, industrial enterprises lacked the sorts of up-to-date products that could be sold well abroad. The following criticism was expressed: "Some (industrial) companies put more effort into accessing and holding on to state support and concessions than, for example, reducing the level of costs and increasing productivity."[4]

Representatives of heavy industry, who in previous decades had enjoyed positions of unchallenged privilege, took these criticisms especially hard. It is well known that the concept of socialist economic development was tightly linked to the primary role of heavy industry, which, during the Cold War, included the necessity of increasing military production.[5] From the late 1940s onward, the general experience of factory directors from these spheres was that heavy industry (mining, electrical energy production, smelting, the machine industry) received most investment. As a result, a heavy industry lobby group evolved that supported itself by the ideological axiom that the leading role in the construction of socialism belonged to the working class. From 1949, in the spirit of this tenet, tens of thousands of industrial workers were "promoted," that is to say, given brief training and placed in leading positions of political, economic, and social life.[6] Many of them nurtured their links with their former enterprises, and, when necessary, would mobilize their relational capital.

The heavy industry lobby therefore was composed not only of the branch ministries (after 1956: the Ministry of Heavy Industry and the Ministry of Metallurgy and Machine Industry) and the leaders of the largest companies, but also of "worker cadres" who had been built into the central or regional party apparatus, and also the National Council of Labor Unions. These functionaries felt that there were considerable numbers within both the party leadership and the apparatus who, from the beginning, had had doubts about, or were even opposed to, the New Economic Mechanism. It was they who, overwhelmingly on the grounds of dogmatism and ideological inflexibility, entered the anti-reform camp. The interest of the heavy industry lobby in opposing the reform arose from the fact that its economic position began to decline after 1968, because of the branch's difficulties in adjusting to market conditions discussed above.

Rezső Nyers remembered the formation of the anti-reform camp as follows: "It was only after the fact that I heard information about an organized counter-attack, but at the time I didn't encounter anything like that personally. . . . Anyway, in a relatively closed system like ours, it was not the 'normal order of things' for an opposition to step forward openly and agitate. Instead, once it had searched out a point which could be attacked by appeals to public opinion, and, in relation to which, the system also hoped to intervene in the interest of power, there it would exert pressure through lobbying in influential circles using critical arguments that concealed their goals."[7]

This quotation points to a very important characteristic of policy-making in the party-state. Because there was no possibility for an open clash of interests, conflicts appeared in the ideological sphere instead.[8] Changes in the preferences of those in power can be traced through the modulations of ideological axioms. Two large themes (property relations and hierarchical subordination) can be highlighted, where interpretations changed as the 1968 reforms were prepared, resulting in a wider room for maneuver for producer cooperatives. The superior status of state property had been for a long time an unchallengeable tenet of the socialist property relations question.[9] Yet, during the conceptual preparation for the 1968 reform, it was stated that "both kinds of ownership—state and cooperative—are equal property forms."[10] Despite this, at the beginning of the 1970s, debate began again in the press over whether cooperative and state property had equal status. Cooperative ownership was criticized mainly for household plots and ancillary enterprises.

Hierarchical subordination was also manifest in the domain of interest relations: individual and group interests (enterprise, producer cooperative) had to be subordinated to social interests (all people's, people's economy). The introduction of the New Economic Mechanism, however, gave scope to the idea that socialist society too could be characterized by the existence of social groups with divergent interests, that is to say, group interest became a concept for "polite society."[11] From the beginning of the 1970s, however, emphasis on the primacy of social interest gained strength once again. What is more, views also appeared calling for action to be taken against those who valued individual and group interest to the detriment of the community or country.

The following case exemplifies the increasingly coordinated actions of the anti-reform forces. In the first half of 1970, the Iron, Metal, and Electrical Energy Industry Workers Union and the Supervision Department of the Ministry of Metallurgy and Machine Industry carried out a joint study of the ancillary industrial activities of producer cooperatives in the Budapest area. In the summary report, which was also submitted to the HSWP Economic Policy Committee, attention was drawn to the problem that workers and employees in the industrial units of producer cooperatives were being paid such high premiums and other forms of workplace supplement that, when taken together with their basic wages, they were significantly higher than the hourly wages and supplements of those carrying out similar activities in state enterprises. On the one hand, this led to an unjustifiable income inequality between cooperatives and large industrial enterprises, on the other, by offering higher incomes, producer cooperative were "siphoning off" skilled workers from the state sector. "Our enterprises have already had to deal for a long time with the labor-siphoning effect of the introduction of cooperative ancillary enterprise activities. The problem was also on the agenda of the meeting between the leaders of our union and the comrade Minister of Metallurgy and Machine Industry. In addition, the question was also raised at the ministerial meeting on Soviet–Hungarian trade, where it was noted that the large-scale labor-siphoning effect on the part of cooperatives is having a negative impact on enterprises meeting our commitments in the direction [of the Soviet Union]."[12]

Over the course of 1971, this and other similar actions finally succeeded in placing in front of the Politburo a number of questions which could be linked as the negative effects of reform. On March 9, the Politburo debated a document titled "The scale, direction and causes of labor migration, as well as the restriction of undesirable labor migration and measures designed to enhance respect for loyal and long-standing workers."[13] Six months later, the non-agricultural activities of producer cooperatives too came before the Politburo.[14] The consequences took on legal form at the end of the year.[15]

The heightened sensitivity of the Kádár leadership in the spring of 1971 can be explained by the Polish crisis and increasingly forceful criticism from Moscow related to it. Kádár summarized the lessons to be learned by the Hungarian leadership as follows: "I would like to state—although I am not superstitious—that we must take the lessons of the events in Poland seriously. However bitter it may be, it is free advice for our task, and ignoring it would be a serious mistake . . . the comrades who are preparing economic measures must think seriously about whether we are going in a direction that is sustainable as a line for ten years, and will not require us to undo anything at all. I am not saying that this is the situation here, but the events in Poland are telling us something."[16]

Events in Poland in December 1970 also posed a serious challenge for the Soviet leadership. The Polish government suddenly announced massive increases in the prices of basic foodstuffs, especially dairy products, following a bad harvest, and these proved to be a major shock to ordinary citizens, especially in the larger cities. Riots and demonstrations ensued, which were put down by the Polish army. At least 42 people were killed and more than 1,000 wounded, forcing party leader Gomulka to resign, and his replacement, Gierek, to promise economic and political change. The price increases were reversed, and wage increases announced. Such instability in the Soviet camp came at a particularly bad time because the Soviet Union was hoping to focus on realizing its foreign policy plans. Of these, the most significant were the German question and preparations for the European Conference on Security and Cooperation.[17] Romania's increasingly independent foreign policy and rapprochement between the USA and China were causing the leaders in the Kremlin concern enough, and they therefore expected the "fraternal parties" in Central and Eastern Europe to act as a secure and calm hinterland. This was the message, wrapped up in an ideological cloak, of the 24th Congress of the CPSU in spring, 1971.[18]

Changing Soviet expectations were not only expressed in official forums, but were also insinuated into the Hungarian Party leadership through less formal channels. At the end of July, 1971, Kádár traveled to the Soviet Union for a rest, and, while he was there, took part in the annual meeting in Crimea of the leaders of the socialist camp. In September, Brezhnev stopped off in Budapest for a brief exchange of views when returning from an unofficial visit to Yugoslavia. The Soviet secretary general stressed that the only way to avoid a shock like the Polish crisis was for the fraternal parties to refrain from diverging from the path of Marxism-Leninism. Hungary did not appear to be unstable either economically or politically, but nevertheless, by this time, it stood alone with its economic reform. It was not only this that stimulated hostile reactions from the leaders of the "fraternal countries," but also the fact that Hungary was trying to strengthen market attitudes within Comecon.[19]

Verbal warnings were soon reinforced in written form. Material arriving from the Soviet Foreign Ministry expressly concentrated on the economic arena. The view was formulated that, because of the New Economic Mechanism, fulfillment of interstate commitments had become uncertain.[20] In 1971, Andropov also visited Hungary. János Kádár informed Rezső Nyers about the meeting, who recalled the following: "By then the discussion with Andropov concerned the whole of Hungarian reform policy—I don't want to use the term debate, although in reality it was a debate, and at this time, Andropov was a partner who still maintained an element of constructiveness toward Kádár. So he reported on all of this. But this conversation was already a sign that a sequel was yet to come. . . ."[21]

The effects of pressure to conform had already made themselves felt in the life of domestic Hungarian politics in the first half of 1971. Leading bodies of the HSWP received one after the other materials which analyzed some tension or other that had emerged as part of the reform, but in previous years these had got stuck at the level of departments and committees of the Central Committee apparatus. In them, two themes were of greatest significance: labor migration and income differentials. Both now came before the Politburo in March 1971.[22] The memoranda were prepared by the Economic Policy Committee, which counted as the highest forum for preparing decisions on matters of economic policy, and where, until 1970–71, leaders supporting the reform had been the majority. The material submitted to the Politburo was neutral, but the debate became heated. The anti-reform forces wanted unambiguously to criminalize labor migration, and they found their scapegoat in producer cooperative ancillary enterprises, claiming that they seduced workers away from the more developed state sector into lower order cooperatives. This reasoning was effectively an attack on the reform itself, and from two sides. First, because easing labor mobility had been an important measure of the New Economic Mechanism, and, second, because the equality of ownership forms had already become accepted during the preparations for the reform themselves. The strength of the anti-reform force offensive is reflected in the fact that, a few months later, the Politburo debated the situation of producer cooperative ancillary enterprises as a separate agenda item.[23]

The March 1971 Politburo meeting is also worthy of note because it was at this time that it could be sensed that the empathy that Kádár had expressed toward the agricultural matters up until then had begun to fade. Furthermore, with the death of Ferenc Erdei, the agricultural lobby lost an intermediary, who could always be counted on when it came to convincing Kádár.[24]

Kádár's changed position was visible in numerous future Politburo meetings, but especially in negotiations about the 1972 economic plan and budget.[25] In 1971, the economy did not perform as well as expected, and it became clear that belt-tightening would be necessary. When it was time to decide who should carry the burden, the industrial and agricultural lobby groups immediately tensed for action against each other. The actors and the arguments were the same as they had been before. Rezső Nyers characterized Kádár's changed attitude as follows: "In the reform period . . . he was fully empathetic toward agrarian problems, that is to say, towards the problems of the peasantry. This lasted until 69–70, then later, when the period of vacillation ensued, he was taken capture by the problems of wages and labor migration. Then his empathy disappeared, and in 1974–75 he had almost turned into the opposite."[26] Reinforced by this, the opponents of reform, arm-in-arm with the representatives of the heavy industry lobby, took aim at the most successful actors in the agrarian sphere, the producer cooperatives. The offensive began at the ideological level: caught in the crossfire were the issues of interest and ownership relations.

The year 1972 began in the spirit of ever more forceful Soviet criticism arriving from ever-higher sources. In February, 1972, Kádár reported to Politburo members on his talks with Brezhnev in Zavidovo: "In one of the phases of the negotiation, comrade Brezhnev—his own, personal opinion throughout—spoke separately and at length about how he is unsettled by certain negative features in the Hungarian economic situation, and various phenomena which, as tendencies, were dangerous. . . . They see processes in which . . . a growing part of our equipment and good labor force is gradually moving from the very important state sector to the looser, cooperative and private sector. Income relations develop such that the income of a relatively small section of the population is rapidly increasing, while that of a significant mass of workers does not, or only to a small degree. Prices are going up and certain consumer items are only available to those with high incomes. This makes the workers dissatisfied, and, with time, social and even political tensions can arise. . . . Generally the center, including the government, must keep under better control the processes and tools necessary to reverse undesirable tendencies."[27]

The effect of direct or indirect criticisms that appeared in various forms was further to strengthen debates within the HSWP between pro- and anti-reform forces.[28] At the same time, the Hungarian Party leadership increasingly found itself on the defensive: toward the Socialist bloc it could not stress enough that it was not aiming at fundamental restructuring, that the reforms did not create an economic system different from those of the other socialist countries, and that no "Hungarian model" existed.

In mid-October, 1972, the HSWP's central newspaper *Népszabadság* felt it necessary to emphasize in a leading article:

> Nowadays one of anti-communism's latest and effective methods has . . . come to the fore: the propagation of various "models" of socialism. . . . Its goal . . . is to inflame nationalism, arouse nationalist separatism, to stir up distrust among the countries building new societies. In accordance with this dual ambition, "models" can be divided into two different groups. One contains the so-called varieties of socialism, which are labeled "democratic," "with a human face" and so on, while the other contains "national types," for example "Russian" or "Hungarian" socialism. . . .
>
> The "national" models of socialism try to pit national characteristics against the general law-like nature of building socialism. . . . With the help of "models," national separateness is "justified" and encouraged, and further it belittles the international significance of the Soviet experience of building socialism. The goal of the theory of the various national models of socialism is to inflame nationalism and anti-Soviet views.
>
> Bourgeois propaganda is also advertising the existence of some kind of "Hungarian model," contrasting it with the construction work of the other socialist

countries. . . . In this situation our position is clear: we reject unfounded conceptions of the emergence of the so-called Hungarian model.

By the fall of 1972, however, position-statements of this kind did not suffice. Exploiting external political pressure from Moscow above all, but also from the GDR, Czechoslovakia, and Bulgaria, the internal opposition to reform succeeded in getting the HSWP Central Committee at its meeting of November 14–15, 1972, to decide to put the brakes on the New Economic Mechanism.[29] The decrees passed at the meeting signaled that power relations between pro- and anti-reform camps had shifted in favor of the latter, especially those which increased the wages of industrial workers and introduced special treatment for the 50 largest industrial enterprises. But the meeting did not demote politicians committed to reform, such as economic policy secretary Rezső Nyers, deputy prime minister responsible for agriculture and interior affairs Lajos Fehér, and Prime Minister Jenő Fock. János Kádár referred to this at the Central Committee meeting: "We say that the Party and the country does not need heads to roll when we speak of mistakes; but they need us to establish precisely what is progressing healthily and appropriately in terms of implementation, and where there are difficulties, where tasks have not been successfully resolved."[30]

The struggle between the pro- and anti-reform forces did not come to a final end with the November 1972 Central Committee decree.[31] In the ensuing period, the dogmatic group centered around Béla Biszku attempted to use "tailwinds from Moscow" to force through the personnel changes that had not taken place in November. To do so they had to prove that the New Economic Mechanism had triggered very dangerous processes. The attack came on two fronts: market-economy attitudes in the agrarian sector and quickly expanding relations with the West. Producer cooperatives were caught in the crosshairs of both forces. For one side, they were positive examples to be used as a model, while, the other side wanted to use them to prove the harmful effects of reforms.

This is how it could happen that, despite the agrarian sphere's visible production results, a press campaign unfolded to discredit producer cooperatives. A spate of articles appeared suggesting that producer cooperatives had achieved their so widely acclaimed results dishonestly, through trickery and speculation.[32] The focus of these criticisms was primarily directed toward ancillary activity, that is to say activity which went beyond basic agricultural activity. Criticism became especially strong from the beginning of the 1970s. According to the newspaper articles, ancillary activities distorted cooperative development, distracted managers and members from agricultural production, and represented unfair competition for the industrial sector, because it siphoned off qualified labor with its higher salaries. Furthermore, focus on food processing was undermining their responsibilities in respect of supplying food. And so on.

ANTI-REFORM REFORMS

The transformation of thousands of collective farms (kolhozes) into sovkhozes in the Soviet Union in the first half of the 1970s provides a suitable point of reference for the re-regulation of producer cooperatives and their leaders.[33] That is to say, the tenet that state ownership was of a higher order came onto the agenda again in agriculture. In the socialist camp, the Soviet example was copied most quickly by Bulgaria (not for the first time), which established extremely large-scale, agricultural-industrial complexes.[34] In the GDR, a process of merging producer cooperatives (Landwirtschaftliche Produktionsgenossenschaften) began, followed later by their specialization: some farms specialized in crop production, while the others specialized in animal husbandry.[35]

There were, therefore, once again, plenty of examples to follow; and keeping a distance was made difficult by several factors. On one hand, there was the fact mentioned above, that, by the 1970s, the majority of socialist countries had given up on economic reforms. This is well illustrated by the fate of the Hungarian reform proposal to improve cooperation within Comecon.[36] On the other, there was a strengthening in Hungarian-Soviet economic relations of processes that increased Hungary's defenselessness in respect of Moscow. From the end of the 1960s, in the course of harmonizing five-year plans, it became increasingly difficult to increase deliveries in the fields of fuel and raw materials.[37] Commodity trade with Comecon partners, in which it sold energy and industrial materials in exchange for instruments, medicine, technological equipment, or consumer goods, was increasingly inconvenient and unprofitable for the Soviet Union.

For Hungary, however, it was vitally important to be able to ensure its energy and raw materials needs from Soviet imports.[38] Furthermore, attention had also to be paid to the Soviets' ever-strengthening requirements for investment credit. In this situation, the Kádár leadership was obliged to make political and ideological concessions in certain questions in order to realize its economic interests. Yet it had great need of the agrarian sector, under ideological assault as it was, because everyone knew that the branch was playing an increasing role in convertible currency exports.

It is this duality that explains why the Hungarian economic leadership sought solutions which, while appearing formally to demonstrate adoption of the Soviet example, did not cause serious disruption to the operation of the economy. One such measure was the organization of agrarian-industrial combines, the first of which were opened on January 5, 1971, in Tokaj-Hegyalja, Bábolna, and later Bóly, Agárd, and so on.[39] When, however, following the Soviet and Bulgarian examples, something had to be done about producer cooperatives, it turned out that simply merging farms would be sufficient to prove that the model was being followed. The industrialization of agriculture and the use of modern technology did indeed require that an appropriate organizational scale be created by merging producer cooperatives which farmed only small areas, but in many cases, mergers were implemented without consulting those affected, on the basis of higher-order decisions, the exercise of power, and, as a result, were accompanied by a great deal of conflict and clashes of interest. It should also be noted that, in many cases, party leaderships used mergers to remove successful, entrepreneurial producer cooperative presidents, with whom they had had many conflicts over the preceding years.

While, in earlier years, there had been an average of 60–70 mergers per year, the rate rose dramatically after 1972. The number of communal farms decreased from 2,314 in 1972 to 1,917 in 1975 and 1,338 in 1980, while their average area doubled, reaching 4,000 hectares. The majority of producer cooperatives were affected by this process, more than half of them on two occasions, but others were merged multiple times. In the first half of the 1970s, producer cooperatives that encompassed six to eight or even more villages were formed across the country, but mainly in the Transdanubian counties. The counties where the number of mergers exceeded the national average were: Veszprém County, where in 1974–75 the number of producer cooperatives fell from 117 to 49; Zala County, where the fall was from 91 to 45; Borsod County, where it was from 174 to 116; Pest County, from 145 to 96; and Szabolcs County, from 203 to 159.[40]

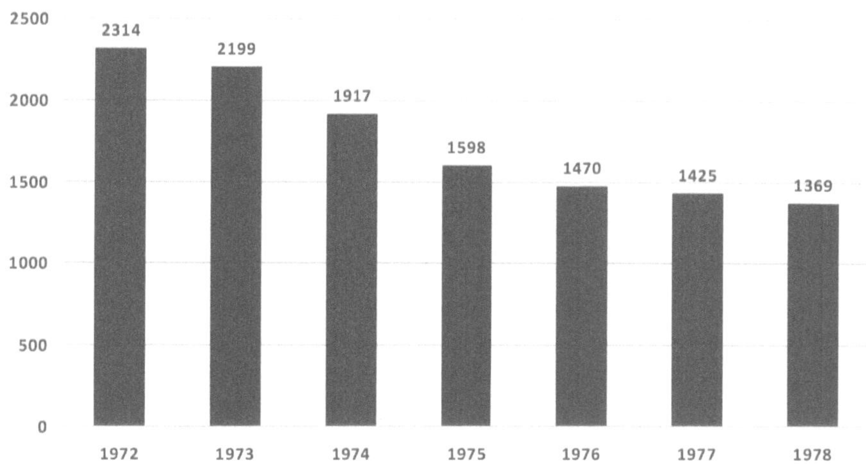

Figure 7.1. Number of Cooperatives (1972–1978). Source: *Mezőgazdasági statisztikai zsebkönyv 1978,* 16.

The leaders of the agrarian lobby periodically drew attention to the negative consequences of the campaign-like implementation of mergers.[41] In 1973, Lajos Fehér himself brought the question up in an extended memorandum sent to János Kádár: "I have become aware that, in some places, forceful moves can be experienced within county and district apparatuses for formal, campaign-like mergers. The essence of this is that farms are merged without restructuring production and farming, and in the following year the bill is submitted to the state, relying on the fact that it will not fail to pay it—because many villages and thousands of people are affected. So far, we have managed to wrestle with these unfavorable phenomena. But if producer cooperative mergers were to become a national campaign, it would take a long time to overcome its consequences, and this would slow down the development of production. In recent years, the pace of development of agricultural production has been 5%, it almost reached the pace of industrial development. A large role in this was played by the fact we concentrated our attention on questions of production and farming methods, and we resolved organizational questions on the basis of these. This is why our practice so far, which tied structural change to the pace of investment and mechanization, is more correct than a nation-wide campaign of producer cooperative mergers."[42]

In 1974, there were so many reports of mergers that had been forced on farms without due legal process, that the Cooperative Policy Working Group reworked its recommendations and warnings. "We must be circumspect in our political preparations for mergers. It is necessary to ensure that, in this essential question, the members be able to decide in the general meeting, in full knowledge of realistic calculations as specified in law, without unfounded promises, strictly adhering to legality. Should any producer cooperative general meeting vote, following legal procedures, to reject a merger, that decision must be respected. *Political preparation for merger—convincing the membership of the advantages of merger—cannot be replaced by any form of administrative measure or violence (wearing members out, convening meeting after meeting).*"[43] [Author's emphasis] A year passed, however, before the national leadership indicated readiness to accept these problems. On the recommendation of the party leadership, the Council of Ministers ordered that, from 1975, the prior approval of the Minister of Agriculture and Food was necessary for a general meeting to be able to put producer cooperative mergers onto the agenda.[44]

COOPERATIVE LEADERS IN THE DOCK

By the midseventies, as a result of transformations in the world economy, Hungary's bargaining position in relation to the Soviet Union had weakened so much that Kádár was obliged to make further political concessions to the Hungarian anti-reform forces, who enjoyed Soviet support. The victory of the Biszku group at the 11th Congress of the HSWP was symbolized by both personnel changes and a new political direction. The two leading figures of the New Economic Mechanism, Rezső Nyers and Lajos Fehér, retained their Central Committee membership, but were excluded from the main decision-making body, the Politburo. Following the Congress, Kádár accepted Prime Minister Jenő Fock's resignation, and at the same time the government was reshuffled.[45] This further weakened the agrarian lobby, because Minister of Agriculture and Food Imre Dimény was removed as part of it.

The "decapitation" of the agrarian lobby opened up the possibility of disciplining its local representatives. This, however, was no easy task, because, after 1967, as a result of the increased independence of producer cooperatives, the police could only investigate a farm if there were grounds for suspicion that a crime had taken place. State supervision of cooperatives differed fundamentally from that of state enterprises, where the state held ownership rights. The state could only exercise control over the legality of cooperative operation via councils, fiscal bodies, and so on, and they only had supervisory powers in their respective functional areas.[46]

There was only one organization that could supervise all facets of the economic activity of a cooperative, and that was the People's Control Commission (PCC). It is worth briefly explaining this organization, because its activities have received very little attention in studies of the Kádár era. It was established in 1957 in order to provide assistance to state bodies in "solidifying state and citizen discipline, defending the people's property and uncovering abuses."[47] The organization had only a small (paid) apparatus, and most of the people's controllers participated on the basis of "social work," that is to say, they received a paid holiday as compensation for their work for a fixed period of time and nothing else. After completing their investigations, PCC could initiate disciplinary action or fines; in more serious situations, they were obliged to submit reports to the police and/or the prosecutor's office. People's Control organizations were also established at district and county levels, and the entire network was held together by the Central People's Control Commission (CPCC). Formally the CPCC reported to the government, but in fact it was under the auspices of the party. The interweaving of the branches of power is also reflected by the fact that the Prosecutor General always attended CPCC meetings, as did regional prosecutors in the district and county level PCC meetings.[48]

The role of initiator in prosecutions, therefore, fell to the People's Control organizations. It seems that, after filtering investigations into the matter in every county and district, from 1973 the PCCs concentrated on the cooperatives that had not made it through the sieve, or had not been allowed to make it through the sieve.[49] A clear tendency is apparent, in that, from the early 1970s, a growing proportion of people's control investigations ended up as criminal complaints. Furthermore, more than two-thirds of these resulted in charges being laid.[50]

The people's control investigations are of particular significance because it was on the information provided by these investigations that the police and prosecutors relied in their legal proceedings against the producer cooperative leaders. Trials instigated against producer cooperative leaders can be categorized for practical purposes on the basis of the themes of the PCC investigations. Very common among them were abuse of ancillary activity, the illegal or inappropriate use of state support, and the violation of storage contracts. There were also a large number of cases of falsifying accounts or official documents, and bribery.

An attempt to summarize the kinds of producer cooperatives that were subjected to court proceedings would reveal that they were very often successful and sometimes nationally renowned producer cooperatives. These were farms that had successfully mined the possibilities of the New Economic Mechanism, headed by leaders imbued with its newly opened entrepreneurial spirit.

Producer cooperative presidents were a special group within the stratum of economic leaders. They were not appointed, like, for example, the directors of state enterprises; rather, they were elected. What is more, since 1967 they had been elected by secret ballot. Producer cooperative presidents, therefore, were responsible not only to the district and county-level party leaders, but also to the farm membership. Numerous conflicts arose from this situation, chiefly when, by representing the interest of the membership, the president contradicted the local political leadership. At the beginning of the 1970s, when the offensive against producer cooperatives was launched in national politics, several local party leaders felt that the time for revenge had arrived. Local factors therefore, not just "high politics," played a role in the initiation of legal proceedings against producer cooperative presidents.

In earlier sections concerning the 1960s, emphasis was placed on the extent of local divergence at county and district levels from the practice of national agrarian policy. This situation had not changed in the early 1970s. This is well illustrated, among other things, by the fact that there were districts where, because of the stance of the party secretary, more "president trials" were created than in other whole counties. Furthermore, this also explains why proceedings of this kind continued to be initiated at the local level in the latter half of the 1970s, by which time the national political line had changed.[51]

Producer cooperative presidents were joined in the dock by other specialists (chief agronomists, chief accountants), often ordinary producer cooperative members too. Another characteristic group of defendants was made up of employees of council, bank, or state organs which had relations with producer cooperatives; these were mainly involved in bribery cases. It is not surprising, therefore, that a common feature of trials was the high number of those accused. There are records of some trials with 19 defendants. A large number of witnesses were brought in too: in one case testimony was heard from 120 witnesses.[52]

Some of the producer cooperative leaders put on trial turned out to be innocent, while there were others who truly were complicit in economic abuse. But even in the latter cases, there were features of the proceedings, both at the stage of initiating prosecution and reaching a verdict, that gave the affairs the characteristics of a show trial.

One striking feature was that prosecution was brought on the same counts in all of the trials, primarily crimes against social property (especially: serious fraud, misappropriation of funds, theft, dishonest handling, negligent handling). In the case of economic leaders, judgment on these crimes was passed in accordance with the stricter interpretations of the amended Criminal Code appropriate for leaders rather than simple members.[53] Furthermore, the fact that the public duty to report had been extended to every one of the crimes of this sort, made it exceptionally easy to raise charges. All that was needed was the testimony of a producer cooperative member or employee to the effect that the producer cooperative president knew about the abuse; and those who did not live up to their duty to report, themselves became complicit in the crime.

Reviewing the documents associated with the investigations, it becomes clear that incriminating testimonies of this kind mainly were made by producer cooperative members who were in prison on remand. The interviews show that the police did not use physical force, but they did persuade them to give false evidence using blackmail and promises. Some were threatened that, if they did not make an incriminating testimony, they would have to remain on remand; others were fed with promises that if they confessed, they would be allowed to go home to their families. Another successful technique was to blackmail them with "everyone else has already confessed." In numerous cases, incriminating testimony coerced in this way became the basis of the indictment of producer cooperative leaders. It is important to add, however, that these false testimonies were often revoked during trial.

In cases of mismanagement and dishonest handling, there was no need to involve producer cooperative members, because, in these cases, only economic managers were implicated. Nevertheless, imprisonment on remand was greatly significant here too. There were instances of remand lasting for one and a half and even four years. The rationale given was usually that there was a danger that the accused would escape or go into hiding, because of the heightened social danger of the crimes and the expected severity of punishment. Given that these cases related to well-known, sometimes nationally renowned, producer cooperative presidents, it is likely that preventing escape was not the main motive. Instead, it is more likely that it was hoped that the stress and psychological tension caused by detainment and isolation would make the suspect crack and confess, so making the job of the organs of justice easier.

The length of time that passed between arrest and the beginning of trials can be explained by delays in preparing indictments. Charges were built upon well-defined notions. Generally, the dominant attitude was that cooperative farming and the rapid increase in peasant incomes that went with it, could not have happened "legally." The prevalent political mood is well characterized by the author of a contemporary piece of sociography: "If a producer cooperative has poor results, that is suspicious, but if its results are good, that is even more suspicious."[54] It was easy enough to construct a charge based on this preconception, but gathering evidence progressed much more slowly. This was why efforts were made to get the accused to make a confession. In interviews, many producer cooperative presidents made reference to the sorts of tools used in this respect in the investigative phase of proceedings. There were cases where their duty lawyer tried to convince them to confess, others where a cellmate mole was introduced to gain a confession.

Research for this volume uncovered several legal infringements not only in the investigative phase, but also during the judicial phase; for example, witnesses for the defense were hardly ever called. Even more significant was the fact that the modified criminal code created several intervention channels through which the subjectivity of judges, and, in this way, political influence, could prevail.

A graphic example of how the political line was realized comes from one of the earliest cases. Because the first level court did not yet sense the new "way the wind was blowing," it was the Prosecutor General who made the necessary adjustment in the appeal process. "The county court was in error when it ruled that the majority of actions were committed in the interests of the producer cooperative membership and that this constituted mitigating circumstances. Such an interpretation of the acts of the accused is incorrect, not only legally but also economically, because prioritizing group interest by dishonorable means is not an isolated phenomenon."[55]

The following passage from the Supreme Court judgment indicates that the Prosecutor General's argument had an effect: "By their actions, defendants number I, II, and III hoped to gain illegitimate advantages for their producer cooperative by adopting methods that are unacceptable in a socialist economic system. . . . Society is greatly endangered by serving the imagined or momentary interests of the producer cooperative at the expense of the people's economy, by misleading the organs of management and control, even when, as in the current case, the perpetrators were not primarily motivated by selfish material interests."[56]

It is equally shocking that the above "group interest flogging" argumentation also appeared in rationale underpinning court verdicts in the midseventies: "Perpetration of the act was not motivated by direct private profit, but by the desire to serve at all cost the concrete cooperative and its members, to maintain at all cost the good reputation of the cooperative."[57]

In the spring of 1974, as noted above, the main representatives of the reform were dismissed: Lajos Fehér, Rezső Nyers and, later, Jenő Fock and Imre Dimény too.[58] This was followed by the nationwide activation of "scapegoat-creators." It is worth noting the response, for example, in Szabolcs-Szatmár County, which counted as Béla Biszku's backyard. In 1974, the county prosecutor said the following at a press conference: "Agriculture continues to be the area in which the highest number of crimes against social property takes place. Damage in this field is 23.4 percent of total damage. . . . In the spirit of the 10th Congress of the HSWP and the November 1972 and 1973 Central Committee decrees, the necessity of heightening the struggle against speculative abuse is indicated by the fact that, compared to 1972, we have submitted accusations against three times as many people for the crime of price-increasing, and two and a half times as many people for the crime of tax fraud."[59] If the sections indicating dates were removed, this quotation would fit perfectly with the combative vigilance campaigns in the 1950s. The "strong-hand policy" reached its apogee in Szabolcs-Szatmár County in 1975, when hardly a month passed without the unveiling of one or two cheating producer cooperative presidents.[60] When a verdict was reached in the county court in the case of the latter producer cooperative president in Nagykálló, an article in the county paper commented on the lessons to be learned: "It is impermissible to subordinate basic farm activities to ancillary enterprise activities of dubious value . . . there is a heavy price to pay for decisions taken exceeding capacities against the community, for the failure to exercise internal and external controls. . . ."[61]

It was already clear from the People's Control investigations that there were very big differences between counties and even within each county, when it came to uncovering strengthening "capitalist" characteristics in producer cooperatives. It cannot be claimed that irregularities and economic abuse did not occur in producer cooperatives. In fact, after 1968, there were many deficiencies in the areas of funds management, the management of stock and remuneration and wage calculations. Discrepancies between legal regulation and economic practice existed before the introduction of the new economic mechanism. However, while this problem was handled constructively by control organs in the 1960s, that is to say, they tried to move legal regulation closer to actual practice, from the beginning 1970s, this duality increasingly became a weapon of attack. Everyday, widespread economic phenomena were criminalized. For example, the common practice of sums of money in brown envelopes facilitating the acquisition of spare parts that were in short supply prompted the charge of "bribery." The charge of infringement of contract with the corn-purchasing enterprise was applied to an equally common practice related to shortage. Farms would sell all of their corn to the enterprise before the end of the economic year so that they could have the necessary cash to pay members bonuses. But the corn would remain in their own barns because the enterprise did not have sufficient storage space. If in the interim, the farm used some of that (already sold) corn to feed its livestock and paid the enterprise the value of lost crop at then current prices, this was nevertheless deemed to be an infringement of the contract. The judicial verdict on such procedures was completely uncertain, depending on how a given county or district interpreted socialist legality: that was how producer cooperative leaders were judged.

Although it would be inaccurate to consider the leaders of Bács-Kiskun county to be anti-peasant at the time in question, there was one district, Kecskemét, where there were more producer-cooperative-president trials than in the rest of the county combined. In his book on producer cooperative presidents, Árpád Pünkösti mentions as examples the cases of the presidents in Kunpeszér and Tiszaalpár, where the exercise of pressure by the district party secretary was proven unambiguously.[62]

The producer cooperatives of the Budapest area were not in a good position either. On one hand, they were always in full view, on the other, because of their circumstances, they were among the first to feel obliged to expand their ancillary enterprises. The authorities blew hot and cold, but the leaders for the most part got away with verbal warnings, disciplinary action or the occasional fines. In 1975, however, the relevant organs in the capital decided that the time had come for them to finally unveil a massive producer cooperative criminal gang. The president of the targeted cooperative, "Rozmaring," counted as a truly "big fish," not just because of the producer cooperative's national reputation, but also because of his political connections. It was common knowledge that he was on good terms with Lajos Fehér, and he was a member of the leadership of the National Council of Producer Cooperatives. The farm had become well known for its floriculture and its network of quality flower shops. Over October and November of 1975, many leaders of the producer cooperative were also arrested, and when, after umpteen interviews, not one of them was willing to testify against the president, on December 5, 1975, the police took the president away for "a little chat," which eventually became more than six-months' imprisonment on remand.[63]

Preparing the indictment took a long time, but in the meantime there was plenty of scope for an intensive press campaign to discredit producer co-operative presidents in the national daily and weekly press. The tone of the articles is vividly illustrated in the following example: "Some employees of the cooperative—for example the deputy head accountant and the head of the labor affairs department—had warned the president several times: if he continues to manage the producer cooperative in this way, he will end up in the dock. President Alajos Kovács did not believe them: 'Exaggerated administration, strict order,' he said, 'would weaken the effectiveness of the professional management.' As is now obvious, bribery was one of the main tools for effectiveness in the Rozmaring Gardening and Agricultural Producer Cooperative. The leaders of the producer cooperative, who according to the indictment had caused almost one million forints' worth of damage to the people's economy, are now on remand, awaiting trial."[64]

At the center of the indictment were fictive salaries as well as manipulations using fake travel receipts. The Budapest Prosecutor' Office set the damage caused by the farm at 940,000 forints. Later in the proceedings, the figure decreased significantly, just as the charges against the producer cooperative president "melted away" as the trial progressed. The Budapest court sentenced the president to 14 months imprisonment and a fine of 5,000 forints. The Supreme Court in its verdict increased this fine to 20,000 forints and dropped the prison sentence.[65] All of which quite reasonably prompts the question of how many versions of justice exist. In the latter case, the party leadership's Public Administration and Administrative Department, which supervised the administration of justice, exercised self-criticism, but only in 1978, after the removal of Béla Biszku.[66] The trial of the leaders of the Rozmaring producer cooperative was reexamined, and the following was established concerning the verdict passed by the Budapest Court: "The verdict was not without error. The court unjustifiably imputed the accused with certain crimes, while, regarding other acts, the guilt of the accused was incorrectly not established. The legal classification of the offenses was not always correct. As a result of all these factors, the punishments meted out to certain of the accused were not legal."[67]

For producer cooperative leaders who were party members, court verdicts were not the end of their accountability. They also had to answer to the party for their actions, even if they had been found innocent. In party logic, they still bore moral responsibility. A separate organization dealt with party punishment. This was the Central Control Commission (CCC), about which there is very little information in the literature to this day. Its key tasks included, on the one hand, examining concrete disciplinary affairs, complaints, and appeals, while, on the other, it analyzed the experiences of disciplinary work in the party and reported its findings to its leading organs. Its activity covered considerably more than supervising the ethical and moral relations of the party membership. In reality, it created an atmosphere of permanent menace: threats of disciplinary punishment and exclusion from the party, so enforcing conformity with central decisions.

CHANGING ECONOMIC ENVIRONMENT—UNCHANGING IDEOLOGY

When the oil crisis of 1973 hit, the leaders of the socialist countries initially announced that it was not restricting their economies, but to no avail. It soon became apparent that they too had to face the effects of the restructuring of the world economy. This was especially so from 1975, when a change was introduced into the mode of payments settlement between Comecon countries: the Bucharest price principle was replaced by a so-called sliding price basis system, a system which established prices annually.[68] The consequence of this was that the impact of changes to world market prices could also be felt in ruble-denominated trade, albeit after some delay. For Hungary, this meant that the level of Eastern import prices increased (by an average of over 25% in 1975), as did energy (which doubled in 1975).[69] Hungary's era of cheap Soviet energy, therefore, came to an end.

So far as trade with the West was concerned, Hungary had to face the fact that the price of everything that it exported had decreased, while, at the same time, modern Western technology had not become any cheaper.[70] Furthermore, because of the recession, it became increasingly difficult to find markets for Hungarian exports. This change in the conditions of trade caught Hungary's foreign trade policy in a dramatic trap. Until 1973, Hungary was able to acquire sufficient convertible currency to finance its imports of Western machines, spare parts, and raw materials by exporting agricultural, metallurgical, ethylene chemicals, and clothing products to the West. These were in turn incorporated into the finished industrial products created with the help of cheap Eastern energy and raw materials imports, which were then exported to the East to balance Soviet energy imports.[71]

After 1973, Hungary was in a situation of dual dependency, caught between the pincers of, on the one hand, a thirst for dollars and, on the other, an unfavorable palette of commodities and prices for Western export opportunities. Because it still could not do without importing raw materials and spare parts from the West, it was obliged to export anything it could possibly sell, at reduced prices, in the shrinking markets of Western countries.[72] At the same time, the Soviet Union was becoming an increasingly tough trading partner, demanding more and better goods in exchange for its increasingly expensive energy. These two factors contributed considerably to a deficit in ruble-based trade.[73]

In this new situation, increasing production to make possible an increase in agricultural and food exports to both West and East became a factor of strategic importance. In the middle of the 1970s, the food economy accounted for 20–23% of all exports, more than its share of national production, and within this, one-third of Hungary's convertible currency exports. In this way, the food economy contributed to the stability of the Hungarian national economy an export surplus of 50–60 billion forints, of which 30 billion was in convertible currency trade.[74]

Table 7.2. The Share of Agriculture in the National Economy 1960–80

	1960	*1965*	*1970*	*1975*	*1980*
Active earners	37.7	27.4	24	204	19.5
Gross production	–	–	16.7	15.9	16.6
Gross domestic product (GDP)	–	–	18.2	16.5	18.1
Investment	13.7	14.3	18	11.8	11.9
Exports	22.1	23.2	22.8	22.6	23.3

Source: Oros, *A falu és a mezőgazdaság*, 164.

These factors obliged the party leadership to put an end to the anti-producer cooperative campaign that had dominated in previous years. As a first step, small-scale agricultural production was "rehabilitated."[75] The Politburo itself debated the necessary steps at its meeting on February 10, 1976. The submission stated, with regard to the potential of household and supplementary plots, that:

> Around half of their products go to meeting their own needs, the rest is sold as commodities. They produce half of our pork. They play a determining role in the production of some vegetables and fruits, eggs and small animal husbandry. An ever increasing number of small-scale farmers rely on the expert, material and technical support of producer and consumer cooperatives, and produce and market in a structured manner. This integrates them into our socialist economic system.
>
> There has been a decline in some places and at some times in household plot and supplementary farm production. A number of factors have contributed

> significantly to this: condescending views concerning household plot production, incorrect practice, occasional local abuses of power, reducing material incentives, and the disorganized state of purchasing. *The Party is taking decisive steps against phenomena that damage equally the interests of producers and the people's economy.*[76] [Author's emphasis]

This attitude characterized the session of the Council of Ministers which duly followed on February 26, and the series of decrees that it passed.[77] In February, the leaders of the Ministry of Agriculture and Food embarked on a national tour.[78] The official rationale underpinning these visits was to consult with county party and economic leaders on the 1976 plan and decide on tasks for the five-year period. In reality, the goal was to inform them of the correction that had been made to agricultural policy.

A further impetus to these moves was given by the emergence, in the spring of 1976, of severe problems in meat supply, and these demanded immediate measures.[79] In addition to ordering meat imports, the government took new steps to develop household plots and supplementary farming. The government extended an earlier concession whereby work spent on household plots (raising cattle and pigs, or growing potatoes, vegetables, and fruit) was considered as cooperative communal labor, provided the members sold the animals, vegetables, and fruit to state or collective organs. In such cases, the producer cooperative approved the workdays for the members concerned, and these days were taken into account by social insurance services, for example, when calculating pensions, social assistance, and paid holidays.[80]

In the fall of 1976, the tax systems for household plots and supplementary farms were unified and simplified.[81] It is appropriate to review briefly what this policy correction entailed, because it was precisely via taxation that activities had been most successfully restricted. According to the new rules, from January 1, 1977, all users of plots no larger than 0.6 hectare would uniformly be taxed at the lower household plot taxation rate. This new tax bracket would remain in force for several years, so long as size of plot and branch of production did not change. The effect of the other tax concessions can be summarized by stating that taxpayers could count on a reduction in their tax burdens in 1977 by a third. Parallel with this, both the Cooperative Policy Work Group and the Economic Committee emphatically drew attention to the propaganda tasks in respect of disseminating information within the local party and council organs.

> It must be made known that the work of agricultural small-scale producers is useful from the point of view of the people's economy and is an activity which has a role to play in our social development. The income derived from it is a supplement to income derived from the permanent work place and is the result

of additional work. Our propaganda and news organs should meaningfully participate in molding public opinion to understand this.[82]

There was still an ideological risk attached to these measures, and it is precisely because of this that the Kádár leadership tried to justify these agrarian sector initiatives too as a strengthening of state property and adherence to the Soviet model. This is how agro-industrial associations were formed in Hungary. The first was the Hajdúság Agro-Industrial Association, established in the fall of 1976 through the participation of 14 large-scale farms, the Kaba Sugar Factory, and the Debrecen Poultry Industry Enterprise.[83] The initiator and leader, that is to say, the managing agent, was the Red Star Producer Cooperative in Nádudvar. Its president, István Szabó, recollected as follows:

> Initially I was not as enthusiastic about it as I was for Corn and Industrial Plant Production Cooperation (KITE). It wasn't even my or our idea, but that of the brains in Budapest, including Kádár, who probably wanted to live up to Soviet expectations. Back then, in the mid-seventies, Soviet agrarian politicians saw the future in large-scale agro-industrial integrations, over hundreds of thousands of hectares, equipped with computer-controlled, chemical-spraying airplanes. Farms like those I was shown in Siberia. I saw a similar one in Bulgaria, which Moscow probably meant as a guinea pig for the Comecon countries. I thought it was nonsense for several reasons. Partly because it did not take household plots into account at all, and they were blooming here in Hungary, and partly because the Soviet technical base was underdeveloped compared to what we had imported from America. *Kádár, however, expressly asked that I organize and manage one of the associations to be created here too as a test, or just as window-dressing.* But in a way that would maintain the independence of the producer cooperatives and other cooperating units. This latter stipulation was reassuring, and so I then took on the task. Besides ours, there were three other similar associations in the country, in Békéscsaba, in the Szigetköz and in Kalocsa.[84] [Author's emphasis]

The increasing status of the agrarian sphere was evident in the fact that Kádár participated in the 3rd Congress of agricultural producer cooperatives in mid-December 1976. The speech of the party first secretary is worthy of note, not only because it was the first time that he had taken part in the producer cooperative congress, but also because he touched on the very topics that had been most hotly debated in previous years. When evaluating agricultural achievements he spoke of income relations. "Agriculture, therefore, has contributed to the increase in living standards, and, at the same time, in accordance with party policy, as the material situation of society as a whole has generally improved, so too has that of agricultural workers: the income levels of workers and peasants have been practically the same for years."[85]

As was discussed in the previous chapter, in the first half of the 1970s, most debates concerning producer cooperative farming had been triggered either by the household plot or by ancillary nonagricultural activities. Regarding the household plot and supplementary farming, the party first secretary acknowledged that they played a significant role in food supply, then continued: "We must more consistently strive to create an organic unity between the communal farm and the household plot in agricultural producer cooperatives." When speaking about cooperatives' ancillary activities, he indicated that both party and government approved of and supported all endeavors that were closely connected to producer cooperative activities, such as repairing machinery in their own workshops, engaging in construction activities and, most important, processing their own food products.[86]

As the above quotation indicates, the correction in agrarian policy did not constitute a complete return to the spirit of the 1967 law on producer cooperatives.[87] This was indirectly expressed when János Kádár turned to cooperative democracy and reminded his audience:

> "We cannot be satisfied, because, often, rights and responsibilities are not realized equally, and there is still a lot of formalism. These mistakes contributed to the fact that the social supervision of cooperatives has temporarily weakened, and this has resulted, in places, in weakened discipline, management errors and offenses against communal property. In the future, democratic life must be made more genuine." He also expressed how he thought this should be carried out. ". . . while respecting the independence of producer cooperatives, the work of state administrative bodies must be better harmonized, increasing their roles in control and assisting production."[88]

Previous sections have discussed at length the extent of economic damage caused by restrictions on household plot farming and ancillary production units. At the same time, it must be emphasized that the production systems that were created as a result of Western model transfer suffered less from the dogmatic turn in economic policy, while this transfer was not organized by authorities or administrative offices, but by economic actors themselves (state farms, producer cooperatives). Furthermore, these were not only capital-rich enterprises, but enterprises whose directors enjoyed significant political capital.[89]

They faced certain restrictions as far as their operation was concerned, but the modernization process was not broken, in fact their production results on a national scale were at their best in the second half of the 1970s. Closed production systems were most widespread in arable crop cultivation. In 1977, the use of crop production systems, including vegetables, extended to almost 30% of arable land, and 20% of plantations for large-scale viticulture and fruit production. In animal husbandry, 36% of cows involved in large-scale dairy farming, 51% of sows, and 87% poultry breeding pairs belonged to systems.[90]

At the same time, it was during this period that the structural problems of industrialized large-scale agriculture were slowly becoming apparent. As already noted above, from the 1960s the development of Hungarian agriculture was characterized by a rapid growth in the use of materials of industrial origin (artificial fertilizer, pesticides, machines, fuel, and so on). In 1968, the ratio of materials of industrial origin used in agriculture was 52.4% of gross production value, while, by 1978, it was already 65%.[91] Over the same period, the costs of materials used increased threefold.[92] This tendency was exacerbated greatly by the opening of the price scissors. Even at the end of the 1970s, four-fifths of agricultural products were in maximized or fixed price categories. As a result, agricultural producers were unable to pass on the majority of the price increases for industrial materials and equipment, and the previous income situation of agriculture and the food industry deteriorated significantly.

The National Association of Producer Cooperatives was at pains to draw attention to this tension. These issues were discussed increasingly openly in professional forums. However, when the HSWP Central Committee discussed the situation of agriculture at its March 15, 1978, meeting, the success-story narrative dominated decisively.[93] Károly Németh, the Central Committee secretary responsible for economic policy, submitted the report on the situation of agriculture, and it is instructive to consider where he placed the emphasis. First, he stressed that the food supply was stable, because this was a basic condition for the party's standard-of-living promises to be realized. Károly Németh went on to evaluate food exports, which "had risen five-fold over the last decade and a half."[94] He expressed his appreciation of the fact that the export of foodstuffs made up a significant part of both dollar and ruble exports. Further, he pointed out the profound transformation that had taken place in the living and working conditions of the peasantry over the preceding decade and a half.[95]

After Károly Németh's success-centered evaluation, Lajos Fehér, former leader of the agrarian lobby who had been forced to retire in 1974 and who had earlier indicated that his comments would be "somewhat different in mood," immediately asked for the floor. His comments are worth quoting at length, because, alongside the successes achieved, he detailed problems and factors that would obstruct further development.

Fehér also began his address by praising the accomplishments of agriculture. He stated: "Averaged over the past five years, the active balance of our agricultural and food industry foreign trade was between 2–3 billion hard-currency forints."[96] He also added that the country acquired at least a half of the hard currency necessary for the development of the people's economy, and an even bigger share on the European convertible currency market, by the ever-growing export of agricultural goods and food industry products. He pointed to a concrete example:

> As far as the significance of corn to the people's economy is concerned, I have data from 1975, according to which the forint value of the total harvest that year exceeded 18 billion forints. This is more than the combined value that year of coal, oil, natural gas, bauxite, quarried stone, pine and deciduous timber. In other words, corn is the most important raw material in Hungary's economy. And this is not poetic phrase-mongering. This is the main base material for meat supplies, and meat in the form of livestock, but we hope in ever growing quantities in processed form too, is our most important raw material, mainly in European convertible export.[97]

Concerning future challenges, Lajos Fehér continued his analysis by pointing out: "it is imperatively necessary that agriculture and the food economy in general be treated appropriately at the level of the people's economy. And in my view this is not the case." He supported this by showing that the ratio of investments in agriculture had declined year by year, it was estimated to be 10–12% in the current five-year plan. By comparison, he noted that in Hungary this ratio was the lowest of the socialist countries. He warned that this low level of investment in agriculture threatened the future: "we would use up that foundation which we laid by our investment so far in the second and fourth five-year plan periods."[98]

He placed the development and modernization of the food industry as top priority of the tasks at hand. Regarding securing necessary investment funds, he said: "Over the past decade and a half, when preparing five-year and annual plans, this was always one of the most important questions in the struggle, and, in these almost tooth and nail struggles, we always lost out."[99]

In the second half of his address, Lajos Fehér turned to problems related to the anti-producer-cooperative campaigns of previous years. He listed the negative effects of the producer cooperative mergers, the impacts of the debates on the right of cooperative property to exist, and then spoke about interference in incentive systems on producer cooperatives.

Finally, he did not avoid what counted as the most uncomfortable question of all:

> Over the last five-six years, a so-called criminal investigation has been launched against the cooperatives. Numerous newspaper articles appeared in our papers that made it seem that producer cooperatives had become veritable breeding grounds for economic crimes and corruption.[100]

He made reference to an investigation in which representatives of the Ministry of Justice and the Ministry of the Interior, along with other bodies, had examined the development of crimes against social property from 1968 to 1975.[101] The study established that crimes of this nature represented 20% of the total in the economy as a whole, while among agricultural producer cooperatives it was about half of this, approximately 11%. The study also revealed that three-quarters of crimes against producer cooperatives were committed not by members but by outsiders (for example, commercial agents). At the end of his comments, Lajos Fehér proposed that a committee be established to determine who was responsible for the anti-cooperative campaign, and that this body initiate the rehabilitation of cooperative leaders who had been unjustly accused.

Not a single participant in the Central Committee session responded, and the committee that Lajos Fehér proposed at the end of his remarks was not established. No one investigated the extent of material loss to the people's economy caused by to the attack on producer cooperatives, nor the degree of moral damage inflicted on producer cooperative presidents, their families, and the entire cooperative sector itself by the torture of show trials. The top political leadership, therefore, failed to exercise self-criticism for the anti-cooperative campaign of the preceding years. Neither Lajos Fehér nor Rezső Nyers returned to power. They had to content themselves with Kádár's dismissal of the two leading figures of the anti-reform camp: Árpád Pullai in April, 1976, and then Béla Biszku in April, 1978.[102]

LIMITS OF THE "HUNGARIAN AGRICULTURAL MIRACLE"

In the first half of the 1980s, the Hungarian agrarian sphere found itself in a paradoxical situation, whereby, thanks to the developments of the previous period, it stood at the international forefront in many areas, yet the domestic economic environment had developed so unfavorably, that cuts had drained its reserves for development.

According to FAO statistics, in 1980, Hungary's per capita meat production was second highest, topped only by Denmark. Five years later, Hungary was in fourth place, behind Denmark, the Netherlands, and Australia, yet in wheat production, it was second to only Canada. It occupied an exceptional position in the mass production of chicken eggs (second to the Netherlands).[103] It is no wonder that leading American newspapers regularly reported on Hungarian success in agriculture. The December 20, 1981 edition of the *New York Times* reported "Hungary became an island of plenty in food-short Eastern Europe mainly by avoiding its comrades' mistakes."[104] One year later, the *Los*

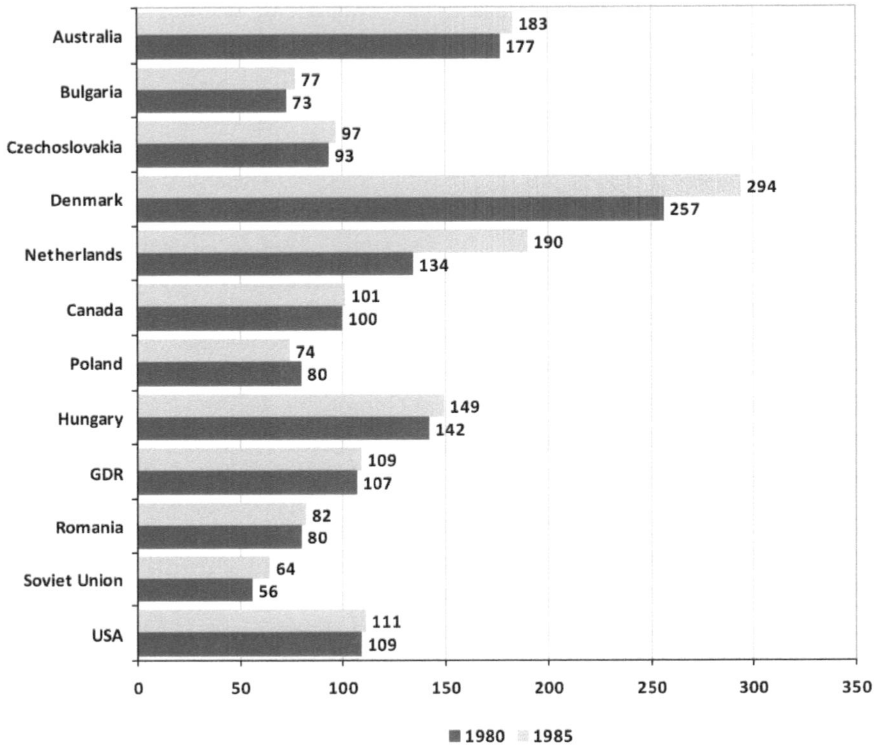

Figure 7.2. Meat Production per Capita (KG) 1980–1985. Source: *Mezőgazdasági statisztikai zsebkönyv 1986,* 280–287.

Angeles Times claimed "Hungary now has the most successful agricultural system in Eastern Europe, providing the nation with hard currency exports and food for the people at home."[105] On April 29, 1985, the *Christian Science Monitor*, with a degree of poetic license, stated: "Agriculture remains the sole bright spot on the economic horizon here. . . ."[106]

Similar praise, albeit somewhat less enthusiastic in tone, also came from the Soviet Union.[107] At the time, the USSR was struggling from severe and permanent food shortages; its food imports increased tenfold in the 1970s, the cost of which, by 1980, had risen to over 7 billion dollars.[108] The Soviet Union, which at the beginning of collectivization had represented the only possible model for the countries of East Central Europe, was, therefore, forced to admit, three decades later, that it still had something to learn.

The publication of an article in *Pravda*, the CPSU's central newspaper, on June 16, 1980, can be interpreted as a symbolic expression of Soviet interest in Hungarian agriculture. The article was entirely dedicated to introducing a Hungarian cooperative, the March 15 producer cooperative in Hernád.[109] The attention of the editors of Pravda was caught by this producer cooperative in Pest County because of its high-level integration of small-scale into large-scale production. The Hernád communal farm had built automatized "mini-chicken factories" in yards of small-scale producers, and had often provided loans for the process. The farm provided the members with day-old chicks and feed, and, further, specified the technology for raising them. After 50–60 days, it transported the grown chickens (about 3,000 from each yard) to the farm's poultry processing unit. The success of the operation was made possible by the fact that the Hernád producer cooperative, as system manager of the Hunniahibrid system, had established poultry production cooperation with 126 producer cooperatives and four state farms, and had built on it vertical channels for cooperative poultry meat production: it organized the operation of the poultry-meat branch from the production of day-old chicks in their millions, through their processing, to their sale (they had ten shops at the time) and their export (30% of their product was exported). The Soviet article also made it clear that the small-scale sector integrated by large-scale socialist agriculture (which the article termed the second line) provided one-third of gross agricultural production in Hungary, and this contributed greatly to its plentiful food supply.

In February 1981, several daily papers reported that Brezhnev, at the 26th Congress of the CPSU, had openly praised the achievements of Hungarian agriculture. In the fall of 1982, not long after his election as First Secretary, Andropov noted in one of his economic policy speeches that "we have much to learn from the fraternal countries, especially from Hungarian agriculture." Gorbachev had already praised the development of agriculture in Hungary when he was Central Committee agriculture secretary, and, after coming to power in 1985, he stated explicitly that Hungarian agriculture could serve as a model for the other East European countries.[110] Although it is not central to the monograph, it would be interesting to investigate the degree to which Hungary served as a technology transit country for the other socialist countries, and which countries adopted which Hungarian agricultural innovations.[111]

Meanwhile, Hungary's debt level reached such a critical point that earlier economic policy priorities had to be completely transformed. Financing growth through foreign loans had failed, and therefore the standard-of-living policy of constantly improving living standards had to be abandoned.[112] The new top priority was debt-servicing and balancing foreign trade. In this situation, the Kádár leadership once again put IMF and the World Bank membership onto the agenda. After a delay of a decade and a half, at its session on October 22, 1981, the HSWP Central Committee agreed, with one vote against, to let the government initiate the accession process.[113] Moscow was only informed officially of the decision after the event, because the Hungarian political leadership realized that the deteriorating economic situation in the Soviet Union meant that it was no longer in a position to meet any Hungarian request for a loan.

Barely a month after the official representatives of the Hungarian government in Washington submitted their request for membership of the IMF and World Bank, Poland declared martial law. Because of growing uncertainty about the socialist countries on the international financial markets, it was impossible to get new loans. This vindicated the decision taken in the fall of 1981.

On May 6, 1982, Hungary won acceptance to the IMF, and on July 9 it became a member of the International Bank for Reconstruction and Development (World Bank). In 1982, Hungary suffered a credit and credit-worthiness crisis so severe that, without the help of the IMF, it would hardly have averted insolvency.[114]

All of these factors placed increasingly heavy burdens on the agrarian sector. Jenő Vancsa, who from 1980 headed the Ministry of Agriculture and Food, recalled several times in his memoirs the intense conflicts of interest between the financial apparatus and the agrarian lobby over five-year plans.[115] The government intended agrarian exports to play an especially large role in order to maintain relative equilibrium in the balance of payments with capitalist countries.[116]

Throughout the 1980s, the annual value of food-product exports on the convertible currency account exceeded the value of Hungary's agricultural imports by 700 million to 1 billion dollars.[117] Furthermore, these exports made it possible for Hungarian industry to continue operating, constrained as it was to import materials, energy, and technological equipment, and weak as it was in exporting, especially to hard-currency markets.

Table 7.3. Foreign Commercial Turnover (Millions of Forints) 1980

	Socialist countries	*All other countries*	*Total*
	Total Hungary		
Import	151,755.4	148,143.1	229,898.5
Export	154,864.1	126,148.2	281,012.3
Balance	+ 3,108.7	–21,994.9	–18,886.2
	Agricultural and food industry share of the total		
Import	5,666.7	19,419.2	25,085.9
Export	34,769.5	28,162.9	62,932.4
Balance	+ 29,102.8	+8,743.7	+37,846.5

Source: Csizmadia, "Élelmiszertermelésünk," 61.

In the middle of the country's increasing external payment obligations, government policy counted on the food industry's capacity to cope with burdens in other respects as well. This became apparent in increasing state extractions from agricultural incomes. A study of the balance between support given to the agrarian sector and extractions from it reveals that the balance deteriorated drastically in the first half of the 1980s, and the main factor in this was an increase in extractions.[118] After 1982, agricultural organizations were ever more likely to reduce their investments, in fact, many cooperatives were forced to replace the working capital necessary for operations by selling property and cutting back their fixed capital and durable capital equipment stocks. From the middle of the decade, a third of large-scale farms had begun to exhaust their productive capacity.[119]

The nominal value of total financial support fell by a small amount in fact, but, within this, completely different tendencies emerged in the patterns of investment and indirect support compared with production support. The fact that, in the mid-1980s, the total sum of investment support did not reach even a third its level a decade earlier had an exceptionally negative effect on agriculture's fixed asset provision. While, in 1975, the state budget financed a third of the gross cost of agricultural investments, this proportion fell to a quarter in 1980, and merely a tenth in 1985, an extraordinarily unfavorable trend. The value of indirect support, which included support for artificial fertilizer and pesticides, fell in 1985 to 30% of its 1975 level, and, within this, support for purchasing pesticides ended entirely in 1985.[120] In contrast to the above, the sum devoted to production support grew significantly, as did their share within total support. In the 1980s, the decisive role in this was played by production cost supplements and forgiving or refunding tax. In this way the state tried to somewhat ease the situation of farms operating under unfavorable conditions.

The total amount extracted from agriculture doubled in the first half of the 1980s,[121] and it was constructed as follows. By the middle of the decade, social insurance contributions represented the largest amount paid into the budget, in that they quadrupled between 1975 and 1985. This was followed by income tax, profits tax, and production tax. In addition to this, the heaviest burden faced by large-scale farms was banking costs. As a result of these changes, the balance of support and extraction for agricultural enterprises turned negative in 1982, and the initial deficit of six billion forint had quadrupled by the mid-1980s.[122] In the second half of the decade the burden of this negative balance between support and extraction was reduced, mainly because investment subsidies increased.

In addition to the intense budgetary squeeze that evolved over the course of the 1980s, note should also be taken of income extraction that took place through the price system. Comparing average sales prices of agricultural products with price changes for industrial materials used in agriculture it can be established that, by international comparison, the price scissors was exceptionally wide and continually opening.[123]

A 1987 Ministry of Agriculture and Food report reflected on these tendencies as follows: "The memorandum establishes that at the time of the sixth five-year plan, the system of economic regulation introduced two distortions into food production that pulled in different directions. On the one hand, the increase in producer prices for food products could not keep pace with the rapid increase in the prices of production equipment of industrial origin, and, because of this, there was a growth in subsidies which compensated for price increases. On the other, because of the increase in budgetary extractions, which even outstripped improvements in efficiency, the budgetary balance improved, but farm incomes remained at their 1980 level."[124]

Two factors played decisive roles in mitigating the signs of crisis which were appearing in large-scale farming units. The first was nonagricultural ancillary activity, while the other was small-scale production:[125] the two main pillars of the officially nonexistent Hungarian model. Producer cooperatives were permitted again to acquire significant income from their ancillary enterprises by exploiting the income-generating possibilities inherent in industrial, food-industry, construction, commercial, and other activities. Generally until 1983, and even afterwards in the case of many of them, producer cooperatives could compensate in this way for the price scissors and increasing state extractions.[126] The dynamic development of ancillary activities had a favorable impact not only on profitability and liquidity, but also on the evolution of employment levels. Economically weaker farms took advantage of this particularly intensively.[127]

The other factor that similarly had a significant impact on the achievements of socialist large-scale agriculture was, paradoxically, small-scale production.

Table 7.4. Changes in the Agricultural Producer Cooperatives' Activities

Activity	*Change between 1978–1989 (%)*
Agricultural production	–13.8
Nonagricultural activity	+48.6
Industrial production within this	63.6
Food industry within this	68.8
Construction industry	–18.2
Transport	–18.2
Commerce	31.5

Source: Gyula Varga, *A magyar mezőgazdaság az idők sodrásában: helyzetkép az EU-hoz való csatlakozás időszakában* [The Hungarian Agriculture in the Succession of the Events: An Overview of the EU Accession Period], Stratégiai füzetek (Budapest: Miniszterelnöki Hiv. Kormányzati Stratek: 2004), 171.

This term encompasses farming on the household plots of producer cooperative members, supplementary farms of producer cooperative employees, the "salary land" granted to state farm workers, and other small-scale producers. Approximately 40% of net agricultural production was derived from household plot and supplementary farming.[128]

Initially, household plot farming assured the self-supply of producer cooperative members and offered a supplement to their incomes, but over the course of the 1970s, commodity production had increasingly come to the fore. Furthermore, household plot and supplementary farming was not just a source of supplementary income, but also a sphere for autonomous economic decision-making and individual deliberation, because, in addition to farming, it was necessary to engage in commercial dealings, exchange information, and so on. In this way, small-scale farming retained and developed the entrepreneurial spirit of village and small town dwellers. What is more, the composition of small-scale farmers had changed over time. By the 1980s, a large portion of small-scale producers were not producer cooperative members, but rather industrial workers and employees.[129] As a result of the policy of locating industrial plants in rural areas, workers by this time made up the majority of village society: as commuting workers and employees in local industrial plants.

Experience accumulated in producer cooperative household plots gained considerable value in the crisis situation that emerged at the end of the decade. The stagnating economy and debt-financing commitments meant that the Kádár leadership could no longer ensure a continuous rise in living standards. Participation in the second economy was liberalized as a way of counteracting this situation.[130] Earlier, second economy activity was widespread, for the most part, in agriculture, in the form of household plot and supplementary farming, but, in the first half of the 1980s, the second economy emerged in industry in the form of enterprise work partnerships (GMK for short). It became possible too to create a variety of forms of small enterprise.

The social groups that were able to take advantage of the various opportunities offered by the second economy were able to maintain their former standard of living, but this came at the cost of increasing significantly their working time of increased self-exploitation. The wide social strata that were unable to connect to the second economy (the majority of pensioners, those at the beginning of their careers) experienced that, after real wages had already fallen, the level of their real incomes also began to fall.[131]

Meanwhile, decreasing investments, curbs on consumption, and restrictive financial policies produced their first results in 1983–84. The external balance in traded goods and the balance of payments stabilized, and the country's external debt decreased by 800 million dollars.[132] Seeing the positive tendency, the Kádár leadership decided that, before their political legitimacy was buried by the upsurge in social dissatisfaction, there should be a return to the growth path that ensured steadily rising living standards.[133] At this point, the opportunity arose to take out new loans from private banks on relatively favorable conditions, and the government grabbed the "lifeline." Learning nothing from its earlier experiences, instead of improving its international competitiveness or carrying out reforms, it once again lavished billions of dollars keeping existing heavy industry plants afloat. Yet things could have been done differently: the loans were not tied to specific goals; they could have been used for anything.[134]

COOPERATIVE SURVIVAL STRATEGIES

Tensions within the agrarian sphere were brought to a head by the unfavorable developments in foreign market conditions of the mid-1980s.[135] At the beginning of the decade, Hungary's net agricultural export surplus in hard currency markets exceeded one billion dollars annually, by 1986 this surplus had fallen to 600 million, despite a drop in the value of the dollar.[136] Hungarian agriculture's earlier successes, and the protected position that it enjoyed at home and in Comecon markets, hid the fact that, with the exception of wheat production (for which geographic conditions in Hungary were very favorable), the country produced more expensively than its market competitors.

In this crisis situation, it became clear that ancillary enterprises and small-scale farming would only be capable of counteracting short term the tensions accumulating in producer cooperatives, and they therefore began to look for solutions that would improve their results. Ever more emphasis was placed on demands for creating true property interests to stimulate an increase in property, for promoting the amalgamation of various property forms, and different scales and structures for farming. The further development of organizational and incentive systems was accelerated by making use of earlier traditions and positive experiences.

At the beginning of the 1980s, agricultural producer cooperatives had already begun renting out arable land; in 1981, this covered only 9.1 thousand hectares, but by 1987 it was 47.1 thousand hectares. From the point of view of large-scale farms, this meant that, in 1981, 4.2% of their land area was farmed by small-scale farmers, while the figure was 5.9% in 1988. A breakdown by production branch reveals that, at the end of the 1980s, more than half of agricultural large-scale producer vineyards was cultivated by small-scale farmers, and in the case of fruit growing, 40% of orchard land was under their use. But in terms of arable land, the figure was 13%.[137] These internal ratios point to the fact that in the case of labor-intensive crops, large-scale farms were endeavoring to establish by degrees more rational farming forms in that, by renting out vineyards and fruit orchards (also on a share-cropping basis), they could significantly reduce their production costs.

The 1980s was also the decade when farms started renting out agricultural buildings, and, to a lesser extent, machinery. Now it was no longer a question of private producers creating undertakings based on a contract covering individual phases of production, rather they could themselves organize the whole farming process, including renting buildings and machinery as necessary. The rental of buildings was most common in the cases of greenhouses (24.7%), sheep sheds (17.3%) and poultry barns (13.9%).[138] The desire to rent on the part of small-scale producers was most common therefore where a single family, relying on its own labor, could tend the livestock in the building or the horticultural products of the given plot of land. Large-scale farms could reduce their production costs by renting out land, or farming it on the basis of share-cropping, and by renting out livestock, buildings and machinery. It was market relations, therefore, even if only to a limited degree, that prompted large-scale farms to implement rational and diversified forms of farming.

The local initiatives reviewed above demonstrate that producer cooperatives did indeed attempt to operate entrepreneurially, to create new entrepreneurial forms inside the farm, but these new solutions in terms of structures and incentives encountered numerous obstacles within the existing framework of large-scale farms.[139] It became necessary to modify and adjust the system of legal and economic regulation.

The following paragraphs review in outline the agricultural reform proposals prepared in the latter half of the 1980s, and how the political leadership related to them. The majority of the plans and submissions under consideration came from the following organs: the Cooperative Policy Work Group working under the auspices of the HSWP Central Committee, the Central Committee's Economic Working Group, the Economic Policy Committee (renamed the Economic and Social Policy Committee in 1988), as well as the Economic Policy Department (renamed the Economic and Social Policy Department in 1988).[140] Many are cited verbatim, despite the dense and convoluted argumentation, to illustrate the strength of the ideological barriers that many struggled to overcome. The materials outlined two directions in which to search for a way out. Some saw the solution in transforming toward simpler cooperative forms, while the others encouraged the further development of incentive systems within the cooperative.

The advantages of simpler forms of cooperative were laid out by the Cooperative Policy Work Group as follows:

> As a result of their activity, there was an increase in the supply of goods and an improvement in the level of service. The vast majority of small organizations

> farmed more effectively than traditional organizations. They are more efficient, they have higher per capita income and profit, and they make better use of equipment. They attained these results by better organization, getting rid of surplus labor, and creating a system of direct material incentives. Their sensitivity to the market and their flexibility is far in advance of those for traditional cooperatives.[141]

These positive experiences encouraged the leaders of the agrarian portfolio to look to simpler forms as a solution for permanently loss-making producer cooperatives.[142] Material support for such producer cooperatives was a permanent burden on every government. For many years, these losses had been settled retrospectively by the state budget, out of a sum ear-marked for the purpose, effectively recognizing the legitimacy of this loss in the annual financial balance. Some of it came in the form of credits, the rest was subventions. Between 1975 and 1985, the total deficit incurred by producer cooperatives approached 12 billion forints.[143] Despite this support, some farms continued to operate at a loss. It is understandable, then, that leaders with a national overview should be searching for possible ways of reducing this source of financial loss.

In the summer of 1986, the leaders of the Ministry of Agriculture and Food and the National Council of Producer Cooperatives stated clearly that, for persistently loss-making producer cooperatives, the only solution could be transformation to a simpler cooperative form (such as specialized cooperative or a small cooperative).[144] This proposal is worthy of note because the specialized cooperative had long been seen as a lower-order cooperative form. Their members devoted more of their activity to individual rather than communal work. Earlier, the tendency of those in power had been to tolerate this form rather than support it.[145] Making it possible for one cooperative form to transform into another (moreover one of a "lower order") required wide-ranging modification of legal regulations, and expert groups were commissioned to work out how it could be done.

While investigating possibilities offered by simpler cooperatives, opinion gravitated around the idea that agricultural small-scale producers too should be provided with a cooperative framework, where activity continued to be based on personal property, but where it was possible nevertheless to implement a form of cooperative activity that was simpler in organization and operation, yet still had legal and economic independence. In the background to this stood the fact that the weight and role of supplementary farms (what today are called "part-time" farms) within small-scale production was increasing (more than 800,000 families), and the bulk of its agricultural production took place, not on the basis of individual farmers, but of privately owned or rented land and machinery, mostly in addition to full-time employment elsewhere or a pension.[146] About a third of these were members of agricultural specialist groups, horticultural associations and small-scale breeders' groups, but it was not possible for groups of this kind to become cooperative forms with a legal identity. The leaders of the Ministry of Agriculture and Food and the National Council of Producer Cooperatives considered that it was feasible to create cooperatives organized on the basis of small-scale production in the framework of "agricultural small-producer cooperatives."[147]

Parallel with this, demands to develop further the internal incentives system appeared with increased force in professional forums. It is worth recalling how great a change had taken place in the conception of interest relations between producer cooperatives and their members, from the initial conception, still tied to the Soviet model, according to which, once members joined they were under a moral obligation to work well and even bring their family members into communal labor. One of the specificities and keys to success of Hungarian cooperative development was precisely the fact that, unlike the kolkhoz form, the authorities at first tolerated local initiatives, then supported them and finally incorporated them into legal regulation.[148]

This trend was reinforced by the appearance of various entrepreneurial forms (specialist groups, the use of separate budget-centers within farms, and so on). Producer cooperative members cultivated ever more vineyards and fruit orchards on the basis of family entrepreneurship. Five to ten percent of large-scale farming livestock was supplied through "outsourcing" forms.

Starting from tried and tested local initiatives, the following proposals were submitted to the party leadership:

> The fundamental aim in the development of forms of internal incentives is the operation of an entrepreneurial form that expresses the interests of both the member and the cooperative, that stays within a cooperative framework, and rests on the principle of self-government. . . . This would be best served by the well-regulated development of units operating as budget-centers and small entrepreneurial groups.[149]

The authors of the submission emphasized the need to develop independence, democracy, self-governance, and the mutual acceptance of risk. They judged that it was important to extend further systems that offered a flat rate for the whole job. They felt share-cropping could be utilized more widely. Moving forward, however, required modifying legal and regulatory systems to make them more flexible. But, for this, decisions at the highest political level were required, and these were always put off. In the middle of the general crisis of Hungarian socialism, the attention of political decision-makers was focused elsewhere.[150] They were only interested in agriculture's ability to gain hard currency. This assertion could be supported by decisions taken on a multitude of occasions, but an illustrative example is the March 5, 1987, meeting of the HSWP Central Committee Economic Policy Committee, because at this meeting the first agenda-item was the program to develop food production. Yet the resolution focused almost exclusively on increasing the ability to acquire hard currency. "The central question now is to improve the country's external balance, and all economic decisions must be subordinated to this. We must, therefore, deal not with branch policy issues, but instead concentrate on those few questions in every field that can improve the ability to acquire hard currency. . . ."[151] The position-paper went on to detail how the agricultural sector's ability to acquire hard currency might be increased. "The development of agriculture and the food industry should continue to be export-oriented, but it should be better adjusted to market needs than has been the case so far by improving the structure of production, improving quality, developing processing, and speeding up transport schedules.[152]

The holder of the agrarian portfolio, Jenő Váncsa, was unable to dislodge the participants from this mode of reasoning, despite the fact that his summary of the proposals that had emerged from specialist circles got to the heart of the matter.

> Food production can only face the international challenges of the past years by increasing its competitiveness and efficiency. This requires a certain shift of emphasis in agrarian policy too. Above all, the internal mechanisms of farms must be made more flexible and simple, internal incentive systems must be modernized, and machinery and land that can no longer be operated profitably on a large-scale basis must be utilized in various entrepreneurial forms. Further, member ties and property interests must be strengthened in cooperatives. Where large-scale agricultural production still cannot be made profitable at the current level of support, opportunities must be offered for transformation into simpler cooperative forms.[153]

Then another year passed before parliament placed the necessary legal amendments on its agenda. In the spring 1988 parliamentary session, decisions were made to amend both the 1971 law on cooperatives and Law III of 1967 on agricultural producer cooperatives.[154] At the very beginning of his exposé, Minister of Agriculture and Food Jenő Váncsa expressed why the law on producer cooperatives, which had been passed twenty years previously, needed to be changed. "In our people's economy, more than ever before, the central question has become to increase performance to a level that would be accepted and appropriately valued by both domestic and international markets."[155]

One of the innovations introduced by the law that should be mentioned is the institution of internal entrepreneurship. On the basis of agreements made between cooperatives and members, land and large-scale production equipment could be put in the hands of internal, entrepreneurial units. At the same time, the law itself placed restrictions on this form of operation by retaining, unchanged, the dogma of indivisible communal property. As a result, the internal entrepreneurial units could not have their own property, and remained completely subordinate to the responsibility as guarantor of the mother cooperative. So the law prevented these units from becoming primary cooperatives or legal persons in other forms, and thus becoming embryos for the development of two-level cooperatives (or secondary cooperative companies).

Another new element in the act was that it allowed for producer cooperatives that consistently operated at a loss, were insolvent, or stood on the threshold of bankruptcy or compulsory financial reorganization, to establish simpler cooperative forms. The rules for transforming producer cooperatives into specialized cooperatives became more flexible, and further, the prohibition on engaging in agricultural activities was removed from the regulations governing small cooperatives (one of the forms of small enterprise created in the early 1980s). The rules for changing from one cooperative form to another were also simplified. During the parliamentary debate, many raised the internal contradictions of the new regulations, mainly in relation to property incentives and the obligation to provide employment. A review of the specialist background materials made available to political decision-makers makes these contradictions even clearer. It is worth getting to know these materials in more detail, as they illustrate the point that reform proposals had reached in late 1987 and early 1988.

First, it is important to recall how experts related to long-stressed, almost unquestionable tenets concerning the existing agricultural system. According to the logic of the model, producer cooperative members were, by virtue of their position, also owners, and they exercised this function in the forums of the system of cooperative self-government. The expert material debated by the Economics Working Group in the spring of 1988 said the following about this situation: "The majority of self-governing bodies function in a rather formal manner, however, while the process of membership alienation is far advanced. The growth in cooperative size accelerated this process. . . . The decisive element of the membership relationship is employment . . . the creation of individual interest in increasing communal property remains unsolved."[156]

This train of thought led to the problem of cooperative autonomy, or rather, the recognition that cooperative independence had been significantly limited by the state regarding both accumulation and income regulation.

> Irrespective of the visible results of producer cooperative development over the past decade and a half, a depersonalization of producer cooperative property has taken place. The de jure ownership collective can be considered increasingly more as a collective of employees, and the membership mostly limits its actions to improving its own income and results. The right to make decisions about cooperative property, on the other hand, is divided de facto amongst many institutions that are not owners in legal terms (the professional leadership, management, certain social organizations). For this reason, their real ownership relations should not be seen as group ownership par excellence, but rather a special, institutional (bureaucratic-managerial) ownership.[157]

With this, we reach the most sensitive of questions: property relations.[158] The official position held that the current structure of agriculture was essentially fully evolved and satisfactory, so, as a consequence, had no need for change. The approach also viewed landownership relations as settled. What is more, it saw the maintenance of the main proportions between state, cooperative, and private sectors as essential to the socialist character of agriculture. Experts, however, listed one-by-one the kinds of problems caused by the indivisibility of communal property in producer cooperatives. It was difficult to integrate members' savings into the development of the communal economy. The creation of individual interest in increasing communal property remained unsolved, there was no mechanism to record individuals' contributions to growth and their share of it if they left or retired, or even remained in membership. Under such conditions, the active property participation of producer cooperative members in the operation of the communal farms could therefore not develop. This was how the essence of the property-related incentive problem was conceived.

1. The expert submission saw the solution in reforming property relations, and marked out three cornerstones for it: The conditions must be laid for the constant reproduction of a flexible, multilateral organizational, and property structure. The ability of agricultural enterprises to adjust their organization and property structures to constantly changing conditions must be promoted not through central measures, but by legal and financial regulation.[159]
2. Interest in property must be given a determining role. The authors of the submission saw the indivisible nature of communal property as the main limiting factor in this respect. A series of proposals were formulated on how to increase the weight of transferable, inheritable ownership rights at the expense of indivisible funds. "It is conceivable, for example, that large cooperatives could be transformed into property-holding companies (cooperative share companies)."
3. They emphasized the necessity for a pluralistic ownership structure. They called above all for a rethinking of the existing system of landownership

and use, in fact for the market allocation of landed property.[160] Special attention was paid to increased support for flexible small organizations, for small cooperatives that could more flexibly adjust to market conditions, for specialized cooperatives and small-scale producers.

The above indicates too that, in the spring of 1988, while legislative work was taking place in the spirit of cautious correction and uncertainty, at the same time the proposals that were being voiced in specialist forums identified problems ever more sharply and ever more openly. There is nothing surprising about this radicalization, if we think back to the events of 1988. Numerous things took place that year that would have previously been unimaginable. At the May HSWP meeting János Kádár, who had led the system for 32 years, was set aside. (Károly Grósz, who handed the role of head of government to Miklós Németh in November 1988, was made first secretary of the party.) This was the year in which the opposition began to take the form of parties, and when these organizations initiated several street demonstrations that were attended by tens of thousands of participants. In the second half of the year reformers within the HSWP became active, and Reform Circles were established across the country. Divisions within the party on "what to do next" became ever sharper, as the economic and social climate deteriorated (the fall in the value of the forint, decreasing wages, abandoning the principle of full employment, etc.).[161] This tendency toward radicalization strengthened further over the course of the fall in animated agrarian debates. Property reform came onto the agenda, and this was closely related to the question of the indivisibility of cooperative property. Criticisms of the relationship between the state and producer cooperatives held that the authors of the regulatory system had forgotten that cooperatives belong to their members, and that capital gains that should go to the owners were being extracted from producer cooperatives by the state in the same way as from state enterprises. At the same time, certain of the opposition organizations, that at this time were forming themselves into political parties, were thinking not merely in terms of reforming the relationship between the private economy and large-scale farms under transformation, but were announcing that socialist agriculture had finally reached a dead end.

The spread of criticism and open discussion provided another impetus for rethinking official agrarian policy. The Ministry of Agriculture and Food prepared a submission on the topic, which was debated by the Central Committee Economic Policy Committee in mid-October, 1988.[162] Signed by the agricultural minister, Jenő Váncsa, the plan was titled, The Renewal of Agrarian Policy [*Az agrárpolitika megújítása*] and it took a position on fundamental issues. Here just a few are indicated. "As a result of tendencies in the world economy, quality, and efficiency will become the defining features in the development of agriculture and the food industry in the future, rather than rapid quantitative growth: incentives must serve this end."[163]

The proposal whittled matters down to four points of agrarian policy. Namely: the population's food demands must be met ever more completely and with ever-lower social costs; an active export-import balance must be maintained in the future, which will help create a positive external balance for the people's economy; the ability of the sector to generate income must be raised by using material and human resources more efficiently; and finally, agrarian and rural development policy should promote the maintenance of ecological potential.

These elements were rearticulated, in a summary fashion, in a toolbox for how the goals might be achieved.

> "The consequence of development is to re-establish the specific cooperative character of cooperative property . . . to do away with the indivisibility of communal property. . . . A multiplicity of ownership should prevail in agriculture too. . . . Space should be given for agricultural small-scale production and individual farming in all areas where they prove to be more efficient than large-scale farming. Group, family and individual undertakings must be stabilized on foundations of legal guarantee. . . . The transformation of organizations that cannot be made viable . . . should not be obstructed by state administrative or informal interventions." Regarding the measures to be taken, the Minister emphasized that the molding force for them "should be the economic compulsion of adjusting to the market."[164]

Several other aspects of the 22-page document could be cited. The point, however, is to draw attention to the fact that these measures came too late. While national and local players of the agrarian lobby had been appearing, one after the other, since the mid-1980s with reform proposals that questioned taboos that had stood for decades, the leading party bodies only put these questions onto the agenda at the beginning of 1989.[165]

At its February 20–21, 1989 session, the HSWP Central Committee paid more attention than ever before to mistakes that had been made in the past.[166] This, however, did not lead to the party leadership taking a constructive approach to finding solutions. For the HSWP's leading bodies, the most important matter remained acquiring convertible currency, and food economy problems were only considered from this perspective. Furthermore, prevarication continued, in that the upshot of the Central Committee session was merely a position statement, which was to be submitted for social debate in the spring. There are many materials available which summarize the experiences of this debate, and they reveal, on the one hand, that there was great interest in it (some passionate debates broke out), and, on the other, how dissatisfied the representatives of the agrarian sphere had become with the position of the party leadership.

The information report prepared for the Politburo established:

> It was emphasized everywhere that the agrarian branch is in a very difficult, and in many respects exposed, position, primarily because of budgetary cuts, reduced support, and the widening of the agrarian scissors. The plan was strongly criticized during the debates, because its concept provides no concrete answer to these concerns. There were requests on numerous occasions that, if the position statement did not want to deal with concrete measures to improve the situation in the branch, then the government should prepare a program at the same time which would remedy agriculture's impossible income problems.[167]

It is worth citing some striking critical observations verbatim. "The current unfavorable situation in agrarian production was brought about decisively not by the agrarian sphere, but by an economic policy on a constrained trajectory and its restrictive, budget-centric measures. Unless the branch is 'purged' of its external burdens (which exceed its capacity), food production will fall, and the HSWP will lose its base in the countryside, which makes up 40 percent of the population." Workers in the agrarian sector therefore required a turn around and urged "the creation of equal conditions in the sector for state, cooperative, corporate and private property. The market should decide which property form is capable of what, this should not take place by guidance and direction from above."[168]

The fate of the expert proposals reviewed above not only demonstrated that the leadership of the HSWP was incapable of renewal, they also made clear the final limits of the specific approach to handling agrarian problems that had been in effect since the 1960s. Until the end of the 1970s, producer cooperatives had been able to correct for the attempts of those in power to siphon off income by modifying material incentives and by household-plot and ancillary activities, and they set to effective work their farms that had been modernized by technology transfer. But when, because of debt-service, producer cooperatives once again found themselves in the role of "internal colony," reminiscent of Stalinist times, their only option was to experiment with creating a new quality of incentive relations. At the center of these lay the expansion of rights of disposal over community and producer-cooperative property. Everyone knew that decisions concerning property relations could only be made at the highest level of power, in the Politburo. Support for these reform proposals in the forums of the party center that prepared economic policy was to no avail, the decision-makers (the Politburo and the Central Committee) did not discuss them. Those in power repeatedly made it clear where the no-entry signs stood. They well knew that once property relations had been "disturbed," the next step might be the questioning of the party's despotic rule.

When the reform measures that the representatives of the agrarian sphere had called for were enacted, in the fall of 1988 and the beginning of 1989, it was too late. This all certainly contributed to the fact the agrarian restructuring after regime change in Hungary took place in the context of enormous loss. This was not the case in Germany, for example, where a reasonable balance was retained between radical property transformation and the preservation of experiences and values accumulated in large-scale production.[169] That, however, is another story.

NOTES

1. Pál Romány, "A 'változatlan agrárpolitika' változásai, 1957–1989" [Changes of the "constant agrarian policy"], in *Ki volt Kádár? Harag és részrehajlás nélkül a Kádár-életútról* [Who was Kádár? About Kádár's life career without anger or favor], ed. Árpád Rácz (Budapest: Rubicon and Aquila, 2001), 122–33.

2. As late as the 1980s a debate was taking place in Soviet agriculture over why indicators tied to plan delivery were too weak as incentives. Alain Pouliquen, "The Contract Brigades: Towards a Neo-collectivism in Soviet Agriculture?," in *Socialist Agriculture in Transition: Organizational Response to Failing Performance*, eds. Josef C. Brada and Karl-Eugen Wädekin (Boulder: Westview Press, 1988), 45–54.

3. Pál Germuska, "Economic Growth and the Industrial Development Policy in Hungary, 1950–1975," in *Industrial Policy in Europe after 1945: Wealth, Power and Economic Development in the Cold War*, eds. Christian Grabas and Alexander Nützenadel (Basingstoke: Palgrave Macmillan, 2014), 321–36.

4. Jegyzőkönyv az MSZMP Központi Bizottság 1968. december 4-i üléséről. [Minutes of the HSWP Central Committee session, December 4, 1968] MNL OL, M–KS 288. f., 4. cs., 97. ő. e.

5. Germuska, "Economic Growth," 321–36.

6. Rudolf Tőkés, *Hungary's Negotiated Revolution: Economic Reform, Social Change and Political Succession, 1957–1990* (Cambridge: Cambridge University Press, 1996).

7. Ferber and Rejtő, *Reform(év)fordulón*, 32.

8. These debates can be easily traced in the periodicals *Társadalmi Szemle* [Social Review], *Pártélet* [Party Life], as well as in the daily *Népszabadság* [Free People].

9. János Kornai, *The Socialist System: The Political Economy of Communism* (Oxford: Clarendon Press, 1992), 89–112.

10. Vass, *Az MSZMP határozatai és dokumentumai 1963–1966*, 402–9.

11. Ibid.

12. A Vas- Fém- és Villamosenergia-ipari Dolgozók Szakszervezetének jelentése a szövetkezetek munkaerő-elszívó lehetőségeinek ellenőrzése tárgyában végzett

vizsgálatok megállapításairól. [Report of the Labor Union of Iron, Metal and Electric Energy Industrial Workers on the Results of the Investigation Regarding the Labor Force Draining Potential of Cooperatives] MNL OL, M–KS 288. f., 15 cs., 192. ő. e.

13. Jegyzőkönyv az MSZMP Politikai Bizottság 1971. március 9-én tartott üléséről. [Minutes of the HSWP Politburo session, March 9, 1971] MNL OL, M–KS 288. f., 5. cs., 548. ő. e.

14. Jegyzőkönyv a Politikai Bizottság 1971. szeptember 7-én tartott üléséről. [Minutes of the HSWP Politburo session, September 7, 1971] MNL OL, M–KS 288. f., 5. cs., 564. ő. e.

15. "41/1971. (XII. 14.) sz. Korm. rendelet a szövetkezetek gazdasági tevékenységének köréről," "1048/1971. (XII. 14.) sz. Korm. határozat a mezőgazdasági termelőszövetkezetek nem mezőgazdasági jellegű tevékenységéről" [Government Decree 41/1971 (December 14) on the scope of economic activities of cooperatives, and Government Decision 1048/1971 (December 14) on the non-agricultural activities of cooperatives], in *TRHGY 1971*, 515–17, 583–86.

16. Jegyzőkönyv az MSZMP Politikai Bizottság 1971. március 9-i üléséről. [Minutes of the HSWP Politburo session, March 9, 1971] MNL OL, M–KS 288. f., 5 cs., 548. ő. e.

17. Csaba Békés, "Hungary the Soviet Bloc, the German question and the CSCE Process, 1965–1975," *Journal of Cold War Studies* 18, no. 3 (2016): 95–138.

18. Jegyzőkönyv az MSZMP Politikai Bizottság 1971. április 21-i üléséről. [Minutes of the HSWP Politburo session, April 21, 1971] MNL OL, M–KS 288. f., 5. cs., 552. ő. e.

19. Huszár, *Beszélgetések*, 315–20.

20. György Földes, "Kötélhúzás felsőfokon. Kádár és Brezsnyev" [String-Pulling of the Highest Degree. Kádár and Brezhnev], in *Rácz, Ki volt Kádár*, 110.

21. Huszár, *Beszélgetések*, 346.

22. Jegyzőkönyv az MSZMP Politikai Bizottság 1971. március 9-i üléséről. [Minutes of the HSWP Politburo session, March 9, 1971] MNL OL, M–KS 288. f., 5. cs., 548. ő. e.; Jegyzőkönyv az MSZMP Politikai Bizottság 1971. március 23-i üléséről. [Minutes of HSWP Politburo session, March 23, 1971] MNL OL, M–KS 288. f., 5. cs., 549. ő. e.

23. Jegyzőkönyv az MSZMP Politikai Bizottság 1971. szeptember 7-i üléséről. [Minutes of the HSWP Politburo session, September 7, 1971] MNL OL, M–KS 288. f., 5. cs., 563. ő. e.

24. István Forgó, *Búcsú Erdei Ferenctől* [Taking leave of Ferenc Erdei], Erdei Ferenc Társaság füzetei 18 (Makó: Erdei Ferenc Társaság, 2006).

25. Jegyzőkönyv az MSZMP Politikai Bizottság 1971. november 16-i üléséről. [Minutes of the HSWP Politburo session, November 16, 1971] MNL OL, M–KS 288. f., 5. cs., 568. ő. e.

26. Huszár, *Beszélgetések*, 308.

27. Jegyzőkönyv az MSZMP Politikai Bizottság 1972. február 22-én tartott üléséről. [Minutes of the HSWP Politburo session, February 22, 1972] MNL OL, M–KS 288. f., 5. cs., 575. ő. e.

28. The debates, however, were never presented to the wider public sphere, to which party unity was presented instead. The same message was conveyed to the party membership. The degree to which this was successful is indicated by an article in the party's theoretical periodical soon after the Central Committee meeting. The author, Valéria Benke, stressed "We had to move against those accounts that held there were separate platforms for representing views, even on essential topics. There were voices before the Central Committee meeting—and scattered about there are those even after the decree—that made it seem there were two fundamental concept followers, with goals antagonistic to one another, with people or groups 'fighting one another.' It is understandable of course that those few with a penchant for simplification or hoping to cause a furor (often external bystanders) spoke of a conflict between 'reformers' and 'dogmatists.'" See: Valéria Benke, "Egységes értelmezés, kommunista kiállás, közös cselekvés" [Unity in interpretation, communist espousal, unity in action], *Társadalmi Szemle* 28, no. 1 (1973): 5.

29. Jegyzőkönyv az MSZMP Központi Bizottság 1972. november 14–15-én tartott üléséről. [Minutes of the HSWP Central Committee session, November 14–15, 1972] MNL OL, M–KS 288. f., 4. cs., 119–120. ő. e.

30. Ibid.

31. György Péteri, "From Purge to scandal: The MEGÉV-affair and changing political style in communist Hungary," in *Muddling Through in the Long 1960s: Ideas and Everyday Life in High Politics and Lower Classes of Communist Hungary*, eds. János M. Rainer and György Péteri, Trondheim Studies on East European cultures & Societies 16 (Trondheim: Trondheim Studies on East European Cultures and Societies, 2005), 109–34.

32. The most critical articles appeared in the HSWP central paper. See: "Félmillió forint jogtalan újítási díj, a termelőszövetkezetek ellenőrizzék rendszeresen közös vállalkozásaikat" [Undue Innovation Fee of HUF 500,000—Producer Cooperatives Should Monitor Their Joint Ventures More Frequently], *Népszabadság*, February 3, 1971; "Szövetkezeti gépekből maszek ócskavas" [From Cooperative Machinery to Private-Sector Scrapheap], *Népszabadság*, December 22, 1971; "A Termoszig szövetkezeti ál-vállalat bűnös üzelmei" [The Criminal Activities of Termoszig, a Fake Cooperative Sub-Company], *Népszabadság* január–február 1972.

33. In the first half of the seventies the number of kolkhoz decreased from 33,600 to 30,000. At the same time the number of sovkhoz increased from 14,994 to 17,717. V. Ya. Romanchenko, "Tipologiia i osobennosti evoliutsii sovkhoznoi sistemy Rossii v usloviakh agrarnoi modernizatsii 1950-kh–1980-kh gg," in *Ezhegodnik po agrarnoi istorii Vostochnoi Evropy 2012*, ed. E. N. Shveykovskaya (Moscow, Bryansk: RAS. 2012), 510–20.

34. Mieke Meurs and Veska Kouzhouharova–Rositsa Stoyanova, "Bulgaria: From Cooperative Village to Agro-Industrial Complex," in *Many Shades of Red State Policy and Collective Agriculture*, ed. Mieke Meurs (New York and Oxford: Rowman & Littlefield, 1999), 111–14; Michael L. Wyzan, "Bulgarian agriculture: sweeping reform, mediocre performance," in *Communist agriculture: Farming in the Soviet Union and Eastern Europe*, ed. Karl-Eugen Wädekin (London and New York: Routledge, 1990), 290–306.

35. Michael Heinz, *Mähdreschern und Musterdörfern: Industrialisierung der DDR-Landwirtschaft und die Wandlung des ländlichen Lebens* (Berlin: Metropol Verlag, 2011).

36. The Hungarian recommendation aimed to replace the inflexible Comecon cooperation system of resource, materials, and product distribution with a flexible system that integrated market mechanisms, and further to exchange economic plan harmonization with continuous economic policy consultations. The intense bargaining process, which lasted for three years, made it clear that the vast majority of Comecon countries had no idea what to do with the recommendations made by Hungarians. Feitl, *Hungarian Plans*, 197–242.

37. Zsuzsa Bekker, *Rendszerválság: Alkalmazkodási folyamatok a kelet-európai országokban 1970 és 1990 között* [System-crisis: Adaptation processes in Eastern Europe between 1970 and 1990] (Budapest: Aula, 1995), 60–67.

38. Földes, *A magyar–szovjet gazdasági*, 1369–75.

39. Varga, *Az agrárium 1945-től*, 315–17.

40. Központi Statisztikai Hivatal, *Mezőgazdasági statisztikai évkönyv, 1978* (Budapest: KSH, 1979).

41. A Szövetkezetpolitikai Munkaközösség 1970. november 18-i ülése. [Minutes of the Cooperative Policy Working Group session, November 18, 1970] MNL OL, M–KS 288. f., 38. cs., 18. ő. e.

42. Fehér Lajos levele Kádár Jánosnak, 1973. november 1. [Memo from Lajos Fehér to János Kádár, November 1, 1973] MNL OL, M–KS 288. f., 47. cs., 756. ő. e.

43. A Szövetkezetpolitikai Munkaközösség 1974. november 11-i ülése. [Minutes of the Cooperative Policy Working Group session, November 11, 1974] MNL OL, M–KS 288. f., 38. cs., 34. ő. e.

44. "A Minisztertanács 32/1975. (XI. 19.) sz. rendelete a termelőszövetkezetek egyesülésének (beolvadásának) közgyűlési napirendre tűzéséhez szükséges előzetes miniszteri hozzájárulásról," in *TRHGY 1975*, 573.

45. Huszár, *Kádár János*, 250–56.

46. Antal Bakóczi, "A társadalmi tulajdon elleni bűncselekmények alakulása" [The State of Offenses against Public Ownership], *Népi Ellenőrzés* 15, no. 6 (1973): 1–4.

47. Boreczky, *Központi szervek, 1950–1970*, 373.

48. M. Ferenc Horváth, "A 'népi ellenőrzés' Magyarországon 1957–1989" ["People's Control" in Hungary, 1957–1989], *Levéltári Szemle* 40, no. 4 (1990): 29–40.

49. Antal Bakóczi, "Az új gazdaságirányítási rendszer és a társadalmi tulajdon elleni bűnözés alakulása" [The New Economic Mechanism and the Offenses against Social Property], *Belügyi Szemle* 11, no. 2 (1973): 3–10.

50. In 1972 criminal complaints that were unresolved made for 38% of all complaints. A year later this dropped to only 18%. See Jelentés a népi ellenőrzési bizottságok 1973. évi munkájáról. [Report of the 1973 Activities of the People's Control Committees] MNL OL, XVII–2–a 5. tétel, 16. d.

51. Havi tájékoztatók a népi ellenőrzés szervei által indított téma és célvizsgálatokról. [Monthly Reports of Targeted Reviews by People's Control Committees] MNL OL, XVII–2–a 22. tétel, I. sorozat, 2.d. 1970–1977.

52. V. K. I. és társai periratai. [Charge Sheet of K. I. V. and Accomplices] MNL OL, XX–10–e–22.098/1973 (379.d.)
53. *TRHGY 1971*, 195–207.
54. Tibor Zám, "Mennyit ér a tsz-elnök?" [How Much Is the President of a Producers' Cooperative Worth?], in *Bács-Kiskunból jövök* [I Come from the county Bács-Kiskun] (Budapest: Szépirodalmi, 1973), 185.
55. P. J. és társai periratai [Charge Sheet of J. P. and Accomplices] MNL OL, XX–10–e–20.065–1974.
56. P. J. és társai periratai. [Charge Sheet of J. P. and Accomplices] MNL OL, XX–5–d–110–1974 (4.d.)
57. Sz. J. és társai periratai. [Charge Sheet of J. Sz. and Accomplices] MNL OL, XX–10–e–22.649/1975–76 (465.d.)
58. Gough, *A good Comrade: János Kádár*.
59. *Kelet-Magyarország*, [Eastern Hungary], April 9, 1974, 5.
60. *Kelet-Magyarország*, February 12, 1975; March 7, 1975; May 11, 1975; December 21, 1975.
61. *Kelet-Magyarország*, November 30, 1975.
62. Árpád Pünkösti, *Kiválasztottak* [The Chosen Ones] (Budapest: Árkádia 1988), 354–63.
63. G. J. és társai periratai. [Charge Sheet of J. G. and Accomplices] MNL OL, XX–10–e 22.278/1977 (539.d.)
64. "'Elvirágzott' vállalkozás" [A faded enterprise], *Esti Hírlap*, October 26, 1976.
65. G. J. és társai periratai. [Charge Sheet of J. G. and Accomplices] MNL OL, XX–10–e 22.278/1977 (539.d.)
66. Rudolf Tőkés, *Kialkudott forradalom: Gazdasági reform, társadalmi átalakulás és politikai hatalomutódlás, 1957–1990* (Budapest: Kossuth, 1998), 115–18.
67. A KB Közigazgatási és Adminisztratív Osztály feljegyzése a Koordinációs Bizottság részére Gergely János és társai (Rozmaring mg. tsz.) bűnügyéről. 1978. május 29. [Memo of the Administrative Department of Central Committee to the Coordination Committee on the case of J. G. (Rosemary Producer Cooperative) May 29, 1978] MNL OL, M–KS 288. f., 31/V/1. ő. e.
68. The Bucharest price establishment principle was amended such that the base period for the establishment of prices was the five years previous to the year at hand. From 1976 the ruble prices in intra-Comecon contracts was changed annually, based on the world economy prices of the previous five years. Thus the base period for 1976 prices was 1971–75, that for 1977 was 1972–76, and that for 1978 was 1973–77. András Éliás, Emília Sebők, and Tamás Ujhelyi, *A mezőgazdasági* és élelmiszeripari *termékek az* új *világgazdasági helyzetben* [The products of the agriculture and food industry in the changing world economy] (Budapest: KJK, 1980), 154–55.
69. Mária Barát, ed., *A magyar gazdaság vargabetűje* [The detour of the Hungarian economy] (Budapest: Aula, 1994), 157; Iván T. Berend, *From the Soviet bloc to the European Union: The economic and social transformation of Central and Eastern Europe since 1973* (Cambridge: Cambridge University Press, 2009), 20–27.
70. This is what is referred to in the literature as exchange price deterioration. Ádám Marton, "Külkereskedelmi áraink az 1970-es években" [Prices of our foreign trade in the 1970s], *Statisztikai Szemle* 58, no. 4 (1978): 341–58.

71. The literature defined this as "dollar–ruble conversion."

72. Hungarian agricultural exports were sensitive to the Common Market's import-restriction moves of the early 1970s. In 1973 Hungary joined the General Agreement on Tariffs and Trade in order to gain access to GATT member state markets without discrimination. Despite accession, the European Community's discriminative trade policy stayed in place until the end of the 1980s. Péter Balázs, "Magyarország és az Európai Unió" [Hungary and the EU], in *Európai közjog* és *politika* [European public law and politics], ed. Tamás Kende (Budapest: Osiris, 2005), 811–38.

73. This was increased by the "dollar content" of Hungarian exports marked for the Soviet Union, and so one of the basic conditions for expanding exports to the East was the ability to import from the West. Katalin Botos, Mihály Patai, and István Szalkai, *Pénzügyek* és *nemzetközi gazdasági kapcsolataink* [Financial issues and our international economic relations] (Budapest: KJK, 1980), 3–10.

74. Központi Statisztikai Hivatal, *Magyar statisztikai évkönyv* [Statistical Yearbook] (Budapest: KSH, 1985).

75. Problems in feed provision, taxation and sales meant that over 1974–75 the liquidation of household cattle stocks accelerated. Due to the same issues the motivation to breed and fatten pigs also waned significantly. In 1975 the stock of sows decreased 29% compared to 1974. Varga, *A mezőgazdasági kistermelés*, 153.

76. Jegyzőkönyv az MSZMP Politikai Bizottság 1976. február 10-i üléséről. [Minutes of the HSWP Politburo session, February 10, 1976] MNL OL, M–KS 288. f., 5. cs., 684. ő. e.

77. The governmental decree on the development of household and small-scale plots was published on March 16. The decree prescribed the support of the important task of developing household and supplementary plots alongside large-scale agricultural facilities—given their social utility. It also stressed that long-term production and purchasing security must be established for small farms, which, in previous years, was lacking in places. See: "A Minisztertanács 1006/1976. (III. 16.) sz. határozata a háztáji és kisegítő gazdaságok termelésének fejlesztéséről," in *TRHGY 1976*, 345–46.

78. *Magyar Hírlap*, February 10, 1976.

79. This sensitive issue was first discussed by the Economic Policy Committee, and then by the State Plan Committee. They established: ". . . the current supply situation is tense, but politically it is still tolerable . . . given the great political importance of adequate meat provision further state interventions to dampen problems are necessary. . . ." See Feljegyzés a Gazdaságpolitikai Bizottság 1976. március 15-i üléséről. [Minutes of the HSWP Economic Policy Committee session, March 15, 1976] MNL OL, M–KS 288. f., 15. cs., 309. ő. e.

80. "A Minisztertanács 13/1976. (V. 27.) sz. rendelete a háztáji gazdaságok termelésének fejlesztését szolgáló egyes intézkedésekről," in *TRHGY 1976*, 283–84.

81. The Council of Ministers discussed the taxation of household plots and supplementary farms during its meeting on October 7, 1976. At the end of October a Finance Ministry decree was published on the execution of the Council of Ministers' decree. It pertained to the execution of the previous. See: "A Minisztertanács 36/1976. (X. 17.) sz. rendelete a háztáji és kisegítő gazdaságok jövedelemadójáról;" Decree "PM 38/1976. (X.31.)," in *TRHGY 1976*, 329–32, 769–78.

82. Feljegyzés a Gazdaságpolitikai Bizottság 1976. január 21-i üléséről. [Minutes of the HSWP Economic Policy Committee session, January 21, 1976] MNL OL, M–KS 288. f., 15. cs., 304. ő. e.

83. Jegyzőkönyv az MSZMP Központi Bizottság 1976. március 23-i üléséről. [Minutes of the HSWP Central Committee session, March 23, 1976] MNL OL, M–KS 288. f., 5. cs., 687. ő. e.

84. Romsics, *Szabó István,* 141–42.

85. "A mezőgazdasági termelőszövetkezetek III. kongresszusa" [Third Congress of Agricultural Producers' Cooperatives], *Népszabadság*, December 16, 1976.

86. Ibid.

87. The same held for the provisions of the Council of Ministers decree 1002/1976 (I. 20.) on non-agricultural activities of agricultural cooperatives. "A Minisztertanács 1006/1976. (III. 16.) sz. határozata a háztáji és kisegítő gazdaságok termelésének fejlesztéséről," in *TRHGY 1976*, 343–44.

88. "A mezőgazdasági termelőszövetkezetek III. kongresszusa" [Third Congress of Agricultural Producers' Cooperatives], *Népszabadság*, December 16, 1976.

89. Romsics, *Szabó István*, 89–114; Schlett, *Sziget a szárazföldön*, 117–25.

90. László Németi, *Magyarország élelmiszer-gazdasága a hetvenes években* [The food economy in Hungary in the 1970s], (Budapest: Mezőgazdasági, 1981).

91. The materials-cost ratios in the agricultural production of state farms had reached 80% in the examined period, and approached 70% in cooperatives. Ibid.

92. Ibid.

93. The Central Committee had last dealt with the situation and developmental tasks of agriculture in 1964, and for this reason the meeting of March 1978, was a kind of stock-taking, or meant to be an evaluation of the last decade and a half. The Central Committee meeting was preceded by thorough preparations. Based on the March 23, 1976, decree of the Political Committee, a comprehensive review of the situation of agriculture and the food industry was undertaken. To carry out this task the Central Committee's Industrial, Agricultural and Transportation Department convened a work committee, which was comprised of eight work groups. The first version of the report was discussed by the Economic Policy Committee on June 6, 1977. See: MNL OL, M–KS 288. f., 15. cs., 354. ő. e.

94. Jegyzőkönyv az MSZMP Központi Bizottság 1978. március 15-ei üléséről. [Minutes of the HSWP Central Committee session, March 15, 1978] MNL OL, M–KS 288. f., 4. cs., 154. ő. e. 47.

95. Ibid., 48.

96. Ibid., 81.

97. Ibid., 81.

98. Ibid., 82.

99. Ibid., 84.

100. Ibid., 95.

101. Jelentés a Titkárságnak a népgazdaságot károsító bűncselekmények tapasztalatairól. [Report to the Secretariat on the Experience of Criminal Acts Damaging the People's Economy] MNL OL, M–KS 288. f., 7. cs., 499. ő. e.

102. Huszár, *Kádár János*, 255.

103. Központi Statisztikai Hivatal, *A magyar mezőgazdaság nemzetközi összehasonlításban* [The Hungarian agriculture in international comparison] (Budapest: KSH, 1987), 25–28.

104. *New York Times*, December 20, 1981.

105. *Los Angeles Times*, November 25, 1982.

106. *Christian Science Monitor*, April 29, 1985.

107. In the official newspaper of the Soviet Communist Party, *Pravda from* the early 1980s a new column appeared with the title: "Sodruzhestvo: fakty, mnenia i problemy" which means "Cooperation: facts, views and problems." The correspondents of *Pravda* regularly gave reports on the latest economic developments of bloc countries. On Hungarian agriculture, see: *Pravda*, 16 June, 1980; 8 December 1980; 16 March 1981; 22 June 1981; 10 May 1982; 7 September 1985, 23 December 1985.

108. Igor Stebelsky, "Food consumption patterns in the Soviet Union," in *Socialist Agriculture in Transition: Organizational Response to Failing Performance*, eds. Josef C. Brada and Karl Eugen Wadekin (Boulder and London: Westview Press, 1988), 98–109.

109. *Pravda*, June 16, 1980.

110. Magdolna Baráth and János Rainer M., eds., *Gorbacsov tárgyalásai magyar vezetőkkel* [Gorbachëv's consultations with the Hungarian leadership] (Budapest: 1956-os Intézet, 2000), 43–77; Kathleen Hartford, "Hungarian Agriculture: A model for the Socialist World?" *World Development* 13, no. 1 (1985): 123–50.

111. Several studies have been written on which experiences the Chinese adopted from Hungarian agricultural plants. Gyula Jordán, "Kína mezőgazdasága ma: változások és tendenciák" [China's agriculture today: changes and challenges], *Közgazdasági Szemle* 32, no. 8 (1985): 30–38; Nigel Swain, "A Post-Socialist Capitalism," *Europe-Asia Studies* 63, no. 9 (2011): 1671–95.

112. Iván Pető, "Változások a változatlanságért: A gazdasági rendszer átalakulása a Kádár-korszakban" [Changes to keep things unchanged: The transformation of the economic system in the Kádár-era], in Rácz, *Ki volt Kádár*, 120–21.

113. Jegyzőkönyv az MSZMP Központi Bizottság 1981. október 22-i üléséről. [Minutes of the HSWP Central Committee session, October 22, 1981] MNL OL, M–KS 288. f., 4. cs., 181–182. ő. e.

114. Földes, *Az eladósodás*, 143–47, 171–80; Ungvárszki, *Gazdaságpolitikai ciklusok*, 60–69.

115. Jenő Váncsa, *Öt évtized a mezőgazdaság szolgálatában* [Five decades in the service of Hungarian agriculture] (Budapest: Magyar Mezőgazdasági Múzeum, 2010), 117–19.

116. This was necessary despite radically decreased world market prices, because exports could not be replaced by other products or branches. The demand to provide subsidies for exports increased, and by the middle of the decade the support of the food economy accounted for more than half of export subsidies. This practice became general practice mostly in food industry branches organising exports and their final release.

117. Központi Statisztikai Hivatal, *Főbb népgazdasági folyamatok, 1986* [The major economic processes, 1986] (Budapest: KSH, 1987), 38.

118. Support in agriculture declined radically in the period 1975–1985, both in terms of percentage of gross production value (56.7% to 28.4%) and absolute value (26.122 million forint to 23.479 million forint). Even more importantly, the balance of support and withdrawals in the last third of the ten years in question turned negative, i.e., withdrawals exceeded support. László Csete, "A termelőszövetkezetek és az állami gazdaságok fejlődése (1976–1985)" [The development of cooperatives and state farms, 1976–1985], *Gazdálkodás* 31, no. 4 (1987): 1–6.

119. Iván Harcsa, Imre Kovách, and Iván Szelényi, "The Hungarian agricultural miracle and the limits of socialist reforms," in *Privatizing the Land: Rural political economy in post-communist societies*, ed. Iván Szelényi (London and New York: Routledge, 1998), 21–42.

120. Gábor Szabó, Margit Szabóné Guttyán, and Katalin Szép, "A mezőgazdasági termelés jövedelmezőségének makro- és mikroökonómiai aspektusai" [Micro- and macroeconomical aspects of agricultural efficiency], *Közgazdasági Szemle* 35, no. 6 (1989): 579–83.

121. Schlett, *Success and Failure*, 104–8.

122. Csete, *A termelőszövetkezetek és az állami gazdaságok*, 10–11; Szabó, Szabóné Guttyán, and Szép, *A mezőgazdasági termelés*, 580–81.

123. Krisztina Makra, Józsefné Németh, and Béla Rózsa, "A mezőgazdasági termelés ár- és költségviszonyai nemzetközi összehasonlításban" [Price and cost relations of agricultural production in international comparison], *Gazdálkodás* 30, no. 12 (1986): 40–44.

124. A Mezőgazdasági és Élelmezésügyi Minisztérium előterjesztése az MSZMP KB Gazdaságpolitikai Bizottság számára az élelmiszertermelés fejlesztésének programjáról, 1987. március. [Submission of the Ministry of Food and Agriculture for the HSWP Economic Policy Committee on the development program of the food economy, March 1987] MNL OL, M–KS 288. f., 15. cs., 538. ő. e.

125. Gyula Varga, "Mezőgazdaságunk nemzetgazdasági szerepváltozásai" [The changing roles of the agriculture in the national economy], in Estók, *1956 és a magyar agrártársadalom*, 128–52.

126. Péter Teknős, "A kiegészítő tevékenység szerepe a mezőgazdasági vállalatok gazdálkodásában" [The role of ancillary activities in agriculture], *Gazdálkodás* 32, no. 9 (1988): 19–23.

127. A chapter in my habilitation thesis dealt with such experiences in Nógrád County. Zsuzsanna Varga, "Konfliktusok és kompromisszumok a hatalom és az agrártársadalom között a Kádár-rendszerben" (Habilitation thesis, ELTE Budapest: 2008), 126–41.

128. Központi Statisztikai Hivatal, *A mezőgazdasági vállalatok gazdálkodása, 1988*. [Economic activities of agricultural enterprises] (Budapest: KSH, 1989), 21–22.

129. Imre Kovách, "Hungary Cooperative farms and Household Plots," in Meurs, *Many Shades of Red*, 125–50; Ernő A. Tóth, *Mezőgazdasági kistermelés, családi termelés* [Small-scale and family-based agricultural production] (Budapest: Mezőgazdasági, 1988), 81–128; Iván Szelényi, *Socialist Entrepreneurs Embourgeoisement in Rural Hungary* (Madison: University of Wisconsin Press, 1988).

130. Tőkés, *A kialkudott forradalom*, 115–17.

131. Valuch, *The Social History of Hungary*, 626–27.

132. Földes, *Az eladósodás*, 223.

133. This orientation was given political backing at the 13th Party Congress held between March 25 and 28, 1985.

134. Földes, *Az eladósodás*, 239–58.

135. This section relies heavily on the following works from the international literature: László Csaba, *Kelet-Európa a világgazdaságban: Alkalmazkodás és gazdasági mechanizmus* [Eastern-Europe in the world economy: Adaptation and economic mechanism] (Budapest: KJK, 1984), 178–99; Csaba Csáki, "A magyar mezőgazdaság nemzetközi versenyképessége" [Competitiveness of the Hungarian agriculture], in *Az európai* és *magyarországi agrárpolitika jövője* [The future of the European and Hungarian Agrarian policy], ed. Ferenc Glatz (Budapest: MTA Történettudományi Intézet, 2010), 99–114.

136. *Főbb népgazdasági folyamatok, 1986*, 38.

137. Imre Kovách, *A vidék az ezredfordulón: A jelenkori magyar vidéki társadalom szerkezeti és hatalmi változásai* [The countryside at the millennium: The major structural changes of the Hungarian rural society] (Budapest: Argumentum, 2012), 66–91.

138. István Molnár and Éva Szabóné Medgyesi, "Mezőgazdasági szövetkezetek, 1990" [Agricultural cooperatives in 1990], *Statisztikai Szemle* 69, no. 11 (1991): 874–77.

139. Donáth, *A munka és tulajdon kapcsolata*, 50–71; János Juhász, *Szövetkezeti modellek a magyar mezőgazdaságban* [Cooperative model in the Hungarian agriculture] (Budapest: Akadémiai, 1988), 75–82.

140. The internal debate materials of the Cooperative Research Institute, the Hungarian Academy of Sciences' Economic Sciences Institute and the Agricultural Economics Research Institute contain valuable information on the investigated reform process.

141. Jegyzőkönyv az MSZMP KB Szövetkezetpolitikai Munkaközösség 1985. június 10-i üléséről. [Minutes of HSWP Cooperative Policy Working Group session, June 10, 1985] MNL OL, M–KS 288. f., 38. cs., 70. ő. e.

142. For various reasons 5–10% of agricultural cooperatives and state farms remained persistently loss-making. Between 1975 and 1985 close to 400 farms had to reschedule their debts. Farms with fiscal balance deficits were concentrated in Borsod-Abaúj-Zemplén, Szabolcs-Szatmár, Hajdú-Bihar, Békés, and Somogy counties.

143. A Mezőgazdasági és Élelmezésügyi Miniszter előterjesztése az MSZMP KB Szövetkezetpolitikai Munkaközösség részére a tartósan veszteséges termelőszövetkezetek helyzetéről. 1985. szeptember 19. [Submission of the Ministry of Agriculture and Food to the HSWP Cooperative Policy Working Group on the situation of permanently loss-making producer cooperatives, September 19, 1985] MNL OL, M–KS 288. f., 38. cs., 71. ő. e.

144. A Mezőgazdasági és Élelmezésügyi Minisztérium és a Termelőszövetkezetek Országos Tanácsának előterjesztése az MSZMP KB Szövetkezetpolitikai Munkaközösségéhez a mezőgazdasági szövetkezetek működése továbbfejlesztésének egyes kérdéseiről. 1986. június 5. [Joint submission of the Ministry of Agriculture

and Food and the National Council of Producer Cooperatives to the HSWP Cooperative Policy Working Group on new forms of small cooperatives in agriculture and the further development of agricultural producer cooperatives, June 5, 1986] MNL OL, M–KS 288. f., 38. cs., 74. ő. e.

145. See: Hann, *Tázlár*; László Maglódi, "A mezőgazdasági szakszövetkezetek jelene és jövője" [The present and the future of the agricultural specialist cooperatives], *Közgazdasági Szemle* 31, no. 5 (1985): 600–607.

146. József Molnár. "'A' háztáji" [The household faming], in Orosz, Für, and Romány, *Magyarország agrártörténete*; Szakács, "A reform kérdése," 98–102; Tóth, *Mezőgazdasági kistermelés*, 177–242.

147. A Mezőgazdasági és Élelmezésügyi Minisztérium és a Termelőszövetkezetek Országos Tanácsának előterjesztése az MSZMP KB Szövetkezetpolitikai Munkaközössége részére: "Az egyszerűbb szövetkezeti formák bevezetése a mezőgazdaságban." [Joint submission of the Ministry of Agriculture and Food and the National Council of Producer Cooperatives to the HSWP Cooperative Policy Working Group on the new forms of small cooperatives in agriculture, June 5, 1986] MNL OL, M–KS 288. f., 38. cs., 74. ő. e.

148. Also see: Varga, *Politika, paraszti érdekérvényesítés*, 71–103.

149. *Az MSZMP KB Gazdaságpolitikai Osztály észrevételei A mezőgazdasági szövetkezetek működése továbbfejlesztésének egyes kérdéseiről című MÉM–TOT előterjesztéshez.* [Remarks of the HSWP Central Committee Economic Policy Committee on the joint submission of the Ministry of Agriculture and Food and the National Council of Producer Cooperatives] MNL OL, M–KS 288. f., 38. cs., 72. ő. e.

150. Ignác Romsics, *Hungary in the Twentieth Century* (Budapest: Corvina–Osiris, 1999), 520–34; Tőkés, *Hungary's Negotiated Revolution*, 263–315.

151. Jegyzőkönyv az MSZMP KB Gazdaságpolitikai Bizottság 1987. március 5-i üléséről. [Minutes of HSWP Economic Policy Committee session, March 5, 1987] MNL OL, M–KS 288. f., 15. cs., 538. ő. e.

152. Ibid.

153. Ibid.

154. *TRHGY 1988*, 13–20.

155. *Országgyűlési Napló*, March 16, 1988, 1838.

156. Emlékeztető a Közgazdasági Munkaközösség 1988. március 28-i üléséről. [Memo of the meeting of HSWP Economics Working Group, March 28, 1988] MNL OL, M–KS 288. f., 16. cs., 40. ő. e.

157. Ibid.

158. Ibid. At the above-mentioned meeting of the Economics Work Community the following heretic statement was made: "The reason . . . for the economy's poor performance must be sought above all in those changes which at the end of the forties began with nationalization, and which in the early sixties closed with the collectivization of agriculture." According to the memorandum written on the meeting the participants deemed this statement "extremist," but at the same time the following two sentences were truly attention-worthy and so finally were entered into the position statement. "The reason our economic system over the past twenty years has been merely functional but has not become competitive must be sought in the fact that as

an objective fact we neglected the existence of capital in the economy. . . . Despite all reform efforts we did not find a successful way of mobilizing state property in an effective manner."

159. Ibid. The submission pointed out that structural problems could not be solved through conserving corporate and ownership structures and mere internal decentralization. Hence, the integration of small-scale production and the unfolding of a more flexible system of internal interests could somewhat ease the tensions present in corporate and ownership structures, but they would not produce a long-term solution.

160. With this the submission touched on another old taboo the inertial force of which is well illustrated by the fact that after twenty years Act I of 1987 on land tried to comprehensively order land regulation, which had become rather complicated. Despite the fact that it repealed two earlier acts, 10 governmental decrees and almost 30 Council of Ministers decrees, the new act was still conceptually unoriginal. Its provisions maintained the commercial rules which made the transfer of land possible in one direction only, toward large-scale producers. (This is illustrated by the provision that cooperatives could still not transfer their property to individuals.) Its only novelty was that it became possible to rent out land that could not be farmed economically on a large-scale basis. Cooperatives could rent such land to private individuals (with no term or spatial restrictions and without need for official authorization). It is also important to mention that the decree which implemented the land act also made it possible to sell cooperative farm-owned land that was unsuitable for large-scale farming and plots suitable for private building using own resources. The law stated that the cooperative members and employees were to be given preference in the transfer, sale, rental, and leasing of cooperative property and land to private individuals. See: *TRHGY 1988*, 3–20.

161. Ignác Romsics, *Volt egyszer egy rendszerváltás* [Once upon a time there was a change of system] (Budapest: Rubicon, 2003), 71–121; Swain and Swain, *Eastern Europe*; Nigel Swain, *Hungary: The Rise and Fall of Feasible Socialism* (London and New York: Verso, 1992); Tőkés, *A kialkudott forradalom*, 279–309.

162. Jegyzőkönyv az MSZMP KB Gazdaságpolitikai Bizottság 1988. október 14-i üléséről. [Minutes of HSWP Central Committee Economic Policy Committee session, October 14, 1988] MNL OL, M–KS 288. f., 15. cs., 563. ő. e.

163. Ibid.

164. Ibid.

165. The MAF submission reviewed above—as mentioned—was written by early October, 1988. Based on this material, in mid-January, 1989, the HSWP Central Committee Economic- and Social-Policy Department finalized the recommendations it was to make to the Political Committee. These were then debated by the Central Committee as well at its meeting on February 20–21, 1989. See Az MSZMP KB Gazdaság- és Szociálpolitikai Osztály javaslata a Politikai Bizottságnak az agrárpolitika megújításának koncepciójára, 1989. január 17. [Submission of the HSWP Central Committee Economic- and Social-Policy Department to the Politburo on the renewal of agrarian policy, January 17, 1989] MNL OL, M–KS 288. f., 5. cs., 1049. ő. e.

166. Anna S. Kosztricz, János Lakos, Karola Némethné Vágy, László Soós, and György T. Varga, eds., *A Magyar Szocialista Munkáspárt Központi Bizottságának*

1989. évi jegyzőkönyvei [Minutes of the HSWP Central Committee in 1989] (Budapest, MOL, 1993), 278–353.

167. Az agrárpolitikai tézisek társadalmi vitájának tapasztalatai, 1989. május. [Experiences of the social debate of the agrarian policy theses, May 1989] MNL OL, M–KS 288. f., 5. cs., 1065. ő. e.

168. Ibid.

169. Jeong Nam Choi, Axel Wolz, and Michael Kopsidis, "Family farm ideology and the transformation of collective farms in East Germany, 1989–2005," in Congost, *Contexts of Property in Europe*, 247–66; Chris Hann and Mihály Sárkány, "The great transformation in rural Hungary: Property, life strategies and living standards," in *The Postsocialist Agrarian Question: Property Relations and the Rural Condition,* eds. Chris Hann and the Property Relations Group (Münster: LIT Verlag, 2003), 117–41; Swain, *Green barons*, 36–43.

Conclusion

This book is the first synthetic analysis of the entire socialist period of Hungarian agriculture in its Eastern European context, based on newly accessible sources. Its findings are of interest not only to those who focus on the history of the socialist bloc, but also to a wider audience interested in modern economic and social history, because it demonstrates two trans-systemic transfers in one country in the Cold War era. The Eastern transfer transplanted the Stalinist system of socialist agriculture into a capitalist agriculture and in a short time triggered a serious crisis in terms of both production and supply. The Western transfer, by contrast, transplanted a capitalist production system in a socialist agriculture based on the Soviet model and quickly generated a dramatic rise in production and thus the end of food shortage in Hungary. The processes of Sovietization and Americanization were analyzed within the framework of transnational comparison, the essence of which is to combine the transfer-approach with historical comparison. The results of the combination of these two methods are surveyed below in relation to the various chapters of this monograph.

Although an enormous specialist literature on the Sovietization of agriculture is available, the attention of researchers has primarily been directed to the struggle between the authorities and the peasantry, and much less on a structural analysis of the new agricultural system that the Soviet Union exported to East Central Europe. The Stalinist system of socialist agriculture therefore, stood at the center of chapter 1; over the course of collectivization, its most characteristic feature became the new hierarchal structure of organizations. This simultaneously ensured the extraction of revenue from agriculture and the control and discriminatory treatment of producers. The structure stood on three pillars: machine and tractor stations; state-owned farms (*sovkhoz*), and artel-type collective farms (*kolkhoz*). The latter became the dominant new form of production unit during Eastern European collectivization. Specialist literature on the subject generally confines itself to a superficial introduction of the kolkhoz, yet this leaves hidden the true content of transfer. This research has returned to the original Russian-language sources, among them the obligatory model charter adopted in 1935.

It was thus possible to expose the discrepancies that existed between the originator of the model and the economic and social relations of the recipient. The most determining of these became the fact that, while in the Soviet Union, as a consequence of the 1917 nationalization of the land, peasants only had to be deprived of their individual land-use rights, in the countries that came under Soviet control, it was a peasantry that enjoyed full private ownership of land that had to be forced into the framework of the new large-scale socialist farms. Furthermore, the post–Second World War land reforms, which the Communist parties of East Central Europe themselves supported, expanded to an unprecedented degree the number of landowning peasants in the region. It is, therefore, not surprising that, a few years later, the Communist parties did not dare to embark openly on nationalizing land. Instead, they employed diverse forms of state force (economic and administrative measures, criminal law, and so on) in order to divest the private-property-owning peasantry of land. Some of these were local "innovations" that were unknown in Soviet practice. The formal retention of private landownership had a great influence on the fact that, in the countries in the Soviet sphere of influence, collectivization became a process that lasted for more than a decade and had to be suspended many times.

The specialist literature has so far devoted little attention to how the East Berlin crisis of 1953 and then the Polish and Hungarian crises of 1956 transformed the way in which the Soviet leadership related to Eastern European realities, particularly those related to food supply. This explains why, when collectivization was complete, Khrushchev was satisfied with a formal transfer of the kolkhoz model and overlooked the failure to adopt completely its original content in the interest of avoiding greater food-supply crises. In fact, it was possible to remain entirely outside it, as the cases of Poland and Yugoslavia demonstrate. Research in Germany has shown that, although the German Democratic Republic is commonly regarded as the country that copied most faithfully the Soviet model, in reality full collectivization was achieved there only in the mid-1970s, because they retained cooperatives of a lesser form longer than elsewhere.

Chapters 2, 3, and 4 were devoted to the Sovietization of Hungarian agriculture in its entirety. The novelty of the approach was that it dealt with this process that extended over more than a decade as a unity of linked periods of collectivization and decollectivization. The first attempt to transfer the *kolkhoz* model was launched in 1949 and ended in failure. This is reflected clearly in the fact that, during the thaw following Stalin's death, 40% of members left producer cooperatives, reclaimed their land, and began to farm privately again. Works of agrarian history have almost completely ignored this decollectivization, but this monograph has studied it intensively. It was therefore possible to identify that, within the leadership of the Communist party, an agrarian lobby group began to form around the new prime minister, Imre Nagy (who was recognized as an agrarian specialist), which radically condemned Hungary's pre-1953 agrarian policy. At the same time, it formulated an agricultural-development program that took Hungarian conditions and traditions into account. This group also supported initiatives taken in still-functioning producer cooperatives to accommodate to local needs and change the rigid structure of the Soviet *kolkhoz* model.

The second collectivization attempt in Hungary, which began in the fall of 1955, also failed after a few months. The forcibly established producer cooperatives began to disintegrate during the summer of 1956, particularly in the western half of the country. By this time, it had become impossible to conceal the fact that forcing the Soviet *kolkhoz* system onto Hungary had plunged its agriculture into a catastrophic situation, an agriculture which enjoyed excellent climatic and soil conditions, and which for centuries had been famous for its exports. Accumulated food-supply problems contributed in large measure to the outbreak of the 1956 Hungarian Revolution.

This was the situation that confronted the Kádár government that came to power, with Soviet assistance, following the defeat of the uprising. Food-supply became a strategic issue for the new régime, which attempted to compensate for its lack of political legitimacy through promises to increase living standards. In order to increase production and provide incentives for agrarian producers, the Kádár government decided upon a correction in agrarian policy that was without precedent in the Eastern bloc. The 1956 uprising thus represents an important caesura not only in political history, but also economic and social history. In November 1956, Hungary became the first country in the bloc to abandon the compulsory-delivery system that was one of the fundamental elements of the Stalinist agricultural system. At the same time, the government halted the formation of producer cooperatives and initiated a new decollectivization phase, the most enduring impact of which was the revival, albeit to a limited degree, of market mechanisms in agriculture.

In late 1958, the Hungarian Party leadership took the decision to resume collectivization as a way of demonstrating its allegiance to Moscow and fitting in with the other countries of the bloc. Bulgaria completed the process of collectivization in 1958, Czechoslovakia in 1959, East Germany in 1960, Hungary in 1961, and Romania in 1962. One of the fruits of de-Stalinization was that, by this time, it was possible for the fraternal countries to learn not just from the Soviet Union, but to draw too upon each other's experiences. The discussion touches on how the Hungarian leadership utilized the collectivization models of other socialist countries, including China.

Local research, using archival sources and oral history, greatly facilitated investigation of the mutual impact of the phases of collectivization and decollectivization. By integrating the micro- and meso-levels, it can be shown how the various groups of peasant society reacted to the collectivization campaigns. Different individual and family survival strategies were investigated, together with their reciprocal influence on the behavior of those who exercised power, and the types of interactions that emerged. Particular attention was paid to how the agrarian lobby was able to get the party leadership to accept grassroots cooperative initiatives, with regard to work organization, remuneration and household plot farming, in spite of the fact that most of them contradicted the original content of the kolkhoz model.

Precisely these questions form a bridge to chapter 5 entitled "Convergence or Divergence?" At its center stands the question of how to make collectivized agriculture work after 1961, and the key actors in this were the producer cooperatives. Since the new large-scale farms were unable for years to produce the results hoped of them, Hungary was obliged to import bread grain and meat until the middle of the 1960s. This situation prompted the Hungarian political leadership to strike a new compromise with the producer cooperative peasantry. Even after the completion of collectivization, it maintained locally established "good practices" that had originally been intended as only temporary concessions. In this way, an increasing number of initiatives moved from being officially prohibited to being tolerated and finally to being supported. Although the party leadership later tried to portray this as its own initiative, in reality divergence from the kolkhoz model took shape that it did as a collective solution to a multifaceted conundrum. The exercise of pressure from the peasantry played a significant role, as did the mediating activity of the agrarian lobby.

Learning from the West represented the other means of addressing post-collectivization problems. Beginning in the late 1950s, the agrarian lobby and agrarian economists were already mediating attempts to establish scientific relations with the Western countries that had the highest levels of agricultural production. The first practical success occurred in 1960, when a Hungarian delegation purchased what was then one of the most modern poultry- and egg-production systems from the West German company, Lohmann. A separate subchapter addressed the initial stages of Western model transfer, presenting the cooperation that developed between the leaders of the agrarian lobby, scientific researchers, and practical specialists.

This early opening to the West naturally could not have taken place without the knowledge and approval of the Soviet leadership. Following the defeat of the 1956 uprising, Moscow accorded greater room for maneuver in certain matters to the Hungarian leadership in order to prove the superiority and viability of the socialist system. The impact of this kind of "exceptionalism" made itself felt particularly strongly in agrarian policy, to which Khrushchev's special interest in agriculture also contributed. Hungary was given an important intermediary role. It was not by chance that the reforms in agriculture preceded by several years the introduction of the New Economic Mechanism on January 1, 1968. They also contributed significantly to the fact that the NEM was the most radical economic-reform in the region, excluding Yugoslavia.

By this time the agrarian lobby had become extremely influential. Chapter 6 focused on how it eliminated the remaining elements of the Stalinist agricultural system as part of the economic reform process, and how, at the same time, it lifted the sector, economically and socially, out of its role as an "inner colony." Comparison of Hungary's 1967 Cooperative Law with the revised rules of operation of Soviet kolkhozes in 1969 clearly demonstrates the differences that had emerged by this time. The Cooperative Law gave legal status to the "good practices" that had become tried and tested on Hungarian producer cooperatives during the 1960s. The leaders of the agrarian lobby were aware that this all required ideological support. The 1967 law was preceded by prolonged ideological debates, over the course of which the agrarian lobby persuaded the Politburo to issue a decree declaring: cooperative property is equal in status to state property and is indispensible in the long term. This set aside a fundamental Stalinist tenet, and one that had remained effective in the Soviet Union.

Knowledge of these economic, social, and legal reform measures is necessary in order to understand how Hungarian producer cooperatives, which had come into being through the transfer of the kolkhoz model, became capable, in the 1970s, of integrating the developed structures of the capitalist agriculture of the time: closed production systems purchased from the United States. The first high-ranking agrarian delegation traveled from Hungary to the United States in 1969, and signed a contract for the purchase of an industrial-type corn production system. This decision was made at the highest level, given that Hungary operated a party-state system, but research confirmed that, unlike the case when adopting the kolkhoz model, Western model transfer was not top-down, but bottom-up; and it expanded horizontally. The Western companies became partners of state farms and producer cooperatives or their associations (the Bábolna State Farm, the Nádudvar Red Star Producer Cooperative, and so on). The large-scale farms themselves, therefore, became the mediators of transfer, not party or state organs. It was they that acted as system administrators and transmitted the developed Western technology to less capital-rich farms. Another disparity between the two model transfers was that when farms took on Western production systems, they had the possibility of choosing between many possible models, economic performance and efficiency being the decisive issues. It is important too to emphasize that the economic actors (state farms and producer cooperatives) were not under an obligation to join, and they could be members of many types of production system at the same time.

Chapter 7 argued that by the 1970s a specific hybrid agriculture emerged in Hungary, where the latest Western (John Deere, Claas and Steiger) brands of machinery cultivated the land of state farms and producer cooperatives that has been created after the Soviet model. Importing this machinery was closely linked to knowledge-transfer, and the necessary conditions for this had been provided by the modernization of intermediate and further agrarian education.

Western model transfer produced a visible improvement in economic performance. In the area of crop production, the greatest success was in grains, particularly wheat and corn (maize). This provided the foundation for a 37% increase in livestock and meat production between 1970 and 1985. Behind this upswing in producer cooperative production lay a specific division of labor between household-plot farms and the large-scale cooperative units. While the large-scale farms produced good results in the highly mechanized branches of arable crop cultivation, household plots specialized in cultivating labor-intensive vegetables and fruit, as well as raising poultry and pigs. This special form of cooperation was investigated in a number of local cases (Bábolna, Nádudvar, etc.).

After the invasion of Czechoslovakia in 1968, the Hungarian reform process stood alone in the socialist camp. As criticism increased, the multifaceted Hungarian cooperative system became the target of dogmatic political forces, not only in Hungary, but within the camp. Following the Polish worker demonstrations of December 1970 especially, there was a strengthening of the view that Hungarian agriculture was developing at the expense of industry and, therefore, of industrial workers. Linked to this was the view that producer cooperatives were "chasing after" mere profit and group interest rather than the interests of society as a whole. There is no doubt that Western model transfer modified the way workers in producer cooperatives thought, their relation to the market and profits, and it was because of precisely this that agricultural producer cooperatives and their entrepreneurially spirited leaders came into the crosshairs of dogmatic, neo-Stalinist political forces. This research has revealed for the first time that show-trial proceedings were launched against more than 1,000 cooperative leaders in the 1970s. These represented the largest number of politically inspired trials in the country since the retributions that followed 1956.

Western model transfer was slowed down temporarily by the offensive of dogmatic forces, but the process could not be stopped. The strength of the agrarian lobby was weakened, however, by the fact that its representatives were squeezed out of the highest-level decision-making bodies. The consequences of this became fully clear only the 1980s, when ever more burdens were heaped on the agrarian sector in order to repay the country's huge accumulated debt. In the first half of the 1980s, producer cooperatives slipped back into the role of "inner colony" reminiscent of the Stalinist period. By modifying material incentives and developing household-plot and ancillary activities, producer cooperatives succeeded for a time in counteracting the increase in state extractions from their revenue and keeping operative their production units that had been modernized by western knowledge and technology-transfer. In these changed internal and external conditions, Hungary's hybrid agriculture reached its developmental limits.

Paradoxically, it was at this very moment that the Soviet leadership began to recognize the achievements of Hungarian agriculture. Gorbachev on numerous occasions pointed to Hungarian producer cooperatives as examples from which other socialist countries might learn, including the Soviet Union. Meanwhile, proposals which saw the solution in a gradual liberalization of property relations were being outlined in Hungarian research institutes and later at economic-policy forums. However, the Politburo did not support these reform plans. It knew that the next step after "upsetting" property relations might be a questioning of one-party rule.

Following system change, the accumulated experience of this specific hybrid, Sovietized and Americanized, agriculture was devalued. Today, when serious economic and social tensions, and occasionally political upheavals, are caused by food-shortage in numerous parts of the world, it is timely to reasses the post-1945 history of Hungarian agriculture. The central message of this book is that it has introduced the case of how a successful alternative for boosting food production can be created through knowledge exchange and technology-transfer between countries with completely different political structures and economic systems when it is mediated by practitioners who are given licence to adapt to local conditions.

Bibliography

PERIODICALS

Belügyi Szemle 11, no. 2 (1973).
Christian Science Monitor, April 29, 1985.
Esti Hírlap, October 26, 1976.
Gazdálkodás 6, no. 4 (1962); 8, no. 1, 6 (1964); 30, no. 12 (1986); 31, no. 4 (1987); 32, no. 9 (1988).
Kelet-Magyarország, April 9, 1974; February 12, March 7, May 11, November 30, December 21, 1975.
Közgazdasági Szemle 13, no. 7–8 (1967); 32 no. 5, no. 8 (1985); 35 no. 5, no. 6 (1989).
Los Angeles Times, November 25, 1982.
Magyar Hírlap, February 10, 1976.
Magyar Közlöny, August 25, December 20, 1948; November 27, 1956.
Magyar Mezőgazdaság 19 (1964); 21, no. 49 (1969); 22, no. 30 (1971).
Medvetánc 2–3, no. 4 (1982) / no. 1 (1983).
Mezőgazdasági Értesítő, January 11, 1961.
Népi Ellenőrzés 15, no. 6 (1973).
Népszabadság, December 15, 1957; December 7, 8, 1961; February 3, December 22, 1971; Januáry–Február 1972; December 16, 1976.
New York Times, December 20, 1981.
Országgyűlési Napló, March 16, 1988.
Pártélet 5, no. 6 (1961).
Pravda June 16, 1980; December 8, 1980; March 16, 1981; June 22, 1981; May 10, 1982; September 7, December 23, 1985.
Statisztikai Szemle 58, no. 4 (1978); 69, no. 11 (1991).
Szabad Föld, August 22, 1948; August 11, 18, 25, September 1, 1957; April 12, 1959.
Szabad Nép, January 26, 29, 1950; March 18, October 16, 1951; July 31, August 7, 1955.

Társadalmi Szemle 16, no. 2 (1961); 21, no. 4 (1966); 23, no. 10 (1968); 28, no. 1 (1973); *Tartós békéért, népi demokráciáért*, December 7, 1948.
Tudomány és Mezőgazdaság 5, no. 5 (1967).

BIBLIOGRAPHY

Adair, Bianca L. "The Agrarian Theses and Rapid Collectivization: Accommodation in Hungarian Agriculture, 1956–1960." *Journal of Communist Studies and Transition Politics* 17, no. 2 (2001): 131–47.

Agrárgazdasági Kutató Intézet. *Az Agrárgazdasági Kutató Intézet története, 1954–1969* [The history of the Institute of Agricultural Economics]. Budapest: AKI, 1970.

Ayatskoy, Dmitriy Fedorovich, ed. *Sobstvennost' na zemlyu v Rossii: Istoriya i sovremennost'*. Moskva: Rosspen, 2002.

Andreenkov, S. N. "Prichiny i alt'ernativy reorganizacii mashinno-traktornyh stantsii 1958 g." *Gumanitarnye nauki v Sibiri* 20, no. 4 (2013): 42–46.

Apor Balázs, Péter Apor, and E. A. Rees, eds. *The Sovietization of Eastern Europe: new perspectives on the postwar period.* Washington, DC: New Academia Publishing, 2008.

Applebaum, Anne. *Iron curtain: the crushing of Eastern Europe, 1945–1956*. London: Allen Lane, 2012.

Artizov, A. N., and György Földes eds. *Sovetsko-vengerszkie ekonomicheskie otnoseniia 1948–1973: Dokumenty*. Moskva: Mezhdunarodnyi Fond Demokratiia, 2012.

Ascher, Abraham. *P. A. Stolypin: the search for stability in late Imperial Russia.* Stanford, CA: Stanford University Press, 2001.

Atkinson, Dorothy. *The end of the Russian land commune, 1905–1930*. Stanford, CA: Stanford University Press, 1983.

Asztalos Morell, Ildikó. *Emancipation's Dead-End Roads? Studies in the Formation and Development of the Hungarian Model for Agriculture and Gender (1956–1989)*. Acta Universitatis Upsaliensis 46. Uppsala: Uppsala University Library, 1999.

Autio-Sarasmo, Sari, and Katalin Miklossy, eds. *Reassessing Cold War*. London and New York: Routledge, 2011.

Babiracki, Patryk, and Zimmer, Kenyon, eds. *Cold War crossings: international travel and exchange across the Soviet bloc, 1940s–1960s*, Introduction by Vladislav Zubok. College Station: Texas A&M University Press, 2014.

Bábolnai Mezőgazdasági Kombinát. *Bábolna: Tények és adatok, 1945–1989* [Facts and Data, 1945–1989]. Vol. 1. Bábolna: Bábolnai Mezőgazdasági Kombinát, 1989.

Bakóczi, Antal. "A társadalmi tulajdon elleni bűncselekmények alakulása" [The State of Offenses against Public Ownership]. *Népi Ellenőrzés* 15, no. 6 (1973): 1–4.

Bakóczi, Antal. "Az új gazdaságirányítási rendszer és a társadalmi tulajdon elleni bűnözés alakulása" [The New Economic Mechanism and the Offenses against Social Property]. *Belügyi Szemle* 11, no. 2 (1973): 3–10.

Balázs, Péter. "Magyarország és az Európai Unió" [Hungary and the EU]. In *Európai közjog és politika* [European public law and politics], edited by Tamás Kende, 811–38. Budapest: Osiris, 2005.

Balogh, Csaba. "Szántóföldi növénytermesztési rendszerek" [Closed production systems in crop farming]. In *A mezőgazdaság szolgálatában: Emlékkönyv Dimény Imre tiszteletére 90. születésnapja alkalmából* [In attendance on agriculture: Memorial volume in honor of Imre Dimény on the occasion of his 90th birthday], edited by Judit Dimény and Péter Szendrő, 95–104. Budapest–Gödöllő: SZIE, 2012.

Balogh, Sándor, ed. *A Magyar Szocialista Munkáspárt ideiglenes vezető testületeinek jegyzőkönyvei* [Minutes of the Provisional Leadership Bodies of the HSWP]. Vol. 1. *1956. november 11–1957. január 14.* [November 11, 1956.–January 14, 1957]. Budapest: Intera, 1993.

Balogh, Sándor, and Lajos Izsák, eds. *Magyarországi pártprogramok, 1944–1988.* [The programs of the Hungarian political parties, 1944–1988]. Budapest: ELTE Eötvös Kiadó, 2004.

Barát, Mária, ed. *A magyar gazdaság vargabetűje* [The detour of the Hungarian economy]. Budapest: Aula, 1994.

Baráth, Magdolna. "Magyarország a szovjet diplomáciai iratokban, 1957–1964" [Hungary in the documents of the Soviet diplomacy]. In *Múlt századi hétköznapok: Tanulmányok a Kádár-rendszer kialakulásának időszakáról* [Everyday life in the 20th century: Studies on the formation of the Kádár-system], edited by János M. Rainer, 55–89. Budapest: 1956-os Intézet, 2003.

———. "Szovjet kézi vezérlés az első Nagy Imre-kormány idején" [Direct Soviet control during the first government of Imre Nagy]. In *Nagy Imre és kora: Tanulmányok és források* [Imre Nagy and his epoch: Studies and sources]. Vol. 4, edited by Levente Sipos. 153–80. Budapest: Nagy Imre Alapítvány, 2006.

———. "Gerő Ernő és Nagy Imre vitája, 1947–1949" [The debate between Ernő Gerő and Imre Nagy, 1947–1949]. In Estók, *1956 és a magyar agrártársadalom*, 67–80.

———. *Kádár János első kormányának jegyzőkönyvei, 1956. november 7.–1958. január 25.* [Minutes of the first Kádár-government, November 7, 1956–January 25, 1958]. Budapest: MOL, 2009.

———. *Szovjet diplomáciai jelentések Magyarországról a Hruscsov-korszakban* [Reports of the Soviet diplomacy on Hungary during the Khruschev-era]. Budapest: Napvilág–Politikatörténeti Intézet, 2012.

———. *A szovjet tényező: Szovjet tanácsadók Magyarországon* [The Soviet factor: Soviet advisors in Hungary]. Budapest: Gondolat, 2017.

Baráth, Magdolna, and János M. Rainer, eds. *Gorbacsov tárgyalásai magyar vezetőkkel* [Gorbachëv's consultations with the Hungarian leadership]. Budapest: 1956-os Intézet, 2000.

Bartha, Ákos. "A két világháború közti csehszlovák, jugoszláv és roman földbirtokrendezés" [The land reallocation in the interwar Czechoslovakia, Yugoslavia and Romania]. *Valóság* 55, no. 10 (2012): 96–111.

Bartlett, Roger P., ed. *Land commune and peasant community in Russia: communal forms in imperial and early Soviet society*. New York: St. Martin's Press, 1990.

Bauerkämper, Arnd, ed. *"Junkerland in Bauernhand?" Durchführung, Auswirkungen und Stellenwert der Bodenreform in der Sowjetischen Besatzungszone*. Stuttgart: Franz Steiner Verlag, 1996.

———. Ländliche Gesellschaft in der kommunistischen Diktatur: Zwangsmodernisierung und Tradition in Brandenburg 1945–1963. Köln–Weimar–Wien: Böhlau Verlag, 2002.

Békés, Csaba. "A kádári külpolitika 1956–1968" [The foreign policy of Kádár, 1956–1968]. *Rubicon* 9, no. 1 (1998): 19–22.

———. "A kádári külpolitika, 1956–1968: Látványos sikerek—'láthatatlan' konfliktusok" [The foreign policy of Kádár, 1956–1968: Visible successes—"invisible" conflicts]. In *Európából Európába: Magyarország konfliktusok kereszttüzében, 1945–1990* [From Europe to Europe: Hungary in the cross-fire of conflicts], 237–56. Budapest: Gondolat, 2004,

———. "Hungary the Soviet Bloc, the German question and the CSCE Process, 1965–1975." *Journal of Cold War Studies* 18, no. 3 (2016): 95–138.

Bekker, Zsuzsa. *Rendszerválság: Alkalmazkodási folyamatok a kelet-európai országokban 1970 és 1990 között* [System-crisis: Adaptation processes in Eastern Europe between 1970 and 1990]. Budapest: Aula, 1995.

Bell, Peter D. *Peasants in Socialist Transition. Life in a collectivized Hungarian Village*. Berkeley, Los Angeles, and London: University of California Press, 1984.

Belyanov, Vladislav Alexandrovich. *Lichnoye podsobnoye khozyaystvo pri sotsializme*. Moskva: Ékonomika, 1970.

Benke, Valéria. "Egységes értelmezés, kommunista kiállás, közös cselekvés" [Unity in interpretation, communist espousal, unity in action]. *Társadalmi Szemle* 28, no. 1 (1973): 3–16.

Berend, Iván T. *Gazdasági útkeresés 1956–1965* [Search for an economic path 1956–1965]. Budapest: Magvető, 1983.

———. *Central and Eastern Europe 1944–1993: Detour from the Periphery to the Periphery*. Cambridge: Cambridge University Press, 1996.

———. *From the Soviet bloc to the European Union: The economic and social transformation of Central and Eastern Europe since 1973*. Cambridge: Cambridge University Press, 2009.

Berend, Iván T., and György Ránki. *Economic development in East-Central Europe in the 19th and 20th centuries*. New York and London: Columbia University Press, 1974.

Beznin, M. A., and T. M. Dimoni, *Agrarnyy stroy Rossii 1930–1980-kh gg*. Moscow: Lenand, 2014.

Blohm, Georg. Új irányzatok a nyugat-német mezőgazdaságban. [New Trends in West German Agriculture]. Budapest: Mezőgazdasági, 1967.

Bokovoy, Melissa. *Peasants and Communists: Politics and Ideology in the Yugoslav Countryside, 1941–1953*. Pittsburgh: University of Pittsburgh Press, 1998.

Boreczky, Beatrix, ed. *Központi szervek: 1950–1970: A magyar állam szervei* [Central organs of the Hungarian state 1950–1970]. Budapest: MOL, 1993.

Borhi, László. *Hungary in the Cold War, 1945–1956: between the United States and the Soviet Union*. Budapest: CEU Press, 2004.

———. *Dealing with dictators: The United States, Hungary, and East Central Europe, 1942–1989*. Bloomington: Indiana University Press, 2016.

Bosznay, László. "Az agrárszakoktatás 50 éve" [50 years of the agricultural special training]. In Orosz, Für, and Romány, *Magyarország agrártörténete*, 601–30.

Botos, Katalin, Mihály Patai, and István Szalkai. *Pénzügyek és nemzetközi gazdasági kapcsolataink* [Financial issues and our international economic relations]. Budapest: KJK, 1980.

Bottoni, Stefano. *Long Awaited West: Eastern Europe since 1944*. Bloomington: Indiana University Press, 2017.

Boyer, Christoph, ed. *Zur Physiognomie sozialistischer Wirtschaftsreformen: Die Sowjetunion, Polen, die Tschechoslowakei, Ungarn, die DDR und Jugoslawien im Vergleich*. Frankfurt/Main: Max-Planck-Institut für Europäische Rechtsgeschichte, 2007.

Bozsonyi, Károly, Zsolt Horváth, and Zoltán Kmetty. "A hatalom hálója: A Kádár-kori hatalmi elit hálózati struktúrája az együttvadászási szokások alapján" [The Power Grid: The Social Network of the Hungarian Elite in the Socialist Era Based on Hunting Habits]. *Korall* 13, no. 47 (2012): 157–84.

———. "The Power Grid: The Social Network of the Hungarian Elite in the Socialist Era Based on Hunting Habits." In *Historische Netzwerkanalysen: Österreichische Zeitschridt für Geschichtwissensschaften*, edited by Albert Müller and Wolfgang Neurath, 186–228. Innsbruck–Wien–Bozen: Studien Verlag, 2012.

Bölöny, József. *Magyarország kormányai, 1948–1992* [The governments of Hungary, 1948–1992]. Budapest: Akadémiai, 1992.

Brada, Josef C., and Karl Eugen Wädekin, eds. *Socialist Agriculture in Transition. Organizational Response to Failing Performance*. Boulder and London: Westview Press, 1988.

Brassley, Paul. "Land reform and reallocation in interwar Europe." In *Contexts of Property in Europe: The Social Embeddedness of Property Rights in Land in Historical Perspective*, edited by Rosa Congost and Rui Santos, 145–64. Turnhut, Belgium: Brepols, 2010.

Brus, Włodzimierz. "Postwar Reconstruction and Socio-Economic Transformation." In *The Economic History of Eastern Europe 1919–1975*. Vol. 2, edited by Michael Charles Kaser and Edward Albert Radice. 564–641. Oxford: Clarendon 1986.

Brzechczyn, Krysztof, ed. *New Perspectives in Transnational History of Communism in East Central Europe*. Berlin: Peter Lang Verlag, 2019.

Burgert, Róbert. *Iparszerű termelési rendszerek szervezése a mezőgazdaságban: Bábolna*. [Organizing industrial-style production in agriculture]. Budapest: Országos Vezetőképző Központ, 1985.

Buza, János, János Estók, Ferenc Szávai, and Zsuzsanna Varga, eds. *Agrártörténet—Agrárpolitika: Tanulmányok Szuhay Miklós Emeritus Professzor tiszteletére* [Agricultural history—agrarian policy]. Budapest: Budapesti Corvinus Egyetem–Budapesti Közgazdaságtudományi Egyetem Alapítvány–Miskolci Egyetem Gazdaságtudományi Kara, 2006.

Choi, Jeong Nam, Axel Wolz, and Michael Kopsidis. "Family farm ideology and the transformation of collective farms in East Germany, 1989–2005." In Congost, *Contexts of Property in Europe*, 247–66.

Conquest, Robert. *The Harvest of Sorrow: Soviet Collectivization and the Terror-Famine*. Oxford: Oxford University Press, 1986.

Crampton, Richard J. *Eastern Europe in the Twentieth Century—and after*. 2nd ed. London and New York: Routledge, 1997.

Creed, Gerald W. "The Politics of Agriculture in Bulgaria." *Slavic Review* 54, no. 4 (1995): 843–68.

Csaba, László. *Kelet-Európa a világgazdaságban: Alkalmazkodás és gazdasági mechanizmus* [Eastern-Europe in the world economy: Adaptation and economic mechanism]. Budapest: KJK, 1984.

Csahók, István, ed. *Fazekas Béla (1922–1994) műveinek válogatott bibliográfiája* [The selected *István* bibliography of the works of Béla Fazekas]. Budapest: KSH Könyvtár és Dokumentációs Szolgálat, 1998.

Csáki, Csaba. "A magyar mezőgazdaság nemzetközi versenyképessége" [Competitiveness of the Hungarian agriculture]. In *Az európai és magyarországi agrárpolitika jövője*, edited by Ferenc Glatz, 99–114. Budapest: MTA Történettudományi Intézet, 2010.

Cseszka, Éva. *Gazdasági típusú perek, különös tekintettel az FM-perre (1945–1953)* [Economic show trials, with special regard to the trial against the leaders of the Ministry of Agriculture]. Budapest: Gondolat, 2012.

Csete, *László*. "A termelőszövetkezetek és az állami gazdaságok fejlődése (1976–1985)" [The development of cooperatives and state farms, 1976–1985]. *Gazdálkodás* 31, no. 4 (1987): 1–6.

Csete, László, and Ferenc Erdei, eds. *A szocialista mezőgazdaság fejlődése Bulgáriában: Három tanulmányút 1959–1960-ban* [The development of the socialist agriculture in Bulgaria: Three study-tours in 1959–1960]. Budapest: Mezőgazdasági Üzemtani Intézet, 1961.

Csizmadia, Ernő. "A vállalati önállóság szervezeti alapjai a termelőszövetkezetekben" [The organizational bases of enterprise independence on producer cooperatives]. *Közgazdasági Szemle* 13, no. 7–8 (1967): 844–50.

———. *Bevezetés az élelmiszergazdaságtanba* [Introduction into the food economy]. Budapest: Akadémiai, 1973.

Csontos, Gábor. *A Hortobágy szélén: nádudvari beszélgetések* [At the edge of Hortobágy: conversations in Nádudvar]. Budapest: Hét Krajcár, 2005.

Dancs, József. *Ez történt a kulisszák mögött* [This happened behind the scenes]. Bábolna: s. n., 1983.

Danilov, Viktor Petrovich, ed. *Tragediya sovetskoy derevni: Kollektivizatsiya i raskulachinanie: Dokumenty i matieriali v 5-kh tomakh. 1927–1939*. 5 vols. Moskva: Rosszpen, 1999–2006.

David-Fox, Michael. *Crossing borders: modernity, ideology, and culture in Russia and the Soviet Union*. Pittsburgh: University of Pittsburgh Press, 2015.

Davies, Robert William. *The Soviet collective farm, 1929–1930*. London: Macmillan, 1980.

———. *The Socialist offensive: the collectivisation of Soviet agriculture, 1929–1930*. London: Macmillan, 1989.

———, ed. *From tsarism to the New Economic Policy: continuity and change in the economy of the USSR*. Ithaca, NY: Cornell University Press, 1991.

Davies, Robert William, Mark Harrison, and Stephen G. Wheatcroft, eds. *The economic transformation of the Soviet Union, 1913–1945*. Cambridge: Cambridge University Press, 1994.

Davies, Robert William, and Stephen G. Wheatcroft, eds. *The years of hunger: Soviet agriculture, 1931–1933*. New York: Palgrave Macmillan, 2003.

Dimény, Imre. *Mezőgazdaságunk és a műszaki fejlesztés* [Our agriculture and technical development]. Budapest: Kossuth, 1972.

———, ed. *Kertészeti termelési rendszerek ökonómiai jellemzői* [Special economic features of the closed production systems in horticulture]. Budapest: Mezőgazdasági, 1980.

———. "A magyar mezőgazdaság sikeressége a 60-as, 70-es években" [The successfulness of Hungarian agriculture in the 1960–70s]. In Nagy and Kovács, *Személyiségek a magyar agráriumban*, 79–105.

Dohan, M. R. "Foreign trade." In Davies, *From tsarism*, 212–34.

Dolbilov, Mikhail D. "Zemel'naya sobstvennost' i osvobozhdeniye krest'yan." In Ayatskoy, *Sobstvennost'*, 45–152.

Donáth, Ferenc. *Demokratikus földreform Magyarországon 1945–47* [Democratic land reform in Hungary, 1945–47]. Budapest: Akadémiai, 1969.

———. "A magyar szövetkezeti nagyüzemi mezőgazdaság kialakulásának vázlatos története (1949–1970)" [A brief account on the history of socialist large-scale agriculture in Hungary, 1949–1970]. *Agrártörténeti Szemle* 14, no. 3–4 (1972): 292–330.

———. *Reform és forradalom: A magyar mezőgazdaság strukturális átalakulása, 1945–1975*. Budapest: Akadémiai, 1977.

———. *A munka és tulajdon kapcsolata az iparosodó mezőgazdaságban: Tulajdon és hatékonyság* [Connections between the labour and the property in the industrialized agriculture]. Budapest: Szövetkezeti Kutató Intézet, 1979.

———. *Reform and revolution: transformation of Hungary's agriculture 1945–1970*. Budapest: Corvina, 1980.

Dragostinova, Theodora, and Malgorzata Fidelis. "Beyond the Iron Curtain: Eastern Europe and the global Cold War." *Slavic Review* 77, no. 3 (2018): 577–87.

Dronin, Nikolai M., and Bellinger, Edward G. *Climate Dependence and Food Problems in Russia 1900–1990: The Interaction of Climate and Agricultural Policy and Their Effect on Food Problems*. Budapest and New York: Central European University Press, 2005.

Éliás, András, Emília Sebők, and Tamás Ujhelyi. *A mezőgazdasági és élelmiszeripari termékek az új világgazdasági helyzetben* [The products of the agriculture and food industry in the changing world economy]. Budapest: KJK, 1980.

Az emberiség békéjéért, jövőjéért: A szocialista országok kommunista és munkáspártjainak nyilatkozata, Moszkva, 1957. november 14–16. [For mankind's peace and future: A declaration of communist and workers' parties of socialist countries, Moscow, November 14–16, 1957]. Budapest: Kossuth Kiadó, 1957.

Enderle-Burcel, Gertrude, Piotr Franaszek, Dieter Stiefel, and AliceTeichová, eds. *Gaps in the Iron Curtain: Economic relations between neutral and socialist countries in Cold War Europe*. Kraków: Jagiellonian University Press, 2009.

Enyedi, György. *Farmok és farmerek: Az amerikai mezőgazdaság* [Farms and Farmers: American agriculture]. Budapest: Mezőgazdasági, 1970.

Erdei, Ferenc. "A szocialista magyar mezőgazdaság sikereinek és nehézségeinek forrásairól" [About the sources of the successes and problems of Hungarian socialist agriculture]. In *Erdei Ferenc összegyűjtött művei: Agrárproblémák* [Selected works of Ferenc Erdei: Agrarian problems]. Vol. 2, edited by Ferenc Fekete and Magdolna Dzúr, 148–65. Budapest: Akadémiai, 1986.

Erdmann, Gyula. *Begyűjtés, beszolgáltatás Magyarországon, 1945–1956* [Compulsory deliveries in Hungary, 1945–1956]. Békéscsaba: Tevan, 1993.

———. ed. *Paraszti kiszolgáltatottság—Paraszti érdekvédelem, önigazgatás* [Peasants' defencelessness—Safeguarding of peasants' interests, self-governing]. Gyula: Békés Megyei Levéltár, 1994.

Estók, János, ed. *1956 és a magyar agrártársadalom* [1956 and the Hungarian agrarian society]. Budapest: Magyar Mezőgazdasági Múzeum, 2006.

Estók, János, György Fehér, Péter Gunst, and Zsuzsanna Varga, eds. *History of Hungarian Agriculture and Rural Life, 1848–2004*. Budapest: Argumentum Publishing House–Museum of Hungarian Agriculture, 2004.

Fairbank, John K. *China: A New History*. Cambridge: Belknap Press of Harvard University Press, 1994.

Farkas, Gyöngyi, "'Gyertek lányok traktorra!': Női traktorosok a gépállomáson és a propagandában" ["Girls, get on the tractor!": Woman Tractor Drivers at the Machine Station and in Propaganda]. *Korall* 4, no. 13 (2003): 65–86.

———. *Lázadó falvak: Kollektivizálás elleni tüntetések a vidéki Magyarországon, 1951–1961* [Rebellious villages: Demonstrations against collectivization in rural Hungary, 1951–1961]. Budapest: Korall, 2016.

Fazekas, Béla. *A mezőgazdasági termelőszövetkezeti mozgalom Magyarországon*. Budapest: Kossuth, 1976.

Feest, David. *Zwangskollektivierung im Baltikum: Die Sowjetisierung des Estnischen Dorfes 1944–1953*. Vienna: Böhlau, 2007.

———. "The Collectivization of Agriculture in the Baltic Soviet Republics, 1944–1953." In Iordachi and Bauerkämper, *The Collectivization*, 79–109.

Fehér, Dezső. "A magyar lótenyésztés, lóversenyzés és lovassport Széchenyi korától napjainkig" [The Hungarian horse-sport from the Szechenyi's epoch to present days]. In Nagy and Kovács, *Személyiségek a magyar agráriumban*, 59–68.

Fehér, Lajos. *A magyar mezőgazdaság fejlődésének útja: Előadás az MSZMP KB Politikai Akadémiáján* [The road of the Hungarian agriculture's development: A lecture given at the Political Academy of the HSWP CC]. Budapest: Kossuth, 1957.

Feitl, István. "Hungarian Plans to Reform the Council for Mutual Economic Assistance, 1967–1970." In *Influences, Pressures Pro and Con, and Opportunities: Studies on Political Interactions in and Involving Hungary in the Twentieth Century*, edited by Zoltán Ripp, 239–71. Budapest: Napvilág Kiadó, 2014.

Fejtő, Ferenc. *A népi demokráciák története* [The history of people's democracies]. Vol. 2. Budapest and Paris: Magvető, 1991.
Fél, Edit, and Tamás Hofer. *Proper Peasants: Traditional Life in a Hungarian Village*. Chicago: Aldine Publishing Co., 1969.
Ferber, Katalin, and Gábor Rejtő. *Reform(év)fordulón* [Reform anniversary]. Budapest: KJK, 1988.
Fischer, Holger. "The non-agricultural activities of the agricultural production cooperatives and state-owned farms in socialist Hungary 1967–1989." In *Agriculture and Rural Life in Finland and Hungary*, edited by Zsuzsanna Varga and Anssi Halmesvirta, 113–25. Loimaa: Sarka, 2018.
Fitzerald, Deborah. *Every Farm a Factory: The Industrial Ideal in American Agriculture*. New Haven, CT: Yale University Press, 2003.
Fitzpatrick, Sheila. "How the Mice Buried the Cat: Scenes from the Great Purges of 1937 in the Russian Provinces." *The Russian Review* 52, no. 3 (1993): 299–332.
———. "Ascribing Class: The Construction of Social Identity in Soviet Russia." *Journal of Modern History* 65, no. 4 (1993): 745–70.
———. *Stalin's Peasants: Resistance and Survival in the Russian Village After Collectivization*. New York and Oxford: Oxford University Press, 1994.
Forgó, István. *Búcsú Erdei Ferenctől* [Taking leave of Ferenc Erdei]. Az Erdei Ferenc Társaság füzetei 18. Makó: Erdei Ferenc Társaság, 2006.
Fóris, Imre, ed. *Mezőgazdasági termelőszövetkezeti törvény: Földjogi törvény* [Law on collective farms: Law on land rights]. Budapest: KJK, 1968.
Földes, György. *Hatalom és mozgalom (1956–1989)* [The power and the political movement, 1956–1989]. Budapest: Reform–Kossuth, 1989.
———. *Az eladósodás politikatörténete, 1957–1986* [The political history of indebtedness, 1957–1986]. Budapest: Maecenas, 1995.
———. "Kötélhúzás felsőfokon: Kádár és Brezsnyev" [String-Pulling of the Highest Degree: Kádár and Brezhnev]. In Rácz, *Ki volt Kádár?*, 103–13.
———. "The Characteristics of the Kádár-Era." In *Regimes and transformations: Hungary in the twentieth century*, edited by István Feitl and Balázs Sipos, 297–324. Budapest: Napvilág, 2005.
———. "A magyar–szovjet gazdasági kapcsolatok 1948–1973" [Hungarian-Soviet economic relations, 1948–1973]. *Századok* 147, no. 6 (2013): 1349–76.
———. Kádár János külpolitikája és nemzetközi tárgyalásai 1956–*1988* [The foreign policy of János Kádár and his international negotiations]. 2 vols. Budapest: Napvilág, 2015.
Garai, Vera, and András Meszticzky. *Tapasztalatok és gondolatok a szántóföldi növénytermelési rendszerekről* [Experiences and ideas on the closed production systems in crop farming]. Budapest: AKI, 1977.
Gaucik, István. "A csehszlovákiai magyarság gazdasági státuszvesztése (1945–1948)" [The economic status losses of the Hungarian minority in Czechoslovakia]. PhD thesis, ELTE TDI, Budapest, 2011.
Gecsényi, Lajos. *Iratok Magyarország és Ausztria kapcsolatainak történetéhez, 1956–1964* [Documents on the history of Hungarian–Austrian relations, 1956–1964]. Budapest: Magyar Országos Levéltár, 2000.

Gergely, István. "Az amerikai tanulmányút tapasztalatai" [The experiences of the American study trip]. *Magyar Mezőgazdaság* 21, no. 49 (1969): 5–7.

Germuska, *Pál.* "Szovjet tanácsadók magyar hadiipari vállalatoknál az 1950-es években," [Soviet advisors in the Hungarian military industry]. *Századok* 142, no. 6 (2008): 1465–81.

———. "Socialist Miracle? Hungarian Industrial Development Policy and Economic Growth, 1950–1975." *The Journal of European Economic History*, 42, no. 1 (2013): 87–134.

———. "Failed Eastern integration and a partly successful opening up to the West: the economic re-orientation of Hungary during the 1970s." In *European Review of History: Revue européenne d'histoire* 21, no. 2 (2014): 271–91.

———. "Economic Growth and the Industrial Development Policy in Hungary, 1950–1975." In *Industrial Policy in Europe after 1945: Wealth, Power and Economic Development in the Cold War*, edited by Christian Grabas and Alexander Nützenadel, 321–36. Basingstoke: Palgrave Macmillan, 2014.

Girnius, Kestutis K. "The Collectivization of Lithuanian Agriculture, 1944–1950." *Soviet Studies* 40, no. 3 (1988): 460–78.

Glatz, Ferenc. *Új vidékpolitika* [The new rural development policy]. Budapest: MTA Társadalomkutató Központ, 2008.

Goldman, Wendy, and Donald Filtzer, eds. *Hunger and war: food provisioning in the Soviet Union during World War II.* Bloomington: Indiana University Press, 2015.

Gorshkov, Boris B. *Peasants in Russia from Serfdom to Stalin: Accommodation, Survival, Resistance*. London: Bloomsbury Academic, 2018.

Gough, Roger. *A good comrade: János Kádár: Communism and Hungary*. London and New York: I. B. Tauris, 2006.

Graf, Maximilian. *Österreich und die DDR 1949–1990: Politik und Wirtschaft im Schatten der deutschen Teilung*. Vienna: ÖAW, 2016.

Maximilian Graf, et al. "A Masterpiece of European Détente? Austrian–Hungarian Relations from 1964 until the Peaceful End of the Cold War," *Zeitgeschichte* 41, no. 5 (2014): 311–38.

Greiner, Bernd, Christian Th. Müller and Claudia Weber, eds. *Ökonomie im Kalten Krieg. Studien zum Kalten Krieg* 4. Hamburg: Hamburger Edition, 2010.

Gruev, Mihail. "Collectivization and Social Change in Bulgaria, 1940s–1950s." In Iordachi and Bauerkämper, *The Collectivization*, 329–68.

Gulyás, Emil, ed. *Az MSZMP agrárpolitikájának fő vonásai* [The main features of the HSWP's agrarian policy]. Budapest: Kossuth–Mezőgazdasági, 1970.

Gunst, Péter, ed. *Hungarian Agrarian Society from the Emancipation of Serfs (1848) to the Re-privatization of Land (1998)*. New York: Columbia University Press, 1998.

———, ed. *A magyar agrártársadalom a jobbágyság felszabadításától napjainkig* [Hungarian Agrarian Society from the Emancipation of Serfs (1848) to the Re-privatization of Land (1998)]. Budapest: Napvilág, 1998.

Gunst, Péter, and Imre Wellmann. *A 200 éves Bábolna múltjából, 1789–1945* [Two hundred years history of Bábolna, 1789–1945]. Bábolna: Bábolnai Mezőgazdasági Kombinát, 1989.

Gyáni, Gábor. "Social History of Hungary in the Horthy Era." In Gyáni, Kövér, and Valuch, *Social history*, 271–507.

———. "A forradalom társadalomtörténeti paradoxonjai" [Socio-historical paradox of the Revolution of 1956]. *Forrás* 38, no. 10 (2006): 27–39.

Gyáni, Gábor, György Kövér, and Tibor Valuch, eds. *Social history of Hungary from the reform era to the end of the twentieth century*. New York: Columbia University Press, 2004.

Gyarmati, György. *A Rákosi-korszak: Rendszerváltó fordulatok évtizede Magyarországon, 1945–1956* [The Rákosi-epoch: The decade of system changes, 1945–1956]. Budapest: ÁBTL–Rubicon, 2011.

Gyarmati, György, and Mária Palasik, eds. *Big brother's miserable grocery store: Studies on the history of the Hungarian secret services after World War II*. Budapest: ÁBTL–L'Harmattan, 2012.

Gyenes, Antal. *A B.-i Mezőgazdasági Termelőszövetkezet: Monográfia* [The Agricultural Producer Cooperative in B.: Monograph]. Budapest: Szövetkezeti Kutató Intézet, 1977.

Gyenis, János. *A nemzetközi szövetkezeti mozgalom története és mai helyzete* [The past and present of the international cooperative movement]. Budapest: Erdei Ferenc Szövetkezeti Alapítvány, 1993.

Halász, *Péter. A termelőszövetkezeti mozgalom története Apátfalván* [The history of the producer cooperative movement in Apátfalva]. Budapest: Akadémiai, 1975.

Hale-Dorrel, Aaron. *Corn crusade: Khrushchev's farming revolution in the post-Stalin Soviet Union*. New York: Oxford University Press, 2018.

Halmesvirta, Anssi, ed. *Kádár's Hungary—Kekkonen's Finland*. Hungarologische Beiträge 14. Kopi-Jyvä: Jyväskylä, 2002.

Halmesvirta, Anssi. *Co-operation across the Iron Curtain: Hungarian-Finnish Scientific Relations of the Academies from the 1960s to the 1990s*. Jyväskylä: University of Jyväskylä, 2005.

Hann, Chris. *Tázlár: a village in Hungary*. Cambridge: Cambridge University Press, 1980.

———. "Morality and economy: work, workfare, and fairness in provincial Hungary." *Archives Européennes de Sociologie* 59, no. 2 (2018): 225–54.

Hann, Chris, and Mihály Sárkány. "The great transformation in rural Hungary: Property, life strategies and living standards." In *The Postsocialist Agrarian Question: Property Relations and the Rural Condition*, edited by Chris Hann and the Property Relations Group, 117–41. Münster: LIT Verlag, 2003.

Hanson, Philip. *Trade and Technology in Soviet–Western Relations*. New York: Palgrave Macmillan, 1981.

Hanson, Philip. "The Soviet Union's acqusition of Western Technology after Stalin: Some thoughts on people and connections." In Autio-Sarasmo and Miklóssy, *Reassessing Cold War Europe*, 16–32.

Hantó, Zsuzsa, et al., ed. *Kitaszítottak* [Outcasts of the socialist society]. Vol. 1. *"Magukkal fogjuk megzsírozni a földet."* Budapest: Alterra, 2001.

Harcsa, Iván, Imre Kovách, and Iván Szelényi. "The Hungarian agricultural miracle and the limits of socialist reforms." In *Privatizing the Land: Rural political economy in post-communist societies*, edited by Iván Szelényi, 21–42. London–New York: Routledge, 1998.

Hare, Peter G., H. K. Radice, and Nigel Swain, eds. *Hungary: A Decade of Economic Reform*. London: Unwin Hyman, 1981.

Hartford, Kathleen. "Hungarian Agriculture: A model for the Socialist World?" *World Development* 13, no. 1 (1985): 123–150.

Haupt, Heinz-Gerhard, and Jürgen Kocka, eds. *Comparative and Transnational History: Central European Approaches and New Perspectives*. New York and Oxford: Berghahn Books, 2009.

Heinz, Michael. *Mähdreschern und Musterdörfern: Industrialisierung der DDR-Landwirtschaft und die Wandlung des ländlichen Lebens*. Berlin: Metropol Verlag, 2011.

Hetzer, Maria, Elisabeth Meyer-Renschhausen, Leonore Scholze-Irrlitz, Laura Stoye, and Viktoria Müller. *Transitzone Dorf: Ein Ort zwischen Bodenreform und Kollektivierung*. Leipzig: Zank, 2015.

Hixson, Walter. *Parting the curtain: propaganda, culture, and the Cold War, 1945–1961*. Basingstoke: Macmillan, 1998.

Hódos, György. *Show trials: stalinist purges in Eastern Europe, 1948–1954*. New York: Praeger, 1987.

Hollos, Marida, and Bela C. Maday, eds. *New Hungarian Peasants? An East Central European Experience with Collectivization*. New York: Columbia University Press, 1983.

Honvári, János. *A gépállomások története, 1947–1964: A gépállomások és a magyar mezőgazdaság gépesítésének története 1947–1964* [The history of the machine and tractor stations: The machine and tractor stations and the mechanization of the Hungarian agriculture]. Győr: Távtan, 2003.

———. *XX. századi magyar gazdaságtörténet: Transzformációk, rendszerek*, Budapest: Aula, 2006.

———. "A klasszikus begyűjtési rendszer változása az 'új szakasz' meghirdetésétől a beadás megszüntetéséig" [Changes in classical system of compulsory deliveries from New Course to the abolition of deliveries]. In Buza et al., *Agrártörténet—Agrárpolitika*, 409–30.

Honvári, János, and Csaba Torda. "Magyarország csatlakozása az IMF-hez és a Világbankhoz" [Hungary's accession to the IMF and the World Bank]. *Archívnet* 9. no. 1 (2009). http://www.archivnet.hu/gazdasag/magyarorszag_csatlakozasa_az_imfhez_es_a_vilagbankhoz_i._resz.html

Horváth, Gergely Krisztián, ed. Életvilágok és társadalmi gyakorlatok a 18–20. században. [Everyday life and social practices in the 18th–20th centuries] Vidéktörténet 1. [The History of the Countryside]. Budapest: MTA Bölcsészettudományi Központ, 2017.

Horváth, Gergely Krisztián, ed. *Vakvágányon: A "szocializmus alapjainak" lerakása vidéken a hosszú ötvenes években* [ford.]. Vidéktörténet 2. [The History of the Countryside]. Budapest: MTA Bölcsészettudományi Központ, 2018.

Horváth, Ibolya, Pál Solt, and Győző Szabó, ed. *Iratok az igazságszolgáltatás történetéhez* [Documents on the history of jurisdiction]. Vol. 4. Budapest: KJK, 1995.

Horváth, M. Ferenc. "A 'népi ellenőrzés' Magyarországon 1957–1989" ["People's Control" in Hungary, 1957–1989]. *Levéltári Szemle* 40, no. 4 (1990): 29–40.

Horváth, Sándor, and József Ö. Kovács, eds. Állami erőszak és kollektivizálás a kommunista diktatúrában [State violence and collectivization in the communist dictatorship]. Budapest: MTA Bölcsészettudományi Központ, 2015.

Huszár, Tibor. *Kádár János politikai életrajza* [Political biography of János Kádár]. Vol. 2. Budapest: Szabad Tér–Kossuth, 2003.

———. *Beszélgetések Nyers Rezsővel* [Conversations with Rezső Nyers]. Budapest: Kossuth, 2004.

———. *Erdei Ferenc 1910–1970: Politikai életrajz* [Ferenc Erdei 1910–1970: Political biography]. Budapest: Corvina, 2012.

Izsák, Lajos, ed. *A Magyar Dolgozók Pártja határozatai 1948–1956* [Resolutions of the Hungarian Workers' Party, 1948–1956]. Budapest: Napvilág, 1998.

Izsák, Lajos, and Miklós Kun, eds. *Moszkvának jelentjük . . . : Titkos dokumentumok 1944–1948*. [Sending our reports to Moscow . . . : Secret documents 1944–1948]. Budapest: Századvég, 1994.

Izsák, Lajos, and József Szabó, eds. *1956 a sajtó tükrében: 1956. október 22.–november 5.* [1956 in the mirror of the press, October 22 and November 5, 1956]. Budapest: Kossuth, 1989.

Izsák, Lajos, József Szabó, and Róbert Szabó, eds. *1956 plakátjai és röplapjai* [Posters and handbills from 1956]. Budapest: Zrínyi, 1991.

———, eds. *1956 vidéki sajtója* [The rural press in 1956]. Budapest: Korona, 1996.

Jarausch, Konrad, and Hannes Siegrist. *Amerikanisierung und Sowjetisierung In Deutschland, 1945–1970*. Frankfurt/Main and New York: Campus Verlag, 1997.

Jarosz, Dariusz. "Polish Peasants versus Stalinism." In *Stalinism in Poland, 1944–1956: Selected Papers from the Fifth World Congress of Central and East European Studies*, edited by Ronald J. Hill and A. Kemp-Welch, 59–77. London: Palgrave Macmillan, 1999.

Jarosz, Dariusz. "The Collectivization of Agriculture in Poland: Causes of Defeat." In Iordachi and Bauerkämper, *The Collectivization*, 113–46.

Iordachi, Constantin. "'Constanta, the First Collectivized Region:' Soviet Geopolitical Interests and National and Regional Factors in the Collectivization of Dobrogea (1949–62)." In *Transforming Peasants, Property and Power: the Collectivization of Agriculture in Romania, 1949–1962*, edited by Constantin Iordachi and Dorin Dobrincu, 103–39. Budapest: CEU Press, 2009.

Iordachi, Constantin, and Arnd Bauerkämper, eds. *The Collectivization of Agriculture in Communist Eastern Europe: Comparison and Entanglements*. Budapest and New York: CEU Press, 2014.

Iordachi, Constantin, and Dorin Dobrincu, eds. *Transforming Peasants, Property and Power: the Collectivization of Agriculture in Romania, 1949–1962*. Budapest: CEU Press, 2009.

Izyumova, L.V. "Gosudarstvennaya politika v kontekste sotsial'noy modernizatsii kolkhoznoy derevni v 1930–1960-ye gg." In *Gosudarstvennaya agrarnaya politika v Rossii XX veka v kontekste modernizatsionnogo protsessa*, 78–101. Vologda: Rus', 2006.

Jordán, Gyula. "Kína mezőgazdasága ma: változások és tendenciák" [China's agriculture today: changes and challenges]. *Közgazdasági Szemle* 32, no. 8 (1985): 30–38.

Juhász, János. *A háztáji gazdálkodás mezőgazdaságunkban* [The household farming in our agriculture]. Budapest: Akadémiai, 1980.

———. *Szövetkezeti modellek a magyar mezőgazdaságban* [Cooperative model in the Hungarian agriculture]. Budapest: Akadémiai, 1988.

Juhász, Pál. "Az agrárértelmiség szerepe és a mezőgazdasági szövetkezetek" [The role of the agricultural intelliegentsia and agricultural cooperatives]. *Medvetánc* 2–3, no. 4 (1982) / no. 1 (1983): 191–224.

———. "Agrárpiac, kisüzem, nagyüzem: Agrárszociológiai tanulmányok" [Agrarian market, small-scale and large-scale farms]. In *Medvetánc: Magyar gazdaság és szociológia a 80-as években* [Bear's dance: Hungarian economy and sociology in the 1980s], selected by Tamás Miklós. 24–50. Budapest: Minerva, 1988.

Juhász, Pál. "Dunaapáti—egy elsüllyedt mezőváros" [Dunaapáti—a sunk agrarian town]. In *Emberek és intézmények: Két zsákutca az agráriumban* [People and institutions: Two dead-ends in the agriculture]. 300–10. Budapest: Új Mandátum, 2006).

Juhász, Pál, and Bálint Magyar. "Néhány megjegyzés a lengyel és a magyar mezőgazdasági kistermelők helyzetéről a hetvenes években" [Some remarks on the situation of Polish and Hungarian small producers in the 1970s]. *Medvetánc* 4, no. 2–3 (1984): 181–208.

Kansikas, Suvi. *Socialist countries face the European community: Soviet-bloc controversies over East-West trade*. Frankfurt am Main: Peter Lang Edition, 2014.

Karcz, Jerzy F., ed. *Soviet and East European Agriculture*. Berkeley and Los Angeles: University of California Press, 1962.

Kecskés, Sándor, Péter Gunst, Éva Mária Fülöp, and Sándor Oroszi, eds., *Az Országos mezőgazdasági kiállítások és vásárok története, 1881–1990* [The history of agricultural fairs and exhibitions in Hungary, 1881–1990]. Budapest: Magyar Mezőgazdasági Múzeum–Agroinform, 1996.

Kenedi, János, ed. *A forradalom hangja: Magyarországi rádióadások 1956. október 23.–november 9.* [The voice of the Revolution: Broadcasts in Hungary between October 23 and November 9, 1956]. Századvég füzetek 3. Budapest: Századvég–Nyilvánosság Klub, 1989.

Kenez, Peter. *Hungary from the Nazis to the Soviets: the establishment of the Communist regime in Hungary, 1944–1948*. Cambridge, New York: Cambridge University Press, 2006.

Keserű, János. "A termelőszövetkezetek gazdaságirányítási reformjának alapelveiről" [Basic principles of the economic management reform of the collective farms]. *Társadalmi Szemle* 21, no. 4 (1966): 3–13.

———. *Parasztsorsfordítók között* [Among Peasant Pioneers]. Budapest: Napvilág, 2007.

Kiss, László, ed. *Nómenklatúra Magyarországon (1957–1989)* [The Nomenclature in Hungary, 1957–1989]. Budapest: ELTE Társadalomtudományi Kar, 2005.

Klenczner, András. "Az állami gazdaságokról" [About the state farms]. In Orosz, Für, and Romány, *Magyarország agrártörténete*, 695–97.

Kibita, Natalia. *Soviet Economic Management under Khrushchev: The Sovnarkhoz Reform*. London and New York: Routledge, 2013.

Kideckel, David A. "The Socialist Transformation of Agriculture in a Romanian Commune, 1945–1962." *American Ethnologist* 9, no. 2 (1982): 320–40.

Kingsbury, Noël. *Hybrid: The History and Science of Plant Breeding*. Chicago: University of Chicago Press, 2009.

Kipping, Matthias, and Ove Bjarnar. *The Americanisation of European Business: the Marshall Plan and the transfer of the US management models*. New York and Oxford: Routledge, 1998.

Kligman, Gail, and Katherine Verdery, eds. *Peasants under siege: the Collectivization of Romanian Agriculture, 1949–1962*. Princeton and Oxford: Princeton University Press, 2011.

Kõll, Anu Mai. *The Village and the Class War: Anti-Kulak Campaign in Estonia*. Budapest: CEU Press, 2013.

Komló, László. *Ipari mezőgazdaság felé* [Toward the industrialized agriculture]. Budapest, Közgazdasági és Jogi Könyvkiadó, 1964.

Komló, László, and Csaba Kovács. "A közös és egyéni érdek a ceglédi Nagy Sztálin Termelőszövetkezetben" [The common and individual interest in the Great Stalin Collective in Cegléd]. *Agrártörténeti Szemle* 21, no. 3–4 (1979): 438–88.

A kommunizmus építőinek kongresszusa: 1961. október 17–31: Részlet az SZKP XXII. kongresszusának anyagaiból [Selections from the materials of the 22nd Congress of the Communist Party of the Soviet Union]. Budapest: Kossuth, 1961.

Konyshev, D. N. "Gosudarstvennaia politika ogranicheniia lichnogo podsobnogo khoziaistva (konets 1950-kh – nachalo 1960-kh gg.)." *Rossiyskaya istoriya* 55, no. 3 (2011): 102–111.

Kopsidis, Michael. "Agricultural development and impeded growth: The case of Hungary, 1870–1973." In *Agriculture and economic development in Europe since 1870*, edited by Pedro Lains and Vicente Pinilla, 286–310. London–New York: Routledge, 2009.

Korbonski, Andrzej. *Politics of Socialist Agriculture in Poland: 1945–1960*. New York–London: Columbia University Press, 1965.

Kornai, János. *The socialist system: the political economy of communism*. Oxford: Clarendon Press, 1992.

Kosztricz, Anna Siklósné. "Magyar ösztöndíjasok a Szovjetunióban, 1945–1960" [Hungarians studying in the Soviet Union, 1945–1960]. PhD-thesis, ELTE, Budapest, 2016.

Kovách, Imre. *Termelők és vállalkozók: Mezőgazdasági kistermelők a magyar társadalomban* [Producers and entrepeneurs: Agricultural small producers in the Hungarian society]. Budapest: Társadalomtudományi Intézet, 1988.

———. "Hungary Cooperative farms and Household Plots." In *Many Shades of Red State Policy and Collective Agriculture*, edited by Mieke Meurs, 125–50. New York–Oxford: Rowman & Littlefield, 1999.

———. *A vidék az ezredfordulón: A jelenkori magyar vidéki társadalom szerkezeti és hatalmi változásai* [The countryside at the millennium: The major structural changes of the Hungarian rural society]. Budapest: Argumentum, 2012.

Kovács, Csaba. "Panaszok a kollektivizálás befejező hullámának időszakából: az egyéni és a szövetkezeti gazdálkodás problémáinak sajátosságai" [Complaints from the final phase of the collectivization]. *Múltunk* 58, no. 3 (2013): 207–51.

Kovács, Ferenc, ed. *A Magyar Tudományos Akadémia Agrártudományok Osztálya 50 éve* [50 years in history of the Department of Agricultural Science of HAS]. Budapest: MTA Agrártudományok Osztálya, 1999.

Kovács, Imre. *Magyarország megszállása* [Occupation of Hungary]. Budapest: Katalizátor Iroda, 1990.

Kovács, Lajos Péter, ed. *A Nagy Imre vonal: Dokumentumválogatás* [The Imre Nagy-line: Selected documents]. Budapest: Reform, 1989.

Kovács, Teréz. "Az 1945 utáni jugoszláv agrárpolitika hatása a délvidéki magyarokra" [The effects of the post-1945 agrarian policy on the Hungarian minority in Yugoslavia]. In Schlett, *Földindulások—sorsfordulók*, 138–46.

Kozári, Monika. *A nyugdíjrendszer Magyarországon Mária Teréziától a második világháborúig* [The pension system in Hungary from Maria Theresia to the World War II]. Budapest: Gondolat, 2012.

Kövér, György. "Az orosz obshchina történetéhez: Áttekintés a hetvenes évek szovjet szakirodalmáról" [The history of the Russian obshchina: An overview on the Soviet historiography of the 1970s]. *Történelmi Szemle* 21, no. 2 (1978): 338–54.

Központi Statisztikai Hivatal. *1949. évi népszámlálás: 3. Részletes mezőgazdasági eredmények* [Census of 1949: 3. Detailed agricultural results]. Budapest: KSH, 1950.

———. *Adatok és adalékok a népgazdaság fejlődésének tanulmányozásához, 1949–1955* [Facts and data for the study of people's economy development, 1949–1955]. Budapest: KSH, 1957.

———. *A szocialista mezőgazdasági üzemek működése* [The functioning of the units of the socialist agriculture, 1956]. Budapest: KSH, 1957.

———. *A mezőgazdaság eredményei 1958-ban* [The agricultural results of 1958]. Statisztikai Időszaki Közlemények 26. Budapest: KSH, 1959.

———. *A mezőgazdasági termékek felvásárlása 1960* [The state purchase of the agricultural products]. Statisztikai Időszaki Közlemények 43. Budapest: KSH, 1961.

———. *Mezőgazdaságunk a szocialista átszervezés idején, 1958–1962* [Our Agriculture in the Time of Socialist Reorganization, 1958–1962]. Budapest: KSH, 1963.

———. *Mezőgazdasági statisztikai zsebkönyv* [Agricultural statistical pocketbook]. Budapest: KSH, 1967.

———. *Mezőgazdasági statisztikai zsebkönyv*. Budapest: KSH, 1976.

———. *Mezőgazdasági statisztikai évkönyv, 1978*. Budapest: KSH, 1979.

———. *Mezőgazdasági statisztikai zsebkönyv*. Budapest: KSH, 1980.

———. *Magyar statisztikai évkönyv* [Statistical Yearbook]. Budapest: KSH, 1985.

———. *Főbb népgazdasági folyamatok, 1986* [The major economic processes]. Budapest: KSH, 1987.

———. *A magyar mezőgazdaság nemzetközi összehasonlításban* [The Hungarian agriculture in international comparison]. Budapest: KSH, 1987.

———. *A mezőgazdasági vállalatok gazdálkodása, 1988* [Economic activities of agricultural enterprises]. Budapest: KSH, 1989.

———. *Magyar mezőgazdaság, 1851–2000* [Hungarian agriculture, 1851–2000]. Budapest: KSH, 2000. CD-ROM.

Kramer, Mark. "The Soviet Union and the 1956 Crises in Hungary and Poland: Reassessments and New Findings." *Journal of Contemporary History* 33, no. 2 (1998): 163–214.

———. "Stalin, Soviet policy, and the consolidation of a communist bloc in Eastern Europe, 1944–1953." In *The Establishment of Communist Regimes in East-Central Europe*, edited by Vladimir Tismăneanu, 51–102. Budapest: CEU, 2009.

———. "Stalin, the split with Yugoslavia, and Soviet East European efforts to reassert control, 1948–1953." In *Imposing, maintaining, and tearing open the Iron Curtain: the Cold War and East-Central Europe, 1945–1989,* edited by Mark Kramer and Vít Smetana, 51–102. Lanham, MD: Lexington Books, 2014.

Kunszabó, Ferenc. *Elnöktípusok a termelőszövetkezetekben* [The types of the presidents on the collective farms]. Budapest: Akadémiai, 1974.

Laird, Roy D. "Khrushchev's Administrative Reforms in Agriculture: An Appraisal." In *Soviet and East European Agriculture*, edited by Jerzy F. Karz, 29–50. Berkeley–Los Angeles: University of California Press, 1967.

Lampland, Martha. *The object of labor: Commodification in Socialist Hungary*. Chicago–London: The University of Chicago Press, 1995.

———. *The value of labor: The science of commodification in Hungary, 1920–1956.* Chicago: The University of Chicago Press, 2016.

László, János. "A gazdaságirányítási reform és a szövetkezetek gazdasági önállósága" [The economic management reform and the economic independence of the collective farms]. *Tudomány és Mezőgazdaság* 5, no. 5 (1967): 71–76.

Laufer, Jochen. "Die UdSSR und die Einleitung der Bodenreform in der Sowjetischen Besatzungszone" In Bauerkämper, *Junkerland in Bauernhand*, 21–36.

Lee, Harold. *Roswell Garst: A Biography*. Ames: Iowa State University Press, 1984.

Lemke, Michael. "Einleitung." In *Sowjetisierung und Eigenständigkeit in der SBZ/DDR (1945–1953)*, 3–14. Cologne–Weimar–Vienna: Böhlau, 1999.

V. I. Lenin művei [Collected works of Lenin] Vol. 30. *1919. szeptember–1920. április*. Budapest: Szikra, 1953.

Leonard, Carol Scott. *Agrarian reform in Russia: the road from serfdom*. Cambridge–New York: Cambridge University Press, 2009.

Lévesque, Jean. "'Part-Time Peasants': Labour Discipline, Collective Farm Life and the Fate of Soviet Socialized Agriculture after the Second World war, 1945–1953." PhD diss., University of Toronto, 2003.

Lewin, Moshe. *Russian Peasants and Soviet Power*. London: Allen & Unwin, 1968.

———. "Taking Grain: Soviet Policies of Agricultural Procurements before the War." In *The Making of the Soviet Union*, 142–77. New York: Pantheon, 1985.

Litván, György. "Imre Nagy's Second Government." In *1956: The Hungarian Revolution and War for Independence*, eds. Lee Congdon, Béla K. Király, and Károly Nagy, 299–310. New York: Columbia University Press, 2006.

Lowitt, Richard, and Harold Lee, eds. *Letters from an American Farmer: The Eastern European and Russian Correspondence of Roswell Garst*. DeKalb, IL: Northern Illinois University Press, 1987.

Macey, David A. J. *Government and peasant in Russia, 1861–1906: the prehistory of the Stolypin reforms*. DeKalb, IL: Northern Illinois University Press, 1987.

———. "'A wager on history': the Stolypin agrarian reforms as process." In *Transforming peasants: society, state and the peasantry, 1861–1930*, edited by Judith Pallot, 149–73. Houndmills, Basingstoke: Macmillan, 1998.

Maglódi, László. "A mezőgazdasági szakszövetkezetek jelene és jövője" [The present and the future of the agricultural specialist cooperatives]. *Közgazdasági Szemle* 31, no. 5 (1985): 600–609.

Magyar, Bálint. *Dunaapáti 1944–1958: Dokumentumszociográfia* [Dunaapáti 1944–1958: Document-sociography]. 3 vols. Budapest: Művelődéskutató Intézet–Szövetkezeti Kutató Intézet, 1988.

A Magyar Szocialista Munkáspárt IX. kongresszusának jegyzőkönyve: 1966. november 28.–december 3. [Minutes of the 9th congress of the HSWP, November 28–December 3, 1966]. Budapest: Kossuth, 1967.

Majtényi, György. *K-vonal: Uralmi elit és luxus a szocializmusban* [Party elite and luxury in the socialism]. Budapest: Nyitott Könyvműhely, 2009.

Makra, Krisztina, Józsefné Németh, and Béla Rózsa. "A mezőgazdasági termelés ár- és költségviszonyai nemzetközi összehasonlításban" [Price and cost relations of agricultural production in international comparison]. *Gazdálkodás* 30, no. 12 (1986): 40–44.

Marchut, Réka. "Land reforms in the little entente states after the first world war and their anti-Hungarian aspects." In *Agriculture and Rural Life in Finland and Hungary*, edited by Zsuzsanna Varga and Anssi Halmesvirta, 97–112. Loimaa: Sarka, 2018.

Marer, Paul. *East-West Technology Transfer: Study on Hungary 1968–1984*. Paris: OECD, 1986.

Markevich, Andrei. "Finding additional income: subsidiary agriculture in Soviet urban households, 1941–1964." In *A dream deferred: new studies in Russian and Soviet labour history*, edited by Donald Filtzer, Wendy Z. Goldman, Gijs Kessler, and Simon Pirani, 385–416. Bern–New York: Peter Lang, 2008.

Marton, *Ádám*. "Külkereskedelmi áraink az 1970-es években" [Prices of our foreign trade in the 1970s]. *Statisztikai Szemle* 58, no. 4 (1978): 341–58.

Mathijs, Erik. "An historical overview of Central and Eastern European land reform." In *Political Economy of Agrarian Reform in Central and Eastern Europe*, edited by Johan Frans Maria Swinnen, 33–54. Brookfield, VT: Ashgate Publ., 1997.

McCauley, Martin. *Khrushchev and the Development of Soviet Agriculture: The Virgin Land Programme, 1953–1964*. New York: Holmes and Meier, 1976.

Medvedev, Roy. *Khruschev: The years in power*. London: Oxford University Press, 1977.

Medvegyev, Roy. *Hruscsov: Politikai életrajz: Hatvanas évek*. Budapest: Laude, 1989.

Merl, Stephan. *Bauern unter Stalin: Die Formierung des Kolchossystems 1930–1941*. Berlin: Duncker & Humblot, 1990.

———. "The role of agriculture in Soviet industrialization." In *Communist agriculture: Farming in the Soviet union and Eastern Europe*, ed. Karl-Eugen Wädekin, 3–22. London–New York: Routledge, 1990.

Meszticzky, András. "Elnökök, szakvezetők, munkavezetők a termelőszövetkezetekben" [Presidents, Managers, and Professional Leaders in Agricultural Cooperatives]. In *Szövetkezeti Kutató Intézet Évkönyve, 1975* [Yearbook of the Cooperative Research Institute, 1975], 279–333. Budapest: Szövetkezeti Kutató Intézet, 1976.

Meurs, Mieke, Veska Kouzhouharova, and Rositsa Stoyanova. "Bulgaria: From Cooperative Village to Agro-Industrial Complex." In Meurs, *Many Shades of Red*, 87–124.

A mezőgazdasági termelőszövetkezetekre vonatkozó jogszabályok: 1958. január 1.–1959. május 31. [Legal regulation of collective farms, January 1, 1958–May 31, 1959]. Budapest: KJK, 1959.

Millar, James R., and Alec Nove. "A Debate on Collectivization: Was Stalin Really Necessary?" *Problems of Communism* 25, no. 4 (July–August 1976): 49–62.

Miller, Robert F. *One Hundred Thousand Tractors: The MTS and the Development of Controls in Soviet Agriculture*. Cambridge, MA: Harvard University Press, 1970.

Mills, Richard M. "The Formation of the Virgin Lands Policy." *Slavic Review* 29, no. 1 (1970): 58–69.

Mitrany, David. *Marx against the Peasant: A Study in Social Dogmatism*. 2nd ed. New York: Collier Books, 1961.

Mitrovits, Miklós. "A népi demokráciától a proletárdiktatúráig: A csehszlovák–lengyel–magyar eset összehasonlító vizsgálata" [From the people's democracy to the proletarian democracy: The comparative analysis of the Czechoslovakian, Polish and Hungarian cases]. In *Sztálin árnyékában: A szovjet modell exportja Kelet-Közép-Európában (1944–1948)* [Under the shadow of Stalin: The export of the Soviet Model to the East-Central-Europe], 9–32. Budapest: Országház Könyvkiadó, 2018.

Molnár, István, and Éva Szabóné Medgyesi. *Az állami gazdaságok Magyarországon* [The state farms in Hungary]. Budapest: Mezőgazdasági, 1987.

———. "Mezőgazdasági szövetkezetek, 1990" [Collective farms in 1990]. *Statisztikai Szemle* 69, no. 11 (1991): 861–78.

Molnár, József. "'A' háztáji" [The household plot]. In Orosz, Für, and Romány, *Magyarország agrártörténete*, 631–44.

Müller, Dietmar. "Bodeneigentum und Institutionenwandel in Ostmittel- und Südosteuropa 1918–1945–1989." *Zeitschrift für Ostmitteleuropa-Forschung* 61, no. 3 (2012): 332–55.

———. "Property between delimitation and nationalization: the notion, institutions and practices of land proprietorship in Romania, Yugoslavia and Poland, 1918–1948." In *Property in East Central Europe: Notions, Institutions and Practices of Landownership in the Twentieth Century*, edited by Hannes Siegrist and Dietmar Müller, 117–43. New York: Berghan, 2015.

Müller, Fruzsina. *Jeanssozialismus: Konsum und Mode im staatssozialistischen Ungern*. Göttingen: Wallstein Verlag, 2017.

Nagy, István. *Nagy Imre és Erdei Ferenc 1956-ban* [Imre Nagy and Ferenc Erdei in 1956]. Az Erdei Ferenc Társaság füzetei 16. Makó: Erdei Ferenc Társaság, 2003.

Nagy, János, and János Kovács, eds. *Személyiségek a magyar agráriumban* [Important Personalities in Agrarian Life]. Vol. 1. Debrecen: Debreceni Egyetem Agrártudományi Centrum, 2005.

Nagy, Miklós, ed. *A magyar külpolitika, 1956–1989: Történeti kronológia* [The foreign policy of Hungary, 1956–1989: Chronology]. Budapest: MTA Jelenkorkutató Bizottság, 1993.

Naimark, Norman M. *The Russians in Germany: a history of the Soviet Zone of occupation, 1945–1949*. Cambridge, MA: Belknap Press of Harvard University Press, 1995.

———. "The Sovietization of Eastern Europe, 1944–1953." In *The Cambridge History of the Cold War*. Vol. 1. *Origins*, eds. Melvyn P. Leffler and Odd Arne Westad. 175–97. Cambridge–New York: Cambridge University Press, 2010.

Németi, László. *Magyarország élelmiszer-gazdasága a hetvenes években* [The food economy in Hungary in the 1970s]. Budapest: Mezőgazdasági, 1981.

Nolan, Peter. "The collectivization in China: some comparisons with the USSR." *Journal of Peasant Studies* 3, no. 2 (1976): 192–220.

Nove, Alec. *An Economic History of the U.S.S.R.* London: Penguin Books, 1975.

———. *The Soviet Economic System*. London: Routledge, 1977.

Orbán, Sándor. *Két agrárforradalom Magyarországon: Demokratikus és szocialista agrárátalakulás 1945–1961* [Two agrarian revolutions in Hungary. Democratic and socialist agrarian transformation 1945–1961]. Budapest: Akadémiai, 1972.

Oros, Iván, ed. *A falu és a mezőgazdaság főbb társadalmi és gazdasági jelzőszámai* [Main economic and social indicators of village and agricultural development]. Budapest: KSH, 1994.

Orosz, István, Lajos Für, and Pál Romány, eds. *Magyarország agrártörténete: Agrártörténeti tanulmányok* [The agricultural history of Hungary: Studies on agricultural history]. Budapest: Mezőgazda, 1996.

Osmond, Jonathan. "From Junker estate to co-operative farm: East German agrarian society 1945–1961." In *The workers' and peasants' state: communism and society in East Germany under Ulbricht, 1945–1971*, edited by Patrick Major and Jonathan Osmond, 135–39. Manchester–New York: Manchester University Press, 2002.

Osokina, Elena. *Our Daily Bread: Socialist Distribution and the Art of Survival in Stalin's Russia, 1927–1941*. Armonk, NY: M. E. Sharpe, 2001.

Ö. Kovács, József. *A paraszti társadalom felszámolása a kommunista diktatúrában: A vidéki Magyarország politikai társadalomtörténete, 1945–1965* [The elimination of the peasant society in the communist dictatorship: The political-socio history of the rural Hungary, 1945–1965]. Budapest: Korall, 2012.

———. "The Forced Collectivization of Agriculture in Hungary, 1948–1961." In Iordachi and Bauerkämper, *The Collectivization of Agriculture*, 215–21.

Pál, Lajos, and Ignác Romsics, eds. *1956 okai, jelentősége és következményei* [Reasons, importance and consequencies of the revolution of 1956]. Budapest: Magyar Történelmi Társulat, 2006.

Pallot, Judith. *Social change and peasant land-holding in pre-revolutionary Russia*. Oxford: University of Oxford, School of Geography, 1982.

Papp, István. "A Begyűjtési Minisztérium az 1956-os forradalom idején és a beszolgáltatási rendszer felszámolása 1956–57-ben" [The Ministry of Delivery during the revolution of 1956 and the abolition of the compulsory delivery system]. In Pál and Romsics, *1956 okai, jelentősége*, 267–89.

———. "A BM II/7. (Mezőgazdasági Elhárító) Osztály" [The Agricultural Anti-Sabotage Department (II/7.) of the Ministry of Interior]. In *A megtorlás szervezete: A politikai rendőrség újjászervezése és működése, 1956–1962* [The organization of reprisal: Reconstruction of the political police and its actions, 1956–1962], edited by Imre Okváth, 181–209. Budapest: L'Harmattan–Állambiztonsági Szolgálatok Történelmi Levéltára, 2013.

———. *Fehér Lajos: Egy népi kommunista politikus pályaképe* [Lajos Fehér: A political biography of Lajos Fehér]. Budapest: Kronosz–ÁBTL, 2017.

Pék, János. "Ötven év a magyar állattenyésztésben—ami száz évet jelentett" [Fifty years in the Hungarian animal husbandry]. In *Falvak, földek, földművesek: Agrárpolitikai, agrártörténeti, településfejlesztési tanulmányok* [Village, land, peasantry. Studies on agrarian policy, agricultural history and rural development], edited by Gyula Pócs, 221–22. Budapest: Agroinform, 2004.

Perkins, John H. *Geopolitics and the Green Revolution: Wheat, Genes, and the Cold War*. New York: Oxford University Press, 1997.

Péteri, György. "Controlling the Field of Academic Economics in Hungary, 1953–1976." In *Academia and State Socialism: Essays on the Political History of Academic Life in Post-1945 Hungary and Eastern Europe*, 207–24. New York: Columbia University Press, 1998.

———. "The field of economic research in Hungary after Stalin, 1953–56." In *Life and the First Crisis of State Socialism in East Central Europe, 1953–1956*, edited by György Péteri, 47–79. Trondheim: Programme on East European Cultures and Societies, 2001.

———. "Nylon Curtain: Transnational and Trans-Systemic Tendencies in the Cultural Life of State-Socialist Russia and East-Central Europe." *Slavonica* 10, no. 2 (2004): 113–23.

———. "From Purge to scandal: The MEGÉV-affair and changing political style in communist Hungary." In *Muddling Through in the Long 1960s: Ideas and Everyday Life in High Politics and Lower Classes of Communist Hungary*, edited by János M. Rainer and György Péteri, 83–108. Trondheim Studies on East European cultures & Societies 16. Trondheim: Trondheim Studies on East European Cultures and Societies, 2005.

———. "Nomenklatura with Smoking Guns: Hunting in Communist Hungary's Party-State Elite." In *Pleasures in Socialism: Leisure and Luxury in the Eastern Bloc*, edited by David Crowley and Susan Reid, 311–43. Evanston: Northwestern University Press, 2010.

———, ed. *Imagining the West in Eastern Europe and the Soviet Union*. Pittsburgh: University of Pittsburgh Press, 2010.

Pető, Iván. "Változások a változatlanságért: A gazdasági rendszer átalakulása a Kádár-korszakban" [Changes to keep things unchanged: The transformation of the economic system in the Kádár-era]. In Rácz, *Ki volt Kádár?*, 114–21.

Pető, Iván, and Sándor Szakács. *A hazai gazdaság négy évtizedének története 1945–1985* [The History of Four Decades of Domestic Economy, 1945–1985]. Vol. 1. *Az újjáépítés és a tervutasításos irányítás időszaka 1945–1968* [The Period of Re-building and Command Economic Planning, 1945–1968]. Budapest: Közgazdasági és Jogi Könyvkiadó, 1985.

Phillips, Ralph W. *FAO: its origins, formation and evolution, 1945–1981*. Rome: FAO, 1981.

Piers, Ludlow N., ed. *Ostpolitik/Westpolitik: European integration and the Cold War, 1965–1973*. Abingdon: Routledge, 2007.

Pittaway, Mark. *Eastern Europe 1939–2000*. London: Bloomsbury Academic, 2004.

———. *The workers' state: industrial labor and the making of socialist Hungary, 1944–1958*. Pittsburgh: University of Pittsburgh Press, 2012.

Ploss, Sydney. *Conflict and decision-making in Soviet Russia: A case study of agricultural policy, 1953–1963*. Princeton: Princeton University Press, 1965.

Pollock, Ethan. "From 'Partiinost' to 'Nauchnost' and Not Quite Back Again: Revisiting the Lessons of the Lysenko Affair." *Slavic Review* 68, no. 1 (2009): 95–115.

Polonsky, Antony, and Bolesław Drukier. *The Beginnings of Communist Rule in Poland*. London–Boston: Routledge & Kegan Paul, 1980.

Pogány, *Mária*. "Nagy Imre és a (volt) népi kollégisták kapcsolatai" [Imre Nagy's relations with the former people's collegians]. In *Nagy Imre és kora: Tanulmányok és források* [Imre Nagy and his epoch: Studies, sources]. Vol. 1, edited by József Sipos and Levente Sipos, 219–40. Budapest: Nagy Imre Alapítvány, 2002.

Poul, Villaume, and Westad Odd Arne, eds. *Perforating the Iron Curtain: European Détente, Transatlantic Relations and the Cold War, 1965–1985*. Copenhagen: Museum Tusculanum Press, 2010.

Pouliquen, Alain. "The Contract Brigades: Towards a Neo-collectivism in Soviet Agriculture?" In Brada and Wädekin, *Socialist Agriculture in Transition*, 45–54.

Pritchard, Gareth. "Workers and the Socialist Unity Party of Germany in the summer of 1953." In *The Workers' and Peasants'State: Communism and Society in East Germany under Ulbricht, 1945–71*, edited by Patrick Major and Jonathan Osmond, 112–29. Manchester–New York: Manchester University Press, 2002.

Pünkösti, Árpád. *Kiválasztottak* [The Chosen Ones]. Budapest: Árkádia 1988.

Rácz, Árpád, ed. *Ki volt Kádár? Harag és részrehajlás nélkül a Kádár-életútról* [Who was Kádár? About Kádár's life career without anger or favor]. Budapest: Rubicon–Aquila, 2001.

Radu, Sorin, and Cosmin Bundeanca, eds. *Countryside and Communism in Eastern Europe: Perceptions, Attitudes, Propaganda*. Berlin: LIT Verlag, 2016.

Rainer, János M. "The Sixties in Hungary: some historical and political approaches. In *Muddling Through in the Long 1960s: Ideas and Everyday Life in High Politics and Lower Classes of Communist Hungary*, edited by György Péteri, 2–26. Trondheim: Norwegian University of Science and Technology, 2005.

———. *Imre Nagy: A Political Biography*. London: I.B. Tauris & Co., 2009.

———. "Magyarország a Szovjetunió árnyékában, 1944–1989," [Hungary in the shadow of the Soviet Union, 1944–1989]. In *Bevezetés a kádárizmusba* [Introduction into the Kadarism], 13–38. Budapest: L'Harmattan, 2011.

Rainer M., János, and Károly Urbán. "'Konzultációk:' Dokumentumok a magyar és szovjet pártvezetők két moszkvai találkozójáról 1954–1955-ben" ["Consultations:" Documents of two meetings of the Hungarian and Soviet party leaders in Moscow]. *Múltunk* 37, no. 4 (1992): 141–48.

Rákosi, Sándor, and Bálint Szabó, eds. *A Magyar Kommunista Párt és a Szociáldemokrata Párt határozatai 1944–1948* [Decrees of the Hungarian Communist Party and the Social Democratic Party, 1944–1948]. Budapest: Kossuth, 1967.

Ránki, György. "Oroszország gazdasági fejlődése, 1861–1917" [The economic development of Russia]. *Századok* 118, no. 3 (1984): 433–85.

Reid, Susan E. "Who will beat whom? Soviet popular reception of the American National Exhibition in Moscow, 1959," *Kritika: Explorations in Russian and Eurasian History* 9, no. 4 (2008): 855–904.

Romanchenko, V.Ya. "Tipologiia i osobennosti evoliutsii sovkhoznoi sistemy Rossii v usloviakh agrarnoi modernizatsii 1950-kh–1980-kh gg." In *Ezhegodnik po agrarnoi istorii Vostochnoi Evropy 2012*, edited by E. N. Shveykovskaya, 510–20. Moscow, Bryansk: RAS. 2012.

Romány, Pál, ed. *Mezőgazdasági üzemekben Skandináviától Itáliáig* [Visiting farms from Scandinavia to Italy]. Budapest: Mezőgazdasági, 1963.

———. "'Feljegyzés a falusi helyzetről:' Erdei Ferenc a szövetkezeti átalakításról, 1957–58" [Memorandum on the village situation: Ferenc Erdei's views on the cooperative transformation, 1957–58.]. *História* 17, no. 9–10 (1995): 32–35.

———. "Az Agrárpolitikai Tézisektől a Nemzeti Agrárprogramig" [The Completion and Partial Dismantling of Collective Agriculture]. In Gunst, *A magyar agrártársadalom*, 357–65.

———. "A 'változatlan agrárpolitika' változásai, 1957–1989" [Changes of the "constant agrarian policy"]. In Rácz, *Ki volt Kádár?*, 122–33.

———. "A 'Nagy Imre-tanszék' és utóélete" [The so-called Imre Nagy's department and its aftermath]. In Estók, *1956 és a magyar agrártársadalom*, 115–27.

Romsics, Ignác. *Hungary in the Twentieth Century*. Budapest: Corvina–Osiris, 1999.

———. *Volt egyszer egy rendszerváltás* [Once upon a time there was a change of system]. Budapest: Rubicon, 2003.

———. *Szabó István életútja Nádudvartól Nádudvarig*. Budapest: Osiris, 2012.

Rothschild, Joseph. *Return to Diversity: A Political History of East Central Europe since World War II*. 3rd ed. Oxford: Oxford University Press, 2000.

Rudolph, Karsten. *Wirtschaftsdiplomatie im Kalten Krieg: Die Ostpolitik der Westdeutsche, Großindustrie, 1945–1991*. Frankfurt: Campus, 2004.

Ruff, Mihály. "A magyar–NSZK kapcsolatok (1960–1963): Útkeresés a doktrínák útvesztőjében" [The Hungarian-FRG relations, 1960–1963: Seeking ways and means in the labyrinth of Doctrines]. *Múltunk* 44, no. 3 (1999): 3–40.

Rychlik, Jan. "Collectivization in Czechoslovakia in Comparative Perspective." In Iordachi and Bauerkämper, *The Collectivization*, 181–210.

S. Kosztricz, Anna, János Lakos, Karola Némethné Vágy, László Soós, and György T. Varga, eds. *A Magyar Szocialista Munkáspárt Központi Bizottságának 1989. évi jegyzőkönyvei* [Minutes of HSWP Central Committee in 1989]. Budapest, MOL, 1993.

Sárkány, Mihály. "A társadalomnéprajzi kutatás hazai története" [The history of social anthropology in Hungary]. In *Magyar néprajz* [Hungarian Anthropology]. Vol. 8. *Társadalom* [Society], ed. Attila Paládi-Kovács, 29–66. Budapest: Akadémiai, 2000.

Sárkány, Pál, ed. *Termelési rendszerek az állattartásban* [Closed production systems in the animal husbandry]. Budapest: Mezőgazdasági, 1975.

Sárközy, Péter. *Szemtől szembe Amerika mezőgazdaságával* [Face to face with the Amerian agriculture]. Budapest: Mezőgazdasági, 1970.

Scherstjanoi, Elke. "'Wollen wir den Sozialismus?' Dokumente aus der Sitzung des Politbüros des ZK der SED am 6. Juni 1953." *Beiträge zur Geschichte der Arbeiterbewegung* 33, no. 5 (1991): 658–80.

———. *SED-Agrarpolitik unter sowjetischer Kontrolle, 1949–53*. München: Oldenbourg Verlag, 2007.

Schlett, András. *Sziget a szárazföldön: A Bábolnai Állami Gazdaság története 1960 és 1990 között*. [An island on the continent: The history of the Bábolna State Farm between 1960 and 1990]. Budapest: Szent István Társulat, 2007.

———, ed. *Földindulások—Sorsfordulók: Kollektivizálás, agrárvilág és vidéki változások a XX. század második felében* [Earthquaking transformations: Collectivization and rural changes in the second half of the 20th century]. Budapest: Szent István Társulat, 2012.

———. "Success and Failure of the Hungarian Agrarian Model." *Arhivele Totalitarismului* [Totalitarianism Archives] 20, no. 1–2 (2012): 96–108.

Schöne, Jens. *Frühling auf dem Lande? Die Kollektivierung der DDR-Landwirtschaft*. Berlin: Ch. Links Verlag, 2005.

Schrerrer, Jutta. "'To catch up and overtake' the West: Soviet discourse on socialist competition." In *Competition in socialist society*, eds. Katalin Miklóssy and Melanie Ilič, 10–23. New York: Routledge, 2014.

Scott, James C. *Weapons of the Weak: Everyday Forms of Peasant Resistance*. New Haven, CT: Yale University Press, 1985.

Siegrist, Hannes, and Müller, Dietmar. "Introduction: Property in East Central Europe: notions, institutions and practices of landownership in the twentieth century." In Siegrist and Müller, *Property in East Central Europe*, 1–28.

Šik, Ota. *A szocialista áruviszonyok* [The commodity relations in the socialism]. Budapest: Kossuth–KJK, 1968.

Simó, Tibor. Érdekérvényesítés a termelőszövetkezetek formális és informális szervezetében [Assertion of interests in formal and informal organization of producer cooperatives]. Budapest: Szövetkezeti Kutató Intézet, 1981.

Simon, Péter. *A magyar parasztság sorsfordulója, 1946–1949* [The Hungarian peasantry's change of fortune]. Budapest: Kossuth, 1984.

Sipos, Aladár. *Agrárviszonyok Nyugat-Európában* [Agriculture in Western Europe]. Budapest: Kossuth, 1967.

Sipos Levente. "Reform és megtorpanás: Viták az MSZMP agrárpolitikájáról (1956–1958)" [Reform and Baulking: Debates on the Agrarian Policy of the HSWP, 1956–1958]. *Múltunk* 36, no. 2–3 (1991): 188–97.

———. "Kolhozosítás vagy szövetkezetesítés: Dögei Imre és Fehér Lajos vitái 1957-ben" [Organizing a kolhoz or a cooperative: Debates between Imre Dögei and Lajos Fehér in 1957]. In Buza et al., *Agrártörténet—Agrárpolitika*, 443–58.

Sjöberg, Örjan. *Rural Change and Development in Albania*. Boulder, CO: Westview, 1991.

Sloin, Andrew, and Sanchez-Sibony, Oscar. "Economy and Power in the Soviet Union, 1917–39," *Kritika: Explorations in Russian and Eurasian History* 15, no. 1 (2014): 7–22.

Smith, Jenny Leigh. *Works in Progress: Plans and Realities on Soviet Farms, 1930–1963*. New Haven: Yale University Press, 2014.

Stanis, Vladimir F. *The Socialist Transformation of Agriculture*. Moscow: Progress Publishers, 1976.

Stebelsky, Igor. "Food consumption patterns in the Soviet Union." In Brada and Wädekin, *Socialist Agriculture in Transition*, 98–109.

Steiner, André. *Von Plan zu Plan: eine Wirtschaftsgeschichte der DDR*. München: Deutsche Verlags-Anstalt, 2004.

Swain, Geoffrey. "Deciding to Collectivize Latvian Agriculture." *Europe-Asia Studies* 55, no. 1 (2003): 39–58.

Swain, Geoffrey, and Nigel Swain. *Eastern Europe since 1945*. 5th ed. London: Palgrave, 2018.

Swain, Nigel. *Collective Farms Which Work?* Cambridge: Cambridge University Press, 1985.

———. *Hungary: The Rise and Fall of Feasible Socialism*. London–New York: Verso, 1992.

———. "The Fate of Peasant Parties during Socialist Transformation." In *Bauerngesellschaften auf dem Weg in die Moderne: Agrarismus in Ostmitteleuropa 1880 bis 1960*, edited by Angela Harre and Helga Schultz, 163–76. Wiesbaden: Harrasowitz, 2010.

———. "A Post-Socialist Capitalism." *Europe-Asia Studies* 63, no. 9 (2011): 1671–95.

———. *Green Barons, Force-of-Circumstances Entrepreneurs, Impotent Mayors: Rural Change in the Early Years of Post-Capitalist Democracy*. Budapest–New York: CEU Press, 2013.

———. "Eastern European Collectivization Campaigns Compared, 1945–1962." In Irodachi and Bauerkämper, *The Collectivization*, 497–534.

Szabó, Gábor, Margit Szabóné Guttyán, and Katalin Szép. "A mezőgazdasági termelés jövedelmezőségének makro- és mikroökonómiai aspektusai" [Micro- and macroeconomical aspects of agricultral efficiency]. *Közgazdasági Szemle* 35, no. 6 (1989): 579–83.

Szakács, Sándor. *Földosztás és agrárfejlődés a magyar népi demokráciában 1945–1948* [Land distribution and agrarian development in the Hungarian people's democracy]. Marx Károly Közgazdaságtudományi Egyetem közleményei 5. Budapest: KJK, 1964.

———. *Állami gazdaságaink helyzetének alakulása 1945–1948* [Development of our state farms, 1945–1948]. Budapest: Akadémiai, 1969.

———. *A népi demokratikus agrárfejlődés kezdetei Magyarországon 1945–1948* [The beginnigs of the democratic agrarian development in Hungary]. Budapest: Akadémiai, 1971.

———. "A nagyigmándi Jókai termelőszövetkezet története" [The history of the Agricultural Producer Cooperative in Nagyigmánd]. *Agrártörténeti Szemle* 17, no. 1–2 (1975): 54–128.

———. *A földművesszövetkezeti mozgalom története 1945–1949* [The history of land recipient cooperatives, 1945–1949]. Budapest: Szövetkezeti Kutató Intézet, 1976.

———. "A Szovjetunió mezőgazdasága (1917–1939)" [The agriculture of the Soviet Russia]. *Agrártörténeti Szemle* 23, no. 1–2 (1979): 95–141.

———. "A reform kérdése és a termelés: Meghatározottságok és adottságok a magyar mezőgazdaságban 1968–1985" [The question of the reform and the production: Determining factors and facilities of the Hungarian agriculture 1968–1985]. *Agrártörténeti Szemle* 31, no. 1–4 (1989): 56–117.

———. "From Land Reform to Collectivization (1945–1956)." In Gunst, *Hungarian Agrarian Society*, 257–98.

———. "A földosztástól a kollektivizálásig, 1945–1956." In Gunst, *A Magyar agrártársadalom*, 339–43.

Szakolczai, Attila, ed. *A vidék forradalma, 1956* [Revolution in the countryside, 1956]. Vol. 2. Budapest: 1956-os Intézet–Budapest Főváros Levéltára, 2006.

Szakolczai, Attila, and László Á. Varga, eds. *A vidék forradalma, 1956.* [Revolution in the countryside, 1956]. Vol. 1. Budapest: 1956-os Intézet–Budapest Főváros Levéltára, 2003.

Szamuely, László, ed. *A magyar közgazdasági gondolat fejlődése: 1954–1978: A szocialista gazdaság mechanizmusának kutatása* [Development of Hungarian economic thinking, 1954–1978: Research into the mechanism of the socialist economy]. Budapest: KJK, 1986.

Szántó, László, and Ferenc Szili, eds. *Az 1956-os forradalom Somogyban: Válogatott dokumentumok* [The revolution of 1956 in the Somogy county: Selected documents]. Kaposvár: Somogy Megyei Levéltár, 1995.

Szemes, Lajos. *A mezőgazdasági termelőszövetkezetek érdekképviselete* [Interest representation for agricultural producer cooperatives]. Budapest: Akadémiai, 1970.

Földművelésügyi Minisztérium. *A szovjet mezőgazdasági artelek minta-alapszabálya* [The model charter of the Soviet agricultural artel's]. Budapest: Földművelésügyi Minisztérium, 1952.

J. V. Sztálin művei [Collected works of Stalin]. Vol. 7. Budapest: Szikra, 1950.

J. V. Sztálin művei [Collected works of Stalin]. Vol. 11. *1928–1929. március*. Budapest: Szikra, 1950.

Sztárayné, *Kézdi Éva.* "Az 1963 és 1989 közötti káderkinevezések elemzése" [Analysis of the cadre appointments between 1963 and 1989]. In Kiss, *Nómenklatúra*, 151–98.

Szuhay, Miklós. "Evolution of Hungarian Agriculture during the Inter-War Years (1918–1945)." In Gunst, *Hungarian Agrarian Society*, 177–90.

T. Varga, György. "Jegyzőkönyv a szovjet és a magyar párt- és állami vezetők tárgyalásairól (1953. június 13–16.)" [Minutes of the negotiations between the Soviet and Hungarian party- and state leaders, June13–16, 1953]. *Múltunk* 37, no. 2–3 (1992): 234–69.

Tamasi, Mihály. "A nyugati tanulmányút hatása Erdei Ferenc gondolatvilágára" [Effects of a Western Study Trip on the Thoughts of Ferenc Erdei]. In *Erdei Ferenc levelesládájából: Müncheni levelek* [From Ferenc Erdei's Letter Box: Letters from Munich], edited by Ferenc Tóth, 19–35. Az Erdei Ferenc Társaság füzetei 8. Makó: Erdei Ferenc Társaság, 1997.

Tanka, Endre. *Az obscsinától a társasgazdálkodásig: Az orosz földviszonyok fejlődési vázlata* [From the obshchina to the collective farming]. Budapest: Szövetkezeti Kutató Intézet, 1988.

Taubman, William. *Khrushchev: The Man and His Era*. New York: W. W. Norton, 2003.

Teknős, Péter. "A kiegészítő tevékenység szerepe a mezőgazdasági vállalatok gazdálkodásában" [The role of ancillary activities in agriculture]. *Gazdálkodás* 32, no. 9 (1988): 19–23.

Thelen, Tatjana. "Violence and social (dis)continuity: comparing collectivization in two East European villages." *Social History* 30, no. 1 (2005): 25–44.

A termelőszövetkezetek megszilárdításáért és fejlesztéséért: Részletes magyarázat a Magyar Forradalmi Munkás-Paraszt Kormány 3004/1958. sz. határozatához [Strengthening and further boosting the collective farms: A detailed explanation on the governmental decree no. 3004/1958]. Budapest: Kossuth, 1958.

Tomka, Béla. *Welfare in East and West: Hungarian Social Security in an International Comparison 1918–1990*. Berlin: Akademie Verlag, 2004.

———. "Fogyasztás a második világháború utáni Kelet-Közép-Európában: politikai meghatározók és transznacionális hatások." [Consumption in East-Central Europe after World War II: political determinants and transnational effects] *Aetas* 34, no. 4 (2019): 62–74.

Tóth, A. Ernő. *Mezőgazdasági kistermelés, családi termelés* [Small-scale and family-based agricultural production]. Budapest: Mezőgazdasági, 1988.

Tóth, Judit. "Kulaks in political cartoons of the Rákosi-Era." In *Countryside and communism in Easter Europe: Perceptions, attitudes, propaganda*, edited by Sorin Radu and Cosmin Budeanca, 637–55. Berlin: LIT Verlag, 2016.

———. "Elimination of the farmer elite in Hungary in the 1950s." In Varga and Halmesvirta, *Agriculture and Rural Life*, 127–37.

Tőkés, Rudolf. *Hungary's Negotiated Revolution: Economic Reform, Social Change and Political Succession, 1957–1990*. Cambridge: Cambridge University Press, 1996.

———. *A kialkudott forradalom: Gazdasági reform, társadalmi átalakulás és politikai hatalomutódlás, 1957–1990*. Budapest: Kossuth, 1998.

Ungvárszki, Ágnes. *Gazdaságpolitikai ciklusok Magyarországon (1948–1988)* [Economic policy cycles in Hungary, 1948–1988]. Budapest: KJK, 1989.

Urbán, László. *Az első termelőszövetkezeti városok agrárpolitikai szerepének kialakulása, változásai, gazdasági és környezeti hatásai* [The agrarian policy role of

the first socialist agricultural towns, and their economic and ecological impacts]. Szolnok: MTA Jász-Nagykun-Szolnok Megyei Tudományos Testülete, 2002.
Vajda, Andrew de. *Adventure, Achievements, Altruism: The story of my life*. Rome: Bonte-Friedheim, 1983.
Valuch, Tibor. *Rekviem a parasztságért* [Requiem for the peasantry]. Határ Füzetek 3. Debrecen: Kossuth Lajos Tudományegyetem, 1988.
———, ed. *Donáth Ferenc: A Márciusi Fronttól Monorig: Tanulmányok, vázlatok, emlékezések* [Ferenc Donáth: From the March Front to the so-called Monor meeting: Studies, sketches, memoirs]. Budapest: MTA Közgazdaságtudományi Intézet–Századvég, 1992.
———. "Agrárkérdések és a magyar falu 1956–57-ben" [Agrarian questions and the Hungarian village in 1956–57]. *1956-os Intézet Évkönyv*. Vol. 8. 286–302. Budapest: 1956-os Intézet, 2000.
———. *The Social History of Hungary in the Second Half of the 20th Century*. Budapest: Osiris, 2001.
———. "Changes in the Structure and Lifestyle of the Hungarian Society in the Second Half of the XXth Century." In Gyáni, Kövér, and Valuch, *Social history*, 511–671.
Váncsa, Jenő. *Öt évtized a mezőgazdaság szolgálatában* [Five decades in the service of Hungarian agriculture]. Budapest: Magyar Mezőgazdasági Múzeum, 2010.
Varga, Gyula, ed. *A mezőgazdasági kistermelés helyzete és jövője* [The present and the future of the small-scale farming]. Budapest: Mezőgazdasági Kiadó, 1979.
———. "Mezőgazdaságunk nemzetgazdasági szerepváltozásai" [The changing roles of the agriculture in the national economy]. In Estók, *1956 és a magyar agrártársadalom*, 128–52.
———, ed. *Erdei Ferenc emlékezete: Válogatott írások, tanulmányok és visszaemlékezések* [Remembrance of Ferenc Erdei. Selected writings, studies and memories]. Szeged: Bába, 2010.
———. "A 'tudományos munkás,'" [The "scientific worker"]. In Varga, *Erdei Ferenc emlékezete*, 325–351. Szeged: Bába, 2010.
Varga, Zsuzsanna. "A Hajdú-Bihar megyei mezőgazdasági termelőszövetkezetek érdekérvényesítési küzdelmei a korai Kádár-korszakban" [Hajdú-Bihar County agricultural producer cooperative struggles to assert their interests in the early Kádár era]. In *A Hajdú-Bihar Megyei Levéltár Évkönyve* [The yearbook of the Hajdú-Bihar County Archive]. Vol. 24. 239–68. Debrecen: Hajdú-Bihar Megyei Levéltár, 1997.
———. "Mezőgazdasági reformmunkálatok (1961–1964)" [Agricultural reform efforts 1961–64]. *Múltunk* 45, no. 2 (2000): 253–82.
———. *Politika, paraszti érdekérvényesítés és szövetkezetek Magyarországon 1956–1967* [Politics, the Assertion of Interests in the Peasantry and Agricultural Cooperatives in Hungary between 1956 and 1967]. Budapest: Napvilág, 2001.
———. "Az agrárium 1945-től napjainkig" [The Hungarian agriculture from 1945 to the present]. In Agrárvilág Magyarországon, 1848–2002 [The rural economy and society in Hungary, 1848–2002], edited by János Estók et al., 261–339. Budapest: Argumentum, 2003.

———. "Agrarian development from 1945 to the present day." In Estók et al., *History of Hungarian Agriculture*, 221–94.

———. "1956 hatása a kádári agrárpolitika kialakulására" [The effects of 1956 on the agrarian policy of the Kádár-government]. In Pál and Romsics, *1956 okai, jelentősége*, 299–315.

———. "The Impact of 1956 on the Relationship between the Kádár Regime and the peasantry, 1956–66." *Hungarian Studies Review* 34, no. 1–2 (2007): 155–76. http://epa.oszk.hu/00000/00010/00041/pdf/HSR_2007_1-2_155-176.pdf

———. "Konfliktusok és kompromisszumok a hatalom és az agrártársadalom között a Kádár-rendszerben" Habilitation thesis, ELTE, Budapest, 2008.

———. "'Földindulás után:' A hatalom és a parasztság Magyarországon az 1960-as évek első felében" ["After the earthquake:" Power and the peasantry in Hungary in the first half of the 1960s]. *Történelmi Szemle* 51, no. 2 (2009): 231–58.

———. "Wartime Agricultural Policy in Peacetime: A Case Study of Hungary, 1940–1956." In *War, Agriculture, and Food: Rural Europe from the 1930s to the 1950s*, eds. Paul Brassley, Yves Segers, and Leen Van Molle, 96–110. New York: Routledge, 2012.

———. *Az agrárlobbi tündöklése és bukása az államszocializmus időszakában* [The Rise and Fall of the Agrarian Lobby under State Socialism]. Budapest: Gondolat, 2013.

———. "Agricultural Economics and the Agrarian Lobby in Hungary under State Socialism." *East Central Europe* 44, no. 2–3 (2017): 284–308.

———. "The Missing Stories from the Rural Hungary in 1956." In *Revolúcia v susedstve: Maďarská revolúcia v roku 1956 a Slovensko*, edited by Attila Simon and Slavomír Michálek, 107–18. Bratislava–Budapest: Fórum inštitút pre vyskum mensín Vydavatelstvo, 2017.

———, ed. *Göröngyös út: Dimény Imre életútja* [A Bumpy Road: the Life of Imre Dimény]. Budapest: Kossuth, 2017.

Vasary, Ildiko. *Beyond the Plan: Social Change in a Hungarian Village*. Boulder, CO: Westview Press, 1987.

Vass, Henrik, ed. *A Magyar Szocialista Munkáspárt határozatai és dokumentumai, 1963–1966* [Resolutions and Documents of the HSWP, 1963–1966]. Budapest: Kossuth, 1968.

Vass, Henrik, and Ágnes Ságvári, eds. *A Magyar Szocialista Munkáspárt határozatai és dokumentumai 1956–1962* [The resolutions and documents of the HSWP, 1956–1962]. 2nd ed. Budapest: Kossuth, 1973.

Verbitskaya, O. M. *Rossiyskoye krest'yanstvo ot Stalina k Khrushchevu, seredina 40-kh–nachalo 60–kh godov*. Moscow: Nauka, 1992.

Viola, Lynne. *Best Sons of the Fatherland: Workers in the Vanguard of Soviet Collectivization*. New York–Oxford: Oxford University Press, 1987.

———. *Peasant Rebels under Stalin: Collectivization and the Culture of Peasant Resistance*. New York–Oxford: Oxford University Press, 1996.

———. "Collectivization in the Soviet Union: Specifities and Modalties." In Iordachi and Bauerkämper, *The Collectivization*, 49–78.

Viola, Lynne, Victor Petrovich Danilov, Nikolai A. Ivnitskii, and Denis Kozlov, eds. *The War against the Peasantry, 1927–1930*. New Haven: Yale University Press, 2005.

Virágh, Ferenc. "A mezőgazdasági termelőszövetkezeti tagság szociális ellátása" [The social insurance of the collective farm membership]. In *Tanulmányok a szocialista mezőgazdaság kialakulásáról* [Studies on the rise of the socialist agriculture], edited by Sándor Orbán and Ferenc Pölöskei, 453–506. Budapest: MSZMP KB Társadalomtudományi Intézete–ELTE BTK, 1988.

Volokitina, T. V. ed. Sovetskii faktor v Vostochnoi Evrope 1944–1953: Dokumenty [The Soviet factor in Eastern Europe, 1944–1953]. 2 vols. Moskva: Rosspen, 1999.

Wädekin, Karl-Eugen. *The Private Sector in Soviet Agriculture*. 2nd ed. Berkeley, Los Angeles–London: University of California Press, 1973.

———. "The Soviet Kolkhoz: Vehicle of Cooperative Farming or of Control and Transfer of Resources." In *Cooperative and Commune,* edited by Peter Dorner, 95–116. Madison: The University of Wisconsin Press, 1977.

———, ed. *Agrarian Policies in Communist Europe: A Critical Introduction*. Studies in East European and Soviet Russian agrarian policy 1. The Hague–London: Allanheld, Osmun Publishers–Martinus Nijhoff Publishers, 1982.

———. "The Agrarian Question in Marxist and Leninist Thought" In *Agrarian Policies*, 4–13.

———. "Soviet Agriculture under Stalin: Collectivization and Its Results." In *Agrarian Policies*, 14–30.

———. "The Early Postwar Period in Eastern Europe." In *Agrarian Policies*, 31–43.

———. "A New Deal for Soviet Agriculture: The Khrushchev Era." In *Agrarian Policies*, 45–62.

———. "Collectivization in Eastern Europe: The Common Pattern and the Deviations." In *Agrarian Policies*, 63–81.

"The re-emergence of the kolkhoz principle." *Soviet Studies* 41, no. 1 (1989): 20–38.

Wheeler, George S. *Az Amerikai Egyesült Államok mezőgazdasága* [The Agriculture of the United States of America]. Budapest: Kossuth, 1959.

Wyzan, Michael L. "Bulgarian agriculture: sweeping reform, mediocre performance" In *Communist agriculture: Farming in the Soviet Union and Eastern Europe*, edited by Karl-Eugen Wädekin, 290–306. London–New York: Routledge, 1990.

Yakhnovskaya, S. V. "'Ochen' mnogo razvelos' skota u rabochikh . . .' Iz opyta gosudarstvennogo regulirovaniya LPKh." *Rodina* 24, no. 3 (2012): 157–160.

Zám, Tibor. "Mennyit ér a tsz-elnök?" [How Much Is the President of a Producers' Cooperative Worth?]. In Bács-*Kiskunból jövök* [I Come from the county Bács-Kiskun]. Budapest: Szépirodalmi, 1973.

Zeitlin, Jonathan, and Gary Herrigel, *Americanization and its limits: reworking US technology and management in post-war Europe and Japan*. Oxford–New York: Oxford University Press, 2000.

Zelenin, I. E. *Agrarnaia politika N. S. Khruscheva i sel'skoe khoziaistvo*. Moscow: Institut Istorii Rossiiskoi Akademii Nauk, 2001.

Zsuffa, Ervin. *A termelőszövetkezetek kiegészítő tevékenységének továbbfejlesztése* [The expansion of non-agricultural activities of collective farms]. Új falu könyvek. Budapest: Kossuth, 1972.

Zyryanov, Pavel Nikolayevich. "Pozemel'nyye otnosheniya v russkoy krest'yanskoy obshchine vo vtoroy polivine XIX–nachale XX veka." In Ayatskoy, *Sobstvennosti*, 153–95.

Index

About the Author

Zsuzsanna Varga received her PhD in agrarian history in 1998. She is head of the Modern Hungarian History Department at Eötvös Loránd University (ELTE) in Budapest and director of the modern Hungarian history PhD program at the ELTE Faculty of Humanities. Her main field of research is the history of socialist agriculture in Hungary. She is chair of the Committee for Agrarian History and Rural Sociology of the Hungarian Academy of Sciences and on the editorial boards of *Agrártörténeti Szemle* (*Agrarian History Review*), *Történelmi Szemle* (*Historical Review*) and *Századok* (*Centuries*). She is a founding member of the European Rural History Organisation (EURHO) and is its vice president. She has written more than 120 publications, including four monographs and six edited collections. Her latest monograph on Hungary is *Az agrárlobbi tündöklése és bukása az államszocializmus időszakában* (*The Rise and Fall of the Agrarian Lobby during State Socialism*, 2013). She jointly edited (with Anssi Halmesvirta) *Agriculture and Rural Life in Finland and Hungary* (2018) and is working with colleagues on an edited volume comparing women's strategies for resilience in the period of socialist farming in Eastern Europe.

www.ingramcontent.com/pod-product-compliance
Ingram Content Group UK Ltd.
Pitfield, Milton Keynes, MK11 3LW, UK
UKHW012118150926
475560UK00002B/173

9 781793 634351